ESSAYS FOR PATRICK ATIYAH

PATRICK ATIYAH

ESSAYS FOR PATRICK ATIYAH

Edited by

PETER CANE

and

JANE STAPLETON

CLARENDON PRESS · OXFORD
1991

Oxford University Press, Walton Street, Oxford OX2 6DP
Oxford New York Toronto
Delhi Bombay Calcutta Madras Karachi
Petaling Jaya Singapore Hong Kong Tokyo
Nairobi Dar es Salaam Cape Town
Melbourne Auckland
and associated companies in
Berlin Ibadan

Oxford is trade mark of Oxford University Press

Published in the United States
by Oxford University Press. New York

British Library Cataloguing in Publication Data
data available

Library of Congress Cataloging-in-Publication Data
Essays for Patrick Atiyah / edited by Peter Cane and Jane Stapleton.
Includes bibliographical references (p.) and index.
1. Law—Great Britain. 2. Law—Philosophy. 3. Atiyah, P. S.
I. Atiyah, P. S. II. Cane, Peter, 1950– . III. Stapleton, Jane.
KD354.E87 1991 349.41—dc20 [344.1] 91-20687
ISBN 0-19-8254105

Typeset by Best-set Typesetter Ltd, Hong Kong
Printed in Great Britain by Biddles Ltd,
Guildford & King's Lynn

Preface

This volume of essays is a small expression of thanks to Patrick Atiyah for his many services to the study of law as tutor, lecturer, supervisor of research students, colleague, first general editor of the Oxford Journal of Legal Studies, advocate of law reform and above all, as scholar, thinker, and writer. His early retirement in 1988 was a serious and much lamented loss to the Oxford Law Faculty in particular, and to the world of legal scholarship in general. The contributors to this volume were invited to write on any subject they chose within the very broad range of interests which Patrick Atiyah pursued in his academic work. So the essays have no unifying theme: they reflect the diversity of Atiyah's achievements. But their authors all have something in common: they share a deep respect and affection for Patrick Atiyah, which each has sought to express by agreeing to take part in the enterprise.

A fitting tribute comes from Guido Calabresi who, because of the pressure of his commitments as dean of Yale Law School, was, to his great regret, unable to write an essay for the volume:

> A Festschrift for Patrick Atiyah, what could be more appropriate, what could be a greater source of joy!
>
> Patrick has been a model for us all of what a scholar should be. Always thorough, comprehensive and careful, he has, nonetheless, been willing to take on topics which were truly daunting and whose examination could never give rise to that 'perfect treatment' in which lesser scholars take comfort. He has been courageous and original, and always ready to revise his own thought (as he effectively criticized the thought of others) in the light of new ideas, further reflections and growth of knowledge.
>
> These qualities which characterize his scholarship, have also defined him as a person. I have been fortunate to be able to count his as a friend. I have learnt an immense amount from him and I look forward to learning more from him, both through his writings and through conversations, over many, many years in the future.

Our thanks are due to Barbara Tearle, Law Librarian of the Bodleian Library in Oxford, for preparing the list of Patrick Atiyah's writings which appears at the end of this volume; and to Oxford University Press for enabling us to honour Patrick Atiyah in this way.

Peter Cane and Jane Stapleton

Contents

List of Contributors

John Bell, Professor of Law, Faculty of Law, University of Leeds, Leeds LS2 9JT, UK

Peter Cane, Fellow and Tutor in Law, Corpus Christi College, Oxford, OX1 4JF, UK

Paul D. Carrington, Chadwick Professor of Law, Duke University School of Law, Towerview at Science Drive, Durham, NC 27706, USA

John Dwyer, QC, Barrister, Owen Dixon Chambers East, 205 William Street, Melbourne, VIC 3000, Australia

John Fleming, Shannon Cecil Turner, Professor of Law, The Law School, Boalt Hall, University of California, Berkeley, CA 94720, USA

Roy Goode, Norton Rose Professor of English Law in the University of Oxford and Fellow, St John's College, Oxford, OX1 3JP, UK

Donald Harris, Director, Centre for Socio-Legal Studies, Wolfson College, Oxford, OX2 6UD, UK and Fellow, Balliol College, Oxford, OX1 3BJ, UK

Jan Hellner, Professor of Law, Stockholms Universitet, Juridiska fakulteten, S-106 91 Stockholm, Sweden

Tony Honoré, Regius Professor of Civil Law Emeritus in the University of Oxford and Fellow, All Souls College, Oxford, OX1 4AL, UK

A. W. B. Simpson, Charles F. and Edith J. Clyne, Professor of Law, School of Law, University of Michigan, Hutchins Hall, Ann Arbor, Michigan 48109-1215, USA

Jane Stapleton, Fellow and Tutor in Law, Balliol College, Oxford, OX1 3BJ, UK

Robert Stevens, Chancellor, University of California, Santa Cruz, CA 95064, USA

Robert S. Summers, McRoberts Research Professor of Law, Cornell Law School, 320 Myron Taylor Hall, Ithaca, NY 14853-4901, USA

William Twining, Quain Professor of Jurisprudence, University College, London WC1H 0EG, UK

S. M. Waddams, Professor of Law, Faculty of Law, University of Toronto, 78 Queen's Park, Toronto, Ontario, M5S 2C5, Canada

1

Reflections on Law in Context

William Twining

Introduction

During 1958–9 Patrick Atiyah was my neighbour in Khartoum. This was my first year of full-time teaching and he closely affected my academic development as mentor, colleague, and friend. That friendship has survived our various wanderings, a second period as colleagues at Warwick, and another recent phase as neighbours in Iffley. Like many others, I owe him an enormous intellectual debt. This paper explores one phase of our relationship: the genesis of the 'Law in Context' series.

The story begins in the Atiyahs' swimming-pool at their house on Sharia el Jamhuria in Khartoum. We used to repair there regularly after work to cool off. That may give a misleadingly neo-colonial impression. Patrick sometimes appears to be larger than life, but the Atiyah 'swimming-pool' was not much larger than a bath. It seemed almost as deep as it was long. The first edition of *Sale of Goods*[1] had already been published, and he was working on *An Introduction to the Law of Contract*.[2] Much as he enjoyed some aspects of life in Sudan, he felt intellectually isolated and he expressed himself memorably in this context. He would swim a length in two or three strokes, stand up, and continuing a passable imitation of a crawl, burst out: 'How can I find out whether English businessmen take consideration seriously when I am isolated in this place?' Splash. 'How can one make sense of *Felthouse* v. *Bindley*[3] in *Khartoum*?' Splash. Or, he might have added, cases about camels in zoos, horses jumping over hedges, circus elephants, Carbolic Smoke Balls, and other features of English life that were conspicuously absent in Sudan.[4]

I do not recall whether terms such as 'context' or 'the law-in-action'

[1] P. S. Atiyah, *The Sale of Goods*, 1st edn., (London, 1957).

[2] P. S. Atiyah, *An Introduction to the Law of Contract* 1st edn., (Oxford, 1961).

[3] (1862) 11 CBNS 869.

[4] This general theme is developed in my 'The Camel in the Zoo' in Issa Shivji (ed.), *The Limits of Legal Radicalism* (Dar-es-Salaam, 1986); see also 'Talk about Realism' (1985) 60 *NYULR* 329, at 359–60.

were used, but the problem of making sense of the common law in Sudan was clear. So too was the relevance of finding out what happens in practice, in England as well as Sudan, as part of understanding any legal doctrine. Patrick juggled ideas and splashed about with equal abandon. And I learned that this was no conventional 'black-letter' lawyer.

Several years later, in 1965, Robert Stevens invited me to join him in planning a new series of law books designed to challenge the existing textbook orthodoxy. We had first developed some of these ideas in Dar-es-Salaam. The need for such a venture seemed obvious to us and we had few doubts about the general approach that we favoured. But there was a problem of choosing a suitable title for the series. 'Law in Society' had been pre-empted by another series that was being launched concurrently. 'Law and Society' was too similar. 'Realism' was a discredited idea in England, and people were still making puns about sociology and socialism. In any case, sociology was too narrow for our purposes. Borrowing the idea from Addison Mueller's *Contract in Context*[5] I had suggested 'Law in Context', which appealed to me more than to my co-editor. Eventually this was accepted *faute de mieux*.[6]

The main problem, as we saw it, was to find suitable authors. To our dismay we soon learned that some of the few obvious candidates had been pre-empted by Otto Kahn-Freund, Bill Wedderburn, and Harry Street for another publisher.[7] When I suggested Atiyah's name, doubts were expressed on the ground that he was an examplar of the tradition we were seeking to subvert. I told of my experiences in his 'swimming-pool', and pointed out that, since he had recently completed several years at the Board of Trade, he was particularly well qualified to explore the relationship between aspects of commercial law, commercial practice, and public regulation. So it was agreed that he should be invited to contribute a book within this general area. However, when I visited him in his rooms in New College he declared that he was bored with contract and commerce (happily this proved to be a passing phase) and wished to write a book on torts. This suggestion was accepted, and within a remarkably short time *Accidents, Compensation and the Law*[8] followed.

As plans for the series developed, I became increasingly concerned about its intellectual foundations. It was clear what it was not, but one of the lessons of the history of the American Realist Movement was

[5] A. Mueller, *Contract in Context* (Brooklyn, 1952).

[6] For details, see 'Talk about Realism' n. 4 above, at 372–8.

[7] 'The Law and Society' series, published by Penguin Books. See the Editorial Foreword in D. W. Elliott and Harry Street, *Road Accidents* (London, 1968). It seems to have been a coincidence that the first book in both series concerned accidents.

[8] P. S. Atiyah, *Accidents, Compensation and the Law*, 1st edn. (London, 1970).

that it had been more successful in its iconoclastic and negative aspects than in providing a basis for constructing coherent alternatives. We decided to hold a one-day meeting for potential authors and sympathetic colleagues, and I undertook to write a general working-paper.

The 'mini-conference' was held in London, at the Oxford and Cambridge Club, on 20 May 1967. Some papers were circulated in advance and presentations were made by Patrick Atiyah, John Griffith, Alan Milner, Patrick McAuslan, and myself.[9] The editors felt that the seminar was a success. Ironically, in the course of a lively debate it was Atiyah's proposal which attracted the sharpest criticism, mainly on the ground that it was 'too traditional'. He had not yet lived down his image.

In the next section my working-paper is reproduced in its original, incomplete form. Some footnote references have been added, the appendices and a lengthy quotation have been omitted, but the text has not been altered. The third section comments retrospectively on the text, with particular reference to the idea of 'a contextual approach' as a juristic concept and the question whether an 'ideal type' of a 'Law in Context' book can be constructed. The essay ends with an examination of the first edition of *Accidents, Compensation and the Law* in relation to that ideal type.

Law in Context: A Tentative Rationale

A. INTRODUCTION: THE STEREOTYPE

Conventional law textbooks tend to follow a stereotyped pattern. 'Law in Context' is envisaged as a series of books that will compete with, supplement, and occasionally even replace this stereotype. The series has been stimulated by a dissatisfaction with the state of legal education, of legal research and, in particular, of legal literature in England. This paper attempts to analyse some of the sources of this dissatisfaction and to provide a tentative theoretical basis for the series.

It is convenient to start with an examination of the stereotype that we seek to attack: the standard pattern of the English textbook. An

[9] The papers were: P. S. Atiyah, 'Torts: Some Preliminary Thoughts'; Patrick McAuslan, 'Modern land Law'; Alan Milner, 'On the University Teaching of Criminal Law', (1963) 7 *JSPTL, (NS)* 192 (already published); William Twining and Robert Stevens, 'Law in Context: A tentative rationale' (reproduced here), together with three appendices: (i) W. Twining, 'Llewellyn's Cases and Materials on the Law of Sales' (a revised version appeared in (1967) *30 MLR 514)*; (ii) Willard Hurst, *Preface to Law and Economic Growth—The Legal History of the Lumber Industry in Wisconsin 1836–1915* (Washington, DC, 1964); (iii) Lawrence Friedman and Stewart Macauley, 'Contract Law and Contract Research: Past, Present and Future' (a revised version was published in (1968) 20 *Journal of Legal Education* 452). Note: hereafter the original footnotes are indicated by an asterisk.

historian has recently commented: 'The lawyer's textbook looks more like a chemistry book than a history book: the law is divided up into a number of elements or rules, and when these are traced back to their origins through strings of cases the logical pattern remains dominant and the separate strands are not woven into coherent history.'[10] Social scientists and others have commented in similar terms and one is sometimes given the impression by laymen that the legal textbook symbolises for them a general aridity, dullness, narrowness and philistinism in the house of intellect of academic lawyers. Law teachers often seem to have a curiously ambivalent attitude towards legal textbooks: they encourage their students to rely heavily upon them, they may write them, they may even make money out of them; yet they disassociate themselves from the intellectual attitudes and educational values that the genre encourages: authoritarian dogmatism, simplification, distrust of speculation on the part of the authors, and for students predigestion, relief from the need to think for oneself, and a high premium on memory-work.

As educational tools textbooks fly in the face of some of the fundamental values of university education and at the same time they are primitive as means of training effective practitioners; as works of scholarship they may be accurate but are rarely exhaustive; they are rarely sufficiently comprehensive to be efficient works of reference; as works of the intellect they are, with rare exceptions, unimaginative; they have no pretensions to be works of art.

That some admirable works have been produced within the convention is not denied. At various points in history treatise-writers have performed a valuable job of creative synthesis, imposing order on a wilderness of precedents or statutory provisions. Not all textbooks have had all the faults listed above. Many are notable for other virtues, most commonly lucidity, accuracy, and a rigorous analytical posture. But if in a legal textbook one finds profundity, originality, imagination, stimulation, or insight it is usually in spite of the tradition of the genre rather than because of it. Perhaps saddest of all is the thought that so many outstandingly able men have devoted so much effort to working within so restrictive a medium.

B. THE CONTEXT

(i) The Juristic Context

The dominant juristic influence in England is still analytical. Courses on jurisprudence, and jurists themselves, may recognize that there is

[10] *Alan Harding, *A Social History of English Law* (Harmondsworth, 1966), 9.

more to jurisprudence than the analysis of doctrine, but to the limited extent that legal theory has been influential in the writing of textbooks, it has been mainly in relation to the analysis of legal concepts. The salient characteristics of the analytical tradition are well known: the emphasis on the autonomy of law as an independent discipline or science; the centrality of doctrine (rules and principles) to the concept of 'law'; the clear differentiation of law as it is from law as it ought to be; exposition and 'neutral' analysis usually given pride of place over criticism and suggestions for reform; and a reluctance to discuss questions of policy in detail. The conservative values of consistency and certainty (in the sense of settled doctrine) repeatedly nudge out other values. In its external relations with other disciplines the closest ties have been with empirical philosophy, which places great emphasis on the analysis of language. Less frequently noted, but for our purposes, significant, is a tendency to maintain a clear-cut distinction between 'theory' and 'practice' and for 'theory' to be associated with a concern with rather general and abstract problems.

Textbook writers under pressure to provide confident statements of 'the law' have to gloss over the problems of interpreting cases and statutes; the blandness of many expositions suggests that even the existence of such problems is not always appreciated. This indifference to their own methodological assumptions is sustained by the authoritarian nature of a tradition that dictates that there is a single correct answer to almost every question.

The main strengths of the tradition have been lucidity, accuracy and intellectual rigour; its weaknesses a narrow formalism, cultural isolationism, a propensity for unjustified dogmatism and a tendency to be divorced from the contemporary world of affairs. A contextual approach which is to be disciplined involves the conscious exploitation of the strengths of both analytical and sociological jurisprudence. 'Law in Context' must proceed from a broader jurisprudential base than does the typical textbook, yet it must seek to preserve as far as possible the rigour associated with the narrower approach.

(ii) The Educational Context: The Textbook and Legal Education

The textbook is still the most used form of students' book. This is largely due to the style of examinations that law students have to undergo; the professional examinations have traditionally been little more than tests of memory; this is largely true of examinations for non-lawyers, even within the universities. Despite a respectable tradition of resistance to parrot-learning by university teachers of law, the information content of university law examinations has tended to be significantly higher than in most other university subjects. This is to be explained in large part by the influence of the profession both direct and indirect. A student who has mastered the textbook in a particular subject can be confident of passing almost any law examination in that subject. It is not surprising that the majority of candidates for law examinations, professional, university or otherwise, rely heavily upon the textbook and its satellite, 'the nutshell'. In the universities students are normally expected to resort to primary sources (cases and legislation), to learned articles in periodicals and, less often, to other kinds of book but very rarely to the extent that the textbook has been considered unnecessary.

The recent growth in importance of the case book in England represents a move away from this pattern. But the English case book tends to differ in function as well as in form from its American namesake. In the United States the main reason for the importance of case books is that the method of teaching is such that each student needs to have the primary sources in front of him in the class-room. The case book therefore contains almost everything that a student needs for a particular course. This is one of the features of American legal education that the editors have no wish to encourage. In England on the other hand case books are only exceptionally used as teaching *materials* (a significant expression) which every student is required to bring with him into the class-room. English case books are mainly regarded as convenient collections of standard cases, the main function of which is to save pressure on the law reports in libraries and to encourage students to resort to the primary sources. Case books are used to supplement rather than replace textbooks.

To return to the textbook. The first point to notice is that the educational objectives that a particular textbook aims to serve are often obscure. Ironically this may have commercial attractions: a work with indeterminate educational aims may be held out as serving several functions at once; for instance as an elementary reference work or as an outlet for original research, or even as a potential authoritative source of law. The standard advertisement by law publishers claims that the advertised product is useful not only to students of several types but also to practitioners and interested laymen. Thus the stereotype textbook often seeks to serve several aims, some of which may be incompatible or at least remarkably difficult to reconcile.

While textbooks have been able to serve non-pedagogical functions, in other respects they have been strongly influenced by patterns of legal education. Not surprisingly they have been closely tied to curricula. Since English law curricula have usually followed a classification which divides law up into fields that are formal in the sense that the divisions do not necessarily reflect significant social categories, textbooks have tended to follow suit. Contract, Tort, Equity are examples of fields which lump together a wide variety of disparate social situations and categories. An approach that purports to relate law to its social context may find that some of the established 'fields of Law' are unmanageable or unsatisfactory in other respects.

In other words, volumes in the 'Law in Context' series may well take some narrow area from a traditional subject and treat it in depth or it may bring together various related social issues traditionally dealt with in different subjects.

Another point worth noting is that university curricula have tended until recently to be narrow in scope and conservative. The subjects offered have tended to be few in number and relatively constant. Taxation, social legislation, international commercial transactions, etc., have only recently started to appear in university calendars. At the same time there are some recognized 'fields', in the orthodox sense, that are badly served or not covered at all by existing textbooks. Here it is worth noting the existence of a vicious circle. When a new subject is proposed to curriculum planners, a commonly raised objection is: 'There is no textbook in the area.' Conversely publishers are reluctant to risk investing in a book on a subject that is not to be found in existing curricula.

In planning 'Law in Context' particular attention will be paid to neglected, new, and unexpected subjects of study. Such subjects are most likely to make their first appearance as options in the final year of the undergraduate curriculum or in postgraduate curricula (although we are equally anxious to develop new volumes with a 'new' outlook for even the most traditional of subjects). At the same time the more senior the student, the easier it should be to loosen the grip of the standard textbook, provided that bad habits have not been too firmly ingrained in his first year or two or study. This is not to say that the series will ignore the needs of first-year students. In particular a strong case could be made out for contextual works on statutory interpretation, procedure and the English legal system which would be appropriate for first-year students.

(iii) The Commercial Context [omitted][11]

(iv) Recent Trends

Recently there has been manifested a growing discontent with the state of legal scholarship and legal education in England, especially among the younger law teachers. One can only speculate about the causes:

[11] This section was never completed. Another section, on 'The American heritage', was omitted from the second draft (see below, n. 30).

increased familiarity with foreign (particularly American) ideas and methods; greater awareness of the need for faster and faster legal change to keep pace with social and technological change; a complex social context, understanding of which can no longer be taken for granted; the inter-disciplinary fashion, which is fast becoming a fad; the belated recognition of psychology and sociology as respectable pursuits. New law faculties are opening, some connected with social science departments; the number of full-time teachers has expanded at an enormous rate during the past few years, especially outside the universities; the paperback revolution, new teaching techniques, Robbins and its aftermath are all part of the picture. On the whole the advance guard of the trend has tended to be cautious; Kahn-Freund insists that, in teaching, each legal problem should be looked at as a social problem needing a solution, but only after it has been treated as a problem requiring a dogmatic 'legal' answer in the accepted manner;[12] Wedderburn has advocated advance 'only a millimetre at a time'; others have been careful to protect their rear from attack by more conservative-minded lawyers. Evolution rather than revolution seems to be the order of the day.

Insofar as this may help us to avoid the otiose polemics of the realist controversy the cautious approach is to be welcomed. There are, however, dangers in such a strategy. The difficulties and problems of a contextual approach may be under-estimated; the urgent need for equipping the younger generation of legal scholars with a whole range of techniques which are unknown to their predecessors may be underestimated (as may be the difficulty of doing this); the crypto-conservative (the unreconstructed realist) may be as much of a threat as Bickel's 'arrested realist',[13] the revolutionary who gets stuck in a groove, his elementary programme elevated to unchangeable dogma. There is one stage in particular in the process of reconstruction where it is particularly easy to stick. The 'convert' has intellectually assented at the level of abstract theory, but he has not realized the full implications of his theoretical ideas for detailed work, still less has he been able to break intellectual habits that are founded on a different theory. (And for the record we should like to say that we are very conscious of this in our own thinking). Habits of mind are hard to break, the necessary materials are not readily available, a field categorised in a traditional manner, like Torts or Equity, may not be well-suited to a contextual treatment, and our formal legal education has not given us all of the relevant technical equipment. Moreover, the research required for a contextual approach may well be more time-

[12] *O. Kahn-Freund, 'Reflections on Legal Education', (1966) 29 *MLR* 121, 125.
[13] A Bickel, *The Least Dangerous Branch* (Indianapolis, 1962), at 81–2.

consuming than traditional legal research. Much work may have to be put into one empirical study to produce a very limited amount of data.

In his *Introduction to Jurisprudence* Lloyd discusses American legal realism with more understanding and sympathy than most English jurists have done. However, he concludes:

> Moreover, there is a great deal of traditional law, such as the rules for the formation and dissolution of contracts, which hardly seems to lend itself to any very profound sociological re-examination or reassessment on the basis of new techniques, and these represent legal spheres with which the ordinary lawyer still remains very much concerned in his daily practice. From this point of view it is not easy to see how the better type of modern textbook can be radically reconstituted in the light of fresh techniques so as better to serve the modern lawyer.[14]

This is a crucial challenge which the series faces.

C. SOME SUGGESTED GUIDELINES

At the very outset it is worth repeating: it is not our intention to replace one stereotype with another. Nor is it our function as editors to tell authors how to write their books. But, for the purpose of provoking discussion, we have not been inhibited or deterred by such considerations from expressing personal opinions on some of the problems of the series, as we see them.

(i) *The Unifying Elements in the Series*

(a) *The Contextual Approach:*

The word 'contextual' has been chosen deliberately for its open-endedness. It is relatively easy to say what 'the contextual approach' is not: it is not narrow-minded, it does not treat law as being 'just there' to be studied in isolation, it is opposed to 'formalism'. But what are these broader aspects? What constitutes the context? Our view is that these need not be, indeed probably cannot be, defined in general terms. Each book will present particular problems of its own in respect of delimitation and presentation of the subject-matter, etc. 'Context' in one case may include the practices and expectations of the people most directly affected by the rules under consideration (e.g. in relation to business law), in another the light to be thrown on particular problems

[14] Dennis Lloyd, *Introduction to Jurisprudence*, 2nd edn. (London, 1965), at 262. This passage was modified in later editions.

by the techniques and findings of other disciplines;[15] in almost all 'context' will include the consideration of policies underlying the rules. That there is plenty of scope within 'the contextual approach' for differences of method, for disagreement and for experiment should be considered a virtue, if a principal object is to liberate legal scholarship from artificial restrictions. But this virtue carries with it the risk for our series that it will be a formless hotchpot of works united only by a negative reaction against a narrow tradition. Quite apart from the weakness of building anything solely on a negative reaction, there is the additional threat in the present case that some works would be 'unreconstructed', with the contextual matter little more than a gloss or an ornament, and that others may go to the opposite extreme, incorporating distortions and exaggerations of the kind which brought the realist movement into disrepute.

One possible solution might be to spell out a theory of law as a basis for the series as a whole. This, however, would almost certainly turn out to be either too vague to be useful or so dogmatic as to be both controversial and constricting—and authors would rightly refuse to be bound by it. Nearly all legal theories are contextual, with the possible exception of Kelsen's Pure Theory and its poor relations. By a 'legal theory' we mean in this context an articulated statement of a coherent set of general ideas about law; an important feature of a contextual approach is that it bears a close and definite connection to legal theories in this sense. For part of the 'context' of any 'legal' discussion is the assumptions presupposed by statements about law, whether these be statements *of* rules of law, or other kinds of statements *about* law. A characteristic of the contextual approach is that these assumptions are articulated, examined, and subjected to critical scrutiny; a characteristic of the tradition we are reacting against is that it is not self-conscious about its assumptions or, when it is, 'theory' is not considered as having a direct bearing on 'practice', which would here include the practice of legal writing.

Viewed in this way any one of a number of legal theories may be acceptable to someone working contextually. Pound, Llewellyn, Bentham, Lasswell and McDougal are just some of those who might provide a theoretical framework for one or more works in the series. The implications of the general ideas of these jurists for the writing of

[15] *e. g., in relation to Evidence, theories of knowledge, the psychology of perception, the weighing of evidence by historians and other specialists in fact-finding and interpretation, the conclusions of the Chicago Jury Project *re* the jury as a fact-finding device; it is significant that *Cross on Evidence*, 1st edn. (London, 1958), only makes use of one 'contextual' work (Gulson's *Philosophy of Proof*, 2nd edn. (London, 1923)) and contains not even a reference to works of leading legal theorists like Bentham, Frank, or Perelman—an interesting contrast is offered by A. Trusov's *An Introduction to the Theory of Evidence* (Moscow, 1963).

law books have not often been spelled out, but there are implications and they can be articulated. There is, of course, a danger that a general theory may be applied dogmatically, instead of being used as a source of ideas and as a guide, but the English tendency is to under-use rather than to over-use theory and we need not be unduly apprehensive of this particular danger.

It does not matter for the purposes of our series what theory, if any, a particular author adopts; what may be important, however, is that what would in a traditional textbook often be left unstated should be articulated. This may be particularly important in respect of (a) the objectives of the book, including educational objectives, if any; (b) the methods employed for attaining (a); (c) the standpoint(s) of the author (see *infra*); and (d) the choice of organizing concepts for classifying the material (See Appendix on Llewellyn's *Cases and Materials on the Law of Sales*)[16]; and (e) the values by which particular legal institutions or doctrines are judged.

It may be wise to leave open-ended the matter of a general theoretical basis for books in the series. It is still possible to ask whether one may not expect some theoretical common ground. This is a difficult question, to which we can only give a tentative answer. Although there is logically no necessary connection between a contextual approach and a teleological view of law, it seems likely (and for the series, desirable), that there will be a close connection in fact. Most authors will probably look on law as a means to an end (they may disagree as to what the ends should be), in which case they will be more likely to make explicit the ends that they consider a particular body of law should be securing and will criticise consistently in terms of such stated ends.

In recent years, much has been written on the relationship of law and the social sciences. Alas the amount of 'doing' has not kept pace with the amount of 'talking'. Thus rather than insist that 'Law in Context' is an attempt to relate law and the social sciences, we would rather put it in a more mundane way. Our purposes in this area are two-fold. We hope to see books in this series relating legal doctrines to what actually happens in practice. (In contract, for instance, trying to find out what businessmen and other participants actually do, what is done in arbitration, the effect of insurance, and the practical importance of such matters as consideration). Second, we should like to see authors being more critical of the policies underlying statutes and judicial decisions, and raising more regularly and more extensively than at present what the law should be.

We are aware that many members of the profession and some

[16] See above, n. 9.

academic lawyers are opposed to exposing students to such material. Obviously we do not share their views. But such critics have to be convinced that the inclusion of such material is not inconsistent with the retention of at least a major part of the advantages to be derived from the current approach to academic law. We think the two are not only reconcilable, but that there exists in England the opportunity for getting the best of both worlds. We trust that 'Law in Context' books will in no way encourage legal sloppiness, or discourage doctrinal analysis; but hopefully they will link this doctrinal analysis to what actually happens in practice, at the same time forcing law students to consider what policies the law should pursue and what the law ought to be.

(b) The Audience

It is the policy of the series that the 'intellectual level' of the books should be that of the 'average' university undergraduate. Implicit in our criticisms of the traditional textbook is the suggestion that such books tend to underestimate the intellectual capacities of undergraduates and to lay too much stress on simplification and handing things to students on a plate. They also try to perform a reference function, which unnecessarily duplicates the efforts of such readily available and more efficient works as *Halsbury*. It is suggested that our image of The Reader should be of an intelligent person who is capable of understanding the How and the Why as well as the What, and who is able to supplement the information provided by 'Law in Context' books by use of standard works of reference. In 'Law in Context' depth should take priority over coverage and detail; this does not mean to say that the information-content of books in the series should be kept deliberately low. The point is rather that, if we are to produce works which are as solid as *Salmond on Torts*, but which aim at a broader perspective and a deeper understanding, then something has to be sacrificed. As has already been suggested, most of our books will try to cover less ground (in terms of legal topics) than *Salmond*—in other words a narrower coverage; but this may not be enough and, in some works at least, the general level of information-content may have to be less detailed as well, although if dramatization or similar devices are used, much more detail may be given in respect of selected instances. One foresees that striking a balance between the competing claims of coverage, detail and depth will be one of the most persistent problems of the series. There is no simple dogmatic solution. We suggest as a general guide that depth should normally be given priority.

If we aim single-mindedly at the undergranduate, the question arises:

should the series have any specific pedagogical aims? Are we, for instance, to look on the books as teaching tools? If so, how is that to affect them? The policy of the series is flexible on this point: it has been decided that the books may vary both in length and form; for instance the series could include a 'Cases and materials' work along the lines of Donnelly, Goldstein, and Schwartz' *Criminal Law*, a monograph like Berle's *The Modern Corporation and Private Property*, a collection of connected essays like Stevens and Yamey, *The Restrictive Practices Court*, or somthing more resembling a treatise, like Gower's *Modern Company Law*, or even a 'contextual' learning programme comparable to Kelso's *A Programmed Introduction to the Study of Law*;[17] similarly, although the aim is to produce substantial works, the series could accommodate a book on a relatively narrow topic of as little as 100–150 pages. Obviously objectives will vary with each book, including pedagogical objectives, and for this reason no general guide can be given for the series as a whole.

(ii) Ephemerality

Within any intellectual tradition it is important to try to seek to differentiate the relatively stable from the ephemeral. Any work which is to have lasting value or wide significance needs to be based on some stable foundation. By and large people working in the tradition of legal formalism find this stable element in the allegedly unchanging principles of the common law. The old law teacher's idea that gentlemen should not study legislation in a university was no doubt rooted in a feeling that one could expect the common law to evolve at a staid and respectable pace, whereas the legislature might overnight at any time abolish a whole field of legal study. The pathos of the German civilian's complaint 'that the politicians could repeal my life work in a day' is matched by the bewilderment of authors and publishers of formalistic books on African Constitutions when a large part of the subject-matter of their work disappears soon after the date of publication, if not on the very day, as happened in the case of Read and Morris' *Uganda*.[18] One of the fatal weaknesses of formalism is its inability to cope with rapidly changing situations. One of the root causes of the present trend

[17] R. C. Donnelly, J. Goldstein, and R. D. Schwartz, *Criminal Law* (New York 1962); A. A. Berle and G. C. Means, *The Modern Corporation and Private Property* (New York, 1932); R. Stevens and B. Yamey, *The Restrictive Practices Court* (London, 1965); L. C. B. Gower, *The Principles of Modern Company Law*, 2nd edn. (London, 1957); C. Kelso, *A Programmed Introduction to the Study of Law* (Indianapolis, 1965).

[18] H. F. Morris and J. S. Read, *Uganda: The Development of its Laws and Constitution* (London, 1966).

away from formalism must surely be the increase in the pace of change in modern life, and in particular, the recent burst of law reform.

How can the contextual approach cope with this problem? In some ways it is harder for it to do so. Social change is notoriously faster than legal change; contextual work necessitates keeping pace with advances in other disciplines; the patient grubber after facts is often as prone to find his research as outdated as the African Constitutional lawyer. 'Law in Context' books are law books and so the problems posed by an increase in the pace of law reform are almost as acute for us as for traditionalists. Almost, but not quite. For insofar as the contextual approach is concerned with Why and How as well as What, it is to some extent concerned with less ephemeral phenomena. Social problems, people's values, even methods tend to change rather more slowly than detailed social facts and legal doctrines. Bentham's *Rationale of Evidence*, for instance, still has contemporary significance because he organised it around a consideration of 'the ends of judicature' and possible ways of achieving those ends.[19] Specific doctrines, many of which have been superseded, were considered in the context of relatively stable problems and objectives. Peake's *Compendium of the Law of Evidence*,[20] the treatise to which he referred non-lawyers and law students, has long since been forgotten.

It is desirable that a high proportion of 'Law in Context' books should be of lasting value, not only because of the obvious attractions of such an objective to authors and publishers alike, but also for basic educational reasons. Insofar as a prime objective of the series is to provide books of more educational value than standard textbooks, and insofar as one of the crucial problems of legal education is how to cope with the ever-increasing pace of change, and insofar as the solution lies in concentrating on that which is relatively stable or which has broad implications—viz. problems, values, methods—books which are written in full appreciation of the problems of working in a changing context are likely to be the most valuable educationally.

The experience of writers on African constitutions suggests some devices for coping with rapidly changing situations. One avenue of escape is to resort to an historical treatment. Dr Claire Palley completed her study of the Constitution of Rhodesia shortly before UDI and she only had time to insert a brief addendum dealing with the event.[21] Unlike many African legal works her book has a good survival potential, for not only is a substantial part of it based on a moving time scale (straight history) but much of the 'flat' description is sufficiently

[19] J. Bentham, *Rationale of Judicial Evidnce*, ed. J. S. Mill (London, 1827).
[20] T. Peake, *A Compendium of the Law of Evidence*, 1st edn. (London 1801).
[21] Claire Palley, *The Constitutional History and Law of Southern Rhodesia, 1888–1965* (Oxford, 1966).

related to an evolutionary pattern that many sections will continue to have a significance that is not dependent upon the law remaining static. History may have to be re-written in every generation, but not every two years. Another device that has been resorted to has been to select particular points of time (e.g. the date of Independence) as the reference point for a detailed study. The basis of selection of the point of time need not be arbitrary, as is usually the case when the cut-off point is related to the date of publication; rather, a moment may be chosen by reference to the same kinds of consideration that affect the choice of subjects of 'case studies'.

To sum up: time is part of the context of almost any study. In periods of rapid change it becomes of critical importance. This is especially so in our present educational situation. One of the most difficult problems is how to equip our students to be adaptable. Insofar as the 'Law in Context' series has pedagogical aims, it should be especially sensitive to this problem.

(iii) Standpoint

One important aspect of lack of self-consciousness in our textbook tradition is that it is often unclear with whom the author identifies himself and what is his image of his audience. To take a simple example: a book on 'Personal injuries and the law' could vary quite considerably in form and content, depending on whether the operative image of the typical reader were a barrister arguing an appeal on a point of law (who might not be able to mention the insurance aspects), a judge hearing the appeal (who might not be meant to know anything about the insurance aspects), a solicitor acting for a client (how much would he need to know that is not in *Salmond*?) or a specialist on accident prevention or a reformer who is interested in (possibly radical) reform of the whole system of distribution of risk in relation to accidents. Differences in standpoint produce different criteria of relevance and of importance. A famous passage on causation from R. G. Collingwood makes the basic point:

> A car skids while cornering at a certain point, turns turtle, and bursts into flames. From the car-driver's point of view, the cause of the accident was cornering too fast, and the lesson is that one must drive more carefully. From the county surveyor's point of view, the cause was a defective road surface, and the lesson is that one must make skid-proof roads. From the motor manufacturers' point of view, the cause was defective design, and the lesson is that one must place the centre of gravity lower.[22]

[22] R. G. Collingwood, 'On the So-called Idea of Causation, (1937–8) *Proc. Aristotelian Society* 85, at 96.

Salmond on Torts, a book which, until the latest edition,[23] never even mentioned the insurance aspects of personal injuries claims, does not make explicit the standpoint of the work. As regards readership the Preface to the First Edition indicates that it is primarily directed towards 'lawyers and students of law';[24] 'the standpoint of the student' is not a clearly differentiated 'standpoint' in the sense the term is used here, because it does not tell us with whom the student is supposed to identify nor what are the objectives of his studying the law of Torts. We may speculate that, in the Oxbridge tradition, there may have been a tendency, perhaps unconscious, to identify with barristers and Lords of Appeal, rather than with solicitors or less senior members of the judiciary or with 'legislators'; certainly the omission of discussion of the insurance aspects is partly explained on this ground. But a complete explanation would also need to include reference to the author's self-image, which, insofar as it is clear, is that of 'the legal scientist' systematically expounding 'legal science', the subject-matter of which is legal doctrine only. The law student reader, it seems, is also expected to identify with 'the legal scientist' in that the basic educational assumption underlying *Salmond* is that the student's main task is to learn the systematically expounded principles of the law of Torts. The fact that this accords most closely with the standpoint of 'the judge' could be treated as being coincidental.

The above analysis should not be interpreted in the first instance as a criticism of *Salmond*, although it could be used as a basis for criticism. Rather it is intended to illustrate the conception of 'standpoint'. *Salmond assumes* certain educational aims and *identifies* fairly consistently with the standpoint of one particular kind of participant in legal processes. The book has probably served those aims admirably. It has also been useful to a wide variety of people. But we must not, for this reason, be led into thinking that *Salmond's* aims are the only possible ones, or that the standpoint of 'the legal scientist' or 'the judge' is the only possible standpoint or even always the most apposite.

At this stage it may be appropriate to look more closely at the concept of 'standpoint' as an analytical tool. Although it is rarely openly described as such, differentiation of standpoint is a commonly used juristic tool for clearing up confusions of thought. Part of the disagreement between 'retributivists' and 'utilitarians' in respect of the justification of punishment has been dissolved by showing that retributivists make most sense when treated as answering 'the judge's question', whereas utilitarians are most commonly concerned with 'the

[23] *R. F. V. Heuston (ed.), *Salmond on Torts*, 14th edn. (London, 1965), 33–8.
[24] *Salmond*, Preface to first edition, reprinted in later editions.

legislator's question'. In other words failure to differentiate between the standpoints of 'the judge' and of 'the legislator' has been the source of some confusion of thought in philosophical discussions of punishment. It is commonly pointed out that Bentham's principle of utility is much less vulnerable to criticism when viewed from the standpoint of 'the legislator' than from the standpoint of the individual actor who has to decide how he alone should act. Examples could be multiplied.[25]

Failure to make clear differentiations of standpoint helps to explain persistent misunderstandings and misconceived criticisms of American jurists, such as Holmes and Llewellyn, when they talk of law in terms of prediction. Brief analysis of a famous passage may help further to elucidate the concept of 'standpoint'.

It will be recalled that one of the first 'realist' writings was Holmes' noted paper 'The Path of the Law'. The context of the reading of this paper is significant; Holmes was addressing [Boston University] law students after dinner during the heyday of Langell's influence at Harvard. Holmes' message was that the way in which the students were taught to look at law was different from the way in which certain types of participants looked at it, and for this reason it was unrealistic. To give punch to what he was saying Holmes set out to shock his audience by use of a vivid and seemingly cynical image:

> Take the fundamental question, what constitutes the law? You will find some text writers telling you that it is something different from what is decided by the courts of Massachusetts or England, that it is a system of reason, that it is a deduction from principles of ethics or admitted axioms or what not, which may or may not coincide with the decisions. But if we take the view of our friend the bad man we shall find that he does not care two straws for the axioms or deductions, but that he does want to know what the Massachusetts or English courts are likely to do in fact. I am much of his mind. The prophecies of what the courts will do in fact, and nothing more pretentious, are what I mean by the law.[26]

This famous passage has been criticised, most commonly on two grounds. First, it is said, Holmes seems to be advocating an amoral attitude to law. This need not concern us here, though it should be pointed out that Holmes' Bad Man looks more like a tax consultant than a character from Genet; second, to look at law in terms of prediction does not take account of the standpoint of the judge or the legislator. There is considerable force in both these criticisms, if Holmes was trying to put forward a rounded philosophy of law that

[25] See now, W. Twining and D. Miers, *How To Do Things with Rules*, 3rd. Edn. (London, 1991), at 64–74.

[26] O. W. Holmes Jr., 'The Path or The Law', (1897) 10 *Harv. LR* 451, 460–1.

accommodated all possible standpoints. But the context of his talk suggests that Holmes' main objective was more modest. He was addressing himself to a specific audience composed, as he saw it, of intending practitioners; the image of the practitioner that he projected in this paper was essentially the image of the office lawyer. The point that Holmes was trying to get across was that the standpoint of such a functionary was significantly different from the kind of standpoint that Harvard law students were being asked to adopt and that this was an unrealistic way of preparing students for private practice. In 'The Path of the Law' the standpoint of the Bad Man and the standpoint of the counsellor are roughly equated and are by implication differentiated from those of the judge, the legislator and even the advocate. Holmes' message can be restated in the following fashion without much distortion: 'You are intending to be private practitioners of law; the standpoint of the private practitioner, especially in respect of his role as counsellor, is very different from that of the judge or legislator. Your legal education, by concentrating on legal rules, tends to teach you to look at law from the standpiont of the judge, insofar as any standpoint is differentiated.'

A similar analysis of the first chapter of Llewellyn's *Bramble Bush* in terms of his picture of his audience as intending private practitioners of law ('the Counsellor' image again predominating) may help to explain, if not totally to justify, some of the passages that have occasioned controversy.[27]

[In a famous passage Pound distinguished between six standpoints from which 'law in the sense of the body of authoritative precepts may be looked at': the lawmaker, the individual subject to the legal precept (whether good citizen or bad man); a judge or administrative official making an authoritative determination; the counsellor or legal adviser; the jurist or teacher; and the enterpreneur or man of business].[28]

Whereas Pound's characterization of different standpoints is quite useful, it is rather crude and is open to the criticism that he does not distinguish clearly between the standpoints of actual people (actual judges, actual members of a legislature, etc.) and the 'standpoints' of constructs which refer to certain functions, no matter who performs them. 'The legislator'for instance may refer not only to one who has power and authority to make law, such as a member of Parliament, but to anyone who is concerned with 'the law as it ought to be'. Actual judges 'make law' and when they do so their standpoint is that of 'the legislator'. The standpoint of 'the legislator' in fact covers at least two

[27] See W. Twining, *Karl Llewellyn and the Realist Movement* (London, 1973), at 140–52.

[28] R. Pound, *Jurisprudence* St Paul, Minn. ii. 129–31. The passage was quoted in full in the text, but has been omitted here for reasons of space.

functions: (i) the formulation or clarification of goals and (ii) the creation or choice of laws or other instruments for achieving these goals. Similarly the standpoint of 'the judge' at least covers the functions of (i) deciding particular cases and (ii) advancing reasoned justifications for such decisions; again a much more differentiated analysis of functions could be made in this respect. There is clearly an overlap or at least a close relationship between many of these functions—in the case of 'persuading' (argument by an advocate on a point of law) and judicial justification, almost complete identity. Pound's suggestion that 'law in the sense of a body of authoritative precepts' can be verified in terms of the standpoint of the judge, should not be taken to mean that the standpoint of the judge can be taken as covering all standpoints for all purposes. For instance, predicting the outcome of a particular case is not normally associated with the standpoint of 'the judge', (although of course an actual judge with an eye to a possible appeal from his decision may be concerned with prediction); nor would preventative counselling or negotiating or drafting, or other functions performed by private practitioners, normally be associated with the standpoints either of 'the judge' or actual judges.

The concept of 'standpoint' may be used with reference either to constructs personifying particular functions ('the legislator', etc.) or to actual or imagined people ('what would a normal solicitor dealing with a typical personal injuries claim arising from a motor accident want to know?'). The former is more intellectualised and accordingly more susceptible to rigorous development; the latter may help to promote a more realistic identification of the author with typical participants in actual processes. But the point must not be overlooked that the extent to which the concept of 'standpoint' can be employed as a tool of refined analysis turns largely on the degree of refinement of the characterization of different standpoints. The difficulty of differentiating between 'judicial', 'administrative' and 'legislative' functions is a familiar illustration of the problem of finding a satisfactory scheme of classification of functions of participants in legal processes. For present purposes it will be adequate to accept Pound's characterization, treating the headings as constructs rather than as referring to actual people.

What is the application of all this to 'Law in Context'? The brief answer is that, if we are right in suggesting that self-consciousness is basic to a 'contextual approach', then it would probably be a healthy exercise for an author to ask: 'Who am I? What am I trying to do? Who is my potential audience?' The first question will help to clarify overall purposes ('I am a legal scientist, scientifically expounding "the law" as it is' (for what purposes?); 'I am a critic of the existing law recommending what the law should be' (ideally or in terms of what is immediately practicable?); 'I am a social scientist-lawyer, reporting on findings I have made' (about what? to what end?); 'I am a collector and organiser of useful information for easy reference' (useful to whom for what?) or a combination of these (to what extent are they compatible?)). The question 'who is my potential audience?' should further clarify purpose and provide criteria of relevance: Am I, in writing about personal injuries, addressing (actual or intending) solicitors, barristers, Lords of Appeal, Law Commissioners, industrial efficiency experts, insurance men, plaintiffs, defendants, social scientists? What knowledge can be assumed? As participants in (typical) processes what do they need to know and understand? (Back to: Who am I?) To what extent am I setting out to give them all they need? And so on. 'Standpoint' is a concept which makes the elementary point that different people have different purposes and roles and needs and that authors of books should bear this in mind.

(iv) Conclusion

These are just some of the ideas that we feel may be helpful in the difficult task of trying to devise 'new' forms of legal literature. We put 'new' in inverted commas because, of course, what is being attempted is only relatively new. There is much relevant experience from which we can learn. In particular American lawyers have been struggling for nearly fifty years with the problems of converting a contextually oriented jurisprudence into concrete work in particular areas. The differences between the American scene and our own, especially in respect of legal education, may point to the conclusion that America may not be able to provide many models for simple imitation on this side of the Atlantic. Nevertheless in many specific respects their successes and their failures may be instructive. There are attached as appendices to this paper, some pieces concerning certain aspects of American legal literature which may be suggestive.[29]

May, 1967 W.L.T.
R.B.S.[30]

Retrospect

If I were to draft a manifesto or rationale for a new series of 'contextual' books today, there would undoubtedly be differences in

[29] See above, n. 9.

[30] William Twining and Robert Stevens. The paper was presented in our joint names as co-editors. I was responsible for the text; Robert Stevens made some comments and censored a section on the American Heritage as being too undiplomatic to present to an English audience.

tone and emphasis and in a few ideas. Among other things the situation has changed. What has surprised me most on rereading this product of twenty-four years ago has been the continuities. Today I might modify a few statements, elaborate on others, but recant on none. However, it is not my intention to explore how far the 'Law in Context' series has lived up to its original aspirations. My concern here is to examine the idea of 'a contextual approach' at a general level and to explore how far *Accidents, Compensation and the Law* exemplifies that approach.

First, a cautionary note. As editors we have tried consistently to encourage authors to write the books they really want to write, rather than conform to a rigid set of criteria or conventions. In the context of a particular publishing venture the label was not meant to be precise or constricting; indeed, one of our aims was to try to encourage a greater diversity in legal literature. Accordingly, too much should not be read into the title as such. Nor would it be likely to be helpful to try to find the lowest common denominator of 'a contextual approach' by analysing the assumptions underlying all the books in the series. This would be repeating the mistake of characterizing 'realism' by looking for ideas shared by a list of twenty legal scholars explicitly selected for their diversity.[31]

However, it would be disingenuous or unduly defensive to claim that 'law in context' and related phrases were intended to have no juristic significance at all. As editors, one test of proposals for the series has been: 'Is it (sufficiently) contextual?' The 'tentative rationale' acknowledged an intellectual ancestry and some specific general assumptions. It may be helpful to proceed by constructing an "ideal type" for a book, research project or other work embodying a contextual approach. Today one might articulate a suggested method for constructing a contextual book in terms of an intellectual procedure along the following lines:

(a) clarify the author's objectives (including educational objectives), vantage-point, role, and intended audience (clarification of standpoint);

(b) formulate the main questions to be addressed;

(c) clarify the general perspective and assumptions to be adopted in addressing these questions, together with the main methods and sources;

(d) choose an appropriate organizing category;

(e) identify the geographical scope of the work (geographical/jurisdictional context);

[31] See above, n. 27, at 75ff.

(f) in the light of (a) and (b) identify the most important relevant contexts in which the particular questions and phenomena will be studied;

(g) construct a broad demographic picture of the phenomena to be studied (total pictures);

(h) summarize the main thesis and themes of the work (the plot);

(i) state how this work relates to and differs from existing literature and what it should add to understanding or knowledge in the area (the literary context). Indicate why you think that the work should deserve attention in ten years' time (the ten-year test);

(j) in so far as particular (kinds of) decisions are a focal point of attention, construct an ideal type of the main kinds of total process which form the context of such decisions (processual thinking).

In considering a proposal or advising an author I have tended to ask such questions regularly, but not as schematically.[32] At first sight most, if not all, of these questions might be asked of any academic book or research project. Supposing that these ten points taken together characterize 'a contextual' approach, one might ask: is there some connecting thread that links all of them? And, what, if anything, makes them characterize a distinctive approach to law? A brief answer to the first question is that all the points are concerned with establishing connections, relating the subject of study and what is said to something else.[33] But we need to look in more detail at some of the categories to be able to give satisfactory answers to either question. Some are clearly points to be taken into account in planning any scholarly work. Formulation of questions (b), clarification of perspective (c), summarizing the argument (h), and relating the work to existing literature (i) are standard elements of designing any book. They feature here as part of the self-consciousness of 'Law in Context'. Clarification of standpoint (a) was dealt with at length in the original paper, but requires a brief further comment along with the other points.

Clarification of standpoint (who am I? At what stage in what process am I? What am I trying to do?) helps to locate the author in terms of vantage-point, purposes, presumed relation to the reader, and so on. Many law books either lack a clear standpoint in this sense, or assume

[32] In practise we suggest to authors that they follow the invaluable advice in Jenny Uglow, 'Preparing a proposal for a book', written for the SPTL Working Party on Academic Law Publishing in 1977.

[33] See further Twining, 'Some Jobs for Jurisprudence' (1974) 1 *Brit Jo. Law and Society* 149, at 164–6 and 'Some Talk about Realism' n. 4 above, at 371ff.

the same criteria of relevance and significance as an appellate-court judge, for no apparent reason. Many 'law in context' books have in practice tended to assume something approaching the standpoint of a legislator or policy-maker. This was the authors' choice, but it is not a necessary corollary of a contextual approach. What is needed is clarity about objectives and vantage-point, for these provide the main criteria of relevance and significance. Writers of avowedly educational works should formulate explicit learning objectives and choose a legal standpoint appropriate to these. In my experience academic lawyers are strangely reluctant to do this or to face squarely why they are giving priority to certain educational objectives. Why, for example, should undergraduate law students be encouraged to think like policy-makers or appellate-court judges? The answers to such questions are too often treated as self-evident.

Choice of an appropriate organizing category (d) has, as a matter of historical contingency, been a matter of conscious concern in 'law in context'. A central idea, borrowed from American legal realism and developed in the late 1960s by Jolowicz and others,[34] was the need to be self-conscious about classification and in particular to question the appropriateness of abstract legal categories for classifying fields of study: for example, substituting 'compensation for accidents' for 'torts' (Atiyah); 'public control of land' for 'real property' (MacAuslan[35]); 'information in litigation' for 'evidence' (Twining).[36] Patrick Atiyah's original proposal for *Accidents, Compensation and the Law* began: 'My principal complaint against the existing textbooks on Tort is that their choice and arrangement of materials is almost entirely governed by conceptualism. This may seem a relatively mild deficiency, but it is in fact a fundamental weakness.'[37]

In practice the re-examination of traditional organizing categories for fields of law and particular topics has not led to a wholesale move to 'fact-based classification', itself a problematic concept, but rather to a self-conscious effort to choose a way of designating and organizing the field or topic under consideration in a way that is appropriate to given purposes.[38] By no means all 'Law in Context' books have involved rejection of traditional legal categories (for example, Trusts, Criminal Law, Contract(s) have all survived).[39] Indeed, titles in the series do not

[34] J. A. Jolowicz (ed.), *Division and Classification of the Law* (London, 1970).

[35] McAuslan n. 9 above.

[36] W. Twining, *Rethinking Evidence* (London, 1990), ch. 11.

[37] Atiyah n. 9 above.

[38] On 'fact-based classification' see Jolowicz and Twining, O'Donovan and Paliwala in Jolowicz (ed.), n. 34 above.

[39] G. Moffat and M. Chesterman, *Trusts Law: Text and Materials* (1988); N. Lacey, C. Wells, and D. Meure, *Reconstructing Criminal Law: Text and Materials* (1990); and H. Collins, *The Law of Contract* (1986).

conform to a single taxonomy and Atiyah himself has stayed with Contract as way of designating a field.

Specifying the geographical scope of a work (e) would seem an obvious task, especially for lawyers conditioned to think in terms of jurisdictional limits. Less obvious is the question: where along the spectrum of general and particular jurisprudence does it belong? Such questions are surprisingly often ducked in academic practice. That they are often difficult to answer is illustrated by disagreements about the 'Americanness' of Ronald Dworkin or the alleged parochialism of critical legal studies.

Choice of appropriate context(s) (f). Whether it is possible to specify *general* criteria of appropriateness is, perhaps, the most problematic and potentially controversial issue, for it raises fundamental questions about the nature of academic enterprises. At one level the purpose of a particular project, enquiry, or book may provide some common-sense indications of what may be appropriate. But one's choice of purpose and method are themselves based on assumptions that are susceptible to critical scrutiny in terms of some more general legal or other theory.

Construction of a demogaphic total picture of the relevant phenomena (g). It is a familiar complaint that traditional expository scholarship tends to treat the atypical, the unrepresentative, and sometimes the trivial as if they are typical, representative, and important. Jury trials are treated as the paradigm of all trials in evidence discourse; appellate cases are treated as representative of all 'cases'; Blackacre was, at least until recently, the prototype of English residential property. The rule of thumb is: set the phenomenon under consideration in the context of some 'total picture' with particular reference to the scale of the relevant phenomena. For example, consider appellate cases in the context of all contested cases, contested cases in the context of all litigation, and litigation in the context of a total picture of all disputes (or dispute-processing) in the relevant society. What percentage of confessions are in practice retracted? Who are the main victims of misidentification—a few persons convicted by juries of serious crimes or hundreds (or more) of juveniles in less visible settings?[40] How much land is there in England and Wales? What are the main uses to which it is put?[41] What is the distribution of people and housing in respect of residential use? How many are owner-occupiers, lessees, licensees, squatters, homeless? What are the main transactions and problems relating to each category? Where does Blackacre and the problems of its spendthrift heir fit into this picture?

[40] See n. 36 above ch. 5.

[41] This demographic approach to land Law was originally developed by Patrick McAuslan.

Relating particular phenomena to some broader total picture is clearly 'contextual' in a straightforward way. Of course, the statistical incidence of a phenomenon is not the sole indicator of its importance or significance (for example, some jury trials are among the most important of all trials; *Re Polemis*[42] *is* conceptually interesting). Thinking in terms of total pictures is a simple heuristic device for countering lawyers' propensity to tunnel-vision.

Thinking in terms of total processes (j). It is a truism that decisions are a focal point of legal discourse and that they take place in the context of processes. The concept of a process as a flow of decisions and events over time has been usefully developed by Harold Lasswell (a prototypical contextual thinker?), although few have been prepared to follow Lasswell and MacDougal in making this the basis for a full-blown theory of law as a process of decision.[43] Looking at particular decisions as part of some longer total process (for example, litigation, an ongoing feud, a political strategy, some other social process) is clearly 'contextual' and equally clearly a necessary part of the intellectual equipment of anyone concerned with law.

These guide-lines are sufficient to ground some elementary points: first, the range of possible connections, and hence of contexts, is almost limitess. Those mentioned are just a sample. Secondly, several of the questions are open-ended. Which of the many possible standpoints, perspectives, and so on is to be adopted is not prescribed. Thirdly, most of these ideas may seem pretty obvious, tempting one to say that they are 'just common sense'. I would agree that they make sense and are sensible, but how common they are in practice, especially in combination, is open to question. Like 'realism', 'law in context' is not a distinctive form of legal theory, nor are these precepts on their own sufficient to constitute a comprehesive methodology for legal scholarship either in general or of a particular kind. However, they embody sufficient good sense to warrant the claim that they should be a necessary part of the equipment of every student of law, and that failure to observe any of them may be a ground for criticism.[44]

Accidents, Compensation and the Law as a Contextual Work

Unlike most authors, Patrick Atiyah delivered his manuscript ahead of schedule. *Accidents, Compensation and the Law* was published in 1970 as the first book in the 'Law in Context' series. We could hardly have got

[42] [1921] 3 KB 560.

[43] See now, Myres S. McDougal and W. Michael Reisman, *International Law Essays* (Mineola, New York, 1981).

[44] This theme is developed in 'Talk about Realism', n. 4 above.

off to a better start. It won almost instant recognition as a brilliantly designed and executed departure from tradition. Now in its fourth edition (edited by Peter Cane) it still holds its own in the market. Atiyah was highly influential in the campaign to establish the Royal Commission on Civil Liability and Compensation for Personal Injury in 1973 under Lord Pearson in the aftermath of the thalidomide affair.[45] The Pearson Commission's proposals were, in Atiyah's view, 'relatively unadventurous',[46] and even these have been largely shelved. So his criticisms of the tort 'system' in England and Wales are as pertinent as ever. The purpose of this section is to explore how far *Accidents, Compensation and the Law* fits the 'ideal type' of a 'Law in Context' book.

Conforming to the requirement to be self-conscious in design and method the first edition contained a foreword to the series (two pages) by the editors and a substantial preface (six pages) by the author. The first paragraph of the Preface gives a clear indication of Atiyah's conception of his enterprise:

> This is a law book but a law book with a difference. It deals with part of the area covered by what is traditionally thought of as the law of torts, namely compensation for the consequences of accidents, but it is at once wider and narrower than conventional books on torts. It is wider in three ways. First, it deals with many aspects of the tort system which are not normally treated as a part of the law of torts at all, and are therefore not included in books or syllabuses on the law of torts. In particular this book attempts to deal with the way in which the law of torts operates in practice, by paying full regard to the relationship between the law of torts and the institution of liability insurance, and also by examining the role of settlements as well as litigation in the compensation process. Secondly, this book is wider than the traditional torts book in that it deals with the many ways in which people may be compensated for accidents otherwise than through the law of torts; it deals with private insurance, with the criminal injuries compensation scheme, and with the social security benefits of the welfare state, and it also touches on the more personal social services which were recently the subject of the Seebohm Report. And thirdly, this book is wider than the traditional torts book in that it is as much a book *about* the law as a book detailing the law. It attempts, in other words, not merely to expound the ways in which people may be compensated under the law, but also to provide a serious attempt to study and evaluate the policies which underlie the different compensation systems operating today. On the other hand, this book is narrower than the traditional torts book in that it does not attempt anything like the same comprehensive coverage of every doctrinal principle that passes under the name of torts. Nothing will be found in this book about the economic torts, very little about nuisance and *Rylands* v.

[45] The Royal Commission on Civil Liability and Compensation for Personal Injury(Cmnd. 7054, 1978).

[46] Atiyah, n. 8 above, (3rd edn.), at 18.

Fletcher, practically nothing about defamation and many other matters discussed in torts books. Moreover, even the discussion of negligence which is not much shorter than that in many torts books, is of a very different kind. This book does not attempt to deal in the same detail with all the myriad rules laid down by the courts in actions of negligence, including in this field problems arising from contributory negligence, remoteness of damage and the assessment of damages. Athough these matters are all dealt with at some length, the treatment is directed towards stating the broad legal position, and evaluating the principal features of the legal position, rather than to a minute statemnt of every detailed rule.[47]

The book is divided into seven parts. The main headings are revealing: 1. The issues in perspective; 2. The tort system; 3. The tort system in operation; 4. Other compensation systems; 5. The overall picture; 6. Objectives; 7. The future.

The 'plot' of the book might be summarized as follows: England and Wales has a plethora of different compensation systems which, like Topsy, have just 'growed' largely independently of each other. These systems are based on different political ideologies and scales of values and their coexistence results in many anomalies and inconsistencies. The tort system does not fulfil its objectives in practice and these objectives are to a large extent incompatible with the objectives of the other main compensation systems. Accordingly, the common-law action for personal injuries ought to be abolished, but there are practical difficulties associated with all the main alternative schemes that have been proposed to date. It can also be anticipated that there will be strong opposition to significant change from the Bar and other powerful interests.

The conception of the book fits most of the elements of the ideal type. So the title indicates a change of organizing category (d); the Preface indicates the implications of this in respect of scope. Although the book was completed in Canberra and draws heavily on American and Australasian materials, the focus is explicitly on the details of the English situation and the implications of the analysis for other jurisdictions are not explored. The tort system is looked at in the context of 'the total compensation picture' in England and Wales (f), and is compared and contrasted with other compensation systems (such as social security and insurance) with devastating effect. A section entitled 'Some facts and figures' (expanded in later editions) gives a brief demography of the main phenomena of accidents and their compensation in England and Wales (g). Part 2 gives an account of the conceptual structure of the law of torts as it relates to accidents. Part 3 looks at this body of law in action in the context of the total

[47] Ibid., at xiii—xiv.

process of personal-injuries litigation, including the operation of out-of-court settlement and insurance (j). Parts 4 and 5 consider critically the phenomenon of the growth of virtually independent compensation systems, how they relate to each other and the anomalies that result ((f) again). Part 6 explores the underlying ideologies of the various systems and proposes a rationale for a single coherent system of compensation for accidents. And Part 7 considers reforms and proposals for reform in other countries and their merits and prospects in the context of England and Wales. The Preface relates the book to existing literature (i). One might say that this is a work that sets the common-law action for personal injuries caused by negligence, both in conception and in practice, in its historical, procedural, economic, ideological, and political contexts, as well as comparing it with other types of compensation and with arrangements in other common-law countries (f). We have already seen that the book passed the ten-year test with flying colours. Ironically this is an indication of its lack of political success. If there had been any significant reform, few would want to read the book as it then stood (or now stands). Most of the anomalies and inconsistencies identified in the first edition still survive. If all or most of the measures Atiyah favoured had been implemented, the book would have had to be almost completely redesigned.

The most difficult points about the relationship of *Accidents, Compensation and the Law* to our ideal type concern the theoretically most interesting questions: in particular, what standpoint, perspective, and methods did Atiyah adopt? *Accidents, Compensation and the Law* could plausibly be interpreted as a book about 'the problem of compensation for accidents' viewed from the standpoint of a mildly Fabian law-reformer, who supports the welfare state in a mixed economy. It diagnoses the problem, it analyses and criticizes current responses as incoherent and inefficient, and considers alternative strategies, though without making very detailed proposals for reform. Unlike an official law-reform document or Terence Ison's *The Forensic Lottery*,[48] it is not mainly an argument directed to resolving a problem or recommending a particular solution. The section on 'The Future' is, significantly, the shortest in the book and, like the rest of the analysis, is rather more detached than the argument of a reformer proposing a particular solution. The reason for this is made clear in the Preface. The enterprise is conceived of mainly as a contribution to legal education and legal scholarship, and only incidentally to reform. The primary audience is law students and academic specialists in torts. Although the author is not explicit about the precise educational objectives, one

[48] T. G. Ison, *The Forensic Lottery* (London, 1967).

can infer that they include critical understanding of the law of negligence. Part of the argument is that the additional (non-legal or at least non-traditional) material, for example about insurance and settlement out of court, is at least as important in understanding the law of negligence as other topics in standard torts courses. The preface emphasizes two further points: that in a university course students should study and debate policy-issues; and that a study of the law of torts through appellate cases (and a few statutes) does not lead to an understanding of this branch of the law as it affects practising solicitors and barristers and claimants. Their criteria of relevance are different from those of appellate-court judges. Thus Atiyah's standpoint is that of an academic lawyer trying to provide the basis for a critical understanding of the law of negligence in action and, incidentally, to indicate points at which that understanding might be advanced by further research. The book is unusually coherent, unlike some other contextual works, because the author sticks consistently to this standpoint.

This formulation may sound almost commonplace today. It was relatively unorthodox in England in the 1960s. What was remarkable was the way in which the objective was pursued at a number of levels. One might be tempted to say that the book sets the law of negligence in context by comparing and contrasting it with other compensation systems. This captures what is perhaps its most original feature, but only gives a partial description of the perspective and method. Perhaps a more balanced account can be made in terms of questions and answers. The opening paragraph of the Introduction outlines the agenda of questions clearly and succinctly:

> This book deals with certain kinds of misfortune, and in particular those arising from accidents. What 'accidents' does the law concern itself with? How does it seek to avoid them? Which accidents are or should be met by payment of compensation? How is that compensation assessed? How should it be assessed? Who pays for the compensation? Who should pay for it? How is a compensation system administered? These are the questions with which we are principally concerned.[49]

In answering these questions Atiyah drew on a wide range of sources from law and other disciplines (and added to them in later editions). He employed a combination of legal, philosophical, and economic analysis. This kind of interdisciplinary approach does not typically involve an articulate, 'scientific' methodology. It is relatively pragmatic and intuitive, and this, for better or worse, has been characteristic of most contextual work by lawyers in recent years. This

[49] Atiyah, n. 8 above, 3.

is a matter which both scientific and ideological purists regard with suspicion.[50].

One may conclude from this analysis that the conception of *Accidents, Compensation and the Law* conformed almost exactly to the ideal type of a 'Law in Context' book, before that ideal type was fully formulated. It was also one of the more systematic, as well as the most brilliant, in respect of execution. One reason why other contextual works differ significantly in conception, however well or badly they are executed, is just because that ideal type is open-ended in so many respects. Atiyah's *Accidents, Compensation and the Law* provides a model of excellence within a genre which accommodates a variety of standpoints, ideologies, perspectives, and methods. 'Law in Context' is neither a distinctive theory of or about law, nor an academic orthodoxy.

[50] See e.g. Campbell and Wiles, 'The Study of Law in Society in Britain', (1976), 10 *Law and Society Rev.* 547.

2

Are Omissions Less Culpable?

Tony Honoré

1. Introduction

In 1977 Jonathan Glover published a powerful attack on the 'acts-and-omissions doctrine'.[1] The doctrine, in his words, holds that in certain contexts failure to perform an act, with foreseen bad consequences of that failure, is morally less bad than to perform a different act which has the identical bad consequences. Harmful omissions are sometimes less culpable than equally harmful acts. Glover denied this and other philosophers have likewise argued that, other things being equal, there is no moral difference between killing and letting die,[2] or between positive and negative instrumentality.[3]

Other things are usually not equal. One who poisons food sent to starving refugees is likely to kill some of them, will cause great resentment, and is a constant menace to others. One who fails to contribute to the refugees' relief-fund is not certain to bring about anyone's death, since others may provide the food. His conduct may be criticized but will not be widely resented, even if he does not care whether the refugees survive. His character is probably little worse than average. But examples can be devised in which these differences are ironed out. It then becomes much less obvious that doing harm is worse than omission to help.

My reason for discussing the acts-and-omissions doctrine afresh is that, though law is strongly committed to it, lawyers have not been very successful in finding a rationale for it. The most plausible arguments for sanctioning acts more severely than omissions have so far been economic. One can refrain from a great many harmful acts, like poisoning, at the same time, while it is difficult or impossible to combine more than one helpful act, like providing food.[4] The benefit of

[1] J. Glover, *Causing Death and Saving Lives* (1977), ch. 7.

[2] H. M. Malm, 'Killing, letting die and simple conflicts' (1989) 18 *Philosophy and Public Affairs* (hereafter 'Malm'), 238, 253.

[3] The phrase is used by J. Bennett, 'Morality and Consequences' (11 *Tanner Lectures*, 1981) (hereafter 'Bennett'), 47, 72.

[4] Bennett, 87.

abstention is also widely distributed, in that if I abstain from doing harm no one is harmed, while the benefit of helpful acts is confined to the few who get the food I can provide. So it imposes a lighter burden on the person concerned, with a more widely distributed benefit to others, to make him abstain from harmful acts than to oblige him to do helpful ones. To require a positive act normally imposes a greater cost in time, effort, skill, and money than a prohibition with similar results.[5] In a society in which most people see to their own subsistence it involves a cost to transfer this responsibility to another. No such transfer-cost is involved in requiring everyone to refrain from harming others.

These are some of the arguments which tend to show that it is on the whole cheaper for society to protect life and health by forbidding harm-doing than by requiring people to help others. It also costs less to distribute the burdensome positive duties so that no one has to undertake more than a limited number of them, and that those are preferably of the sort which they would be inclined to undertake anyhow. It is cost-effective (including psychological costs) for parents to look after their own children and only in special circumstances other people's.

If we assume that it is morally worse, because more selfish, to refuse to incur a small cost in the interest of others than a large expense, it follows that it is usually worse to do harm than to fail to help. It is also worse to fail to help those whom one is naturally inclined to help than to fail to help others. Whatever the force of these arguments, societies in practice adopt the acts-and-omissions theory, even when they have sophisticated welfare systems. In both criminal and tort law liability for an omission is exceptional. In the language of duty, which is central to legal thinking, there is liability for omission only when one can show the breach of a duty to act owed to some individual or to the state, over and above the (mainly negative) duties we all owe to one another as fellow human beings.

But it does not follow from the fact that it is cheaper to regulate society mainly by forbidding harmful acts that these acts are morally worse than omissions, apart from the fact that it costs little to abstain from them. If it turns out that, apart from considerations of cost, not contributing to the relief-fund is morally just as bad, or almost as bad, as poisoning the relief food, we shall have to ask whether law and conventional morality is justified in making so sharp a distinction between acts and omissions on the basis of cost alone.

I shall argue that, when conduct is judged from the standpoint of responsibility for the harm it brings about, the acts-and-omissions

[5] Not always: see Section 4 below.

doctrine is broadly sound. Nothing will be said about the relative culpability of acts and omissions apart from their consequences, or of acts and omissions which violate social convention rather than morality or law. Rude conduct is often judged according to the distress it creates; and one can ask whether positive discourtesy (making a rude gesture) is on a par with negative discourtesy (cutting someone in the street) if the distress caused is similar. The answer—if it is possible to give one in general terms—must await another occasion.

Since writers use slightly different terms in discussing omissions, it is as well to explain at the outset how the term is used in this essay. Conduct can be divided into doing and not-doing. Sometimes conduct is contrary to a norm. A doing contrary to a norm is a commission, a non-doing an omission. Omissions are therefore those not-doings which violate norms. Norms are divided for this purpose into ordinary norms and norms which impose distinct duties, a concept which will be explained shortly. Omissions which violate distinct duties may be termed distinct omissions.

Positive acts, I contend, are often worse than omissions which violate ordinary norms, because they create the primary harms and risks of harm which omissions fail to remedy. But on the 'distinct-duties' theory, omissions which violate distinct duties are usually on a level with positive acts which violate those duties. The distinct-duties theory holds that we have, besides the background duties which we owe to all, distinct duties to other people and associations, including the state, which vary from person to person according to individual circumstance and past dealings between them. Examples are the duties of parents to children, of citizens to their state, of those who endanger others to the persons endangered, and of those who can rescue others in an emergency to the victims. How these distinct duties are thought to come into being is discussed in Section 3.

If the distinct-duties theory is right, positive acts are on a level or nearly on a level with omissions in contexts where the person concerned—the agent as he may be called—is under a distinct duty like that of parent to child. It then makes little or no difference whether the agent breaks his duty by a positive act or an omission. Beating and starving one's child are equally culpable when the harm to the child is equal (say, comparable suffering culminating in death). They are equal because the distinct duty counteracts the otherwise greater significance of positive acts by requiring the person subject to it to devote time, trouble, or money to fulfilling the duty, and in that way eliminates or reduces the moral significance of the cost difference. On the distinct-duty theory, distinct duties are stronger than the backgound duties we owe to everyone and take priority over them. Moreover, distinct duties can have varying strengths among themselves. Though both the parent and the householder have distinct duties, a parent's duty to a child may be stronger than a householder's to a visitor. It may have a higher priority and require more of the person subject to it.

But when background duties are in issue, positive acts are normally worse than omissions. Background duties are indeed largely (though not exclusively) duties to abstain from doing harm or creating an unjustified risk of harm. Beating someone else's child and not feeding it are not on a level, even if the harm to the child is the same (I may know that some child will suffer if I do not contribute to a relief-fund just as much as it would from a beating). Even if one has some background duty to care for other children, it is a weaker duty than that of caring for children who are dependent on one. So beating that other child is worse than not giving money to feed it.

The distinct-duties theory attracts lawyers, and also philosophers who attach weight to rights and obligations. Other philosophers reject the theory, and give little weight to talk of duties. Utilitarians and other consequentialists think not merely that conduct should be commended and judged by its likely outcome, but that the consequences to everyone should count. On some theories, the welfare and so forth of each person counts equally and must be added up (maximizing theories); on others the less-well-off count for more (distributive theories). Let us call all these theories in which an agent's duty is to produce the best overall result, whether the best is the maximum or the best-distributed, 'optimizing theories'. Optimizing theories make redundant the notion of duties owed to particular individuals or bodies. According to them, for example, that parents should look after their children counts not as a duty but at most as a rule of thumb, arrived at on the basis that if they do so that is likely on the whole to optimize overall happiness or welfare, or that it is too costly to get people to abandon their natural commitments even for something which is in principle better.

On optimizing theories there is no intrinsic moral difference between acts and omissions. One must behave so as to bring about the optimum good, for example, the optimum overall welfare. The best (and hence the right) way of doing this may sometimes be by abstaining from action and sometimes by a positive act. There can be no systematic preference for one over the other, but at most a rough indication based on a rule of thumb. It follows that it cannot in any systematic way be more culpable to fail to optimize welfare or satisfaction by a positive intervention than by an abstention. When the resulting shortfall from the optimum is the same, and the cost of refraining or doing is similar, acts and omissions must be equally bad. The optimizing theories, therefore, lead to a different conclusion about the relative culpability of acts and omissions from the distinct-duties theory.

The discussion which follows is intended to defend the acts-and-omissions doctrine, at least in certain contexts, and to show the connection between it, the notion of intervention, and the distinct-duties theory.

I believe my enterprise is appropriate to a volume in honour of Patrick Atiyah. It has indirectly a bearing on his theory of contract, an aspect of his work which has rightly been seen as original and challenging. At times Atiyah argues that to make a promise is no more than to admit or fix the extent of a duty based on some other ground, such as benefit or reliance.[6] On this view, promises are no more than evidence, sometimes conclusive evidence, of the promiser's obligation. In other passages Atiyah seems to allow some independent weight to promising, but treats not keeping a promise as a rather trivial default, unless the making of the promise induced the promisee to rely on its being kept and so to incur expense or forego opportunities.[7]

Not keeping a promise counts as an omission (Section 2) for which on the distinct-duties theory (Section 3) the promisor is liable by virtue of the positive act of making a promise. But the duty to keep the promise may rest on more than one ground. The promise may merely create an expectation in the promisee that it will be kept; or it may induce him to incur loss by reliance on the promise. If the promise is not kept, the promisee is in the first case no better off than before but in the second is actually worse off. It is presumably worse to make the promisee worse off than not to make him better off. People resent having their position made worse more than not having it improved as they expected, though in monetary terms the shortfall may be the same. Harm is worse than disappointment; compare a wage-cut with the refusal of an increase. The contrast, as explained further in Section 3 (a) and (e), depends on the differing grounds of the duty to keep the promise in the two cases: creating a risk of harm and giving an undertaking respectively. This difference has some bearing on the reasons for holding acts to be in general worse than omissions which bring about the same harm (Section 4).

My plan of campaign will be as follows. Some logical groundwork is first called for (Section 2). The next stage (Section 3) is to analyse the reasons for imposing distinct duties, by which people often have a duty positively to intervene in the interest, individual or collective, of others. The final part (Section 4) seeks to assess the relative culpability

[6] *Promises, Morals and Law* (Oxford, 1981), ch. 7.

[7] Atiyah's third head of liability in this area, benefit, usefully reminds us that responsibility need not be based on the conduct of the person held responsible. A person can be responsible not because of what he did or did not do but because of a benefit received or, more widely because of his position in society. It is not true (Bennett, 47–9) that 'because he did' and 'because he did not' are exhaustive of prima facie responsibility (Section 3(d) below).

of acts and omissions, something which is easier once account is taken of the social context of the conduct in question.

2. Positive Acts, Not-doings, Omissions

'If a child is neglected, it is not only his father who omits to look after him; everyone else omits to look after him also', says Glanville Williams.[8] That is plainly wrong, and violates ordinary use, which here marks a useful distinction. Only those parents, relatives, foster-parents, managers of a children's home, baby-sitters, and so on who are charged with looking after the child can be said to omit to do so. 'Omit' is both a normative and a pejorative term. An omission is not-doing-something, but not every not-doing-something is an omission. To omit implies that one ought to have done what was not done.[9] Often the 'ought' is legal or moral, as in the case of the neglected child, but it need not be. Apart from omitting to look after a child in one's charge one can omit or forget or leave out the bicarbonate of soda in the cake recipe. I can fail to take a coat when it would be wise to do so because cold weather is expected, and neglect to shake hands when shaking hands would be polite. In these informal contexts we often speak of failing or neglecting rather than omitting, 'omit' being a rather formal equivalent of the other terms. In sum, one can omit to do something only when, for whatever reason, the situation calls for it to be done.

The 'ought' which is needed to turn not-doing-something into an omission to do it can be a simple matter of prudence, courtesy, or conformity to a rule or recipe. On the other hand, a person who changes his habits does not merely by doing so omit to do what he did previously. The tippler who usually goes to the Fox and Hounds for a drink at six-thirty does not omit to do so if one day he decides to stay at home. He does not go to the inn; but, unless he has promised or is required by ties of friendship to be there, he does not omit to go there. The mere fact that he knows that someone will rely on his presence may give rise to a duty to warn the person concerned that he will not be there. In that case he will be open to criticism for omitting to give the warning rather than omitting to be present.

An omission violates a norm. Omissions therefore entail responsibility, but at times this is of the minor sort involved in being forgetful, imprudent, or impolite rather than legally or morally at fault. It is the sort of responsibility that often calls for nothing more than an

[8] *Criminal Law: The General Part*, 2nd edn. (London, 1961), 4.
[9] E. Weinryb, 'Omissions and responsibility' (1980), 30 *Phil Q.* 1, cf. Bennett, 50.

apology. On other occasions—and there is no very clear borderline—omissions are legally and/or morally significant. They are so when the norm violated is legal or moral, but not otherwise. In law this point is expressed by saying that an omission is legally significant only if there is a legal duty to act. This raises the question, to which we must return in Section 3, of the sorts of reason which give can rise to a moral or legal duty to act.

But there is more to the analysis of omissions than the fact that they must be contrary to some norm. An omission is a species of not-doing, of negative conduct, by which I mean conduct which is in its relevant aspect negative, an instance of negative instrumentality.[10] In analysing omissions we cannot avoid an inquiry into the difference between doing and not-doing. The inquiry should aim at a distinction between doing and not-doing, between positive and negative conduct, which is morally and normatively neutral. Otherwise the answer to the question whether harm-causing omissions are less culpable than positive acts will be built into the definition.

There is, however, in my view a limit to the neutrality that can be achieved. In particular it is a mistake to think that by finding a normatively neutral distinction between acts and omissions it will be possible to show that utilitarianism or some other optimizing theory, according to which there is no moral distinction between the two, is correct. If a distinction such as that between doing and not-doing is prominently marked in thought and language it is sure to mark a difference in social evaluation too, and that difference is not likely to be arbitrary.

Let us, for convenience, call the person whose conduct is in question the agent, whether the agent's conduct was positive or negative. Not-doing-something is not an easy notion to analyse. Strictly speaking, conduct itself cannot be negative, since only phrases and propositions are negative. Conduct can of course be described by a proposition which contains a negative, as in 'James did not stop speaking', but that does not settle that James's conduct was negative, for one could convey the same sense by saying 'he went on speaking'. The point of 'he did not stop speaking' is likely to be that James was expected to stop but did not. The alternative, positive way of putting it does not carry the same implication, or not so strongly. But whichever form is used refers to the same flow of words on James's part.

Clearly what is at stake in the contrast of doing and not-doing must be to do with the behaviour itself and not merely with the way in which it is described. Corresponding to every positive description of conduct there is an equivalent negative one: shooting is equivalent to

[10] The phrase is Bennett's.

not refraining from shooting. The converse is not true, at any rate not in a straightforward way. There is no positive expression which means the same as not going to the cinema. One could if necessary invent the (positive) verb 'discinematize' to express the idea ('she decided to discinematize and concentrate on her work').

So it is possible, if not always natural, to describe conduct with positive and negative expressions which have the same meaning. Apart from this point about the resources of language, the same conduct can be described in an indefinite number of ways which have different meanings. Some of these would naturally be put in a positive form, others negatively. We can say of a motorist who drove at 90 mph that he did not drive at 70 or 110 or any speed other than 90 mph. Sometimes there is point in the negative expression (for example, if the speed limit is 70 mph, or most motorists drive at that speed). But most of the possible negative descriptions of conduct will sound unnatural and be pointless. Whatever the agent's conduct, the list of negative propositions describing it—the list of things the person did not do on that occasion—will outstrip the list of possible positive descriptions. But the list of the things a person was not doing at a given moment is endless and, shorn of a special rhetorical point,[11] boring.

To whittle down the list of propositions describing conduct, the first step is to eliminate those that are irrelevant in the context. We are here interested in conduct which brings about harm, whether it would ordinarily be said strictly to cause it or to contribute to or occasion or facilitate it. Our concern is not with what are sometimes called 'pure' omissions but with those which have harmful consequences. To eliminate causally irrelevant descriptions will drastically cut down the list of propositions describing conduct. For example, it may be clear that driving at 90 mph was a cause of the accident, but far from clear that not driving at 70 or 110 mph was. The propositions that the motorist did not drive at 70 or 110 mph leave open too many possibilities, some of which would not have brought about the harm which occurred but worse harm or none at all. Those propositions have to be rejected as not specific enough in the context.

The exact sort of harm in issue will influence the appropriate description in another way. A judge has said that a doctor's wrong diagnosis (a positive act) may be equivalent to his failure to make a proper diagnosis (an omission).[12] This suggests that in the context of responsibility for the consequences either description of the doctor's conduct is acceptable. That is not the case. Suppose a doctor diagnoses

[11] For example, listing some of the things which the Prime Minister ought to have been doing instead of playing cricket.

[12] *Harnett* v. *Bond* [1924] 2 KB 517, 541.

cancer rather than AIDS. If the harm to the patient comes about through his not getting the proper treatment for AIDS, the appropriate proposition about the doctor's conduct is that he did not diagnose AIDS. If, on the other hand, the patient suffers through being mistakenly treated for cancer, with bad side-effects, the relevant proposition is that the doctor mistakenly diagnosed cancer. The harm in these two cases is not the same.

The appropriate description of the conduct must be sensitive to the connection of the conduct with the exact harm for which the agent is said to be responsible. But when the harm is the same, the difference between doing and not-doing does not depend on the causal process by which the harm is brought about. There are negative as well as positive conditions of human welfare (absence of poison, availability of food), and the same is true, with the necessary adjustment, of keeping property in good condition. So harm can be done by either intrusion or deprivation: by introducing something noxious into the body or soil or by removing or not supplying something necessary to its health. But whether harm comes about by intrusion or deprivation does not determine whether, if the causal process is traced further back, it will prove to have come about through doing or not-doing. Though often intrusions result from positive acts (beating, shooting, spraying, discharging effluent) and deprivations from not-doing-something (not feeding, not fertilizing), the inverse is possible. One can bring about starvation by destroying the food supply, a positive act. A doctor can allow a patient to be poisoned by a not-doing, for example, by not intervening when he knows that the nurse is about to give the patient a lethal dose by mistake.[13] In that case his not-doing results in an intrusion.

But what is it about the relevant description of conduct that makes it in substance positive or negative? It is widely thought, in my view rightly, that the distinction between doing and not-doing is ultimately connected with bodily movements, and that doing involves bodily movements in a way in which not-doing does not. But the connection is not straightforward. Of the causally relevant descriptions of an agent's conduct on a given occasion, some may involve conscious bodily movement, others not ('the surgeon cut the artery' and 'the surgeon did not see where the knife was going' are both relevant if the surgeon cut the artery because he did not see where the knife was going). Confronted with such ambigities, how can we say whether the relevant proposition describing the conduct is positive or negative?

Though his detailed argument is rather complicated, a suggestion by Jonathan Bennett offers a useful hint in all but freakish cases. His

[13] Cf. Malm, at 253.

suggestion is along the following lines. For an agent's conduct to be regarded as positive: (i) he must have moved in a way which was relevant to the outcome in the sense of causing it or raising the probability that it would occur, and (ii) only that movement or a small number of closely related movements would have had the same outcome.[14] Thus, if the agent removes a rock from behind the wheel of a truck so that it slides downhill, his conduct can be described as positive because only that very movement or a small number of related movements by the agent would have ensured that the rock was removed so that the truck slid downhill. If, on the other hand, the agent refrains from putting the rock behind the wheel when he could do so, and the vehicle runs downhill in consequence, his conduct counts as negative. This is because there are many alternative bodily movements which the agent may have been performing (going for a walk, eating a sandwich, mending a leaking tap) such that, if he was doing them at the relevant time, he was not preventing the vehicle running downhill.[15] So it would not be wrong to say that the vehicle ran downhill because he was going for a walk or doing any one of a thousand other things. (The same would, of course, be true if he was not doing anything, but it is not essential that he should have been doing nothing.) It is the range of movements relevant to the outcome that determines whether his conduct is positive or negative. If there are a small number of related movements such that they would have ensured the outcome which came about, and the agent performed one of them, the conduct is positive; if a large number, it is negative.

The distinction suggested, though serviceable, is not infallible. Bizarre cases can be suggested, for example, those in which only immobility on the agent's part will bring about a harmful consequence.[16] Take a case in which John is searching for Dick to shoot him. The slightest movement on Bill's part will alert Dick to John's threat, in which case Dick will escape. If Bill remains immobile, and Dick is shot, was Bill's immobility a positive or negative instrumentality in Dick's death? On the suggested test it is negative, in that it does not involve movement, but positive in that there is no range of (alternative) movements which would have brought about the same outcome. In fact, any movement would have brought about a different outcome. It is worth noting, however, that fanciful cases do not make for sound judgment.[17] Our thought and language may mark out workable

[14] Bennett, 55 f. Bennett confines his formulation to raising the probability of the harm. I have put it in what seems a more plausible form.

[15] The examples come from Bennett, 52–3.

[16] Bennett, 66; Malm, 253 has an (implausible) example in which both immobility and activity (rowing) will cause harm, but to different people.

[17] Bennett, 74.

distinctions even though on freakish hypotheses they give indeterminate or counter-intuitive results. We should perhaps frankly concede that, on the suggested definition, Bill's conduct could be classed as either positive or negative.

The suggested distinction between positive and negative conduct, which depends on the way in which the agent's conscious bodily movements (or lack of them) are related to the outcome in which we are interested, is morally neutral. But it does in my view, at a deeper level, reflect a certain view of what it is to intervene in the world, and hence of responsibility. Why should bodily movement mark such a divide in our thought and language? Has the distinction a rationale?

A close study of causal language and thought suggested that the reason why movements feature so prominently in our assessment of responsibility is that we have a picture of a world as a matrix into which, by our movements and especially our manipulation of objects, we introduce changes.[18] By moving their bodies people change the world, though they may not know or foresee exactly what changes will come about. It is inherent in this world-picture that positive acts count as interventions in the outside world and attract at least a minimal responsibility for their outcomes.[19] On the other hand, non-movement is prima facie not an intervention in the world, so that the agent is not responsible for its consequences. But superimposed on this picture of the world is a refinement of it, which treats disruptions of the normal course of events as similar to interventions which bring about change,[20] though the change is not now a change in the existing state of affairs but rather in the normal or expected sequence of events. The regular course of things may take the form not only of recurrent natural events, but of regular human conduct such as clearing the street when the snow stops falling. If this regular or expected conduct fails to occur, the failure then counts not, as the first world-view would suggest, as a non-intervention but rather, on a wider view of what amounts to change, as a sort of intervention in the world. If, as is often (though not always) the case, the break in routine violates a norm (the person who does not sweep up the snow may or may not have a duty to do so), it is a form of not-doing which amounts to an omission and is a potential ground of responsibility.

I suggest, therefore, that what explains the difference between doing and not-doing is the notion of intervening in the world so as to bring about change; and that at a secondary level this notion extends to the interruption of human routines. If the human routine is required by a

[18] H. L. A. and Hart A. M. Honoré, *Causation in the Law*, 2nd edn. (Oxford, 1985), 28–32.

[19] Honoré, 'Responsibility and Luck' (1988), 104 *LQR* 530.

[20] *Causation in the Law*, 33–8.

norm, the violation of it is an omission which will entail responsibility.

It was said at the begining of this section that 'omission' is a pejorative term. The point may now be spelled out. A not-doing which contributes to a favourable outcome, even if it has normative significance, does not count as an omission. If I refrain from vetoing a project which I have a right to veto, and the project is successful, my not vetoing it may be morally or legally significant, perhaps praiseworthy, but it is not an omission. If on the other hand I refrain from vetoing a disastrous project, which I had the right to veto, that might be an omission; but if it was, the reason would be that it was not merely my right but my duty to intervene. Not-doing when one has a duty to act and not-doing when one has a right to act are not symmetrical notions.

3. Omissions and Distinct Duties

This section concentrates on distinct duties. It deals with the grounds on which distinct duties are imposed by legal systems and moral theories, and argues that, when a distinct duty is violated, acts and omissions are on a par, or very nearly so. Legal systems and moral theories do, of course, differ greatly in detail both among themselves and *vis-à-vis* one another as regards the circumstances in which they impose a distinct duty. My contention is not that they coincide, but that, if distinct duties are recognized at all, legal systems and moral theories agree on the broad grounds for imposing such duties to act. For example, they agree that the fact that someone is better placed than anyone else to help another is sometimes a ground for imposing a duty on him to help the other. But they may not agree on whether a motorist who, without fault, has run someone over has a duty to give aid to the victim.

I shall say no more about the optimizing theories (Section 2) since these do not recognize distinct as opposed to background duties. On the optimizing theories there is never a moral difference between acts and omissions where the outcome is the same. According to the optimizing theories, the agent has a general duty to intervene whenever to do so would optimize the chosen good. But these theories are oppressive, since instead of allowing an area of freedom where the agent can do as he likes within the limits of the largely negative background duties he owes to others, they require the overall optimum to be kept in sight every minute of the day. They make it impossible for people to pursue their own projects without continual distraction.

Those committed to law or to moral theories which embrace distinct duties argue differently. For them, an important class of omissions arise from distinct duties, which usually require both positive acts and abstentions. Distinct duties are limited and heterogeneous. The breach of such a duty to act will be a (distinct) omission, the breach of a duty to abstain a (distinct) commission. Alongside distinct duties there remain background duties to avoid doing harm and to help others in situations outside the limits set. But the background duties are weaker than the distinct duties, and the latter may themselves be of differing strengths.

Five types of situation which yield distinct duties can be listed.[21] Such a duty is often imposed on: (a) a person who performs a harmful or risk-creating act; (b) a person who occupies an office or position of responsibility or social role; (c) a person who is better placed than others to meet the need of someone dependent on him; (d) a person who has received a benefit from another; and (e) a person who has undertaken the duty in question. There is a good deal of overlap between these grounds of duty, and often more than one is present. In discussing these grounds I introduce a few examples from legal cases by way of illustration only. The grounds are as much moral as legal, assuming that the moral outlook adopted gives weight to duties. Only the extent of their application varies from society to society and, for practical reasons and out of respect for freedom, is usually broader in morals than in law.

A. HARMFUL AND RISK-CREATING ACTS

An important ground of duty is that the agent, by a positive act, has intervened or proposes to intervene in the world in such a way as to do harm, or create or substitute a new risk of harm, or increase an existing risk to others.[22] The agent then often has a duty to minimize the risk of harm or, if it has occurred, to mitigate it by means which may be either positive or negative, usually both.

This duty is in principle distinct from any duty the agent may have violated in doing the harm or creating the risk of it in the first place. It is true that the two are in practice often run together, so that creating the risk of harm and failing to take steps to avoid it are seen as part of a single course of wrongful conduct (for example, driving and not slowing down at the traffic lights). But that the duty to avoid threatened harm or minimize actual harm is secondary may be seen from that fact that the harm-doing or risk-creating act may not itself be culpable.[23] If I

[21] There is a good discussion of duties in tort law in *Prosser & Keeton on Torts*, 5th edn. (St Paul, Minn., 1984), para. 56; cf. *Restatement of Torts (Second)*, topic 7, 'Duties of Affirmative Action', paras. 314–28.

[22] *Prosser & Keeton*, 377.

[23] *Restatement of Torts (Second)*, para. 321.

lend a car to a friend and later discover that the steering is defective, I must warn the friend even though I did nothing wrong in lending the car. A motorist who without fault runs someone over has morally, and in many systems legally, a duty to summon help,[24] even though he was not at fault in running the victim over.

Quite apart from these everyday instances,most economic and domestic activities, from building, manufacture, transport, and marketing, to running a home, shop, school, or business create some risk to others. Those who engage in these activities are often required to take steps to minimize the risks involved, steps which vary from country to country and activity to activity according to the level of wealth and social consciousness and the specific requirements of local law and custom.

This reaction to risk-creating acts and activities accounts for the legal doctrine that prior positive conduct can generate a duty to act. So to state the matter is misleading, because the positive act need not precede the time at which the precaution should have been taken. When the duty arises from doing harm, for example, running over a pedestrian, the positive act does precede the duty. But when the duty arises from creating a risk of harm, this need not be the case. True, a driver who takes a vehicle on the road must from then on keep a proper look-out, but he must not take the vehicle on the road in the first place unless it is roadworthy. He must ensure that it is roadworthy before taking it on the road. This duty is imposed not because of a previous act but because of a prospective, future act. Nothing turns on the sequence in time of risk-creating act and precautionary duty. The crucial factor is that the act, past or future, carries with it a danger to the person or property of others and so may impose on the agent positive as well as negative duties.

This ground of duties to act is of the greatest conceptual and practical importance. Acts which do, or create risks of, harm are the prime example of noxious or potentially noxious human interventions in the world. Harmful omissions normally presuppose and are predicated on positive interventions, which they fail to counteract. Failure to react appropriately cannot be equated with doing harm or creating a risk of it in the first instance. This is an argument for the view that, in many contexts, positive acts are morally and socially worse than omissions.

The ground of duties imposed to counteract doing harm or creating risks presupposes a voluntary element. There must have been a conscious bodily movement on the agent's part, often with a deliberate plan behind it. But the agent need not have agreed to assume or even have known of the duties which his act or activity would impose on

[24] Ibid., para. 322.

him. Society subjects him to them willy-nilly if he does the act or engages in the activity in question. It offers him a stark choice. He may not do A without also doing or having done B. He may not drive without keeping a look-out, invite visitors before taking steps to see that his property is safe, sell food without having checked that it is fresh, run a company without publishing annual accounts. Freedom in a social framework, which is the only freedom on offer, is limited and conditional.

B. OFFICE OR POSITION OF RESPONSIBILITY

A second ground is that the agent occupies a position or office or fills a role which may require him to act positively. Parents,[25] friends, employers,[26] managers, owners, and possessors of property,[27] officials public and private have duties of this sort and are guilty of omission if they fail to discharge them. The legal liability of innkeepers, common carriers, and possessors of land falls under this heading.[28] In contrast with the previous risk-creating type of situation, the person who has a duty to act need not have created the danger himself. For instance, it seems reasonable that a landowner on whose premises a fire starts, but who did not start it himself, should take steps to put it out.[29] As with (a), there is a voluntary element in this ground of duty. The person in question has chosen to fill the office or position or take on the role, but again, once he has done so he is saddled with the duties attaching to the post whether he agreed to them or knew of them or not. The freedom to take on offices, roles, and positions is, once again, limited and conditional.

C. DEPENDENCY: BEING WELL PLACED TO MEET A NEED

The second ground of duty shades into a third, where society imposes a duty to act positively because of a need which the agent is well placed, often better placed than anyone else, to fulfil. Dependency, permanent or temporary, then generates a duty of help and protection. The dependency may be due to the choice of the person concerned, who puts himself in a position where he is better placed than anyone else to fulfil a certain need, for example by taking custody of someone so as to deprive him of normal opportunities for looking after him-

[25] Ibid., para. 316.
[26] Ibid., para. 314B.
[27] Ibid., para. 318.
[28] Ibid., para 314A.
[29] *Commonwealth* v. *Cali* (1923) 247 Mass 20, 141 NE 510; *Goldman* v. *Hargrave* [1967] 1 AC 645.

self or being looked after.[30] But the dependency need not have been chosen. Parents who have become so by mistake and not choice still have duties to their children. Temporary dependency is important when Samaritan-type duties to rescue are in issue and is mainly a matter of chance. Very often the case for saying that there is a moral or legal duty to rescue or help someone in danger is that the person who could help is at hand and better placed to do so than anyone else. Whatever the extent of Samaritan-type duties ought to be,[31] an important ground for imposing them at all is dependency.

Even if the person on whom the duty is imposed is not in the best position to meet it but merely in as good a position as others, there can be a strong case for imposing a duty to act, if necessary by selection. An example is compulsory military service. In this context we are not free; social needs override our wishes.

D. BENEFIT RECEIVED

A fourth ground of duty which often includes a duty to act positively, and so may lead to responsibility for omission, is the receipt of a benefit. It is a commonplace that the receipt of a gift or of hospitality imposes an obligation (not usually legal) on the recipient. The law of restitution is concerned with the duty of the recipient of money or property to restore benefits which there is no good reason for him to retain. The same ground helps explain why those who earn or receive money or enjoy facilities within a social framework are subject to tax liability. Progressive taxation illustrates ground (c), by which those who are better placed to meet collective needs are subject to a greater burden. This ground of duty often embraces a voluntary element, in that the person concerned has a choice whether to receive the benefit. Once he has done so he cannot escape from the resultant duty. His freedom is once more conditional. This type of duty does not always presuppose any positive conduct on the part of the person subject to it. A person who passively receives a benefit may be bound as a result.

E. UNDERTAKING

There is no sharp divide between undertaking an office or receiving a benefit which carries duties with it and undertaking duties directly. But promising in particular gives the person undertaking the duty greater freedom to fix its content than in (a), (b), and (d). Promising depends on the invention of forms of words for binding oneself, and such an

30 *Restatement of Torts (Second)*, para. 314A.
31 See the author's *Making Law Bind* (Oxtord, 1987), ch. 13.

invention is possible only within a social context in which people understand definite duties which stem, as it were, naturally from the structure of a community, as they do in (a) to (d) above.

Promising is not the only form of voluntary undertaking. There can be conventions to the effect that non-verbal conduct carries with it a duty, and there is no very clear line between non-verbal undertakings on the one hand and taking on a role or receiving a benefit which involves duties on the other. One who in a supermarket puts goods on the check-out counter is taken to agree to pay for them. One who boards a bus must pay the fare to his destination. Is this because boarding a bus conventionally carries this meaning, or because the passenger has the benefit of the ride, or because he assumes the role of passenger? The categories overlap, and non-verbal conventions are often unclear in their implications. A good example, important in practice, is that of a householder who allows someone, family, friend, or stranger, into his home for a cup of tea, or as a guest at a party,[32] or for a shorter or longer visit. Opening the door and inviting in is significant, but what duty does it import if the vistor wants to stay on, or falls ill, or is reluctant to leave because of the weather, or has no alternative accommodation? Whatever undertaking is involved in inviting a person in may in the end merge into a dependency as in (c) above.[33]

The grounds set out for imposing distinct duties, including positive duties the violation of which amounts to an omission, do not fall into any neat pattern. The needs of the community (office-holding, risk-creation, dependency), justice between its members (benefit, dependency), and respect for the choice of those who freely agree to take burdens on themselves (undertaking, risk-creation, office-holding) all help to explain one or more grounds. They seem not to derive from or be reductible to a single principle. It is worth noting that the three alleged grounds of contractual liability, benefit, reliance, and expectation, are all represented: benefit under (d), reliance (causing loss by inducing expense) under (a), and expected gain under (e). There is no particular reason to suppose that the strength of the duties arising under these three heads need be the same.

4. Relative Culpability

It is time to return to the question whether an omission, other things being equal, is less culpable than a positive act which brings about the

[32] *Parrish* v. *Troman* (1979) 124 Ariz 228, 603 P 2d 120, 121 says no duty to protect the guest against assault by three men who were allowed in and started a fight.

[33] *R* v. *Nicholls* (1874) 13 Cox 75.

same or a similar outcome. On the optimiszing or overall-duty view of morality, acts and omissions always stand on a level. All depends on whether in a given situation the optimizing course is to act or to abstain from action. In settling this question costs have to be taken into account. They will often tilt the balance in favour of not-doing as less culpable, not in principle but in the particular case.

This optimizing view is counter-intuitive. It leaves unexplained why, as mentioned earlier (Section 1), acts and omissions are seldom equal in the resentment they cause. By and large, positive acts cause more resentment than omissions with similar results, though resentment is also affected by what is seen as the motive of the agent. I feel worse about Mark if he hits me than if he does not intervene, as he easily could have, to stop James hitting me (Mark is much stronger than James). The difference is not simply accounted for by the effort and danger involved in intervening in a fight. Here resentment has partly to do with the feeling that Mark's blow points to a worse vice than his standing aside: ill will rather than lethargy or cowardice. But this may be because our assessment of vices reflects the distinction between positive acts and omissions. At any rate, feeling is in practice more often directed against the person who did the harm than the person who abstained from preventing it. Even when the harm is equal (despite the diaparity of strength, Mark and James hit equally hard on this occasion) the agent is not regarded as on a level with the non-intervener. The reaction is more nearly equal when the abstainer is felt to have a distinct duty to intervene. If Mark is a friend of mine he ought to have protected me from James, but even so it was a worse provocation on his part actually to hit me. Indeed, I shall then resent Mark's blow more than James's. Though the blows are equal in the sense of equally painful, the blow from a friend is more insulting. Harm is here agent-relative. Mark makes my position worse not just physically but from the point of view of friendship, whereas James does this only physically; and, as stressed earlier (Section 1), worsening one's position is more greatly resented than not making it better. It is an inroad on security, as opposed to an inroad on expectation.

On the distinct-duties theory my resentment of Mark's blow is justified, because that theory recognizes the distinct duties attaching to friendship. On that view omissions are sometimes morally the same or nearly the same as acts which bring about similar harm; but in other cases they are less culpable. They may be equally culpable when a person, by virtue of his office or role, has a distinct duty to a defined person or persons. Take the case of Susan, a nurse whose duty is to give a patient a certain medicine at six o'clock. Without a valid excuse she gives the wrong medicine or fails to give any medicine at all. Can her legal or moral culpability be different in the two cases, assuming that the impact on the patient's health is equally bad and that her character does not appear in a worse light in one of them (because, for example, in the second case she went off to watch a TV programme). Her duty is to use the means, positive and negative, which will enable the patient to be restored to health. The same will be true if for some reason no nurse is available and Adrian, a chemist who knows what he is doing, undertakes to give the patient the proper medicine. It is equally bad of him to give the wrong medicine and to fail to give any medicine, again assuming the harm to the patient and motivation to be similar. Suppose again that Adrian does not promise to give the medicine but that he is the only person available to do so in an emergency. The act and omission will again be morally on a par. As this example shows, when a distinct duty exists, the fact that positive acts make greater demands on the person concerned than abstentions does not support the view, as it otherwise would, that an omission is less culpable than a positively harmful act. The argument from distinct duty counteracts the argument from cost.

Judgement is, however, clouded by the fact that it is very difficult to think of instances when the outcome of the acts and omissions are the same or closely similar. In the medicine example it is hardly plausible that giving the wrong medicine will have the same impact on the patient as failing to give any medicine at all. This difficulty has led to the devising of bizarre examples like that of the runaway trolley, of which more in a moment, in which an act and an omission do have very similar outcomes. One reason why it is not easy to think of examples in which the outcomes are the same is that an omission can often be more easily parried than a positive act. If A gives B the wrong medicine, his intervention may be irremediable. There may be no antidote. If A does not give B the right medicine someone else may do so, or he may do it himself later. So the equivalence holds, at most, when no one but A is in a position to intervene, and that is precisely the sort of case in which, on the distinct-duty theory, A may well have a duty to intervene.

There is, therefore, much to be said for considering a banal example in which an act and an omission have the same effect and it would cost the same or much the same to avoid either. Take the problem of litter in the streets. If a person is employed by the local council to keep the streets clean, it can make no noticeable difference to the appearance of the street whether he drops a wrapper in the street himself or fails to pick up a wrapper dropped by someone else. The outcome in each case is that there is one more wrapper in the street than there would otherwise have been, and the urban scene is to that extent less tidy. It is nevertheless probably worse for him to drop a wrapper than to fail to pick one up, since he is in that way adding to the very conditions he is employed to remedy.

The difference is more obvious if we consider an ordinary pedestrian, who either drops a wrapper or fails to pick one up which he or someone else has dropped. Here dropping the wrapper is surely morally and socially worse. The litter problem exists only because people drop wrappers and other rubbish in the street and so disfigure the scene and, if the things are greasy, create a risk of slipping. Wrapper-dropping is antisocial in a way in which not picking up wrappers is not, because if nobody dropped wrappers the nuisance would not exist, whereas if everyone picked them up, or there was an efficient cleansing service, the nuisance would still exist until the wrappers were picked up. Conversely, for an ordinary pedestrian to pick up a wrapper is better than not dropping one, since to pick one up is to do more than one's duty, whereas it is no more than one's duty (a background duty) not to drop wrappers in the street.

This example is a good illustration of the greater moral blame attaching to positive acts, because the trouble involved in disposing of a wrapper neatly in a bin or bag is much the same as the trouble involved in picking a wrapper up. The cost of not dropping the wrapper is therefore close to that of picking one up. The positive act of dropping the wrapper is worse, not because its outcome is more harmful or the alternative more costly, but because of the sort of harm- or risk-creating act it is.[34] It is an intervention which changes things for the worse. Only if one looks at items of conduct atomistically rather than in their wider setting—a fault of some lawyers and moral philosophers—do acts and omissions appear equivalent.

The litter problem is a paradigm. It is primarily by positive acts that people do harm and create risks of harm to others, in the sense of changing things for the worse, whether by violence, pollution, speed of movement, destruction of property, or in a score of other ways. Of course this view of the primary threats to our individual and collective well-being depends on our living in a relatively stable (as it were, Newtonian) world, in which people and objects on the whole continue as they are unless something intervenes to change them. People reasonably attach importance to this continuity since their survival and that of others depends on it. This aim of survival in a stable state and the flourishing of which it is a condition is one that people can generally ensure, provided that others do not intrude on them or destroy what they need. Security in this sense is therefore a prime human value, and any conduct which threatens to change it for the worse a prime evil.

[34] Conversely, positive acts which constitute achievements and improve the world are socially and morally better than abstention from obstructing the achievements.

This helps to explain, I believe, why positive-harm doing is on the whole viewed as worse than harmful abstention, which threatens our security interests only indirectly. Though in a particular instance a harmful abstention may have equally noxious results, in general positive acts of intrusion and destruction are the more menacing, and it is reasonable to judge them more severely from a social and moral point of view. To say this is not to recommend a form of rule-utilitarianism, though it is certainly a sound principle of conduct to abstain from harmful intrusions and acts of destruction. It is rather that harmful positive acts have a general destructive significance different from that of harmful abstentions.

The great value placed on security explains why making someone's position worse is for good reason seen as worse than not making it better. The latter threatens not security so much as the expectation of improvement, which is a different but secondary value, because it presupposes stability. Atiyah is therefore, in my view, right to argue that in contract law expectation-damage is less significant, and calls less urgently for compensation, than loss through reliance.

The value attaching to stability also helps to explain when omissions and abstentions are seen as threatening, which they clearly sometimes are, for otherwise disruptive strikes would not be feared. They are so judged when security has come to depend on homoeostatic routines, and when disruptions of security by harmful and risk-creating acts are remedied by similar routines, which then fail.

Viewed against this background in which security is the prime value, worsening interventions—acts which make things worse or create a risk that they will be worse—must generally be more objectionable than failures to intervene. The latter are for the most part secondary in one of two ways. Either they fail to make things better rather than making them worse, and so violate our secondary rather than our primary interests; or they constitute failures to react against worsening interventions. Their secondary character seems to justify the judgement that harmful abstentions are normally less culpable than positive acts, even though in the context of distinct duties, as we have seen, the two are usually on a level.

In conclusion, it may be worth while turning briefly to one of the dramatic examples which have been invented to test the relative culpability of positive acts and omissions. These are examples where intuitive judgment is to be mistrusted. If the examples are very gruesome they numb our sensibilities,[35] and if very remote from everyday life outstrip our moral resources. Suppose the agent has a choice between A's death and B's. A trolley-car[36] is out of control and

[35] R. Trammell in *Killing and Letting Die*, ed. B. Steinbock (1980), at 167.

[36] J. J. Thompson, 'The Trolley Problem', *Essays in Moral Theory* (Harvard, 1986), 94–116.

will crush Tom unless I pull a lever, in which case the trolley will crush Sam. If we know no more than this—there is no information about my role and how I come to be in a position to intervene—the right conclusion is that I should not intervene. The act of pulling the lever and crushing Sam would be worse than letting the trolley take its course. As Malm points out, I could in no way justify my intervention to Sam's family and friends.[37] On the other hand I can justify my non-intervention to Tom's family, because I had no authority and no business to intervene. This judgment of course presupposes that harmful interventions have to be justified, even if I am redirecting the harm rather than increasing it.

The reason against pulling the lever is not happily expressed by saying that I should not play God. There are many less exalted roles which would justify intervention. If I am an official of the trolley company in charge of the lever mechanism, I may well have a reason connected with the overall effect on the system to pull the lever. In that case the consequences of intervention and non-intervention are not the same, and this difference will have to be taken into account in reaching a decision. Again, if an army commander diverts the enemy fire from point A to point B, where an equal number of casualties is to be expected, he may be justified in doing so because of the tactical advantage to be gained. Indeed he may be justified even if heavier casualties are likely. Here again the outcome is not the same.

To revert to the trolley-car, if the person who pulled the lever was Tom's father, this would at least make his intervention less culpable than if he were a stranger to both Tom and Sam, for the outcome to him if Tom dies is then different from that if Sam dies. But these examples point to the importance in making the comparison between act and omissions of two factors. One is the social role of the agent, which may carry with it a distinct duty which adds to the reasons in favour of intervention. The other is that, in the trolley-car type of case, intervening by a positive act is worse than not intervening unless the outcome of not intervening is worse than that of intervening for some reason other than that one person dies. When outcomes are equal, abstention is the appropriate course for those who lack the right or duty to intervene. It would be strange to think otherwise.

[37] Malm, 245–8.

3

Scandinavian Legal Realism in the Law of Contract

JAN HELLNER

1. Introduction

Scandinavian legal realism seems to be a fairly well-known body of ideas in so far as it is often mentioned in general surveys of jurisprudence.[1] However, it has never had any strong influence outside Scandinavia and there are few who adhere strictly to it nowadays. The founder of the school was the Swedish philosopher Axel Hägerström (1868–1939).[2] His best-known Swedish followers were Vilhelm Lundstedt (1882–1955) and Karl Olivecrona (1897–1980). The Dane Alf Ross (1899–1980) is generally considered to belong to the school as well and he is perhaps the one who is most read at present. Ross began as a follower of Kelsen and retained in his later writings many of the ideas that he absorbed during this period. There is also an influence from logical positivism in his chief work, which has been translated into English under the title *On Law and Justice* (1958). This illustrates the fact that, in spite of their being considered to form one school and in spite of the influence of Hägerström on these legal scientists, they exhibit important differences among themselves.

The legal scientists mentioned wrote numerous works not only on jurisprudence, but also on various subjects belonging to their special fields of law. Lundstedt held a chair at Uppsala on the law of obligations, Olivecrona one at Lund on the law of procedure, and the main

[1] See e.g. E. Bodenheimer, *Jurisprudence* (Cambridge, Mass., 1962), 120 ff., G. C. Christie, *Jurisprudence* (St Paul, 1973), 751 ff., R. W. M. Dias, *Jurisprudence* (London, 1976), 369 ff.; W. Friedmann, *Legal Theory* (London, 1967), 304 ff.

[2] Hägerström's main works in legal theory have been translated into English by C. D. Broad, edited by K. Olivecrona (Stockholm, 1953). There is an extensive study of Hägerström's legal philosophy, dealing also with problems connected with special branches of the law, by E. Pattaro, *Il realismo giuridico Scandinavo I. Axel Hägerström* (Bologna, 1975), which also includes a list of unpublished manuscripts in the Uppsala University Library. Hägerström's research in Roman law has been studied by C. Faralli, *Diretto e magia, Il realismo di Hägerström e il positivismo filosofico* (Bologna, 1987).

subject of Ross's chair in Copenhagen was public law. Their treatment of special subjects was, especially in the cases of Lundstedt and Olivecrona, strongly influenced by their general views on law and jurisprudence.

To lawyers the more specialized works are in many ways more interesting than the contributions of these jurists to general jurisprudence. They illustrate how far general ideas are connected with questions of legal method that have an impact on practical issues. From a philosophical point of view, on the other hand, the conclusions may be less original and therefore less interesting. As I shall deal now with the law of contract I shall be concerned mainly with Lundstedt's writings.[3] Some of his ideas may be originally attributable to Hägerström and it is even possible that he exercised an influence on Hägerström, due to their close personal contact. As just mentioned, the law of obligations was the subject of Lundstedt's professorship. He wrote extensively on the law of torts, particularly during the later period of his life.[4] Other, somewhat earlier, works deal with contracts, although some of his main ideas are common to both torts and contracts.[5]

It may be debatable how original the views of the Scandinavian realist school were. The writers were certainly all of them opposed to natural law, but so are legal positivists in general. It may be argued that Scandinavian legal realism is just one, extreme branch of legal positivism in spite of the recurring criticism of this school. As for the works on special subjects, a connection with other Scandinavian writings in the field was inevitable since these writings dealt with the rules of the same legal systems. Furthermore, German legal science exercised a strong influence in Scandinavia, and this fact is reflected in all the writings. The connections with previous legal science were mostly negative, in the sense that the protagonists of realism opposed what they considered to be generally accepted doctrines. However, to some extent the connection was positive in so far as the views proffered agree substantially with those of earlier or contemporaneous writers. This is not surprising, because Scandinavian legal science had long had a realistic trend although not founded on any philosophy of the kind

[3] Lundstedt's main work in English is *Legal Thinking Revised*, published posthumously (Stockholm, 1957). In my opinion this work gives an unsatisfactory picture of Lundstedt's achievement. It was written late in his life and is much concerned with polemics against writers who were supposed to hold ideas resembling his own. Lundstedt wants to stress the originality of his own views. In what follows I shall refer mainly to his writings in Swedish.

[4] See *Grundlinjer i skadeståndsrätten Part 1, Culparegeln* (Uppsala, 1935), *Part 2, Strikt ansvar*, vol. 1, (Uppsala, 1944), vol. 2: 1, (Uppsala, 1948), vol. 2: 12, (Uppsala, 1953). I commented on Lundstedt's writings on tort liability many years ago in an essay, 'Legal philosophy in the Analysis of Tort Problems', *Scandinavian Studies in Law* (1958), 149 ff.

[5] See *Obligationsbegreppet*, vol. 1 (Uppsala, 1929), vol. 2 (Uppsala, 1930).

that Hägerström and his followers embraced.[6] Moreover, their work influenced a number of writers in Scandinavia who did not, either in their own opinion or in that of the true adherents of Hägerström, belong to the same school. Part of the importance of the work of Hägerström and his followers was that it made a number of legal scientists examine their methods and arguments, in order—often unsuccessfully—to escape from the more or less justified criticism for untenable arguments that Lundstedt and Olivecrona in particular raised. In what follows I shall concentrate on Lundstedt's work but try to fit it into the context of the general development of the law of contract. I will treat Scandinavian legal realism as a wider movement than the jurisprudential school associated with this expression.

From a present-day point of view Lundstedt's work on contracts appears to lie in the mainstream of the Scandinavian treatment of contract law, in spite of the fact that he strongly opposed much of it. Lundstedt sought out for analysis topics on which he could oppose his views to those of his predecessors while leaving other parts of contract law untouched. Although many of his ideas appear to be grossly exaggerated or even absurd they may, if set out in their proper context, be found to be valuable or at least to offer interesting alternatives to other views. The focus here will be not on the philosophical foundations, however, important they may have been to Lundstedt himself, but on the practical conclusions that he drew from them, especially in so far as the conclusions of his work agree with other views and methods that are found in Scandinavia.

The most important part of Lundstedt's work, from the present point of view, is his preoccupation with questions of the validity of arguments that are found in legal discourse. He opposed all arguments which in his opinion were fallacious and sought to find a tenable basis for work within legal science. However, the conclusions as regards the validity of arguments cannot be understood except in the context of Lundstedt's general ideas concerning the law of obligations.

2. The Concept of Obligation

Lundstedt's main work in the law of obligations is entitled *Obligationsbegreppet* (the concept of obligation).[7] Far from being a general treatise on the law of obligations, it contains an analysis of some theoretical and practical issues in contract and tort that have only

[6] The tradition can be said to go as far back as to the Danish jurist A. S. Ørsted (1776–1860): see K. Illum, 'Some Reflections on the Method of Legal Science and on Legal Reasoning', *Scandinavian Studies in Law, 1968*, 29 at 57.

[7] See n. 5 above.

a loose connection with each other. The title is obviously inspired by Hägerström's work on Roman law *Der römische Obligationsbegriff im Lichte der allgemeinen römischen Rechtsanschauung*.[8] Lundstedts starts, as Hägerström did, from the description of an obligation in the *Institutiones* (I. 3, 13 pr.); *Obligatio est iuris vinculum quo necessitate astringimur alicuius solvendae rei secundum nostrae civitatis iura.*[9]

The importance of this start to the work—besides stressing the connection with Hägerström's work—consists mainly in the fact that it indicates the extreme realism which is to be the basis of the whole study. The only fact that is admitted as creating an obligation is a coercion to pay money, subject to two conditions: that there is something that can be considered to be a breach of the obligation (which generally includes that the obligee has suffered a loss); and that a claim can successfully be enforced by a lawsuit and a subsequent execution of the judgment.[10] This analysis is, in Lundstedt's view, fundamental. Understanding of this fact is, in his opinion, necessary for lawyers and laymen for an understanding of how law works. Illusions that there is something more in an obligation are, in his view, a source of misunderstanding of the law. Subsequently he offers the same type of analysis of the concept of a right.[11]

Lundstedt's analysis is quasi-sociological in that it tries to reduce the concept of an obligation to the very simplest kind of reality. The utility of this type of concept analysis may be open to doubt. But even as a sociological description of what corresponds to that which lawyers mean by an obligation, the analysis is far from satisfactory. It covers too much to be useful. If this analysis is accepted everyone will be constantly under all sorts of obligations. The description is useless in delimiting what is generally considered to be an obligation arising from tort or contract. Lundstedt in fact admits as much, but he insists that coercion of the kind mentioned is a *conditio sine qua non* for everything that is styled obligation; whereas other elements which are generally present can be replaced by others.[12] One of Lundstedt's aims is, therefore, to point out that there is no real difference between an obligation in tort and one in contract.[13] Later Scandinavian legal science has not been strongly impressed by Lundstedt's analysis of the concept of an obligation. This is not surprising for the reasons just mentioned. How-

[8] Vol. 1 (Uppsala, 1927). Vol. 2 appeared posthumously, edited by Karl Olivecrona, (Uppsala, 1941). It appears from the study by Dr Faralli (n. 2 above) that this work is not only a study of Roman law, but also has a place in the general development of the positivist thinking of its time.

[9] *Obligationsbegreppet*, vol. 1 (n. 5 above), 9.

[10] Ibid., 42 ff.

[11] Ibid., 68 ff.

[12] Ibid., 52.

[13] Ibid., 51. Cf. *Legal Thinking Revised* (n. 3 above), 118 ff.

ever, indirectly Lundstedt's rejection of any fundamental difference between claims based on tort and claims based on contract seems to have exercised an influence. Under some legal systems, it may be necessary to make such a distinction, for historical reasons and because it is generally accepted. Scandinavian law, on the other hand, does not seem to be bound by any such presuppositions. It may well be argued that it is an advantage to be able to discuss for example, liability for *culpa in contrahendo* and even products liability, without being bound by any theoretical considerations a priori considering differences between tort and contract.

3. Morals, Justice, and Social Welfare

The relationship between law and morals is a favorite topic in modern legal philosophy. It is also discussed in relation to contract law, particularly by P. S. Atiyah.[14] Lundstedt, on the other hand, does not seem to take an interest in this issue. As far as I can see, Lundstedt never deals with the moral aspect of contract law. He deals only with law, and sees contracts from the point of view of a legal scientist who wants to explain rules that are found in statutes and applied by the courts. This can be considered as a consequence of the sociological (or quasi-sociological) view of the law that was mentioned in the preceding section. From this point of view, law and morals are regarded as two different systems whose norms and concepts migh coincide but which should nevertheless be kept apart. Lundstedt is, in this way, a legal positivist in a wide sense, although he rejects all notions of law being the will of the state or the legislator, or anything of that kind.

Scandinavian legal science mostly agrees with Lundstedt (and a great number of other philosophers and lawyers) in separating law and morals. Personally I do too, for several reasons. One is that I believe that it leads to greater clarity. A legal positivist in the wide sense is, of course, free to discuss whether there are moral reasons for legal rules or moral reasons for rejecting legal rules, and when and where legal and moral norms coincide, and whether there is a moral norm prescribing that legal norms should be followed. But personally, I feel little qualified to discuss most of these questions, and would, therefore, separate them from the legal questions whenever possible. I do not believe that this position prevents me, or anyone else holding similar views, from discussing questions of legal method arising in the law of contract on a common basis with those who attribute a moral aspect to law. On the contrary, as far as I can see the main differences of method

[14] *Promises, Morals and Law* (Oxford, 1981). See also *Essays on Contract* (Oxford, 1986).

arise from other sources, chiefly perhaps the different traditions of legal systems.

On the whole, discussions of moral questions do not seem to have attracted much interest from Scandinavian lawyers. The question of whether a promise, in addition to being legally binding, should also be considered to have a moral character, is mostly left to philosophers. On the other hand, it is not denied that a number of promises which are not legally binding, perhaps because they are not in writing when such a form is required, may be morally binding.[15] Even then, however, most stress is laid on the fact that if such a morally binding promise is broken, it will lead to extra-legal sanctions, including the difficulty of continuing business for one who becomes known as inclined to act in this way.[16]

It appears that the corresponding problem in Lundstedt's world of ideas (although it is dubious whether the connection is strong) is the role of *justice*.[17] To be subject to a rule based on justice is in some ways equivalent to having a moral obligation. However, Lundstedt contrasts justice with *social welfare*, and an important part of his position involves the entire rejection of justice as a foundation for law.[18] In his opinion, social welfare provides the whole explanation of the legal system and its various rules. Much law is, in Lundstedt's opinion, unjust in any ordinary sense, but it is upheld by the courts because of its social utility. As a consequence, it is impossible in the long run to resist the force of social welfare. Lundstedt's views on the foundations of the legal system, therefore, lead to a normative view on how law should be applied in order to promote social welfare.[19] Whereas he rarely criticizes legal rules and court decisions, he will constantly object to the reasons given for them, especially by legal writers. When Lundstedt notices and comments on differences among legal systems he explains some of them by the variety of social conditions.[20] Social welfare if, therefore, not the same everywhere and for all times but may be different for various periods and for various countries.

Lundstedt's views are, on the best possible interpretation, a tremendous over-simplification which can only partly be explained by a reac-

[15] It is sometimes argued that when there is no legal obligation, the moral obligation is even stronger, since it is impossible to have the promise enforced in court.

[16] I have dealt with some such issues in *Kommersiell avtalsrätt*, 3rd edn. (Stockholm, 1989).

[17] See *Legal Thinking Revised* (n. 3 above), 123 ff.

[18] The expression 'social welfare' is used in *Legal Thinking Revised*, and in consequence I have adopted it here. However, 'social utility' seems to cover Lundstedt's Swedish expression *samhällsnytta* better. Perhaps the translator rejected it because it is associated with utilitarianism in the philosophic sense.

[19] *Legal Thinking Revised* (n. 3 above), 195 ff.

[20] This is particularly evident in *Strikt Ansvar*, vol. 1 (n. 4 above), in which Lundstedt deals with French, English, and American tort law.

tion against some German and German-inspired legal science of the nineteenth century. It is significant that Lundstedt himself was one of those most strongly inspired by German legal science before he converted to the faith of Hägerström. His attempt to take account of facts leads to a conservatism reminiscent of the ideas of Hegel: what exists is proved by its very existence to be useful, and thus justifiable. While Lundstedt aspired to revising legal thinking, he had little ambition to change or develop the law. Lundstedt's conclusions are more interesting than his ideas. A prominent example from his later writings is his argument that deterrence must be the fundamental aim of rules imposing liability to pay damages in tort and contract. He believed it to be more important to deter people in general from causing losses than to provide indemnity to the minority that suffer losses. If one looked at justice alone it would, in Lundstedt's opinion, often be manifestly unjust to impose on the tortfeasor liability to pay damages. This example demonstrates a main feature of Lundstedt's arguments: the long-run effects of a rule that is consistently applied by the courts are considered more important than its consequences in particular cases which would be judged in terms of the aim of achieving justice.

Lundstedt's influence on Scandinavian legal science can be seen in the fact that arguments based on the long-run effects of legal rules continue to figure prominently. As for contract law, however, there has been a change of emphasis, since the consistent application of rules by the courts can hardly be invoked as an argument in countries where there is as little litigation on contracts as in Scandinavia. Instead, the *functional* aspect of rules as applied in business practice is taken into account. There is nothing new in this approach.[21] An outstanding example is found in the leading commentary on the Scandinavian Sale of Goods Act dating from the beginning of the twentieth century by Tore Almén.[22] This commentary reflects a general functional tradition in Scandinavian legal writing and has had an immense influence on Scandinavian law. Lundstedt criticized it on a particular point to which I shall return (Section 5 below). This criticism may be justified, but in the main Almén's commentary is remarkable for the understanding it displays of the functional issues in sales law and in contract law in general.

Concentration on the long-run effects of legal rules also leads to

[21] Lundstedt admits the insight into this function which appears in a statement by the Danish Jurist Julius Lassen, at p. 138 of *Obligationsbegreppet*, but immediately finds fault in another statement of Lassen's.

[22] T. Almén, *Om Köp och byte av lös egendom*, 4th edn. by R. Eklund (Stockholm, 1960). There is a German translation by F. K. Neubecker, *Das skandinavische Kaufrecht* (Heidelberg, 1922), which has exercised considerable influence on the treatment of sales law in German legal science.

mistrust of arguments based on justice. Long-run effects are accepted by Lundstedt without empirical proof as part of his general view on law. Justice is rejected because Lundstedt believes that it conflicts in certain cases with the requirements of social welfare. The possibility that justice plays some role in cases other than those mentioned, or that it reappears on another level when the long-run effects have been exhausted as an explanation of the rules, does not present itself to Lundstedt. Any idea that rules might have substantive legitimacy based on their contents as opposed to the formal legitimacy provided by their application by the courts, is apparently considered by Lundstedt to be unfounded or possibly irrelevant.

Considerations of function, which are more or less based on Lundstedt's ideas, have become a characteristic of Scandinavian legal science, particularly in the field of contract law. There are different aspects of this functional approach, some of which have been stressed by later writers more than by Lundstedt himself.

One such aspect is the influence of legal rules on human behaviour in general, as opposed to decisions on disputes by courts. This aspect appears most clearly when law develops by legislation or by other means. For this development, those rules can often be considered most successful that do not give rise to any litigation in court but provide business with suitable instruments for its work and facilitate the settlement of disputes.

Such development can take place by the work of private organizations, as when the International Chamber of Commerce issues the 'Incoterms' and the 'Uniform Customs and Practices for Documentary Credits'. The most important development is, of course, that undertaken by the legislator when issuing new statutes. The task will then be to foresee the effects in the long run for business and for people in general, as well as to provide guidance for the courts when deciding on particular cases.

Another aspect is the one which comes into focus when the contents of legislation are considered. There is a difference between an approach which favours justice between the parties to a contract rather than the functions of the rules and the consequences which ensue when the rules are practised. This aspect gains a new interest if we look at some issues in the law of sales. For example, in the law of sales we face the question whether the same principles should apply to breaches of contract by the seller and breaches by the buyer. The UN Convention on International Sales of 1980 seems to be based on the notion that remedies for breach by either party should follow the same pattern even if they need not be the same.[23] This corresponds to the

[23] This feature appears clearly in the whole structure of the UN Convention as well as in particular provisions. Compare e.g. Art. 49, concerning breaches of contracts by the

tendency of Continental Codes to promote general principles and symmetry both in substance and form. The English Sale of Goods Act of 1979, as well as the Scandinavian Sale of Goods Acts from the beginning of this century, take an entirely different approach, and there is a considerable difference between the remedies available to a buyer and those available to a seller, on the other party's breach.[24] This latter approach, which is found in legal writing as well as in the text of relevant statutes, is clearly based on a functional approach as opposed to considerations of abstract justice.

The Scandinavian tradition which appears most clearly in the Sale of Goods Act has been to try to find practical solutions to practical problems on the basis of an analysis of what rules are suitable to the various situations that arise.[25] This attitude is not due to Lundstedt, as it existed long before he wrote; but opposition to arguments based on abstract justice has in all probability been reinforced by the kind of criticism that he made. As Lundstedt's influence has decreased, the willingness to accept rules based on abstract justice has increased in Scandinavia.[26] At all events, a preference for arguments based on the function of legal rules as contrasted with arguments of abstract justice, may be considered to be mainly a psychological matter of heuristic importance. It seems unlikely that, in the face of convincing evidence of the difference between a seller's breach of contract and a buyer's breach, anyone would maintain that they should be treated alike solely on the ground that justice requires it. Mistrust of general arguments of justice would, in such situations, only have the importance of directing our analysis towards asking about the function of the rules. On the other hand, too strong an emphasis on long-run consequences of legal rules might lead us to assume that such consequences exist, without sufficient proof. As mentioned, Lundstedt assumed that the deterrent effects of liability were the most important ones without any empirical proof.[27] The same sort of reasoning might be used in other cases.

The problem does not end here, but raises more fundamental questions. Consider the argument that, *ceteris paribus*, the price of

seller, with Art. 64, concerning breaches of contract by the buyer. Cf. J. Hellner, 'Das internationale Kaufrecht aus dem Blickwinkel der Gesetzgebungstechnik', *Zeitschrift für Gesetzgebung* (1988), 249–66.

[24] Cf. regarding the Swedish Sale of Goods Act of 1905, J. Hellner, 'Contracts and Sales', in S. Strömholm (ed.), *An Introduction to Swedish Law* (Stockholm, 1988), 233 ff.

[25] There is little general discussion of this theme, as the policy underlying the statutes appears most clearly from the statutes themselves. The character of Scandinavian legislation, as opposed, on the one hand, to Continental European codifications and, on the other hand, to the English emphasis on judge-made law, was stressed by the Dane J. Lassen in a lecture published posthumously in *Udvalge Afhadlinger*, ed. F. Dahl (Copenhagen, 1924), 37 ff.

[26] There is a difference between the older Scandinavian Sale of Goods Acts, dating from the beginning of this century, and the new ones (the Finlandian one of 1987, the Norwegian one of 1988, and the Swedish one which was enacted in 1990).

[27] Cf. section 3 p. 59 above.

goods sold or services rendered should be equivalent to their value in order to achieve balance in the performance of the contract; and that remedies for breach of contract should have the aim of maintaining such balance.[28] When studying the rules of a particular legal system, the value of the argument depends on how far it can explain rules that are found in case law or statutory law. When preparing an international convention—such as the UN Convention on International Sales—this attitude is not sufficient, since different national systems may have different rules. Sometimes the answer to the question whether such balance should be required is simply that further analysis is necessary, and resorting to the argument of balance is a way of trying to reach a solution without properly analysing the problem encountered. Such may be the case at least with early discussion of the remedy of reduction of the price which was introduced into the UN Convention on International Sales.[29] But sooner or later we arrive, I believe, at a stage in the discussion in which no such analysis can assist us and we are forced to a resolution. How far can an argument based on considerations of justice assist us then?

Numerous other such examples could be found. But it would probably require Lundstedt's obsession with his own ideas to deny that arguments of justice can be relevant. Even those who give most weight to long-run considerations employ arguments based on justice when there is substantial similarity between factual situations which justifies treating them similarly. However, personally, I must admit to some scepticism. One's sense of justice may be based on sentiments that have been acquired by familiarity with one particular system and which are irrelevant against the convictions of those who have been educated in another legal system. Sometimes a rule may or must be explained simply by the necessity of having a rule, be it the one or the other, to which parties can adapt their behaviour or which they can change by agreement if necessary. But this is not the place to discuss the fundamental problems of method and value in contract law.

4. The Binding Force of a Promise

In order to understand Lundstedt's views on the binding force of a promise and the discussion which took place in Scandinavia on this topic, it is necessary to put them into their historical context. In the

[28] See e.g. A. von Mehren, 'Contractual Justice', in *A General View of Contract, International Encyclopedia of Comparative Law*, vol. vii, ch. 1 (Tübingen, 1982), 64 ff.

[29] Cf. E. E. Bergsten and A. J. Miller, 'The Remedy of Reduction of Price', *American Journal of Comparative Law* (1979), 225 ff.

first place, the doctrine of consideration was unknown to the jurists who took part in the discussion—or rather it was known only as a principle which was accepted in common-law systems. Secondly, the discussion which had taken place in German law influenced Scandinavian lawyers. In German law (whose origins in this respect need not be examined) the contractual promise was identified with a declaration of will. Traditional German doctrine as exemplified in the leading textbook by Bernhard Windscheid, held that the will of the promisor to be bound was the basis of the obligation in a contract.[30] Against this doctrine another, which emerged somewhat later, held that a promise is binding because of the reliance which it generates.[31]

Lundstedt examined and rejected both these propositions. His main objection to the theory of the will's binding force was that the will could not bind the promisor unless there was a legal system which upheld the effects of a declaration of will. It was, therefore, according to Lundstedt, a *petitio principii* to argue that the binding force of the promise is derived from the will of the promisor.[32] The same point has been made by others as well, independently of Lundstedt.[33] The will theory is rarely advanced nowadays by Scandinavian legal writers. The doctrine of reliance is more important. It was found fallacious by Lundstedt on grounds similar to those advanced against the will theory. In the first place, says Lundstedt, it presupposes that the promisee relies on the binding force of the promisor's will and is thus indirectly based on the will theory. Secondly, reliance would be justified only if it was protected by the law. There is thus, according to Lundstedt, an additional *petitio principii* in finding the basis of the legally binding force in reliance.

There are a number of objections of Lundstedt's criticism of the reliance theory as presented in earlier German and Scandinavian legal theory.[34] Perhaps the most important is that there may very well be reliance even if there is no legal rule to justify it. The criticism of *petitio principii* then fails. However, the reliance theory as a theory applicable to all legal systems that recognize the binding force of a promise, seems to depend for its details on the particular rules of each legal system. For instance, a promise may be binding even if there is no reliance on it. An example of this type was given by the Norwegian jurist Fredrik Stang.[35] In his example, a Norwegian promises a Swede a

[30] See B. Windscheid, *Lehrbuch des Pandektenrechts*, vol. 1, 4th edn. (Leipzig, 1873), 174 ff., vol. 2, 3rd edn. (Leipzig, 1873), 156 ff.

[31] The main work is S. Schlossmann, *Der Vertrag* (Leipzig, 1876).

[32] *Obligationsbegreppet*, vol. 1 (n. 5 above), 128 ff.

[33] See P. S. Atiyah, *Promises, Morals and Law* (n. 14 above), *passim*.

[34] The role of the reliance element in English law, which in this respect differs from Scandinavian law, is discussed by Atiyah, *ibid.*, *passim*.

[35] F. Stang, *Innledning til formueretten*, 3rd edn. (Oslo, 1935), 258.

gift. The Swede does not believe that the promise is valid and does not rely on it because, according to Swedish law, the promise of a gift is not binding. However, according to Norwegian law it is. There is no doubt that the Swede can enforce the promise (provided that Norwegian law is applicable). On the other hand, if a Norwegian relies on such a promise given by a Swede and Swedish law is applicable, his reliance does not help him. The most that can be said is that the role of the reliance depends on the rules of the legal system concerned.

However, the method whose use and application Lundstedt criticized had already gone out of fashion in Scandinavia when he presented his criticism. I refer to the method of justifying a legal rule by pointing to one particular circumstance among those that are relevant according to the rule, and singling this circumstance out as being the basis of the obligation. This method can give rise to endless and useless disputes as to the 'real' basis of the obligation.[36] However, even if leading writers do not adduce reliance as being the basis of the obligation they may, in arguing in favour of particular rules, present reliance as if it were such basis. Indeed, the main discussion aroused by Lundstedt's criticism concerned such an approach. Lundstedt's adversaries argued that, whatever earlier ideas there had been regarding the basis of the bindingness of a promise, 'reliance theory' had become in Scandinavian law simply the name for a particular rule.[37] If a person by mistake, in writing or in a similar manner, presents a declaration of will that does not express his true intention, the declaration can yet be enforced by a person who in good faith believes it to express the true intention of the declarer (Sec. 32, para. 1, of the Scandinavian Contracts Act). This rule is supposed to embody the reliance theory. Lundstedt, on the other hand, maintained that various writings by leading legal scientists proved that the theory of reliance involved reference to more than a particular rule.[38]

This controversy may seem rather insignificant, and indeed it now belongs to legal history. In Scandinavia, 'reliance theory' is now the accepted name for a special rule relating to a special kind of mistake.[39] In my opinion, this is somewhat unfortunate because it means that a particular rule is given a general name. It becomes more difficult to

[36] I have commented on the use of this method in tort law in 'Legal Philosophy in the Analysis of Tort Problems' (n. 4 above), at 154 ff.

[37] This view was presented very clearly by Ö. Undén, 'Om Julius Lassens tillitsteori', *Svensk juristtidning* (1929), 342 ff.

[38] *Obligationsbegreppet* vol. 2 (n. 5 above), 149 ff.

[39] Stang, n. 35 above 254 ff., prefers the name *erklæringsprinsippet* (principle of declaration) as being more adequate, partly because it avoids the error of indicating that reliance is the basis of the binding force of the promise. On the whole, Stang's analysis of the will theory and the reliance theory is very enlightening. In any case, the name 'theory' for a rule, or possible a principle, is a misnomer.

discuss the merits and demerits of the rule when it is given such a name. However, its function as a name proves once more that the importance of reliance depends on the special rules of the legal system concerned. In this field there are numerous differences among legal systems, and it is not easy to say which is the best, even supposing that an impartial view is possible. There is a German rule according to which reliance on a mistaken promise is protected by giving the promisee a right to damages for his reliance interest (*negatives Vertragsinteresse*) when the promise is void but the promisor acted negligently.[40] Who can say whether this rule is better than the Swedish rule which, as mentioned, has been given the name of 'reliance theory'?

The question remains, how much value we should attach to the argument that a certain rule promotes or protects reliance. This question may be raised with regard to a number of rules other than the one just discussed. In my opinion, which follows from what was just said about the differences between legal systems, the argument should be viewed with some suspicion. It avoids the general problem, which is to decide when reliance should be protected and in what way. We must admit that legal systems differ on many points of contract law, and we cannot decide on the superiority of any system or any rule simply by reference to reliance. If a rule is good for other reasons it does not add much to its value to say that it protects reliance. Nor does it detract from the value of another rule which is found good on the whole to say that it does not protect reliance. To take a well-known example, there are considerable differences between legal systems as to the possibility of revoking an offer before it has been accepted by the offeree.[41] It does not strengthen the arguments in favour of irrevocable offers to say that the irrevocability protects the reliance of the offeree.[42]

Consequently, it is in my opinion impossible to discuss questions regarding the role of reliance without considering the legal system to which the discussion refers. It is possible historically that the aim of avoiding a *petitio principii* played a part in judging the role of the theory

[40] German Civil Code, Articles 118, 122.

[41] It may be noted that even staunch supporters of the will theory did not draw the conclusion that an unaccepted offer should be binding. Windscheid considered only the accepted offer to be binding, as expressing the *consensus* of the offeror and the offeree: see n. 30 above, vol. 2, 156 ff. When the German Civil Code adopted the rule that an offer is irrevocable unless it indicates otherwise (Civil Code, Article 145), the reasons given referred to the practical advantages of the rule. This rule had been adopted previously for commercial contracts by the Commercial Code, Art. 319: see Mugdan, *Die gesammten Materialien zum Bürgerlichen Gesetzbuch für das Deutsche Reich*, vol. 1 (Berlin 1899), 443.

[42] This argument is advanced, among others, in support of the Swedish rule that the offer is irrevocable (Article 1 of the Contracts Act of 1915); see for the *travaux préparatoires: Nytt juridiskt arkiv II* (1915), 163.

of reliance in Scandinavian law, and in so far as there is any tendency towards *petitio principii* this aim is still worth pursuing. But the main point is to draw the attention to differences between legal systems: German law is different from Scandinavian law, and both are different from English law. There is no common doctrine of reliance that can cover all legal systems.

We arrive at a conclusion that is somewhat similar to the one that was drawn from Lundstedt's ideas on the importance of the long-run effects of legal rules. The basis of his original criticism of the doctrine of reliance is outdated. However, it is still worthwhile to examine what is meant when reliance is used as an explanation of various contract rules. There is little value in referring to a notion that is consistent with a great number of legal rules that have little factual affinity. What is needed is a diversification with regard to the various practical issues and the differences between legal systems.

5. The Fictitious Guarantee

As appears from the preceding section, part of Lundstedt's critical analysis of earlier writings consisted in finding circular arguments. Another favourite object of his criticism were *fictions* as the professed basis of rules in them. What he reacted against was not the use of fictions as it occurs in primitive or formalized legal systems as a method of developing the law, nor the use by courts of fictions of intention to deal with matters to which the parties assuredly did not pay any attention when they entered into a contract.[43] Rather, Lundstedt criticized the use of fictions as an explanation of statutory rules. Such an explanation is empty; moreover, by the choice of a fiction almost any rule can be justified. The importance of a fiction becomes apparent when conclusions are drawn from it. The conclusions may be unwarranted and even unsuitable to practical situations.

Lundstedt's main criticism is directed against use of the notion of a fictitious guarantee to 'explain' the seller's strict liability when unascertained goods are not delivered in time (Article 24 of the Scandinavian Sale of Goods Act of 1915).[44] The use of such a fiction may appear unnecessary to an Anglo-American reader but it is explained by the hold of the *culpa* rule, derived from Roman and German law, on Scandinavian law at the end of the nineteenth and the beginning of the twentieth century. According to the Sale of Goods Act

[43] The classical study of fiction in primitive law is H. S. Maine, *Ancient Law* (London, 1861), ch. 2.

[44] See 'Kan härskande tolkning av 24 § köplagen anses riktig?' (1921) *Svensk juristtidning*, 325 ff.

(Article 23), the seller of specified goods was, in principle, liable to pay damages if he was negligent, although the burden of proving that he was not negligent lay on him. As for unascertained goods, strict liability was considered by Almén to require special justification since it constituted an exception to the *culpa* rule. He found such justification in the explanation that the seller had silently guaranteed that the goods were to be delivered on time.[45] The seller was excused for not delivering only when it was impossible because of an unforeseeable event to deliver the goods in time. This exception which regulates *inter alia* the consequences of *force majeure*, is the important part of the rule. Lundstedt's analysis did not refer to the exception but only to the main rule and to a certain conclusion drawn from it in order to deal with a somewhat special situation. This situation was where a seller of unascertained goods had concentrated his efforts on one particular batch of the goods, which then perished because of an unforeseeable accident—which was, however, not of a *force majeure* type—immediately before the time for delivery. The discussion of principle was, in an unfortunate way, intermingled with the problem of how this particular situation should be handled. Those who opposed Lundstedt's treatment of the fictitious guarantee were, in fact, mostly concerned with treatment of this particular situation.

This matter may also be considered to belong to legal history, since the fictitious guarantee has long ago been abandoned as an explanation of the main rule of liability for delay in the delivery of unascertained goods.[46] However, it took a considerable time for fictitious guarantees of this kind to disappear entirely from legal arguments in Sweden. Under earlier Swedish law, an employer was liable for an injury suffered by an employee only if it had been caused negligently by someone in a responsible position. This rule—which was abandoned by legislation in 1972—was 'explained' by the employer being considered to have undertaken a guarantee for the actions of his employees in a superior position but not for those of a common worker.[47] The emptiness of such an argument may be obvious to us but apparently it was not at the time.

However, even if fictitious guarantees of the kind that Lundstedt

[45] See Almén, n. 22 above, 286 ff.

[46] The special situation of a seller having concentrated his efforts on one special delivery that perishes accidentally, is uncertain even under the new Scandinavian Sale of Goods Act, which was enacted in Finland in 1987 and in Sweden in 1990. This situation seems to continue to hold a fascination for Scandinavian lawyers, which is out of proportion to its practical importance, and which testifies to the continuing influence of Lundstedt's writings. Cf. J. Hellner, 'Kontrollansvaret', in *Festskrift Curt Olsson* (Helsinki, 1989), 114 ff., at p. 131.

[47] See the opinion of Judge Stenbeck in the case reported *Nytt juridiskt arkiv I* (1929), 550 (at 553).

criticized seem to have disappeared from Swedish legal discussion, the same is not true for equally fictitious references to the parties' intentions. It is easy for a court to base its decision on the presumed intentions of the parties even when there is no basis in fact for such presumptions. Such a procedure may seem innocuous, but it conceals the reasons of policy which may have been decisive. In this respect, it seems possible to proceed further towards realism.

6. Conclusions

From the preceeding survey, it appears that in the field of contract law the main results of Scandinavian legal realism can be summarized in three propositions. The long-run effects of rules and the functions of rules in business life are emphasized, in contrast to considerations of justice in individual cases. Circular reasoning is revealed whenever possible. Justification of legal rules by fictions is rejected.

These are the good sides of the work carried out, and I have done my best to present them in as favorable a light as possible, pruning the countless exaggerations and misplaced criticisms in Lundstedt's writings. As will have appeared, I consider it a real merit to have drawn attention to these pitfalls of legal arguments, although others may have done the same independently of Scandinavian work. However, even if we admit that there are merits here, the limitations are considerable and it should not be argued that the merits alone constitute a sufficient basis for legal science as Lundstedt seems to have believed. The analysis is mostly negatively critical and directed against what are believed to be prevailing errors. Some of the errors had already disappeared when the criticism was advanced. The main targets of the criticism were writings by legal scientists which may not have been very influential in practice. The criticism was methodological rather than factual. The aim of the criticism was destructive rather than that of laying the foundations for the creation of new and valuable rules, or of developing the law. The empirical foundations of general statements regarding the effects of rules were entirely neglected; it was simply assumed that such effects occurred even if they were not proved. Questions concerning the legitimacy of legal rules were omitted altogether, or rather were considered to be non-existent. Although I have tried to carry the analysis somewhat further than Lundstedt did, the main trend has been the one indicated by him. This leads us to the question of the present situation.

The core of legal realism in Scandinavia is, as I see it, the aim of examining critically the validity of arguments proffered by legal writers for the purpose of discovering arguments that are untenable on theoretical grounds. This aim seems to have been assimilated by Scandinavian legal scientists in general, although it is, of course, by no means always carried through. The influence of legal realism is indirect rather than direct; which is understandable given that the polemics which occupy the main part of Lundstedt's work are hopelessly outdated. It is also possible that a new generation is not so strongly impressed by the old arguments, even when they are familiar with them.

The main reason why most of the ideas of the Scandinavian realists seem less interesting today than when they were first advanced lies in the limitations which I have pointed out. New problems have emerged that attract the attention of legal scientists. The reliance theory, in the narrow sense that Scandinavian legal theory finally gave to this concept, may seem rather uninteresting when the protection of consumer interests on the one hand, and the emergence of new types of business contracts and business relations on the other, engage our attention. On a somewhat higher level of discussion, the passive acceptance of established law is not sufficient and the value of present law must be examined. Yet, if we stay within the boundaries which the realists drew for themselves, their work is still worth being considered.

4

Statutes and Contracts as Founts of Formal Reasoning

ROBERT S. SUMMERS[1]

Introduction

In this essay, which I dedicate to my friend and co-author,[2] Professor Patrick Atiyah, I seek to demonstrate that, in American law, the overall level of formality of those reasons for decision (or other action) that derive from contracts is generally lower than the formality of reasons deriving from statutes. I also explore the importance of this fact, and here and there speculate on the explanations for it. I provide brief accounts of the varieties of formality involved, as well. I believe these efforts, which are partially programmatic, enable us to understand somewhat more fully the distinctive nature of statutes and contracts (which I here consider to be a type of law), and the special character of the reasoning that these types of law generate.

The American jurist, Oliver Wendell Holmes, Jr., and many of his followers have thought that statutes, contracts, and other forms of law are merely predictions or bases for predictions of official action. It was Holmes who said that, 'the duty to keep a contract . . . means a prediction that you must pay damages if you do not keep it—and nothing else'.[3] A valid contract, however, is not merely a basis for predictions. Like a statute, a valid contract is normative in character and thus also generates what Professor Atiyah and I call formal reasons that may guide and justify action.[4] A formal reason may be defined roughly as a legally authoritative reason which can justify acts of private par-

[1] Arthur L. Goodhart Visiting Professor of Legal Science, Cambridge University, 1991–2; McRoberts Research Professor of Law, Cornell Law School. The author has had fruitful discussions with Dr G. Marshall, The Queen's College, Oxford University. Mr John Moscati, jun, Cornell Law School Class of 1992, also provided valuable assistance. The author is also indebted to the editors of this volume.

[2] P. S. Atiyah and Robert S. Summers, *Form and Substance in Anglo-American Law* (Oxford, 1987).

[3] Holmes, 'The Path of the Law' (1897) 10 *Harv. LR* 257, 462.

[4] See generally, Atiyah and Summers, n. 2 above ch. 1.

ties, judges, and others.[5] In Atiyah–Summers parlance, the expression 'formal' reason is not pejorative. Of course, a particular formal reason might be a bad reason. For example, it could be over-formal, that is, formalistic. And a formal reason may go awry in other ways, as well.[6]

Formal reasons are to be differentiated from substantive reasons. A substantive reason standing alone is a merely moral, economic, political, institutional, or other consideration, devoid of legal authoritativeness.[7] (It, too, may or may not be a good reason.) A formal reason does not stand alone. It presupposes a statute, a contract, or other valid form of law. A formal reason, unlike a merely substantive reason, derives some force from the fact that it arises from a legally authoritative source.

But no law can exist without material content, and substantive reasoning must determine or inform that content. The substantive reasoning that influences the content of a statute, a contract, or other species of law also figures thereafter in the content of the formal reasons that derive from or arise under such law. For example, substantive reasoning about the ends and means of having a safe and quiet public park informs the statute: 'No vehicles may be taken into the park.' The content of this statute thereafter shows itself in formal reasons deriving from it.

Even the simplest statute may give rise to hundreds of different formal reasons for action on the part of many citizens. For example, the statute providing that 'No vehicles may be taken into the park' may, on a single day, generate numerous reasons including: 'since a pram is not a vehicle, it is permitted'; 'since a skateboard is a vehicle, it is prohibited'; 'since a pony is not a vehicle, it is permitted'; 'since a battery-driven scooter is a vehicle, it is prohibited'; 'since a pair of roller-skates is not a vehicle, it is permitted'; 'since a horse-drawn carriage is a vehicle, it is prohibited'; and so on, and on, and on. Of course, these formal reasons may prove not only to be reasons for citizens to act, but also for administrators such as park superintendents and for judges, too.

A formal reason, then, may be analysed in terms of formal attributes and substantive content. Thus, one formal attribute is authoritativeness. Moreover, as we shall see, the formal reason that a statute, a contract, or other form of law generates also generally prevails against

[5] See H. L. A. Hart, *Essays on Bentham* (Oxford, 1982), 243–68.

[6] See generally, Summers, 'Theory, Formality and Practical Legal Criticism' (1990) 106 *LQR* 407.

[7] Contracts bring a special subclass of substantive reasons into play, namely, those having to do with the personal preferences of contracting parties. Such reasoning naturally informs the content of contracts, but it is not usually appropriate for statutes to incorporate this kind of reasoning, except in so far as it overlaps with principles and policies of a more public-regarding or social nature.

any contrary substantive reasons that emerge from the facts at point of application, that is, in Atiyah–Summers parlance, it has high 'mandatory formality'. Thus, for example, it generally won't do for youngsters riding prohibited skateboards to reply to the park superintendent: 'But we are having an exceptionally good time, parks are for play, and we're not hurting anyone.' In short, formal reasons are not only authoritative; they are also highly mandatory, that is, relatively unmodifiable by officials at point of application, despite even strong countervailing substantive considerations emergent there.

In the various processes whereby statutes, contracts, and other forms of law are created and applied, at least five formal attributes combine with the substance of the law to generate formal reasons (in light of the facts).[8] The varieties of formality that figure in these formal attributes include the following:[9]

1. constitutive formality, which contributes authoritativeness to a particular statute, contract, or other law;
2. expressional formality, which is largely a function of the precision with which the law is formulated;
3. close-ended formality, which consists mainly in the completeness of the law at inception;
4. interpretative formality, which is largely a function of the extent to which the applicable interpretative methodology adheres to the law's express wording;
5. mandatory formality, which is the degree of unmodifiability of the law by a judge or other official at point of application.

A somewhat different form–substance contrast figures in each of these five varieties of formality, a matter to which I will return. These varieties of formality do not all enter legal processes relevant to the ultimate generation of formal reasons at the same stage. Constitutive formality, expressional formality, and close-ended formality enter mainly at the law-making stage, whereas interpretative formality and mandatory formality come into play at point of application. We will see, too, that the level or degree of formality in each variety may be relatively high or relatively low. Indeed, my main thesis here is that, in the American system, the level of formality of each of the above five varieties is generally lower in regard to contracts than in regard to statutes. These differences of level are important. Among other things, they affect the availability and nature of formal reasons ultimately

[8] See generally, Atiyah and Summers, n. 2 above, ch. 1.

[9] Here I depart somewhat from the categories of formality first adumbrated in Atiyah and Summers, n. 2 above.

arising under a statute or a contract.[10] Nor are these differences of level mere accident. As we shall see, various rational explanations suggest themselves.

Constitutive Formality

A statute, a contract, or any particular law must have substantive content. But it does not follow that having some particular substantive content is necessarily required for putative law to constitute valid law. It is logically possible that the applicable legal standards defining what constitutes a valid statute or valid contract could be entirely independent of substantive content. That is, those standards could be purely formal. For example, they could be 'source-oriented', and thus require only that a putative statute or contract derive from a legally appropriate source, such as a duly elected legislature following proper procedures or, in the case of a contract, two contracting parties of sound mind, legal age, and so on. In the American system, however, the validity of putative statutes and of putative contracts is governed both by formal standards and by substantive standards. I will first argue that the formality of the formal standards of validity—constitutive formality—is generally higher for statutes than for contracts.

In the American system, a federal or a state statute must generally satisfy two different kinds of formal requirements to be valid. Such a statute must: (1) satisfy applicable 'source-oriented' standards of validity, that is, be duly adopted by a duly elected legislature and duly signed (or the like) by the executive; and (2) have a single, definitive, linguistic formulation. Both types of requirements are formal in the sense that they are entirely independent of the substantive content of the statute. Similarly, a prima facie valid contract must at least satisfy applicable source-oriented standards of validity, for example, be entered into by persons of sound mind and legal age, and so on. But while a statute must have a single, definitive, linguistic formulation—one that may itself accommodate any substantive content—in the case of a contract there is really no general parallel requirement. The nearest counterpart in the case of a contract consists simply of the actual substantive agreement of the contracting parties, however proven. In general, no single, definitive, linguistic written formulation is required for the validity of a contract. (Certain statutorily prescribed contract clauses, such as those to be found in the field of insurance, are partial exceptions to this.)

[10] I do not here go into substantive reasoning as it influences levels. For such see, Summers, n. 6 above.

Neither the presence of a statute-of-frauds requirement nor the operation of a parol evidence rule alters this general analysis. It is true that a statute of frauds, when applicable, requires a signed writing. But this requirement does not apply to all contracts, and when it does apply it does not require that the contract be expressed in any single, definitive form or even that it be embodied in a single authentic writing. It does not even require that all of the contract's essential terms be stated in the writing. The most modern American version of a statute of frauds requires very little by way of written terms.[11] All the rest can be proven by oral or other evidence.

It is true that a parol evidence rule may operate to define the subject-matter of a contract. Such a rule, in its most modern American version,[12] applies to a writing that the parties intended to be a complete and exclusive embodiment of their substantive agreement. When it applies, it excludes evidence of terms outside the writing, and thus operates to define the subject-matter of the agreement. The rule does not apply to oral contracts, and moreover, in applying the rule to an agreement in writing, many a court today will go behind an apparently complete contract—one in which the agreed-upon terms are apparently all in the writing—to find further terms of the contract in extrinsic evidence, at least when the court is convinced from all the evidence that the parties did not intend the writing to be a complete and exclusive embodiment of their agreement. The effect of this way of administering the rule is often to deprive the 'contract' of anything like a single, definitive, linguistic formulation.

A statutory 'writing' is very different and much more formal. Moreover, courts do not, except in cases of obvious drafting mistakes in grammar, punctuation, or the like, go beyond the formal wording of the statute itself and insert new or revised wording or punctuation into the definitive linguistic formulation of the statute as adopted by the legislature. (This is not to say that courts never look behind the statute to 'legislative intention' when interpreting it, on which more later.)

Plainly, the nature of the authoritative version of a statute or a contract affects the availability of formal reasons thereunder. In general, only the words of a statute can ultimately anchor a formal statutory reason. And a formal reason can not arise from a term not 'in' a contract, expressly or by implication. Moreover, what is taken to be the authoritative version of the statute or contract affects the content and thus the nature of the formal reasons arising under it.

I have said that, in the American system, both statutes and contracts are subject to substantive standards of validity, as well as to source-

[11] See *Uniform Commercial Code*, s. 2-201.
[12] Ibid., s. 2-202.

oriented ones. Thus, statutes in the American system must not violate substantive constitutional provisions. Similarly, contracts must not offend constitutions, violate the criminal law, be unconscionable, and the like. Such standards of validity are content-oriented, and thus substantive. Obviously, insofar as standards of validity require that the law have or not have particular substantive content, this also affects the formal reasons that may ultimately arise under the law.

In my view, substantive, that is, content-oriented tests, generally play a larger role, overall, in the validity of contracts than in the validity of statutes. Thus the validity of statutes is, in this respect too, less a matter of substance than of form, compared to contracts. First, in regard to contracts, there are not only substantive tests of validity deriving from constitutional law, the criminal law, regulatory laws, the law of unconscionability, public policy, and the like. There are also many statutes and regulations which impose, prohibit or otherwise regulate the specific content of contracts. Some bodies of law actually prescribe, sometimes as a condition of validity, part of the substantive content of contracts, thereby necessarily shaping the content of the formal reasons that arise thereunder. These bodies of law relate to contracts of insurance, of carriage, of storage, of certain loans, and more.[13]

It is possible to overstate here the role of constitutions as direct sources of content-oriented standards for determining the validity of statutes. Unlike bodies of law prescribing the content of certain types of contracts, these constitutional provisions seldom precribe the actual content of any particular statute. They mainly consist of content-proscriptions, not content-prescriptions.

Secondly, prima facie valid contracts are defeasible. They may be invalidated on a vast array of further substantive grounds besides unconstitutionality, illegality, unconscionability, and the like, grounds which have no counterparts in statute law. For example, they may be invalidated for fraud, undue influence, mutual mistake, and the like. Plainly, these are substantive rather than formal grounds of invalidity, and they may operate to restrict or eliminate formal reasons that would otherwise come into play. Most contracts invalid on such grounds generate no formal reasons at all. (But even invalid contracts may contribute to reasons of a restitutional nature.)

Expressional Formality

As its name implies, expressional formality relates to how law is expressed. The level of such formality is higher to the extent that the

[13] See E. W. Patterson, 'Compulsory Contracts in the Crystal Ball' (1943) 43 *Colum. LR* 731.

law is written, and to the extent that it is expressed in legal or other technical terms formulated with precision and conciseness in accord with canons of formal draftsmanship.[14] When expressional formality is high, as with many statutes, the substantive 'means–end' relations of the law may not be at all apparent to the untutored eye and ear. Indeed, the essential substance of the law will often not even be intelligible to the lay citizen. When expressional formality is low, as with most contracts, the law is not expressed in legal or other technical terms, is not cast in highly precise and concise language, and is not rigorously and economically drafted in accord with canons of formal draftsmanship. As a result, the substantive 'means–end' relations of the law so expressed emerge as much more intelligible. A court may also, in the case of contracts, resort to what is only 'implied in fact' to round out the substance of such law.

The expressional formality of contracts generally is much lower than that of statutes. For one thing, many contracts are not even written. Of those that are, many are prepared by lay people, and are thus informally expressed. Of course, some contracts do exhibit very high levels of formality. (Statutes may even prescribe this formality.) On the other hand, some statutes are expressed rather informally. But this does not alter the broad truth that contracts generally are far less formal, in expressional terms, than statutes. At the very least, statutes are in writing (in print) and, are usually drafted by lawyers in more or less formal terms. Indeed, if a statute is expressed in an overly informal way, courts in America may invalidate it.

The relatively low expressional formality of many contracts affects the nature of the reasons that derive from them. For one thing, oral and informally written contracts may generate rather indeterminate formal reasons. Even when the reasons are determinate, we may still be uncertain whether they are truly grounded in the contract. Furthermore, informally written contracts require a lower level of interpretative formality, which, as we will see, can affect the reasons that may ultimately arise under such contracts.

Close-ended Formality

The formal attribute of close-endedness consists mainly of the degree to which a given statute or contract is complete in its legal content at inception—at time of creation. If entirely complete, it is totally close-ended. For example, a statute in the form of a truly 'hard and fast' rule

[14] See generally, R. Dickerson, *The Fundamentals of Legal Drafting*, 2nd edn., (Boston, 1986).

with no exceptions or with all exceptions duly specified is complete in its legal content at inception, and thus totally close-ended. On the other hand, a statute in the form of a broad grant of discretion to the courts is open-ended. That is, it is essentially dependent for its complete legal content on an infusion of substance at point of application, and thus displays a much lower level of what I call close-ended formality.

Although some statutes confer broad discretion or are otherwise open-ended, most statutes take the form of rules. Many of these statutory rules are relatively hard and fast, that is, quite close-ended, and thus in little need of infusions of substance at point of application in order to fill out their overall content so as to be relatively complete as laws. On the other hand, most contracts are not just incomplete but are radically incomplete at inception, and judges or others may have to fill these gaps.[15] In some branches of the law of contracts these gaps can be filled with 'stand-by' terms taken 'off the rack' of the general law,[16] so to speak, while in other branches of the law judges must play a much larger law-making role in filling these gaps.

This basic difference between the levels of close-ended formality in contracts and in statutes also affects the formal reasons that emerge from each type of law. For example, in so far as a contract is incomplete at inception, formal reasons of relevance to the incomplete aspects may have to be made up at point of application. That is, the judge may have to put contractual fragments together with other justificatory resources available in the circumstances (such as custom, for example) and act accordingly. Private parties must do likewise. With statutes, on the other hand, which are more often close-ended or nearly so, judges will more often have at their disposal formal reasons, the nature of which is determined more fully by the antecedent law (and the interpretative method) under which those reasons arise.

Interpretative Formality

Interpretative formality resides more in the methodology of interpretation than in the law being interpreted. Yet the two cannot be divorced. The nature of what is being interpreted affects the methodology of interpretation. For example, the generally higher expressional formality of statutes is congenial to a higher formality of

[15] See S. Narasimhan, 'Of Expectations, Incomplete Contracting, and the Bargain Principle' (1986) 74 *Calif. LR* 1123.

[16] For examples of such gap fillers, see J. J. White and R. S. Summers, *Uniform Commercial Code*, 3rd edn. (St Paul, Minn. 1988), ch. 3. See also *Restatement (Second) of Contracts*, (1981), s. 204.

interpretative method than is the lower expressional formality of contracts.

An interpretative methodology is formal: (1) insofar as it does not recognize interpretative arguments that go behind and diverge from the ordinary, technical, or special meanings of the authoritative language in which the law is expressed; or (2) in so far as such arguments *are* recognized, the methodology nevertheless accords in cases of conflict between arguments, cancelling force, priority, or overriding weight, to those arguments arising from the ordinary or technical or special meanings of the written or printed words used to express the law being interpreted.[17] An interpretative methodology is less formal is so far as it goes behind the express words of the law either to take account of the substance of the intended meaning (including the purposes) of those who made the law, or to take account of relevant substantive reasoning that happens to appeal to the interpreter though it is not truly grounded in the text.

The general law on interpretative method both in regard to statutes and in regard to contracts is not uniform in the United States. Even so, there are widely observed judicial doctrines with regard to both. Here, I will rely mainly on authoritative US Supreme Court cases on statutory interpretation, and in regard to contract interpretation, mainly on the second Restatement of Contracts.

The authoritative methodology of contract interpretation is far less formal than that of statutory interpretation. As a result, the interpretation of statutes differs greatly from the interpretation of contracts, a fact that many, including the perceptive American jurist, Lon L. Fuller, have overlooked.[18] To see this, it is enough to compare three of the leading types of interpretative arguments, as applied to statutes and to contracts. First, the formal argument from the standard ordinary or technical meaning of the specific words used in the statute or contract in issue has much lower standing in contract interpretation than in statutory interpretation. That is, the American law of contract interpretation allows the interpreter to go behind the meaning of written words either to take account of extrinsic evidence of the substance of any agreement, or of substantive social policies or principles, far more extensively than the American law of statutory interpretation allows the interpreter of a statute to go behind its words.

To begin with, the express wording of a purported written contract

[17] See D. N. MacCormick and R. S. Summers (eds.), *Interpreting Statutes—A Comparative Study* (1991), ch. 12.

[18] Lon L. Fuller, *Anatomy of the Law* (New Haven 1971), 102: 'In case of dispute the courts interpret and apply . . . [contract] terms much as they would the enactment of a legislature.'

may be entirely in order on its face and have an objective ordinary or technical meaning, yet one party be allowed to show that no contract was formed at all because evidence of the subjective understandings of the parties reveals a mutual misunderstanding going to the root of the transaction. For example, A may, in a writing that describes 'Greenacre', promise to sell such property as is described to B, but the evidence of prior negotiations show that A intended to sell Blackacre and B intended to buy Whiteacre.[19] When extrinsic evidence outside the writing reveals a material misunderstanding, and neither party had any more reason than the other to know of it, there is simply no contract, even though the parties signed a writing having a perfectly obvious objective meaning to all third parties. The law here considers the two parties to be the appropriate persons to decide on their obligations. As the Restatement says, the 'operative meaning', if any, is to be found in the substance of the transaction between the parties, 'rather than in the law or in the usages of people other than the parties'.[20] There is simply no parallel statutory doctrine. Even though the addressees of a statute may interpret it in radically different ways, the statute remains a statute, and if it has an objective ordinary or technical meaning, this will generally control.

Moreover, even when the parol-evidence rule operates to confine the valid contract to the words appearing in the writing, and even when the language has an objective ordinary or technical meaning, judges and others may still be allowed to resort to any evidence of prior or contemporaneous agreements, negotiations, and circumstances in order to interpret the meaning of the words in the writing. For example, if A contracts in writing to buy 'your wool' from B, A can introduce evidence from the negotiations to show that 'your' was in fact meant by both parties to include not only wool being grown on B's sheep at time of contracting, but also any wool that B happened to contract to buy later from others long after the making of the contract between A and B.[21]

The parallel doctrine with regard to statutes is, according to many (though not all) American cases, to the contrary. These cases take the view that, if the language of the statute has a clear objective meaning (ordinary or technical) for the case, then extrinsic evidence from legislative history supporting a different meaning will generally not be given effect.[22] Some cases, however, do hold that, if extrinsic evidence of contrary legislative intention is 'clearly expressed', then this

[19] *Restatement (Second) of Contracts* (1981), s. 201(3); s. 212, comment a, Ill. 1.
[20] Ibid., s. 212 comment a.
[21] Ibid., s. 214(c) comment b, Ill. 2.
[22] See e.g., *Kaiser Aluminum Chemical Corp.* v. *Bonjorno* (1990) 110 S. Ct. 1570, 1575.

extrinsic evidence operates to displace the ordinary or technical meaning evident on the face of the statute.[23] Here, though, the evidence must often meet relatively stringent standards to qualify as 'clearly expressed'. In contract cases, there is no such standard at all. The evidence of intention need only be probative under the Restatement.

In addition, even though a word or phrase in a written contract has an objective ordinary or technical meaning, if extrinsic evidence shows that each party attached a different subjective meaning to the word or phrase at the time of the transaction, the contract will be interpreted in accord with the subjective meaning attached by one party at the time of contracting, if, among other things, that party did not know of the meaning adopted by the other party, and the other party knew of the meaning adopted by the first party.[24] If a word or a phrase in a contract has an objective ordinary or technical meaning, it is to be interpreted in accord with that meaning only in the absence of extrinsic evidence that *one* party's subjective meaning at time of contracting should control, as above, and in the absence of any extrinsic evidence of contrary *shared* subjective meaning.[25]

Finally, if there is an omission in the language of a contract, the court will look first to extrinsic evidence of shared subjective understandings of the parties to fill it. If the evidence indicates the parties did not agree, the court is to supply a term which is substantively reasonable in the circumstances.[26] Here again, statutes are often treated very differently. Even though it appears that there is a gap in the statute, and this gap could be filled in light of the substantive reasoning informing the statutory scheme as a whole, if there is relevant common law in the background many courts will give effect only to the explicit statutory words and leave the gap to be filled by pre-existing common law not specifically displaced by the statute.[27] This relatively formal solution is simply not an option with most gaps in contracts. There is not and could not be such general law in the background that could similarly fill gaps of the particular kinds that so frequently arise with contracts.

Overall, it may be said that in American law, arguments from extrinsic proof of subjectively shared meanings or understandings have primacy in contractual interpretation over the objective meanings of the words used. Indeed, the general 'rule' is sometimes phrased in pre-

[23] See e.g., *Public Citizen* v. *US Dept. of Justice* (1989), 109 S. Ct. 2558, 2566, 2572.
[24] *Restatement (Second) of Contracts* (1981), s. 201(2)(a).
[25] Ibid., s. 201; 202(3).
[26] Ibid., s. 204.
[27] *Norfolk Redevelopment and Housing Authority* v. *Chesapeake and Potomac Telephone*, (1983) 464 US 30, 35.

cisely these terms.[28] But in statutory interpretation, primacy is much more often accorded to any objective ordinary or technical meanings, a relatively formal approach.

This basic difference is not difficult to explain or rationalize. Contracts are essentially private agreements deriving from shared intentions and understandings, and it is their actual substance rather than their mere outward expression that the law ultimately purports to enforce. (Of course, the two commonly coincide.) Statutes, on the other hand, are public legal enactments, and their authoritativeness resides primarily in the enacted words. Moreover, legislative intentions behind statutory words are more problematic conceptually than are shared contractual intentions, and their relevance is more controversial. In the case of legislative intentions, there is often a problem about which of several intentions is to count as authoritative—that of the sponsor of a bill, of the committee to which it was referred, of the floor leader, and so on. This problem is less significant in contract interpretation. Further, it is highly controversial whether statutes should be interpreted contrary to objective ordinary or technical meaning where there is evidence of contrary legislative intent. Among other things, it is said that the words of a statute just are the best evidence of intent and that the legislature and the executive assent to the language of bills, not committee reports or the like. It is far less controversial, however, that courts should, within limits, enforce the discernible subjective agreement of the parties even though this may be contrary to the language of a writing they signed. After all, the ultimate aim of the law of contract is to enforce the actual agreements of contracting parties, not mere verbal expressions.

So far, I have concentrated largely on the comparative standing of the argument from the standard ordinary or technical meaning of the words used *in the part of the statute or contract in issue*. I now turn briefly to a second powerful type of argument in statutory interpretation, namely, the argument from harmonization with the overall linguistic context. Here, a court interprets the words in issue in the part of the statute concerned in light of: (1) words in the rest of the statutory section involved; (2) words in the other sections of the same statute; (3) words in sections of statutes *in pari materia*; and (4) the language of the general law of which the statute forms a part. This type of argument may even be sufficiently powerful to cancel or displace a standard ordinary or technical meaning of the very words at issue in the statute.[29] In its focus on the express linguistic

[28] '*Unless a different intention is manifested*, where language has a generally prevailing meaning, it is interpreted in accordance with that meaning.' *Restatement (Second) of Contracts* (1981), s. 202(3)(a) (emphasis added).

[29] See MacCormick and Summers, n. 17 above, at ch. 11, p. 433.

context, this type of harmonization argument is, in my terms, formal.

But again, in regard to contract interpretation the general story is very different. Admittedly, courts do sometimes interpret contract language so to harmonize with the contract 'as a whole',[30] and, occasionally, to harmonize with related contracts between the same parties. But far more often any such harmonization argument is subordinated to contrary extrinsic evidence of actual shared meanings or intentions of the parties, largely for reasons of the kind already identified. Moreover, contextual harmonization arguments turning on the wording of related parts of the contract or of related contracts tend to have less force here than in statutory interpretation. This is mainly because most contracts are not written with the same relatively high level of expressional formality as statutes usually are. Finally, contextual harmonization arguments are simply less often available in contract. The very concept of contracts *in pari materia* is itself problematic, and such contracts are not common. Similarly, courts rarely seek to 'fit contracts into the fabric of generally related law' in the way they seek to harmonize a statute with related statutes.

A third basic type of argument frequently encountered in American statutory interpretation cases is the argument from that interpretation which would best serve a statutory purpose.[31] To the extent that this argument is confined to evidence of purpose on the face of the statute, it is, in my terms of reference, relatively formal, and many cases confine purposive argumentation with regard to statutes in this way (though there are cases the other way, too). Many cases also invoke the argument from purpose only where the statute is ambiguous, vague, or otherwise unclear. Again, with contracts, the story is very different. American courts readily go behind the words of a contract to extrinsic evidence of a shared common purpose in order to interpret the agreement.[32] In this regard, too, contract interpretation may be said to be less formal than statutory interpretation.

In sum, interpretative method in regard to contracts is, overall, much less formal than it is in regard to statute law.

Mandatory Formality

We now assume that the law is valid, complete, that is, has no relevant gaps, and that it has been duly interpreted and, as so interpreted, has generated a formal reason with determinate bearing on the issue posed

[30] *Restatement (Second) of Contracts* (1981), s. 202(2).
[31] See e.g., *Mills Music, Inc.* v. *Snyder* (1985) 469 US 153, 172–3.
[32] *Restatement (Second) of Contracts* (1981), s. 202(1).

by the facts. In my terms, the mandatory formality of such law and the reasoning arising under it is higher to the extent that courts at point of application have less power to modify its content in light of substantive reasoning emergent there and not as such taken account of when the law was first made. On the other hand, mandatory formality is lower in so far as courts are empowered to modify the content of the antecedent law and thus the formal reasoning arising under it in light of such newly emergent substantive considerations.

Judges generally disclaim any power to *rewrite* statutes,[33] except when there is a very obvious drafting error or when statutes are plainly obsolete because of some technological change or the like. Similarly, judges generally disclaim any power to *rewrite* contracts.[34] Despite these similarities of disclaimer, the formal mandatoriness, that is, unmodifiability, of a contract and the formal reasoning arising under it, is lower than that of statute law. That is, courts more readily rewrite contracts on substantive grounds than they rewrite statutes on such grounds.

There are at least two basic ways in which courts rewrite contracts. First, they rewrite them to make them conform more fully to what the parties probably wanted, where unforeseen circumstances or the like have arisen, or where outward expressions fail to express the intentions of the parties adequately in the first place.[35] Here the substantive reasoning that prevails takes the form of actual or probable preferences of the contracting parties. Secondly, judges rewrite some contracts to make them conform more fully to various public policies, that is, substantive considerations.[36]

Judges do not generally go so far with regard to statutes, and this is not difficult to explain. First, judges cannot so readily assume that a legislature has overlooked a matter, or failed to express its intentions adequately in the first place. Secondly, to revise statutory language is to revise a public legislative act. For a court to revise the language of private parties is far less daunting.

Conclusion

The formality of formal reasons arising from contracts is significantly lower than in the case of statutory formal reasons. This is generally

[33] See e.g., *Branch* v. *Dubois* (1976), 418 F. Supp. 1128, 1131.

[34] See e.g., *Joseph Martin, Jr. Delicatessen, Inc.* v. *Schumacher* (1981), 436 NY 2d 247, 417 NE 2d 541.

[35] See e.g., *C & J Fertilizer, Inc.* v. *Allied Mutual Insurance Co.* (1975), 227 NW 2d 169, 177; *Nanakuli Paving Co.* v. *Shell Oil Co.* (1980), 664 F.2d 772, 805.

[36] See e.g., *Wood* v. *May* (1968), 438 P. 2d 587, 591; *McCutcheon* v. *United Homes Corp.* (1971), 79 Wash. 2d 443, 486 P. 2d 1093, 1099; *Dwyer* v. *Jung* (1975), 133 NJ Super. 343, 336 A. 2d 498, 500.

true with regard to each of five major varieties of formality which are attributes of both types of reason. This overall difference is important because, as we have seen, it affects the availability and nature of the formal reasons arising from these fundamentally different sources of law. This difference is also not mere accident, and here and there I have suggested rational explanations for it.

It must not be thought, however, that formal reasons arising under statutes display the highest formality of all types of legal reason. Reasons arising under *official orders* probably display the highest. Nor should it be thought that formal reasons arising under contracts display the lowest formality of all types of legal reasons. Reasons arising under *customary law* probably display the lowest. As we can see, this entire subject awaits a more comprehensive, more systematic, and still more thorough analysis than I am able to provide here.

5

Conceptions of Public Policy

JOHN BELL[1]

Section 24 of the Social Security Act 1975 provided that, if a woman was under pensionable age when her husband died and he had made sufficient national insurance contributions, '[a] woman who has been widowed shall be entitled to a widow's allowance at the weekly rate specified in relation thereto in Schedule 4, Part I, paragraph 5 . . .' Along came Mrs Connor, who satisfied the age requirement and her husband had satisfied the contribution requirements. Yes, he was dead and she was a widow, so could she please have the widow's allowance? One snag, a jury at Leeds Crown Court had found her guilty of the manslaughter of her husband, in that the cause of his death was a wound made by a knife which Mrs Connor was wielding. The Divisional Court in *R.* v. *National Insurance Commr., ex. p. Connor*[2] had no difficulty in refusing Mrs Connor her widow's allowance on the ground that 'public policy demands the court to drive the applicant from the seat of justice'.

Appeals to 'public policy' in legal reasoning give the impression that at key points the law is open to some explicit wide-ranging consideration of public welfare in deciding the content of legal rules. The *Connor* case illustrates a typical situation in which this is misleading. Reference in that case to 'public policy' amounts simply to an argument of (legal) common sense, that all legal rules are subject to qualifications introduced by certain general principles of law. The justifications offered here demonstrate little willingness to engage the non-legal audience and its concerns.

Yet is 'public policy' just another kind of legal rule? To suggest this might seem to reflect an undue formalism of reasoning which Atiyah has criticized in a number of writings. Indeed, he has suggested that judges often are hiding their real creative role in the formulation of

[1] This chapter develops a working-paper presented as part of the ESPRIT working group on 'The Foundations of Legal Reasoning' at its Cork meeting in June 1990. My thanks are due to all the members of the working-group who commented on the paper and to the ESPRIT programme for giving the opportunity for such discussions.

[2] [1981] 1 All ER 770.

policy behind formal arguments based on legal rules.[3] On the other hand, Atiyah and Summers have stressed the importance of formal reasons in organizing social affairs in an orderly manner and in promoting the values of the rule of law.[4] How 'public policy' arguments are deployed may already reflect an implicit theory of the judicial function to which the apparent formal position is to give effect. The suggestion in this chapter will be that different views of the rule of law offer different interpretations of the point of an acceptable practice of appealing to arguments of public policy.

In their thought-provoking study of reasoning in Anglo-American law, Atiyah and Summers contrast the English approach of treating law as a set of hard-and-fast rules with the American willingness to see legal rules as 'guide-lines' for decisions.[5] I will argue that public policy is not best conceived as a specific set of legal rules or principles, but as a set of goals or objectives which form a framework within which legal decisions are made. The point of such decisions is to ensure that the purposes of the legal order as a whole are pursued in the application of specific rules to the resolution of disputed cases. There may well be the reluctance to perceive the law in this way which Atiyah and Summers note, but this is, none the less, an important facet of a legal order in practice.

Despite the common equation of the two, formalism and a rule-centred approach to law are distinct ideas. A rule-centred approach focuses on the kind of society we wish to create, for example, one in which legal certainty has paramount importance. Formalism, by contrast, is about the kinds of legitimate argument which may justify decisions taken according to law. By excluding a whole range of substantive arguments from debate, we can have a manageable way of providing common reasons for action and dispute-resolution in a heterogeneous society.[6] A proper conception of the rule of law can include formalism without commitment to a rule-centred approach to law, and public-policy arguments provide an illustration of how this works.

I will consider both French and English law in this area, for two reasons. First, the point I am making is not confined to English law, but is about law in western democratic countries in general. As part of the civil-law tradition, French law provides a convenient test of conclusions drawn from a common-law system. Secondly, both the French and English legal traditions are very formalistic in the general sense.

[3] See P. S. Atiyah, 'Judges and Policy' (1980) *15 Israel LR* 346.

[4] P. Atiyah and R. Summers, *Form and Substance in Anglo-American Law* (Oxford, 1987), esp. 25.

[5] Ibid. 88–9.

[6] Ibid. 25.

Rule formality may be greater in England than in France, and formality in the justification of judicial decisions may be far greater in France than in England. All the same, compared with the American tradition, both lie on the formalist end of the legal spectrum in terms of the reasons given for judicial decisons. Decisions are justified often by reference to precise legal standards, rather than by reference to the reasons justifying them. Both seek to treat the law as a closed system requiring only limited external justification. The way public policy operates in such systems provides a sterner test for my suggestions about a proper conception of the rule of law than illustrations of more clearly substantivist reasoning drawn from a country like the United States.

Public Policy as a Legal Argument

THE MEANING OF PUBLIC POLICY/ORDRE PUBLIC[7]

Long ago it was said that public policy involves 'political arguments, in the fullest sense of the word, as they concern the government of the nation'.[8] At the same time, this idea is usually differentiated from the wide range of arguments which can be invoked in parliament. A popular line is drawn by Malaurie in his thesis of 1953,[9] which suggests that the legislator develops a revolutionary and directory public policy, trying to engineer society in new directions to achieve a competitive economy or more social justice. In this sense, the public good and public policy are synonymous. On the other hand, the legal idea of public policy is more conservative, seeking to preserve the essential foundations of existing society. It is merely a subset of arguments which could be used in the governance of the country. The reality of such a dichotomy may be called into question, but there is significant validity in the emphasis which Malaurie wishes to bring out. In part, this is simply a feature of the division of labour between legal and political institutions which exists within western legal systems. Writing

[7] 'Public policy' and *'ordre public'* are not exact equivalents. All the same, for the purposes of this discussion *'ordre public'* (use as embracing *'bonnes mœurs'*) can be viewed as functionally equivalent to public policy in the kinds of legal involved.

[8] *Chesterfield* v. *Janssen* (1750) 1 Atk., 339 at 352 *per* Lord Hardwicke LC.

[9] P. Malaurie, *Les Contrats contraires à l'ordre public* (Paris, 1953), 38–41 and 52. Also J. Shand, 'Unblinkering the Unruly Horse: Public Policy in the Law of Contract' [1972] *CLJ* 144 at 147; K. Simitis, *Gute Sitten und Ordre public* (Marburg, 1960), 98. R. Pound, *Jurisprudence* (St Paul, Minn., 1959) argues to similar effect that public interests 'ultimately . . . come down to a social interest in the security of social institutions, of which political institutions in the world of today have taken the first place' (p. 236).

in the same year as Malaurie, Lloyd suggested much the same idea in relation to the laws of England and France:

> [Public policy] must be something which the very structure and character of the community demands; not merely something which people as a whole think desirable or otherwise, which they would pretty generally agree to accept or reject. It is indeed no more than the recognition that legal rules are built upon certain implicit moral and social assumptions which cannot be readily or precisely formulated in advance and which may change fundamentally from time to time.[10]

In this perspective, public policy represents part of the fundamental framework of social values and institutions out of which specific laws come. It helps to define the character of the social enterprise which is taken for granted in the specific activities of law. Only in rather special circumstances does that background have to be made explicit. If, as Atiyah rightly claims, law is a purposive enterprise,[11] it is proper that issues about this purpose should surface from time to time in legal debates.

The reason for invoking a generalized notion of 'public policy' is that specific legal rules and principles have failed to make clear some assumptions on which legal liberties or rights were granted. This was true in *Connor* of the law on social security, which failed to make clear that a person may not profit from his or her own wrong. In that the values of society can and are formulated to a significant extent in any society, the appeal to public policy may well, as in this case, refer to a specific recognized value. In other cases there may be less on which the lawyer can rest his case. The fundamental values may be settled in very general terms, but significant aspects are subject to public controversy. In this case, public policy refers to the changing exigencies of social stability in general.

A good example of this has occurred in recent French cases on the legality of associations formed to help sterile couples obtain children through the use of surrogate mothers. In two decisions, the highest French courts have ruled that such associations are contrary to public policy.[12] Reading the arguments of the *commissaire du gouvernement* and the *rapporteur* in the respective decisions, great weight seems to have been given to the negative opinion given in 1984 by a special ethical commission set up to examine the question of surrogacy. But the judges had to decide the requirements of public policy in an area

[10] D. Lloyd, *Public Policy* (London, 1953), 127–8.

[11] *Pragmatism and Theory in English Law* (London, 1987), 144.

[12] CE Ass. 22 Jan. 1988, *Association Les Cigones*, AJDA 1988, 163; Cass, 1re civ., 13 Dec. 1989, *Association Alma Mater c Procureur-général d'Aix-en-Provence*, D 1990, 273, rapport Massip.

where no decisions had been taken formally by public authorities. Various possible legal arguments seemed tenable to support particular solutions, but the underlying factor was a choice of social policy which the judges had to decide upon.

PUBLIC POLICY AS A LEGAL STANDARD

If these are the sorts of function which public policy performs, how should we conceive of public policy as a genre of legal argument?

One view suggests that public policy, like equity, is the name for a precise set of legal standards which lie at the bedrock of the legal system. They encapsulate the values which the legal system is designed to serve, and are brought to the surface in specific cases. Thus, Dworkin's analysis of *Riggs* v. *Palmer*[13] is that the maxim 'no man may profit from his own wrong' is a legal principle, a legal standard of higher generality and less precise application than a legal rule. The public policy invoked in that case and in *Connor* is not an extra-legal consideration, but merely a different character of legal standard than the statutory rule which it qualifies. In a similar but more qualified way, Atiyah has written that:

> The doctrine of public policy [in contract law] is strictly limited by precedents. It cannot be too strongly emphasized that it is not open to a judge to reject a contract merely because he may personally think that it is contrary to the public interest. It is only when a contract falls under one of the well-established categories stigmatized as being contrary to public policy that the judge can interfere . . . But public values do change, and change these days sometimes seems to come about very quickly; provided that the courts avoid idiosyncratic views there seems no real reason why they should not treat agreements as contrary to public policy in wholly new situations.[14]

In other words, there are rules which govern most situations, and the creative role of the judge is to create further rules where new situations so require.

An alternative view would be that public policy, in law as in politics, is nothing more than a framework within which conflicts between competing social interests are resolved.[15] Given the open texture of public-policy rules, the key feature of rules permitting decisions based on 'public policy' is that they authorize decision-making by particular individuals (often judges) to settle conflicts of interests. Though the nature of the judicial process may not appear legitimate for such an activity, Atiyah has noted that the issue of legitimacy is more com-

[13] *Taking Rights Seriously* (London, 1977), 23.
[14] P. S. Atiyah, *An Introduction to Contract*, 4th edn. (Oxford, 1989), 360–1.
[15] B. Smith, *Policy-Making in British Government* (London, 1976), 15.

plex than some (including myself) have suggested, and may not work against the suitability of the judicial function in this regard[16].

A way of escaping these problems of public policy as a framework for resolving conflicts of interest is to envisage it as an ideal which judges seek to implement either by qualifying or expanding existing rules. If the law is to fit into community ideas of fairness and justice, then appeal to such ideals would be appropriate ways of handling the inadequacy of specific formulations of the law in statutes or judicial decisions.

PUBLIC POLICY AND THE RULE OF LAW

What differentiates these perspectives is a view about the enterprise of law and the ability of rules to limit discretionary power. On one interpretation, the rule of law provides stability and guidance for citizens, offering clear solutions around which they can plan. In this way a common set of standards can be provided for a heterogeneous society.[17] Public policy, like equity, should operate as a form of rule-based justice which can be clearly located on the legal map. It may be general in formulation and defeasible in particular circumstances, but it is at least statable and containable. As such it does not fall outside the predictability of law.

In contrast, a more Kelsenian view of the rule of law focuses on the way in which law serves to validate and confer (legal) legitimacy on state exercises of power. To have this legitimacy, an exercise of power must be validated by a higher legal norm, but its specific content is left to the discretion of the decision-maker. Rather than ask questions about the correctness of an interpretation of the law, as in the first model of the rule of law, we are left simply with issues of legality—is this a bona fide exercise of power within the scope authorized by law and does it conform to the law's objectives? On this view, public policy is a form of corrective or dispensing power to bring the detailed operation of the law within its overall objectives. Since the statement of these objectives is rather general and contestable, judicial discretion is the central feature of this aspect of the law. Rules of public policy provide some guidance for the exercise of this discretion, but they function basically as a framework for decision-making.

The idea that judges are pursuing an ideal is more contestable. As Winfield put it:

[16] P. S. Atiyah, 'Book Review' (1985) 33 *Am. Jo. Comp. Law* 342, 346–7.

[17] Atiyah and Summers, n. 4 above, pp. 71 and 73; N. MacCormick, 'On "Open Texture" in Law', paper to ESPRIT working-group on 'The Foundations of Legal Reasoning', Tübingen meeting, Dec. 1990.

Some judges appear to have thought [the unruly horse of public policy] more like a tiger, and refused to mount it at all, perhaps because they feared the fate of the young lady of Riga. Others have regarded it like Balaam's ass which would carry its rider nowhere. But none, at any rate at the present day, has looked upon it as a Pegasus that might soar beyond the momentary needs of the community.[18]

But that is to take the notion of an ideal too far. As has already been stated, we are dealing with a conservative, rather than a visionary notion. All the same, it is not inappropriate to talk of ideals in such a context. Public values are reflected not only in the penal function of law. Law is a way of stating not only the limits of individual action, but also of society's values. To adapt Lucas, legal decisions 'indicat[e] what the values of society are and the authorities' determination to uphold them'.[19] To disapprove of conduct is a communication of the values of society and an effort to elicit support for the law among the public in general. That judges wish to consider themselves spokespersons for social consensus is well known, though their ability to achieve this may well be doubted.[20] Equally, the law is perceived (by traditional lawyers at least) as a neutral backbone of social stability, a reflection of the values of society. Specific legal rules are meant to exhibit this feature, and it is not all that surprising that the background idea comes in as a corrective of the law through the notion of public policy. To quote Honoré,[21] if law exists to reinforce people's reasons for conformity to certain standards, then to perform this task, it must be able to react against the law being used as either an instrument of unfairness, or contrary to other cherished values in the community. In this way, conformity to public (better 'institutional') values may be more important than simple conformity to rules. It is this idea of the rule of law which Raz alludes to in his description of the rule of law as 'principled . . . application of the law' in which judicial decisions are justified by reference to the 'common values and shared practices of the legal culture'.[22] Specific rules have to be related to the common values of the legal system as a whole.

Public Policy in Legal Practice

The plausibility of the first conception of the rule of law comes from the formalist character of the French and English legal systems. It may

18 'Public Policy in the English Common Law' (1928) 42 *Harv. LR* 76, 91.
19 J. Lucas, *On Justice* (Oxford, 1980), 132.
20 See J. Bell, *Policy Argument in Judicial Decisions* (Oxford, 1983), 10–7 and ch. 7.
21 'Real Laws', in P. Hacker and J. Raz (eds.), *Law, Morality and Society* (Oxford, 1977), at 104.
22 J. Raz, 'The Politics of the Rule of Law' (1990) 3 *Ratio Iuris* 331, 335–6. See also Dworkin's idea of integrity: *Law's Empire* (London, 1986), ch. 6.

be right to note that formulations of legal standards in the two systems are different—more principled in France and more detailed in England. But this does not detract from the essentially formalist approach of both systems. Public policy finds a place in a number of areas, and the rule-based idea focuses on the way in which it merely expresses established and defined standards inherent in the legal system, even if not expressed in a particular detailed rule. Following the approaches of standard textbooks, it is possible to sketch the outline of the case for treating public policy as essentially rule-based. Two of the principal areas will be discussed—the interpretation of statutes and the limitations placed on voluntary transactions. What is seen through both is the way public policy affects norms created by both legislators and private individuals.

THE CONSTRUCTION OF STATUTES

When used in the interpretation of statutes, 'public policy' is used to denote arguments which do not have their source either in the text of the statute or in the general principles of law which regulate a specific branch of law. By resort to systemic principles of public policy (which might be regarded in some legal systems, like the French, as general of law), an interpretation contrary to the text may be given without expressly violating parliamentary sovereignty.

Unexpressed Limitations on Statutes

The *Connor* decision is a good example of the use of public policy to introduce limitations on the apparently clear words of a text. Nothing in the law of social security pointed to this solution, yet I doubt if many lawyers question it. Another clear example comes from the recent decision in *R.* v. *Registrar General, ex. p. Smith.*[23] Section 51 of the Adoption Act 1976 provides:

> . . . the Registrar General shall on application made in the prescribed manner by an adopted person a record of whose birth is kept by the Registrar General and who has attained the age of 18 years supply to that person on payment of the prescribed fee (if any) such information as is necessary to enable that person to obtain a certified copy of the record of his birth.

Smith was such a person, but the Registrar General refused to give him the necessary information because he was a patient in a secure mental

[23] [1990] 2 All ER 170.

hospital (Broadmoor), having been convicted, *inter alia*, of the manslaughter of a cell-mate whom he mistook for his foster-mother. The Registrar was afraid that Smith would use the actual record of his birth to trace his real mother and perhaps to do violence to her. The Divisional Court had no difficulty in upholding the decision of the Registrar General. The statutory right was effectively denied where there was a real risk that it would be used for future criminality. To treat the right as absolute would outrage the public. It did not matter that there was no precedent for the Registrar General's argument: 'If what we deem to be an appropriate head of public policy is apparently novel and wanting until now of expression being given to it, that is no reason at all to deny it a place in the relevant law.'[24] Although this might be seen as an example of ellipsis, in practice it is not the deliberate omission of the obvious by a draftsman, but his inability to foresee all contingencies.

Penalties for Breach

A statutory provision may require qualification for reasons other than that it has failed to express (obvious) limitations on the rights granted. Many statutes declare conduct unlawful without adequately specifying the consequences. For example, in the French surrogacy associations cases, the article of the Penal Code lays down a criminal penalty for whoever, 'for gain', causes parents of a child to be born to abandon it. Even if, as the French courts found, that provision applies to the activities of surrogacy associations, it says nothing about the legality of such associations. The penalty has to be added by the decision-maker. The logic of the argument, if fully articulated, would be that, if the legislator has decided to penalize the conduct by a criminal penalty, that purpose must also require the prohibition of agreements ancillary to the crime.

Indeed, in most cases, the public policy argument will centre around the 'intention of the legislator', rather than specifically about 'public policy'. After all, the judges are trying to give meaning to a text, and the legislator is primarily responsible for defining public policy. The interpretation of the text is offered as a continuation of the legislator's thinking. But such arguments are tenuous. The purpose and wording of the statutes is directed towards creating a criminal penalty. To expand the statute beyond that to create a civil penalty is really to apply the statutory purpose by analogy, not to deduce an answer from the obvious or even inferred intention of the legislator.

Such a problem is encountered, for instance, when contracts involve

[24] Watkins LJ, ibid. at 175.

the commission of a crime. A contract to commit a crime is clearly contrary to public policy.[25] A more difficult problem is posed by contracts which actually, but not necessarily, involve the commission of a crime. Does the maxim that no one may profit from his own wrong still apply? English law suggests that where the statute's purpose was to outlaw such contracts, then the contract is unlawful, but where the criminality is merely incidental, then it will not normally be presumed that the legislator intended to make the contract unlawful.[26] French law will take a similar view. A contract whose purpose involves the commission of a crime has a clearly illicit *cause*. Where, on the other hand, there is a mere breach of a legal obligation in the making or performance of the contract, then the penalty may only be criminal.[27] The difficulty lies in deciding whether a criminal penalty alone suffices. For example, if an insurance policy covers the insured for the damages he has to pay as a result of a criminal act in driving is this unlawful as against public policy? Both English and French law have held that it is not. On the other hand, a person who killed another with a gun was not able to rely on his liability insurance polciy to indemnify him for the damages he had to pay to the widow of his victim.[28] The distinction is the result of a judgment of social policy. The judge has to balance the need to compensate the victim, the need to penalize the wrongdoer, and the seriousness of the antisocial act. As Diplock LJ suggested in *Hardy* v. *MIB*,[29] 'the Court has to weigh the gravity of the anti-social act and the extent to which it will be encouraged by enforcing the right sought to be asserted against the social harm which will be caused if the right is not enforced'.

French law is, however, more willing to extend a statute by analogy. For example, the setting of maximum prices by statute has been taken to make unlawful the refusal to sell even at the maximum price. (Otherwise customers might be effectively forced to pay over the maximum in order to get any of the goods at all.)[30]

The approach of the courts in these cases very much suggests that public policy is used to fill out details of a statutory scheme in relation to the wide objectives both of the statute and of the law in general, even if this involves some departure from the express words of the

[25] See *Everet* v. *Williams* (1725) noted (1893) 9 LQR 197: a partnership action between parties 'skilled in dealing in several sorts of commodities' who turned out to be highwaymen seeking a division of their spoils!

[26] See e.g. *Anderson* v. *Daniel* [1924] 1 KB 138; *St John Shipping Corp.* v. *Joseph Rank Ltd* [1957] 1 QB 267.

[27] Malaurie and Aynès, *Droit civil—les obligations* (Paris, 1985), n° 344.

[28] Compare *James* v. *British General Insurance Co Ltd* [1927] 2 KB 311, and *Gray* v. *Barr* [1971] 2 QB 554. See also *Geismar* v. *Sun Alliance & London Insurance* [1978] QB 383.

[29] [1964] 2 QB 745.

[30] Cass. crim., 20 June 1846, DP 1846.1.44; Cass. crim., 13 July 1847, DP 1847.1.48.

statute. There are some established ideas to which the law gives effect, but the appropriateness of doing so remains a matter of judgment.

VOLUNTARY TRANSACTIONS

Malaurie[31] suggests that public policy functions typically to restrict individual freedom in the general interest. Just as prima facie statutory rights to benefits or to information can be denied where their exercise would be clearly contrary to the common good, so the same is true for general liberty rights, such as to own property, or to make contracts or gifts. This is made clear in Article 6 of the French Civil Code: 'Private transactions may not derogate from laws concerning public policy and good morals.' In a western capitalist society, individual freedom of action, initiative, and enterprise are necessary to the improvement of the general welfare through the market economy. Likewise, the free disposal of one's goods is an aspect of a free society. All the same, there are limits to these freedoms which the law grants to individuals. Traditionally, there have been political and moral rules of public policy governing the organization of political institutions and good social morals. More recently, as French authors put it,[32] there has been the growth of economic and social public policy which has sought to protect specific categories (consumers, workers, and so on) from injustices caused by the free operation of market forces. By and large, such developments have been the result of specific legislative interventions which have regulated or outlawed certain practices, and which, in some cases, have imposed contracts on parties whether they wish to contract or not.

Public Policy drawn from Legislative Policy

Although often not directly expressed as a problem of public policy, the issue of private derogation from legal protection is a major concern of the law. For instance, in *Johnson* v. *Moreton*,[33] in which it was held (despite the absence of express wording) that a tenant could not contract out of the right of appeal given by the Agricultural Holdings Act 1948. By contrast, French courts have held that an employee can contract out of some employment rights, such as to money in lieu of a weekly rest-day.[34] The issue is whether the policy of the statute is best given effect by allowing freedom of contract, or by restricting it. This,

31 See Note 9 above at 19.
32 Ibid., 52; J. Ghestin, *Droit civil—Le contrat* (Paris 1980), n° 117.
33 [1980] AC 37.
34 Soc. 18 Mar. 1955, D 1956, 517 note Malaurie; also Poitiers, 18 Dec. 1953, D 1954, 519 note Malaurie (contracting out of statutory maximum prices for electricity).

in turn depends on whether the restriction is best seen as for the protection of an individual or for the public good. In the employee's case, the legal rights were there for the good of employees. By contrast, the Agricultural Holdings Act was held to have been passed for the improvement of the productivity of agricultural land.

Common-law Public Policy

More scope for judicial development of the law occurs in the area of the general principles of the common law (whether based on judicial precedent or on the general provisions of the Civil Code) in which traditional principles of public policy operate. Within the principles of freedom in transactions, the intervention on grounds of public policy which invalidate otherwise effective transactions poses problems. The resolution of the difficulty lies in identifying the values which operate in this area, and the extent to which they are predictable.

In broad terms, the effect of public-policy restrictions in traditional areas is to outweigh the reasons for enforcing contracts or provisions. They introduce incapacities. The incapacity may relate to a person—for instance, in English law a barrister may not contract for his services in court, nor a local authority for the performance of its statutory powers. In other cases, as in the surrogacy cases or parental rights, it will be argued that certain subject-matter is outside the realm of voluntary transactions. More problematic are the cases where a person has capacity to purchase a subject-matter which the law permits, yet the transaction as a whole is part of a scheme which the law refuses to countenance. For instance, an adult may purchase champagne, yet the law will not enforce a transaction of this kind which forms part of the arrangements for entertainment in a brothel.[35] Here the purpose of the transaction has to be identified in order to ascertain whether it constitutes an abuse of the law. Only proximate and direct purposes are taken into account. All the same, this is one of the few situations in which the law investigates the purposes of a transaction in order to determine its validity. The law is concerned to prevent itself being abused by the fraudulent or improper purposes of individuals.

SPECIFIC AREAS OF TRADITIONAL PUBLIC POLICY

Common-law public policy is concerned with the extent to which parties can alter the background values, either from statute or common law, which would normally apply to their arrangments. If the performance of a voluntary transaction (contract or gift) would harm

[35] *Taylor* v. *Chester* (1869) LR 4 QB 309; Trib. com. Seine, 1 May 1888, GP 1888.1.797.

certain established interests, then it will be held contrary to public policy. Given that certain categories of public policy have been recognized for a long time, it is possible to draw up a list of these interests, while recognizing that it is by no means exhaustive. All the same, it offers the possibility of a 'negative check-list' against which agreements can be verified rapidly. This can be illustrated by a few traditional examples drawn from both England and France which illustrate the fundamental similarity of the values protected in the two legal systems.[36]

Harming Governmental Institutions

Although many harms to governmental institutions are specific crimes, such as treason, others are not. Public policy offers a ground for outlawing conduct which improperly seeks to affect the operation of the political and governmental processes. Thus, 'treating' electors by offering free drinks, or offering money with a view to obtaining public honours such as a knighthood have been held to be contrary to public policy.[37] Likewise, payments for a person to exercise influence with the administration are struck down for similar reasons.[38] Although statute did not specifically proscribe such conduct, it was, by common assessment, improper conduct. The line between undesirable and unlawful conduct is, however, difficult to draw, and this illustrates the importance of judicial choice in this area.

Protecting Recourse to Judicial Institutions

Judicial institutions are regarded as the guardians of rights, a principle now enshrined in Article 66 of the 1958 French Constitution. The denial of recourse to the courts to enforce rights is generally frowned on, unless it involves simply giving priority to an alternative method of dispute resolution, such as arbitration. People cannot be completely deprived of their rights of access to the courts. Equally, agreements to stifle a prosecution or otherwise to prevent a proper use of the legal process have been held illegal.

Protecting the Institution of the Family

The French surrogacy cases are but recent illustrations of the desire of the law to protect the institution of the family and the traditional

[36] See generally P. S. Atiyah, n. 14 above, chs. 17 and 18; Malaurie and Aynès, n. 27 above, n°s 237 ff.

[37] Respectively, Trib. civ. de Tarbes, 14 Mar. 1899, S. 1900.2.219; *Parkinson* v. *College of Ambulance* [1925] 2 KB 1 and *Egerton* v. *Brownlow* (1853) 4 HLC 1.

[38] Req. 5 Feb. 1902, DP 1902.1.158.

values associated with it. As in France, contracts to transfer parental rights and duties have been held contrary to public policy in England.[39]

A specific problem occurs in relation to gifts or contracts which restrict freedom to marry. In principle, the freedom to marry is a fundamental right which cannot be lost by a voluntary transaction (other than marriage itself). There may, however, be good reasons why advantages should be attached to the voluntary restriction of this freedom. A gift made on condition of future celibacy may be valid if made with the intention of benefitting the donee, or for some other good motive, but not simply to gratify the wishes of the donor, and the same goes for contracts.[40] Although significant changes in values have occurred with the advent of divorce and *unions libres*, the preservation of certain features of family life, especially parental obligations, remains an important aspect of public policy.

Protecting Economic Institutions

The function of the law in protecting competition, thereby protecting the fundamental free market out of which freedom of contract springs, has been a traditional function of the law. Although these days this is largely superseded by EC and national legislation, there remain residual rules which may serve as a safety-net to catch unacceptable agreements which do not infringe more specific legislation. Contracts in restraint of trade have long been penalized by English law, either because they are unfair in the interests of parties or in the interests of the public generally. The liberty rights of individuals play a significant role here, and the doctrine is frequently used to outlaw post-employment terms which unduly restrict the future freedom of an employee to seek work.[41] But the public interest in having a sufficiently competitive market is also protected by this doctrine, even if the agreement is in the interests of the parties.[42] A more controversial area has been the protection of the currency. In the past, judges were opposed to gold clauses or other ways of index-linking contractual obligations on the ground that this was a factor

[39] *Humphreys* v. *Polak* [1901] 2 KB 385.

[40] See P. Malaurie and L. Aynès, *Droit civil—libéralités, les successions* (Paris 1989), n° 369; Paris, 30 Apr. 1963, D 1963, 428, note Rouast (nullity of a clause in a contract of employment imposing celibacy on air hostesses), cf. Cass. Ass. plén. 19 May 1978, JCP 1978 II 19009 (a Catholic school could dismiss a teacher who remarried after divorce).

[41] See e.g. *Empire Meat Ltd* v. *Patrick* [1939] 2 All ER 85; Soc. 21 Apr. 1971, JCP 1971.IV.138. For an argument that much of the law is based on fairness, see Atiyah, n. 14 above, ch. 16.

[42] *Lyne-Pirkis* v. *Jones* [1969] 1 WLR 1293; *Esso Petroleum Ltd* v. *Harper's Garage (Stourport) Ltd* [1968] AC 269.

contributing to monetary instability, though this economic theory has been rejected in more recent years.[43]

Protecting Constitutional Values

Certain values are established, even though they may not be associated directly with any specific social institution. An agreement with a creditor which unduly restricts personal liberty (sale of property, changing employment, and so on) will be treated as contrary to public policy, though a less restrictive agreement made in the interests of the person restricted may be enforceable.[44]

More problematic are values of equality. All contracts and gifts involve freedom of choice, and thus the preference of one person against another. At the same time, the law does not wish to enforce certain discriminations. Statute has now outlawed discrimination on grounds of race or sex, though the common law did find some such discriminations contrary to public policy. Discrimination on grounds of religion remains controversial. English law will uphold such discrimination, whereas French law is more willing to strike it down.[45]

Good Morals and Contracts

No account of public policy would be complete without reference to contracts invalidated as being contrary to good morals. Take, for example, the story of the 'Lady Birds', four Danish striptease artistes. Their agent made contracts for a tour of Italy and France during which the dancers would give a number of performances. The impresarios cancelled the tour and the agent sued them for breach of contract. The French court[46] raised the issue of illegality of its own motion 'by reason of its mission of social health' given by Article 6 of the Civil Code. Since it would be scandalous to have specific performance of such contracts if a woman refused to perform because she had 'returned to her natural sense of propriety', the contract must be void as contrary to public policy.

[43] *Treseder-Griffin* v. *Co-operative Insurance Society Ltd* [1956] 2 QB 127; Ghestin, n. 32 above, n° 130. But see now P. Malaurie and L. Aynès, n. 27 above, n°s 624–7; *Multiservice Bookbinding Ltd* v. *Marden* [1979] Ch 84.

[44] Compare *Horwood* v. *Millar's Timber* [1917] 1 KB 305 (restrictions quashed when imposed by a creditor) with *Re Denny* [1919] 1 KB 583 (restrictions upheld on friendships and the use of alcohol imposed on a profligate son in an effort to reform him).

[45] *Blathwayt* v. *Cawley* [1976] AC 397 (discrimination against Catholics); *Re Tuck's S.T.* [1978] Ch 49 (discrimination against Jews); cf Trib. civ. Seine, 22 Jan. 1947, D 1947, 126 (nullifying a clause revoking a gift if the donee married a Jew).

[46] TGI Paris, 8 Nov. 1973, D 1975, 401 note Puech. See also Paris 21 Jan. 1972, GP 1972.1.375 (illegality of a contract by an individual to reveal details of their sex-life).

Law reports are replete with cases concerning entertainment or work in brothels, or the sales of such institutions. Anything connected with the provision of prostitution is considered to be living off immoral earnings and is thus void. Only services which do not partake of the immoral character of the activity, for example, window-cleaning, are not illicit.

A similar established area is contracts or gifts for the pursuit of an extra-marital relationship.[47] Changes in social values have meant that the courts are prepared to uphold gifts made between extra-marital partners both during and at the end of a relationship, provided that they are not given directly in return for sexual favours.[48]

Preventing Fraud

Much wrongdoing in trading or dealings between individuals is specifically prohibited by statute. All the same, public policy is used as a ground for outlawing other fraudulent practices. For example, where a doctor agreed to prescribe certain patent remedies which had been developed by persons with no medical qualifications and for which exaggerated claims were made, the French court[49] had no difficulty in striking down the contract as contrary to public policy, even in the absence of statute. The difficulty here lies not so much in the idea that fraud should be sanctioned, but in deciding what is fraud. After all, if the remedies in the case of the doctor had been homoeopathic, would the same result have bee reached?

Summary

Although the above list is not exhaustive and by no means clear-cut in its content, it does demonstrate the way in which many issues of public policy are, as Malaurie suggests, concerned with the protection of fundamental social institutions. Whether particular agreements or clauses will have such an effect is to be resolved as a matter of judgement on fact and policy in particular cases. Though there is a broadly settled framework of public-policy issues, its content, as Atiyah suggests, is subject to significant change over time.

[47] See e.g. contracts for someone to become a mistress: *Frances* v. *Bolton* (1797) 3 Ves. 368; Soc. 4 Oct. 1979, D 1980 IR 267.

[48] Malaurie and Aynès, n. 27 above, n°s 340 & 343; Paris 19 Nov. 1974, D 1975, 614 (gift to buy house), *Tanner* v. *Tanner* [1975] 1 WLR 1346 (licence of house to mistress), Cass.civ. 6 Oct. 1959, D 1960, 515 (gift at end of relationship).

[49] Cass. civ. 4 Dec. 1929, DH 1930, 50.

Public Policy as a Legal Standard

The above sketch would seem to provide a plausible account of public policy as a structured concept. It reflects either the purpose of legislation (read in the light of the purposes of the law in general) or the background limits within which freedom of individual transactions is permitted to operate. The existence of established categories might appear to give comfort to the rule-centred analysis.

The difficulty in viewing what has been sketched as rules of whatever degree of generality is that their content is broad in key particulars. Except in relation to very specific provisions, we are not dealing with the kind of hard-and-fast rules which Atiyah and Summers identify as central to much of the English perception of law.[50] In both England and France, we have what amount to statements of values or objectives around which courts reason, rather than precise standards. The objectives of the legal system are too fluid to be captured by specific rules. Indeed, this is an inevitable feature of an aspect of the legal system which serves to relate specific rules and principles to the fundamental functions of the legal order. The formality of legal doctrine and reasoning requires that decisions be fitted into these overall objectives. But what does this involve? The objectives must be generally stated, and previous decisions (whether binding or not) are neither exhaustive of the objective nor do they pre-empt future decisions. Even in the English precedential system, changes in values may undermine previous decisions so that the inherent revisability of public policy introduces a dynamic element into the legal system. The mode of reasoning in specific cases is incremental, in that earlier decisions may serve as analogies for the future, but typically in a tentative and incomplete manner.

Unlike rules or principles which state more general legal values and which justify a number of specific rules of law, goals or objectives found in areas like the law on public policy are more like frameworks into which a variety of arguments can be fitted according to time and place. What might be involved in protecting family or governmental institutions will change over time. The kind of guidance provided for a decision-maker is general and leaves much to her own initiative.

Public policy in this context is not just an ordinary form of 'open-textured' rule or principle, in applying which judges could be characterized acting as the assize of the nation. Their task goes further. Within a framework of objectives, the judges must define the wrongs which the law must penalize. They are creating offences of abuse of rights, if not of public mischief which might appear a contestable

[50] Atiyah and Summers, n. 4 above, 73.

judicial function. Of course, any such decisions, like any public power, are not unconstrained. Broadly defined objectives and existing rules of law must be respected. Nevertheless, public policy includes a broad power to adjust otherwise applicable rules to avoid what are considered undesirable outcomes. The various values serve as objectives for and constraints on the discretion of the judge in defining the content of public policy. The suggestion is, in short, that public policy is best conceived of not as a set of rules to be put into the equation alongside the rules of statutes, codes, or the common law. We are dealing with a judicial power to adjust the law to fit its overall purposes and role.

As regards the purpose of legislation, we are dealing with a set of default ideas which apply when the text does not provide the necessary link with the purposes of the law. The law has certain general objectives such as punishing wrongdoers, preventing crime, and compensating the victims of wrongs, and these are considered as infusing specific legislative actions. The judicial approach is apparently exegetical but involves (at least in Dworkin's analysis)[51] the construction of an account of the text as a normative instrument which most advances the values it is designed to serve. But such a broad remit is parallel with the duties of the government (for example, in Article 21 of the French Constitution) to ensure the implementation of laws. The purposes of legislation and the general objectives of the law are so broadly stated as to require more than judgement in their implementation. Substantive concretization of the higher norm is necessary, a decision which may be controversial. After all, if social-security payments are there to meet needs, is there no argument that Mrs Connor has a clearly definable need as a widow? She may have to suffer a criminal penalty, but does society have to inflict penury on her as an additional punishment?

Any application of a text requires judgement, and to that extent a choice of solutions. What is suggested here is that the use of public-policy arguments in determining the normative scope of a provision is more akin to a form of subordinate legislation—a tidying-up of legal prescriptions. The judge is not acting as an office-boy who faithfully carries out whatever instructions he is given, without responsibility for the outcome. Rather, he or she is the manager who has to co-ordinate and reconcile policy decisions given at different times into a coherent and workable strategy. It is inevitable that such judgements will down-play certain aspects of the job and promote others. The idea of the judge as a mere 'refiner, finisher, and polisher' of legislation[52] is

[51] See Dworkin n. 22 above, ch. 9, esp. 337–8.

[52] Donaldson J, *Corocraft Ltd* v. *Pan-Am* [1968] 3 WLR at 732; Lord Mackay, 'Finishers, Refiners, and Polishers: The Judicial Role in the Interpretation of Statutes' [1989] *Stat. LR* 151.

plausible only where minute adjustments have to be made in precise programme texts. More obviously when public policy is a criterion for the interpretation of statutes, the role of delegated legislator is more appropriate as a description.

When it comes to protecting certain essential features of society against the effects of private arrangements, then it is more abundantly clear that the values involved are very general in content. That is not to say that certain more limited and specific factors cannot be identified. They most certainly can. But the point is that the general underlying values may still be asserted, even if specific rules cannot be found. In other areas of the law we may say, for instance, that dishonesty is bad, but we do not treat all dishonest acts as necessarily unlawful—in general there must be a specific crime or legal rule which outlaws it. But we are prepared to permit ideas like the prevention of fraud to constitute a feature of public policy, without confining it to specific rules.

Sources of Arguments

FORMS OF REASONING

The plausibility of a rule-centred approach to public policy seems helped by the formal character of judicial justifications. As Atiyah and Summers suggest,[53] English courts tend to appeal to rules rather than to the purposes behind them. The French judiciary appears even more formal in the judgements handed down by superior courts, which appeal simply to rules without attempts at further justification. But such formalism in the giving of reasons does not indicate necessarily an absence of substantive justification. More often, it is a matter of coming to clear decisions which can be followed in lower courts. The *conclusions* of the *commissaire du gouvernement* or the report of the reporter judge, although technically merely preparatory documents for the decision, and from which this last may depart in significant particulars, are frequently publicized in order to demonstrate the kinds of substantive justifications which lie behind the formal statement of reasons.

Of course, the formalist structure of decisions may be a convenient way of failing to confront the questionable character of the exercise of discretionary power in the use of public policy. On the other hand, it may reveal an impression that everything is so obvious and uncontrovesial that no justification of a specific kind is necessary. Indeed, cases such as *Connor*[54] and *Smith*[55] base their views of public

[53] See n. 4 above, 75. [54] See n. 2 above. [55] See n. 23 above.

policy on self-evidence, and few would contest the general ideas of public policy on which they are based. By contrast, the recent surrogacy cases are in a more delicate area of public controversy (though not one where divisions are on party-political lines). The sources of arguments used here are of some interest for the analysis of public policy and the judicial role.

SURROGACY CASES

In the French cases, the civil and administrative courts had different bases for decision. The decision *Alma Mater* of the *Cour de cassation* in 1989[56] was directed to the legality in the light of public policy of an association formed to assist surrogacy arrangements. The arguments of the *rapporteur* Massip fall into two parts: there are arguments based on the interpretation of legal texts and there are arguments of a broader kind. The former arguments, specifically picked up in the judgment, have four strands. First, it is argued that contracts concerning the human body are not permitted (a reference to Article 1128 of the Civil Code, which states that objects not in commerce cannot be the subject-matter of contracts). Secondly, civil status is inalienable (Article 311-9 of the Civil Code) and a surrogacy association has the objective of enabling surrogate mothers to transfer the status of a child to the commissioning parents. Thirdly, such arrangements would involve dealing in parental authority, proscribed by Article 376 of the Civil Code. Finally, the association would be acting as an intermediary in adoption by the ordering parents, even though it did not have the necessary legal authorization (Article 100-1, *Code de la famille*). These legal grounds are repeated in the typically terse judgment of the court as justifying the decision.

But in the report of Massip, he considers whether these interpretations of the general legal texts are the right ones from the point of view of common opinion and social policy. In the first place, he considers what has been done in other courts in France, notably the *Conseil d'État*. Secondly, he considers legal academic opinion, which also broadly favours the outlawing of surrogacy. Thirdly, he examines moral and religious opinion in France. Both the Catholic Church and the medical profession had publicly condemned the practice of surrogacy, while the smaller Protestant churches had been more nuanced. In addition, the National Consultative Committee on Ethics in 1984 had also criticized such a practice as improper. This common opinion had given rise to a proposed bill to outlaw the practice which had not yet

[56] Cass. 1re civ., 13 Dec. 1989, *Association Alma Mater* c *Procureur-général d'Aix-en-Provence*, D 1990, 273, rapport Massip.

been passed into legislation. Such a solution broadly coincided with practices in other countries. A final set of arguments concerned the consequences of giving legal sanction to the practice of surrogacy. Conflicts between parents and the surrogate mother would occur, as in the American experience, which would be undesirable. These could only harm the child, who might also suffer psychologically when the identity of the surrogate mother is known. Furthermore, it was considered an undesirable practice because the women 'enrolled' by such an association would often be poor, performing the task out of financial necessity.

In the *Conseil d'État* case on the legality of surrogacy associations, 《Les Cignognes》[57], the applicable law of Alsace-Lorraine was interpreted as permitting the prefect to refuse to register an association only if it had a criminal objective. The main discussion in the conclusions of *commissaire du gouvernement* Stirn concerned whether the acts done or encouraged by the association were criminal. The text in question, Article 353-1 of the Penal Code, penalizes those who, for profit, procure or act as intermediaries in the procurement of parents to abandon future or living children or giving them in adoption. Since freedom of association is a constitutionally recognized principle, the restrictions had to be narrowly interpreted. The legal argument was that surrogate motherhood does involve the surrogate mother agreeing to give the child in adoption to the requesting couple, and she does receive money. On the view adopted, this came within the crimes set out in Article 353–2. All the same, since the law in this area was undeveloped (and this was the first supreme court decision to be made in France), Stirn looked more widely to the policy of the law in this area. He noted that government committees in France as well as abroad had insisted on strengthening medical guarantees and prohibiting profit-making intermediaries. In particular, the 1984 report of the National Committee on Ethics had condemned the whole process of surrogacy. In such a case, there was no argument for a more flexible interpretation of the criminal text which excluded this association. Stirn also proposed additional arguments of public policy which he did not think necessary for the decision in the instant case, and which the *Conseil* did not take up. The arguments were that the human body was not capable of being the object of a contract, even if blood and organs were, since it concerns the use of the body of the surrogate mother and the whole body of the child. Such an approach would fit into currently developing principles of personal privacy and family life in the case law of the *Conseil d'Etat*.

In both cases, public-policy arguments appear to restrict the freedom of association. In the 1990 case of *Baby Elise*, the Court of Appeal of

[57] CE Ass. 22 Jan. 1988, *Association Les Cignognes*, AJDA 1988, 163.

Paris examined the same public-policy arguments in relation to a specific contract of surrogacy and tookd a different view.[58] The child was ordered by a French couple from an American woman. When the child was born, she was given in adoption to the French couple and a court in Kentucky made an adoption order in their favour. The issue in the French courts was whether French public policy prevented recognition being given to the adoption order and to giving the child French nationality. The Paris court rejected any such argument. An agreement that the child would be adopted was not a prohibited contract about a person's status since it was a voluntary transfer, and the arrangement was no more artificial than others recognized in France where a child could obtain a more favourable status after a formal recognition of paternity. It also took the view that the contract did not deal with a subject-matter outside commerce, in that the sale of blood and organs was already permitted, so why not this contract concerning the capacity of a woman to give birth? No social harm for the woman or the child was demonstrated, nor did such an arrangement interfere with the exercise of rights by the rest of society. Even if the promise itself might be unenforceable if the surrogate mother refused to transfer the child, this did not prevent enforcement of the contract once the transfer had been performed. To recognize such a contract would be consistent with the recognition of the right to family life in the European Convention on Human Rights. Though not formally contradicting the earlier cases, it does go very much against their spirit.

In the English case, *Re an Adoption Application (Surrogacy)*,[59] the issue was similar to that in the last French case—did a surrogacy agreement act as a bar to the adoption of the child by the ordering couple? Latey J took the opinion of counsel for the Attorney-General appearing as *amicus curiae* that, apart from the statutory provisions of the Surrogacy Arrangements Act 1985, there was no formulated public policy on surrogacy arrangements. A White Paper was in existence and there were deliberations in parliament which might lead to such policies. But Latey J was of the view that: 'It is there, in my opinion, that questions of morality and ethics should be weighed. There is no requirement in the instant case for the court to weigh them, which it is not equipped to do and should not attempt.' The adoption was ordered in favour of the ordering couple simply considering the interests of the child. The failure of any public-policy argument had an important effect on the attitude of the court to the surrogacy agreement. It enabled it to treat the contract as no amounting to an illegal payment or reward for

[58] Paris, 15 June 1990, *Dalloz* 1990, 540, note Boulanger.
[59] [1987] 2 All ER 826. See also *Re P (Minors) (Wardship: Surrogacy)* [1987] 2 FLR 421.

adoption to section 50 of the Adoption Act 1958 or at least to treat it as 'venial'.[60] In this case, the British Medical Association repudiation of surrogacy did not come until after the court made its decision.

COMMENT

What job is public policy performing in such novel cases? It is certainly a criterion relevant to the decision in a new case, and it operates to defeat the otherwise relevant principles of freedom of contract, freedom of association, and the welfare of the child. It might be argued, as Ian White has suggested,[61] that judgments are overdetermined, and that public policy in such cases in not really performing a significant role. After all, the decisions of the *Conseil d'État*, the Paris Court of Appeal, and the English High Court were all resolved on other grounds. Public policy was either a supporting argument or a rejected counter-argument. Was it that, out of deference to counsel or for some other ancillary motive, the court felt it necessary to consider a peripheral argument? I think not. That it was necessary for the *Conseil d'État* and the English High Court to obtain argument on public policy to be satisfied about the legal rightness of their decisions is evidence enough for its importance in novel cases. The situation is rather as Alexy suggests, that in order to test the applicability of established rules it is necessary to resort to general practical reasoning, even if, at the end of the day, this argues in favour of applying those rules to the new case.[62]

When one looks at the justifications for the decisions, a number of different kinds of argument are deployed. Those based on specific legal texts predominate, in that they provide the structure for the whole debate. The legal rules provide a background which public-policy arguments seek to defeat in their application to the instant case. Legal rules and principles may also provide the basis of more specific arguments to defeat the prima facie rules, such as the freedom of association. Beyond these, there is heavy reliance on 'prevailing opinion' in terms of government committees, the medical profession, and so on. Legislation (whether actual or proposed) also provided for the French judges authoritative indications of social trends. In typical English fashion, Latey J looked for a precise, enacted rule or general principle—in the absence of these, there was no public policy. Reports of official or prestigious committees, such as the Warnock Report, were

[60] Latey J., ibid. at 830–1; S. De Cruz, 'Surrogacy, Adoption & Custody: A Case-Study' [1988] *Family Law* 100.

[61] 'Policy or Reason', paper presented to ESPRIT working-group on 'The Foundations of Legal Reasoning', Cork meeting, June 1990.

[62] R. Alexy, *A Theory of Legal Argumentation* (Oxford 1989), 279 and 284–6.

accorded less weight in England than the National Committee on Ethics in France. Apart from illustrating differences of legal method, it also illustrates a different approach to the judicial function. The highest French courts seem to be seeking a consensus among social institutions on these social and moral questions, while the English seem to want to intrude only in a limited way into a moral area of controversy. To a great extent, these philosophies of the judicial role are implicit in the practice of decision-making, but this is not to say that they are deliberately concealed.

It might be asked whether judges are making new independent decisions here, or merely recording and implementing a prevailing trend among other decision-makers?[63] I think it can be maintained that there is sufficient independence of thought to justify the view that we are dealing with a decision. The decisions in the cases of the children show a greater willingness to evade some of the public-policy issues, and an ability to take decisions appropriate to individual situations. A degree of deference shown by all the courts does not deny the ability to make one's own decisions. By seeking out the views of social authorities, the judges are able to appear not as idiosyncratic, but as responsible decision-makers, whose views can be defended by objective evidence of public benefit or harm determined by other institutions or, failing that, by legal tradition.[64] While some, like Devlin, may argue that seeking public policy from the doctrines of morality and religion might deny the creative function of judges, it is perhaps significant that he includes in his sources for judicial development of the common law 'the rules of public policy which [the judges] believed all reasonable men would hold'.[65] The French too seem to be taking refuge in the same idea, in that they demonstrate the reasonableness of the decision from common (informed and authoritative) opinion. But the argument appears more as a comfort than as a source for the decision reached, because it follows, rather than precedes, the principal basis for the decision and is accorded limited authoritative status.

Conclusion: An Institutionalized Rule of Law

Public policy offers an illustration of the way legal systems, even formalist ones like the English and French, operate by conferring on

[63] C. Alchurron and L. Bulygin, 'Limits of Logic and Legal Reasoning', paper presented to ESPRIT working-group on 'The Foundations of Legal Reasoning', Cork meeting, June 1990.
[64] See Bell, n. 20 above, 175–6.
[65] *Samples of Lawmaking* (London, 1962), 116.

those who have to implement the legal system the task of integrating specific rules with broad statements of social objectives. However much the idea of hard-and-fast rules may dominate lagal thinking, this more wide-ranging set of values cannot be ignored, and this says much about our ideas of legality and the rule of law.

Legal certainty is an important value in the rule of law. It enables people to predict with a fair degree of accuracy the way in which the law will impinge on the activities which they wish to undertake. As a formal value, it requires merely that the law be specific, coherent, set out in advance, with sufficient clarity to guide individuals before disputes arise which may have to be resolved in court. This value is met by a (theoretically) programmable set of rules and exceptions, and moves in the direction of routinized, bureaucratic administration. But there are other values which the law must also further. Most notable among these are fairness, the reflection of public values, and social control.

In order that these other values can be a common basis in a heterogeneous society, it may be that they have to be institutionalized through law. Within the institutional framework of law, otherwise pertinent questions can be ignored or down-played. Public policy becomes reduced to a set of rather conservative values which are taken to be agreed in society, whether this is in fact true or not. This is an important lesson to draw from those who have stressed this institutional character of law, and the formalism of legal reasons which is linked to it.[66] The institutional character of law in itself provides a form of stability and certainty. This already furthers ideas inherent in the rule of law, in that power is to operate within this institutional framework and is legitimated by it. Precise rules and other standards have an important role within such an institutional setting. But public policy illustrates ways in which the purposes of the institution of law may feature more directly in the way decisions are taken according to law. It acts as a kind of 'safety valve' concept in the implementation of more precise legal standards. It may be used in a rather tentative and pragmatic way, but this is not a failure of approach, merely a reflection of the rather diverse circumstances in which it may be appropriate to use it. None the less, the rule of law is served in that the judge is required to make specific legal decisions fit coherently with the underlying purposes of the legal system. It may be that the various values expressed in doctines of public policy are more ideal than actual in the current state of the law, as are ideas of integrity and coherence. But such an ideal aspect to law is important as a regulative device

[66] See esp. D. MacCormick and O. Weinberger, *An Institutional Theory of Law* (Dordrecht 1986).

within the institution of law. It encourages decision-makers to make the law more fully fit the ideal. In this way, public policy as an ideal notion fits into the idea of public policy as a framework for decision-making.

Such an ideal of the rule of law depends on those who implement the system. It gives power, for which an account must be given. If English and French judges exercise such power with circumspection, this may not be because they wish to hide what they are doing, but because traditional ideals of the judicial function do not give them adequate legitimacy for what they perceive it necessary to do. In such a context, a better account of the rule of law as it operates in the institutional framework of law is necessary.

The judicial function reflects the complexity of what is required from law as a social institution. Judges are focal decision-makers in the western legal tradition, whether in the common law or in the civil law. Although the bureaucratic, rule-based model is more officially enshrined in the civil law, there is much left for decision by judges in practice, and public policy provides an important juncture at which the roles of judges and legislators interact. In protecting social institutions, judges are concerned to ensure that rights and freedoms do not harm society as a whole. Judges and other officials need freedom to exercise control in order to preserve the system as a whole. To that extent, interventions cannot be totally predictable, and the courts need to be able to look beyond the form of statutory texts or voluntary transactions to substantive values and purposes. Such tasks are not contrary to the rule of law, but are required by a proper understanding of it.

6

Aftermath

PAUL D. CARRINGTON[1]

The attainments of so distinguished a scholar and legal theorist as Patrick Atiyah are not only his by reason of his own talents and efforts, but are also attainments of the legal tradition in which he writes and of the culture of which that tradition is part. This is, of course, no less true for the attainments of American legal and political theorists: theory is everywhere more outcome than cause of political and social institutions. Few readers are likely to dispute this assertion. Yet the point is at moments overlooked.

Such a momentary oversight occurs in the elegant comparative work published in 1987 by Professor Atiyah with his American colleague, Robert Summers.[2] To an important degree, the very point of their work is the one stated in the preceding paragraph, yet they forget it just long enough to suppose that Americans who write about legal theory have a substantial influence on the shape of American law and legal institutions, and thus a significant influence on American culture itself.[3]

I write to dispute this supposition: what a people think about their law is usually and largely a product of time, place, or circumstance, a manifestation but seldom a cause of their governance, and is all but impervious to theoretical deliberation. I do not challenge the distinguished authors merely to be quarrelsome or in any way to diminish their well-deserved status, but because their momentary lapse seems to reflect a widely shared forgetfulness, a state of mind observed in America perhaps with increasing frequency, reflected in a current preoccupation or even obsession of American law teachers with the romance of abstraction, to the possible neglect of the more modest but

[1] The author is grateful for comments on earlier drafts by Francis Allen, David Barnhizer, George Christie, John Frank, Walter Gellhorn, Martin Golding, Erwin Griswold, Stanley Hauerwas, Wythe Holt, Kenneth Karst, Richard Maxwell, Jeffrey O'Connell, Jefferson Powell, Thomas Rowe, Theodore St Antoine, and Harold Shapiro, and for the support of the John Simon Guggenheim Foundation and the E. T. Bost Trust of Duke University, that have supported the work of which this essay is a part. None of these persons or entities bear responsibility for the contents.

[2] *Form and Substance in Anglo-American Law* (Oxford, 1987), henceforth cited as *Form and Substance*.

[3] Ibid. 407.

significant role that most are called to play in the distinctive American culture.

Law and Culture

In *The Spirit of Laws*, Baron Montesquieu argued, against existing belief, for cultural relativism. He insisted that positive law is good or bad only in relation to the culture of which it is both product and part.[4] Although the baron somewhat inconsistently indulged himself in preferring some cultures to others (he did not care for despotism), he was prepared to approve legal institutions in one social and political context (even a little slavery) that he would disapprove in another.

The baron's relativism no longer startles readers;[5] some now embrace it as a means to deny claims to abstract justice,[6] others as a step in the resistance to injustice that is said to surround us.[7] On the other hand, as our world shrinks and its diverse cultures are brought closer together, his insight seems less valid to many. As we reject the baron's (albeit limited) tolerance of slavery, we are drawn to the legal philosophers' pursuit of the single truth, the one great theoretical design for positive law (might we call it Justice?) that will best advance our increasingly unified human condition.[8]

The pursuit of the single truth in law implies, however, the existence or at least the desirability of a hierarchy empowered to bring the social and political universe into conformity with the truth when found. It conflicts with the democratic principle of self-government that seems increasingly to be a characteristic of the common world culture, and itself a premier human right, one especially valued in America. Cultural relativism is the necessary basis for mutual respect in a pluralist world respecting rights of self-governance. Lengthening the lists of human rights or principles of natural law is a form of non-violent imperialism, depriving as it does the choice of social arrangements open to a self-governing state or community.

At least until the one great, comprehensive, universal, political truth is revealed and accepted, every legal system is an expression of the culture that called it into being. Each is a system among a network of

[4] Bk. I, Ch. 3, S. 12 (1748), T. Nugent trans. (London, 1750).

[5] For a contemporary treatment of the complexities of cultural relativism, see A. MacIntyre, *Whose Justice? Which Rationality*? (1988).

[6] Cf., R. Rorty, *Contingency, Irony and Solidarity* (Cambridge, 1989).

[7] Cf. B. Smith, *Contingencies of Values* (Cambridge, Mass., 1988); J. W. Singer, 'Should Lawyers Care About Philosophy?' [1989] *Duke L. J.* 1752.

[8] An illustrative yielding to this temptation is the Universal Declaration of Human Rights of 1948, a proclamation that the whole world should resemble as nearly as possible suburban middle-class America.

interdependent systems functioning together to form that culture. The interdependence of systems creates resistance to change and increases the risks that planned change will bring unplanned consequences. While social change may come rapidly in moments of crisis, when all or most systems are in flux, it is seldom the product of choices except those narrowly confined by circumstance. Law is one means by which cultures respond to stimuli, adapt, and even exercise choice when presented, but law is rarely a primary cause of significant change even in the institutions of the law itself, for these are generally reactive to impulses generated elsewhere in the culture or coming from an external source. Law is more aptly viewed as an aftermath than a precursor of its culture, not unlike an exhaust-system to its engine, serving an essential role in keeping the whole going, but not its central, driving feature.

Atiyah and Summers made this point freshly and well. English and American law are very different, despite superficial similarities derived from common language reinforced by the nominal reception in America of English common law.[9] The differences are rooted in the contrasting cultures of which they are parts. Courts, judges, legislators, and lawyers function quite differently in relation to one another within the two polities; and this is so because law performs quite different roles in the quite different governances of two quite different cultures.

In large measure, these cultural differences in legal institutions are determined by causes other than the law itself. Thus, positive law is far more important in America than in England. Among the causes for this enlarged role may be the absence of an aristocracy, the hetereogeniety of the population, the unsettling presence in the formative years of the frontier and its interminable land disputes, the continental scale of the national enterprise, and a handful of deliberate choices made in the decade following the conclusion of the Revolution. Few decisions made since 1800 have had a major effect on the deep differences between American and English polities that were established in the late eighteenth century.

American Law and Culture: The Position of American Legal Education

One culturally determined difference between English and American legal traditions emphasized by Atiyah and Summers is the contrast in

[9] For a more recent empirical study of the contrasts, see R. Abel, *American Lawyers* (New York, 1989) and *The Legal profession in England and Wales* (London, 1988).

educational traditions.[10] The authors contend that élite American law schools are 'the most important' legal institutions competing to influence the American legal tradition, in contrast with English 'law schools' that are described as 'least important'.[11] This assessment is based primarily on the observation that the literature produced by the American legal academy is often cited by persons in authority and is said by the authors to be the major source of ideas about appropriate legal method.[12]

The authors' assessment is congenial to members of American university law schools, especially those having élitist pretensions, but it is, sadly, incorrect. American legal education is an expression of the legal tradition of which it is a part in much the way that that legal tradition is an expression of its culture. Legal education is an aftermath of an aftermath, consequential but largely derivative.

I do not question the authors' comparision. In contrast to the English legal academy, the American legal academy can fairly pretend to greater status and greater influence on its legal institutions.[13] To an outsider, the traditional attitude of English courts toward English academic literature has been offensively condescending,[14] an attitude possibly reciprocated in some respects by a monastic self-isolation of the academy.[15] The influence of the American law schools is surely greater than that of the English, but is ineffable, and scarcely grand. It is surely not 'the most important influence' on American law.

American law schools may influence the legal system of which they are a part in at least three ways.[16] First, they train the professionals who staff the system, and hence have the opportunity to influence, among other things, the standards of professional conduct that their

[10] *Form and Substance*, 384 ff.

[11] Ibid. 407.

[12] For a similar assessment, see W. Chase, *The American Law School and the Rise of Administrative Government* (Madison, 1982).

[13] But not to be compared to the great influence of academicians on the development of the civil law in Italy after 1200 or in Germany after 1500. At those times and places, law professors became themselves central features of their legal systems, dominating the weak judiciaries. Indeed, these men were often so deeply involved in adjudication that education was a secondary activity. For descriptions, see J. Dawson, *The Oracles of the Law* (Ann Arbor, 1967) (hereafter cited as *The Oracles of the Law*), 126 ff (Italy after 1200) and 199 ff (Germany after 1500).

[14] *The Oracles of the Law*, 96–7.

[15] Dawson describes such a circumstance of mutual disdain in nineteenth-century France, *The Oracles of the Law*, 390. If such a withdrawal to the monastery occurred, it may be correcting itself with the rising academic interest in empirical study of law: *Form and Substance*, 399.

[16] There are others. As gatekeepers to the profession, American universities exercise some influence on the size and demography of the legal profession, and perhaps on the quality of legal services. For reflections on the tension between the schools' responsibilities for the cost of entry into the profession and for the quality of services, see P. D. Carrington, 'The University Law School and Legal Services' (1978) 53 NYULR 402. This paper does not address these possibilities for institutional influence because they

students bring to their public responsibilities. Some may doubt the prospects for such moral education. There is indeed good reason to doubt the effect of moral education on the private or interpersonal morals of adult students. But even mature adults tend to share the standards of professional conduct of those who initiate them into their professional roles.[17] Insofar as American law schools are to some degree the professional preceptors of their students,[18] they enjoy an opportunity for influence that English universities appear to lack. This opportunity may carry with it some unwelcome obligations.

Secondly, American law schools provide a pulpit for individual law teachers, who are afforded, almost luxuriously, the time and job-security to enable them to serve legal institutions as ministers without portfolio, bearing obligations only to the common interest as best they can know it. To the extent that individual law professors exploit this special opportunity, their schools may be said to influence the law.

Thirdly, there is the possible influence of legal scholarship. American legal scholarship has effects, but these may be easily exaggerated, in much the way that a bugler might suppose that he effected a cavalry charge with the force of his breath. Academic literature is often an aftermath of an aftermath of an aftermath. Superficially influential literature generally expresses currents that operate quite independently of academic expressions. Yet I affirm that even reactive academic writing can marginally affect law much as editorial writers and political cartoonists affect politics.

All these opportunities for influence are themselves the product of the cultural forces that shaped American legal institutions, including the law schools. They sometimes compete for the resources and commitment of the schools.[19] Before considering each of these methods more fully, I propose to put them in historical and cultural perspectives, explaining the deep differences between university law teaching in America and in England.

American Legal Institutions, Products of Revolution

American higher education in law was established as a direct consequence of the American Revolution, its form and content

have only indirect bearing on how lawyers and judges think about the law and their work, and adequate treatment would greatly overextend the space allowed here. For an illuminating and somewhat different taxonomy of the law teachers' means of influence, see D. R. Barnhizer, 'Prophets, Priests, and Power Blockers: Three Fundamental Roles of Judges and Legal Scholars in America' (1988), 50 U. *Pitt. LR* 127.

[17] E. Durkheim, *Professional Ethics and Civic Responsibility* (London, 1957).

[18] Cf. R. C. Cramton, 'The Ordinary Religion of the Law School Classroom' (1978) 29 *J. Leg. Ed.* 247.

[19] Therein lie the difficulties ruefully enumerated in Carrington, *'Why Deans Quit'* [1987] *Duke LJ* 342.

entwined in the post-Revolutionary culture that created the nation's institutions and decreed their operative method and theory. The educational aim was to provide fit leaders for the nation's new legal institutions.[20]

The founding instruments of the American legal tradition, the Declaration of Independence and the Constitution, were written in English and executed by men most of whom bore English names. Many has trained as apprentices in English law as it was administered in Colonial America. A few had trained as lawyers in England. A very few had attended English universities. But they were united by their commitment to make a body of public law quite different from what they knew of England's. They had read William Blackstone but reviled his royalism;[21] they knew the English aristocracy and did not aspire to replicate it.[22] Their intention to depart from the English legal tradition was of course cemented by the blood-sacrifice of their neighbours and, in some cases, even their brothers or sons.[23]

The American Revolution was, if nothing else, a rejection of a premiss of monarchical government that may survive in modern English government re-centered on an omnipotent legislature. Atiyah and Summers report that the English people 'still think of law as something imposed from above, rather like a command. Although

[20] P. D. Carrington, 'The Revolutionary Idea of University Legal Education' (1990) 31 *W. and M. L. Rev.* 527. See also C. R. McManis, 'The History of First Century American Legal Education: A Revisionist Perspective' (1981) 59 *Wash. ULQ* 597.

[21] 'Blackstone by his famous treatise confirmed the ruling classes of England in their overweening conceit of power and flattered them by expressing entire content with the law and constitution of England, as they then existed', C. Andrews, *The Colonial Background of the American Revolution* (New Haven, 1924), 208. Most offensive was his definition of law as a prescription of the 'supreme power in a state', a power said by American politicians not to exist: 1 *Commentaries*, 44. For the reaction of Revolutionaries, see J. Waterman, '*Thomas Jefferson and Blackstone's Commentaries*' (1930) 27 Ill. LR 629. See also *Works of James Wilson*, ed. McCloskey., (Cambridge, 1979) i. 66 and ii. 21. On the other hand, Americans of the time may well have believed that the idea of separation of powers that was the centre-piece of their Constitution had English origins; if so, it is likely that they were misled by Montesquieu who mistakenly attributed the idea to the English Constitution: *The Spirit of Laws*, Bk. XI. That Montesquieu misunderstood the eighteenth-century English Constitution was abundantly demonstrated in W. Bagehot, *The English Constitution* (London, 1867).

[22] An American assessment of English aristocracy in the time of George III was made by Abigail Adams: '[R]etiring to our own little farm feeding my poultry and improving my garden has more charms for my fancy than residing at the Court of Saint James's where I seldom meet with characters so inoffensive as my hens and chickings, or minds so well improved as my garden. Heaven forgive me if I think too hardly of them. I wish they had deserved better at my hands'. Letter to Thomas Jefferson, 26 Feb. 1778, *Papers of Thomas Jefferson* ed. J. Boyd (vol. 12, Princeton, 1955), 624, 625.

[23] While the war was fought on a modest scale by the standards of a later time, and engaged the military services of few Englishmen, the cost to the American states was substantial. There were 170,000 males aged 15–24 counted in the 1775 census of the colonies; 33,700 were killed or wounded in the war. Only the Civil War, among American wars, entailed a greater loss in comparison to the population.

political power may be as diffused in Britain as it is in other democracies, it seems to us that, in the English vision of law, neither law itself nor political sovereignty is conceived of as something that comes from the people'.[24] That was, of course, the central complaint voiced in the Declaration of Independence,[25] a voice whose echo can still be heard in many lands.

The Constitution, however, represented a retreat from at least some of the assertions of the Declaration. It reflects mistrust of popular decision-making. The founders were apprehensive about the moral capacity of the American people to exercise sovereignty.[26] They feared that greed fed by demagoguery would soon lead to despotism. Some even contemplated a monarchy for Washington. But, in the end, the Constitution did not so mistrust the people that it abandoned the idea of popular sovereignty; rather the Constitution sought to constrain the popular will, to divide and weaken it, thereby reducing its dangers. It remains a cardinal tenet of the American tradition that law is *not* something imposed or received from above, but comes at least indirectly from the people who are asked to obey it.[27]

Accordingly, the Constitution rejected most features of the English Constitution of 1688 so extolled by Blackstone.[28] Federalism, the limitation of the national legislative power to enumerated purposes, was such a rejection. The separation of the executive power from legislative control to compel compromise between these branches was another such rejection. The division of the legislative power to compel frequent compromise between the houses resembled but did not follow English practice. The system of concurrent judicial responsibilities and jurisdictions requiring co-operation between levels of sovereignty and between judicial powers was another departure.

Most important for present purposes was the role created for the

[24] *Form and Substance*, 226. Lord Mansfield had put the matter: 'The supremacy of the British legislature must be compleat, entire, and unconditional.' Accordingly, he urged that America must either submit to the absolute power of Parliament or become independent. For more of this and other like comments, see J. Miller, *Origins of the American Revolution* (Boston, 1943), 201–20.

[25] For a lively and comprehensive treatment of the legal premises of the Revolution, see J. Reid, *Constitutional History of the American Revolution: The Authority of Rights* (Madison, 1986).

[26] Perhaps most ardent in his concern was John Adams. See *A Defense of the Constitutions of the Government of the United States* (1788, ed. De Capo, New York, 1971), vol. 2, 504–5.

[27] The declining rate of participation of Americans in elective politics, and the reduction of campaigning to competition between television commercials and sound-bites may, however, suggest a weakening of this conviction.

[28] It may be that the Declaration of Independence was intended to claim for colonists the rights of Englishman as described by Blackstone. G. Wickersham, 'Presentation Address of Blackstone Memorial' (1924) 10 ABAJ 576; but see Waterman, n. 21 above at 651.

federal judiciary in enforcing this complex scheme of divided responsibilities and authority, a role alien to the English judiciary[29] or perhaps to any other then known.[30] This role necessarily followed from the several divisions of power, for these could not be maintained without an enforcement mechanism. The revolutionaries thus subjected American politics to law, thereby conferring novel political responsibilities on American legal institutions.

Moreover, in separating powers and dividing the legislature into houses substantially equal in power, the founders impeded efforts of American lawmakers to achieve coherence in their enactments. As Atiyah and Summers observe, no American legislative system is structurally capable of acting regularly with the singleness of purpose and coherence often achieved by an omnipotent parliament led by its own executive.[31] This cumbersomeness of formal American lawmaking was deliberately designed in 1787 to forestall implementation of policy gaining momentary acceptance in the corridors of power. In so assuring the impotence of American legislation, the revolutionaries created a vacuum often embodied in indeterminate texts of legislation that would inevitably be occupied by the other two branches of government. Thus, in this respect as well, the founders quite consciously ensured that American judges should make decisions often laden with social and political consequence.

In subjecting politics to law, the founders necessarily subjected law to politics. Who amongst the American people were fit to hold a political-judicial office? Not those with social status. Only in Virginia and South Carolina was there even a semblance of a social élite who could have lent to American judicial institutions status of the kind long enjoyed by the English judiciary. It was inevitable that the selection of the federal judiciary would quickly become and remain a political battleground.

The appointment of John Marshall to the Supreme Court was a politically contentious act of the outgoing President Adams. Unsurprisingly, the successor president was inclined to remove Marshall and

[29] *Form and Substance*, 228. Americans were of course familiar with the 'vague flourishes' of Blackstone on the matter of judicial review. See I *Commentaries*, 91. More significance was attached to Coke's dictum in *Bonham's Case*, Co. Rep. 118a (1610), and to his romantic enlargement of the significance of Magna Carta. See P. Kurland, 'Magna Carta and Constitionalism in the United States: "The Noble Lie"', in *The Great Charter: Four Essays on Magna Carta and the History of our Liberty*, ed. S. Thorne, (New York, 1965), 50. For a recent review of the literature, see J. Sosin, *The Aristocracy of the Long Robe* (Westport, 1989), 7 ff.

[30] A possible exception is the highly political Parlement of Paris as it operated in the decades preceding the French Revolution. See *The Oracles of the Law*, 358 ff.

[31] *Form and Substance*, 400. The authors also suggest that American legislators and administrators may be relatively less competent than their English counterparts.

some of his colleagues by impeachment.[32] Marshall's troubles with President Jefferson were but the beginning of a major feature of America law, political disputation over the personnel of the judiciary, that was flourishing as recently as the Bork confirmation hearings in the fall of 1987. To secure federal judicial appointment, a lawyer must generally be a person of some political attainment. Only irregularly would a judge be selected primarily on account either of social status or exceptional technical competence. This is even more true of the judiciaries of many states, partly as a result of the efforts of nineteenth-century Jacksonians and Populists to secure direct popular election of judges.

The nature of American courts so established dictated a legal method and theory elevating substance over form. If such courts were to win and maintain public trust and acceptance for decisions having grave political consequence, they had to persuade the people to be governed that they were deciding for reasons that commanded respect, if not agreement. Indeed, to be persuasive in justifying the exercise of the judicial power on the scale conceived by Madison and the other architects of American government, it would be necessary to explain decisions so that they could be understood, to rest them as far as possible on the first principles or premisses of the political scheme, and not on arbitrary selections among possible interpretations of the available legal texts. Formalism that separates the legitimate exercise of power from the expression of the social and political values bearing on the decision could not serve the need of American courts to justify themselves, however comfortable such formalism might have been to those familiar with English legal traditions. Moreover, political influence being a necessary credential for the judicial appointment, it would be surprising if American judges were inclined, even if they were able, to justify their decisions in formalist, avowedly apolitical terms. It would even seem to require a reversal of character for elected judges in American state courts to make a full embrace of the politically sterile style embraced so heartily by their English brethren. Thus, by the design of the politicized judicial office, the founders of American courts rendered it unlikely that the formalism becoming the fashion in England[33] would be the customary style of America case law. They made it more likely that what Karl Llewelyn was later to name the Grand Style or Manner[34] would be, over time, the predominant American legal method, even if formalism might hold sway for a few decades.

[32] The story is fully told by R. Ellis, *The Jeffersonian Crisis: Courts and Politics in the Young Republic* (New York, 1971). See also G. Haskins and H. Johnson, *Foundations of Power: John Marshall, 1801–1815* (New York, 1981), 207–45.

[33] I here use a troublesome term in the manner prescribed by *Form and Substance* at 28 ff.

[34] K. Llewellyn, *The Common Law Tradition: Deciding Appeals* (Boston, 1960), 64–72.

This became apparent as soon as the politically embattled Marshall Court was required to decide cases of political consequence on the basis of opaque Constitutional texts, texts themselves the products of intensely contested political compromises. The situation forced Marshall to lead, for good or ill, toward a legal theory and method that engaged the Court in the overt consideration of first principles and basic political values.[35] The very preservation of the republic demanded a substantive or 'pragmatic instrumentalist'[36] legal theory and method, and Marshall's style answered that demand of reality.

It was in this necessitous circumstance that Marshall invented the opinion of the Court, that is, the practice of giving a single opinion as that of the whole Court.[37] To gain moral and political stature, his Court often acted unanimously,[38] with Marshall or a colleague giving a reasoned and authoritative exposition of the law underlying each decision. Implicit in this practice was an obligation of all members of the Court not only to pursue the national common interest, but to maintain institutional coherence in that pursuit, to sacrifice pride of opinion to institutional, national, or community need. The professional morality embodied in the practice of delivering a single opinion for the whole Court visibly differed from that of the English judiciary of the time, who were entrenched in the custom of *seriatim* expression of their individual views, a custom that disavowed shared responsibility.

The effectiveness of the opinion of the Court as an instrument enhancing the political weight of the judiciary was recognized at once, with hostility by Thomas Jefferson,[39] with appreciation by his close ally James Madison,[40] and with the admiration of emulators in the courts of

[35] On the relation between the American constitutional scheme and the American legal method, see L. Fuller, *The Law in Quest of Itself* (Chicago, 1940), 88–99; see also his 'Jurisprudence', 13 *Encyclopedia Britannica* (1965), 149, 152.

[36] This is the term applied in R. Summers, *Instrumentalism in American Legal Theory* (Ithaca, 1982) to describe an approach to legal theory that subsumes but antedates and survives Legal Realism. Summers describes it (p. 35) as 'the only indigenous general theory of law'.

[37] The first appearance of the opinion of the court came in the first decision rendered after the appointment of Marshall. The story is told in G. Haskins and H. Johnson, n. 32 above, at 383–7. There was a precedent for such a device in the opinions of the Privy Council giving advice to the Crown, but the Council was not primarily a judicial institution, at least until the Privy Council Appeals Act of 1832. *Report of the Select Committee of the House of Lords on the Appellate Jurisdiction* 27 (1872). See generally J. P. Dawson, 'The Privy Council and Private Law' (1950) 48 Mich. LR 627.

[38] The Court was not so unanimous as may appear. It was the tradition of the Court in those years of fragility to suppress dissent: E. White, *The Marshall Court and Cultural Change, 1815–1835* (New York, 1983), 186 ff.

[39] Letter from T. Jefferson to W. Johnson, 27 Oct. 1822, *Writings of Thomas Jefferson*, ed. P. Ford, (1899), vol. 10, 222.

[40] Great was the difference between the views of Madison and Jefferson toward the role of American judges. See e.g., Letter Madison to Jefferson, *Letters and Other Writings*

every American state. Indeed, it was the development of this institution that confirmed for most Americans the belief that a single opinion of a court is itself a source of law,[41] a belief not then held in England[42] or on the Continent, where judicial opinions were not then considered to be authoritative legal texts, but mere signs of what the omnipresent law might be.

This belief in the importance of judicial opinions in turn created a market for reliable reportage that seems not to have existed except in America. Official reporters of judicial decisions were in place in most American jurisdictions in 1815, decades before such a function was known to England,[43] France,[44] or Germany.[45]

The compelling need of the American judiciary to reassure its public also indicated the use of the broadest possible range of authoritative materials. As Thurman Arnold explained, American judges needed and sought the appearance of learning as a substitute for red robes and wigs.[46] Classical learning, including Roman law, was often advanced to justify judicial action.[47] No doubt, especially in the formative decades, this broader learning was more than a costume and sometimes structured the thinking of American judges.

In addition to shaping the legal method and literary style of the courts, the American scheme of government also sustained the development of a legal profession bearing the stamp of these politicized courts. Given the nature and importance of decisions being made in American courts, it was all but certain that the officers of those courts would become a political élite, as Tocqueville soon observed them to be.[48] It was a related even that all but two of the men elected president of the United States from 1796 to 1868 were lawyers.[49] It

of James Madison ed. Rives and Fendell (Philadelphia, 1865) vol. 3, 326–7. Thus, Madison joined Jefferson in his negative reaction to *McCulloch* v. *Maryland*, 4 Wheat. 316 (1819) (taking expansive view of power of Congress to provide for the general welfare), but on quite contrary grounds, including the use of the opinion of the court in a case that Madison regarded as better suited to *seriatim* treatment. D. McCoy, *The Last of the Fathers: James Madison and the Republican Legacy* (New York, 1989), 99–100.

[41] F. G. Kempin, 'Precedent and Stare Decisis' (1959) 3 Am. J. Leg. Hist. 28. This is not to say that this theoretical issue was easily or fully settled in America.

[42] *The Oracles of the Law*, 78; C. Allen, *Law in the Making*, 6th edn., (Oxford, 1958), 207 ff.

[43] An official reporter was appointed in England in 1865: *The Oracles of the Law*, 82. See also J. Baker, 'Records, Reports and the Origins of Case-Law in England' in J. Baker (ed.), *Judicial Records, Law Reports, and the Growth of Case Law* (Berlin, 1989), 15.

[44] French case law was made regularly accessible by private reporters in the 1830s: *The Oracles of the Law*, 402. See also A. Wijffels, 'Legal Records and Reports in the Great Council of Malines (15th to 18th Centuries)' in *Judical Records*, n. 42 above.

[45] Regular annual reports commenced in Prussia in 1847: *The Oracles of the Law*, 438.

[46] *Fair Fights and Foul* (New York, 1965), 252 ff.

[47] R. Ferguson, *Law and Letters in American Culture* (Cambridge, Mass., 1984), 72–8.

[48] 1 *Democracy in America* trans. H. Reeve, ed. J. Spencer (New York, undated), 304–5.

[49] General Harrison and General Taylor were the exceptions.

was not unrelated that many men of American letters were also lawyers.[50]

Not least of the consequences of the Constitution for the legal profession in America has been the right to jury trial. In creating in the Constitution such a politically powerful judiciary, the founders evoked a popular outcry. In order to secure ratification of the Constitution, it was necessary to set in Constitutional cement the right to a jury in civil as well as criminal proceedings in federal courts.[51] This represented yet another division of power, this one within the judicial branch between the professional judge and the lay jury, each having their assigned roles, the purpose being to limit the awesome political power of the federal judge.

In significant respects, the civil jury is no longer the institution that it was two centuries ago,[52] and matters once in its purview may now be handled by administrative agencies. But while there are complaints about the institution,[53] there has been no occasion in the entire two hundred years of its Constitutional life when serious consideration was given to its retirement. The civil jury was an institution quickly entrenched within the American legal tradition as a means of diffusing responsibility and gaining popular support for the making of many public decisions.[54] This institution contributes directly to the substantive, non-formalistic character of American law.[55] It has also powerfully shaped the personae of the American bar. Jury argument, or in some minds jury demagoguery, is for most laymen and many professionals the paradigm of American law practice.[56] It also dictates the main outlines of American civil procedure, including, for example, the discovery-rules designed to enable counsel to prepare for dramatic trials. In so shaping the bar and the courts, the right to jury trial has also materially affected American thinking about legal method and theory. The American law of torts is in important respects an outgrowth of the American civil jury.

Almost as an afterthought to these many portentous decisions, the revolutionary generation established the precursors to American

[50] See generally R. Ferguson, n. 47 above.

[51] The right to jury trial in criminal cases is assured by the Sixth Amendment; in civil cases, by the Seventh Amendment. For expression of the views of those opposing ratification, see especially. C. Kenyon (ed.) *The Antifederalists* (Boston, 1966). 49–51.

[52] P. D. Carrington, 'The Seventh Amendment: Some Bicentennial Reflections' [1990] *Univ. Chic. LF* 33.

[53] For a recent expression by a person in high authority, see W. E. Burger, 'Thinking the Unthinkable' (1985) 31 Loyola LR 205.

[54] On the role of the American jury in deciding questions of law arising in civil litigation, see Carrington, n. 52 above, at 43–7.

[55] *Form and Substance*, 174–7.

[56] See generally Carrington, n. 52 above, at 67–71.

university law schools. Law-teaching in America was a response to the fear that the Revolution would dissolve into disorder and despotism, the same fear that gave rise to the Constitution. A republic could stand only so long as the people maintained a measure of mutual trust. This appeared to require, at the very least, leadership that would merit general public trust. To win such trust, it was believed, the legal and political élite would need to pursue the classical republican virtue of making and supporting public decisions based on selfless concern for the interests of all. Divisions of power alone, the founders recognized, would not suffice if the leaders were ideologues or demagogues unsuited to compromise and accommodation of competing values.

Montesquieu had emphasized the special need of a republic for education,[57] presumably conducted by the republican family,[58] that would inculcate this morality of civic virtue in all republican citizens. It was Jefferson's contribution to suggest that such moral education could be reinforced, if not provided, in the existing American colleges. It was his hope, shared by many others, including even arch-Hamiltonians such as James Kent,[59] that a legal and political élite, if not the people at large, could be socialized to a sense of shared public responsibility and trained to persist in the attempt at disinterested analysis of public issues. The goal of law-teaching was, therefore, to create a class of public men fit to occupy judicial and other high office; their claim to status would derive not from technocratic competence, income, or social status, but from their morality with respect to public affairs. Such an élite as that envisioned appears to have had no particular English origins;[60] if there was a model, it was in the traditions of the Roman senatorial class providing the jurisconsults who advised Roman courts and lent intellectual authority to Roman legal institutions.[61]

[57] *The Spirit of Laws*, Bk V. chs. 2–8. On Montesquieu as the chief contemporary expression of this concern, see P. Spurlin, *Montesquieu in America, 1760–1801*, 2d edn. (1969).

[58] *The Spirit of Laws*, Bk. IV, ch. 1, s. 1 and Ch 5, s. 5–7.

[59] 'An Introductory Lecture to a Course of Law Lectures' (1903), 3 *Colum, LR* 330, 338, 341. The lectures were delivered in 1796.

[60] It has been widely asserted that American legal education was inspired by the English model in the person of William Blackstone. Most widely quoted to this effect has been J. B. Thayer, 'The Teaching of English Law at Universities' (1895), 9 *Harv. LR 169. But Blackstone was scarcely a role-model for Jefferson and Wythe. For Blackstone, the royalist, the pursuit of self-interest was the source of natural law and the basis therefore of all English law. For comment, see D. Boorstin, The Mysterious Science of the Law* (Cambridge 1941) 52–3. Thus it was that Blackstone's readers were adjured to admire the common law, and to refrain from changing any part that they did not understand well enough to admire. Cf.: 'We ought to understand [the law] according to our measure; and to venerate where we are not able presently to comprehend . . .', 'An Appeal from the New to the Old' (1791), in *Works of Edmund Burke* (London, 1903), vol. 3, 114.

[61] *The Oracles of the Law*, 109–11.

Achievements and Travails of Teaching Republican Morality

American colleges were, then, called to validate the status of this élite by teaching them public law.[62] Academic law-teaching was initially undertaken to effect moral education, to transmit republican virtue to democratic leaders. Moral education, the first of the three means of public influence of law teachers, was historically primary. The roles of the law teacher as public person and as scholar-author were distinctly secondary.

American colleges, then as now, were part of an academic tradition or system quite apart from law but, like it, integral to the culture. To the extent that English and American institutions of higher education differed, these differences would inevitably be reflected in the corresponding differences in the legal education they would provide. American law had no Oxford; but then English law had no William and Mary; thus George Wythe would have been a different teacher at Oxford, as William Blackstone would have had a far different career at William and Mary, had either been able to secure the other's appointment.

The American colleges of the time were not ill-suited to the task of moral education. They were actively engaged as a primary mission in preparing young Americans for the clergy, and it was perhaps a modest step for them to train a secular clergy, the priests of public virtue who would protect the electorate from the selfish and destructive bickering to which it would be prone. The role proved no less attractive to fledgling *public* colleges that were striving to justify a claim on the public purse.

The first college to assume this role was William and Mary, which undertook it in 1779 at the command of Governor Jefferson by the appointment of the Governor's mentor in law, George Wythe, a signer of the Declaration. William and Mary was soon followed by most American colleges.[63] For the first century, law-teaching in American colleges, with rare exception,[64] has as its clear aim preparation for public leadership.

Most of the teaching was performed by men of some public attainment; many of them were judges, and several of those had

[62] Carrington, n. 20 above.

[63] Including Yale, Princeton, Pennsylvania, Columbia, North Carolina, Brown, and Dartmouth in the eighteenth century, and Maryland, Dickinson, Transylvania, Georgia, Middlebury, and Vermont in the early years of the nineteenth century before the War of 1812. Ibid.

[64] The Harvard Law School before the appointment of Joseph Story was such an institution. See A. Sutherland, *The Law at Harvard* (Cambridge, Mass., 1967), 43–91.

distinguished public careers.[65] Perhaps the professionally least-experienced young man appointed to teach law in an American college in the first century was Henry Clay, who soon went on to pursue perhaps the most significant American political career of the first half of the nineteenth century.[66] Several of the most distinguished college presidents of the antebellum era personally undertook to provide instruction in law; some of them were, in fact, clergymen who studied the Constitution and public law to enable themselves to contribute to the public morality of the nation.[67] The line between professional training and general education was seldom clearly drawn; the classics, Shakespeare,[68] and political economy were seen as part of a young man's preparation for public life. Only Harvard and Yale referred to their law programmes as independent 'law schools'.

Early American law students were often required by their teachers to develop forensic competence by means of class participation. The literature assigned them to read often included Blackstone, but generally in an American edition, which was often that of Professor St

[65] Wythe was Chancellor of Virginia, and all but one of his antebellum successors at William and Mary was a member of the Virginia judiciary. Robertson and all but two of his Transylvania colleagues were members of the Kentucky judiciary. Kent was chancellor and then chief judge of the New York Court of Appeals. In addition to Justice Story, Harvard was served by several members of the Massachusetts judiciary. Several Connecticut judges served on the Yale faculty. A chief justice of New Jersey served as a professor of law at Princeton. Pennsylvania was served by Justice Wilson and later by members of the state judiciary, including Judge Sharswood. Other examples can be found at Indiana, Lafayette, Dickinson, Mississippi, and Louisiana. David Hoffman at Maryland, Francis Lieber at South Carolina, John Barbee Minor at Virginia and Timothy Walker at Cincinnati were significant exceptions, law teachers who were not judges.

[66] A recent account and evaluation is M. Peterson, *The Great Triumvirate* (New York, 1987). To summarize for English readers, Clay was first elected senator in 1807 at the age of 29. As the leader of the War Hawks, he was instrumental in pushing the Madison administration into war with England in 1812. He was the *bête noire* of President Andrew Jackson, among other issues on the rights of native Americans. Almost alone, he struggled successfully as a senator to cause the American government to adopt the policy of the Monroe Doctrine, allying itself with Latin American democracy. He was a slave-state senator who opposed slavery. He was the principal champion of the protective tariff. He led the peace movement against war with Mexico in 1845, an engagement in which his oldest son was killed. He is generally credited with negotiating the major compromises of 1820, 1833, and 1850, that held the Union together during antebellum times. He narrowly failed of election as president on three occasions; it was said that if women had voted, he would have won every presidential election from 1816 through 1848.

[67] E.g., Stiles and Woolsey at Yale, Smith at Princeton, Nisbet at Dickinson, Holly at Transylvania, Wayland at Brown, Swain at North Carolina, Cooper at South Carolina and Bishop at Miami.

[68] Francis Lieber observed that American lawyers were blessed in their access to Shakespeare: 'A public man cannot read him too much', *Political Ethics* (1838), 2d edn, ed. T. Woolsey (New York, 1875) vol. 2, 292. Abraham Lincoln agreed, claiming to have read Macbeth 'as frequently as any unprofessional reader', J. Duff, *A Lincoln: Prairie Lawyer* (New York, 1960), 11.

George Tucker, who elided Blackstone's royalisms and provided his own insights into American public law.[69] In time, Blackstone was generally replaced by Kent, whose work as judge and writer greatly diminished the influence of the English law of property in America.[70] Primary emphasis was given to the study of American constitutional law, *The Federalist* often serving as a basic text. All Princeton students, and perhaps others, were for a time required to memorize and recite the text of the Constitution.[71] Often included in the curriculum were international law, comparative law, and political economy. Only a few of the small number of law teachers from the era between the Revolution and the Civil War wrote other than as judges, but the works of David Hoffman,[72] Thomas Cooper,[73] James Kent, and Francis Lieber[74] are impressive for their intellectual breadth. Hoffman's elaborate and widely acclaimed outline for law study[75] confirms the aspiration of those training this political élite to give their students the broadest possible intellectual experience in order to enhance their receptivity and their capacity for making public decisions rooted in a broad appreciation of public values and a balanced assessment of the public interest. The patterns of legal education thus tracked the Grand Style adopted by the judiciary.

The early legal institutions of higher education in law were few and small. In 1830, the largest American university, with the largest enrollment in its law department (seventy-one) and the largest law faculty (three) was Transylvania University in Lexington, Kentucky.[76] This institution, in many ways a reflection of its trustee and former professor, Henry Clay, enjoyed significant if now forgotten prominence. It was the flagship of the American colleges' efforts to

[69] Tucker's edition was published in 1803. For a contemporary review, see E. White, n. 38 above, 81–7.

[70] *Commentaries on American Law*, 4 vols. (New York, 1826–30).

[71] S. Smith, *The Lectures, Collected and Improved, which have been Delivered for a Series of Years in the College of New Jersey on the Subject of Moral and Political Philosoph* (1812), vol. 2, 329.

[72] See T. L. Shaffer, 'David Hoffman's Law School Lectures 1822–1833' (1982) 32 *J. Leg. Ed.* 127, and especially D. Hoffman's *Legal Outlines* (Baltimore, 1836).

[73] Cooper was perhaps at his best as an editor, producing American editions of works in Chemistry, Political Economy, and Roman Law, translating major works from German, French, and Latin. Jefferson described him before he went to South Carolina as the 'greatest mind in America'. See generally D. Malone, *The Public Life of Thomas Cooper, 1783–1839* (New Haven, 1926).

[74] See for examples his *Manual of Political Ethics*, 2 vols., (Boston, 1838); *Legal and Political Hermeneutics* (Boston, 1838); *Civil Liberty and Self Government* (Philadelphia, 1854).

[75] *A Course of Legal Study Addressed to Students and the Profession Generally* (1817). For the acclaim, see Story, 'Book Review' (Nov., 1817), *The North American Review* 76.

[76] See generally, P. D. Carrington, 'Teaching Law and Virtue at Transylvania University: The George Wythe Tradition in the Antebellum Years' (1990) 41 *Mercer LR* 673.

train a legal and political élite to lead the exercise of popular sovereignty and prevent its tendency to excess.

By graduating as many as thirty United States Senators, Transylvania may have provided Clay with an extra personal bond to political adversaries that enabled him to assemble the great compromises of 1820, 1833, and 1850, preventing the premature collapse of the federal union. Three of its teachers (not including Clay) were authoritatively identified in 1908 as among the 77 'Great American Lawyers' whose lives were worthy of biography.[77] What Transylvania sought to do, and may have succeeded in doing by its teaching, was to impart to students headed for public careers a moral tone and a commitment to the national interest. It is even possible that Transylvania's success in this endeavour provided the margin of public dedication that enabled the nation to survive.[78] Whatever Transylvania achieved was the product of its teaching, not its scholarship, and assuredly not its enrichment of American legal theory.

Transylvania was an offspring of William and Mary and of George Wythe. Wythe could be said to have had the most important teaching career Socrates.[79] Before his academic appointment he had tutored young Jefferson, becoming his 'second father'. Among his first students at William and Mary was John Marshall.[80] After he left the professorship, Wythe tutored Henry Clay, acquiring a grandparental relationship to him. Others of the two-hundred or so students he taught served in high office, and several founded the Transylvania Law Department. Wythe had been trained in the classics by his Quaker mother, and was thereafter self-educated in law and politics, mastering Roman law and the literature of England, France, Germany, and Italy. As a lawyer, it was said that 'no dirty coin even got to the bottom of George Wythe's pocket'.[81] As a judge, he was compared with Aristides

[77] *Great American Lawyers*, 3: 232 (J. Boyle); 4: 365 (G. Robertson); 5: 301 (T. Marshall) (ed. W. Lewis, 1908).

[78] This assumes that 'Transy' was the difference in enabling Clay to effect the compromises that held the nation together. There is little doubt that if the Southern states had seceded in 1820, there would have been no war, and the semi-feudal society of the South would have survived at least the nineteenth century. This was probably true even as late as 1850. Had there been war in 1850, it seems highly likely that the South would have succeeded in defending itself, for it was only in the decade following that the North's advantage in manpower and economic productivity became overwhelming, and, even in 1860, the outcome of the war was a very near thing: J. McPherson, *Battle Cry of Freedom: The Civil War Era* (New York, 1988), 857–9.

[79] A. Dill, *George Wythe: Teacher of Liberty* (Williamsburg, 1979); I. Brown, *American Aristides* (Rutherford, 1981).

[80] Wythe was less close to Marshall, but a decade after Marshall's student days, Chancellor Wythe declared unconstitutional an enactment of his former student sitting as a member of the Virginia legislature, thus providing a model for Marshall's own later decision in *Marbury* v. *Madison*. *Commonwealth* v. *Caton* (1782) 4 Call. 5.

[81] I. Brown, n. 79 above, at 35.

or with an angel, so great was his reputation for disinterestedness.[82] He was in these respects exceptionally well qualified to provide training in republican virtue. By his fruits one would suppose that he did that well. In this respect, as a teacher, his influence on American law and politics was as great perhaps as any person's will ever be.

The tradition of American legal education established by George Wythe abides. Although Wythe himself left behind meagre writings,[83] his teaching aims and those of his followers were clearly and fully stated in the 1837 work of Francis Lieber, then of the University of South Carolina.[84] In short, Lieber extolled reasoned disinterest and willingness to engage in mutual sacrifice of compromise to save the integrity of the polity. While no law teachers today would adhere to the whole of Lieber's teachings, it is still an important, if seldom stated, aim of American university law-teaching to train students for public responsibilities in a democracy. This is evidenced in case-books or the 'cases and materials' that invite the balanced assessment of competing interests, each claiming an entitlement to public concern, and in the traditional classroom discussion designed to prod most students to active engagement in disinterested or balanced discussion of significant disputes.

Undeniably, the aim of teaching republican virtue has been bruised and crowded over two centuries of experience, but generally by causes that have been external to the institutions of legal education, and indeed even external to America. I here note four such difficulties encountered along the way by those who would teach law as a means to the public morality needed to sustain democratic institutions.

First came the French Revolution. The barbarism and mass homicide that followed the Revolution[85] confirmed the worst fears of the American revolutionaries regarding the disintegrative tendency of republican government[86] that had given rise to the establishment of legal education; in this respect, the mayhem underscored the need that law-teaching was intended to meet. On the other hand, it was

[82] John Randolph said of Wythe that: '[H]e lived in the world without being of the world . . . he was a mere incarnation of justice—his judgments were all as between A and B; for he knew nobody; but went into court as Astaea was supposed to come down from heaven, exempt from all human bias.' Quoted *in* W. Lewis (ed.) *Lives of Great American Lawyers* (1907), vol. 1, 275.

[83] *Decisions of Cases in Virginia by the High Court of Chancery, with Remarks upon Decrees by the Court of Appeals Reversing Some of those Decisions* (1795).

[84] See P. D. Carrington, 'Republican Virtue and American Patriotism: The Teaching of Francis Lieber' (forthcoming)

[85] S. Schama, *Citizens* (New York, 1989), 786–92, elaborates these horrors, including the systematic poisoning of wells in the Vendée region by the revolutionary 'government'.

[86] American reaction to that event was not far different from that of Edmund Burke expressed in *Reflections on the Revolution in France* (1790).

sometimes thought that the event may have served as a model for the widespread disorder that infected American colleges in the early years of the nineteenth century; Princeton, for example, was seized by 'Jacobinic' students in 1800, and in 1807 the college expelled seventy of its 125 students for riotous conduct.[87] A lesser effect was to chill any taste for things French, and to rekindle the remaining embers of Anglophilial sentiments, especially in New England.[88] It became less fashionable to speak of republican virtue, as even such New Englanders as John Adams had, for it was a term that was frequently on the lips of those who manned the guillotine, Marat, Danton, St Just, and Robespierre.[89]

A second and more troublesome impediment to law-teaching as training in public morality came with the resurgence of slavery, the blight that America inherited from some of its English founders. Montesquieu proclaimed that the institutions of slavery could not coexist with the institutions of a republic,[90] and the revolutionary generation recognized this to be so. They spoke freely of the emancipation of the slaves. Indeed, law Professor Tucker led the emancipation movement in Virginia.[91] Clay and others associated with Transylvania led it in Kentucky. There was no opposition when President Jefferson in 1809 led Congress to the abolition of the slave-trade on the first day that this could be done under the terms of the Constitution.[92]

However, the rise in the world demand for cotton and the resulting prosperity of cotton agriculture renewed the enthusiasm of Southern planters for slavery. The fugitive-slave issue gave rise to increasing bitterness on both sides. The text of the Constitution obligated all states to honour the property-claims of slave-owners. What could be said by law teachers to nurture the spirit of compromise that marks the practice of republican virtue within such a constitutional scheme? Especially if the professor taught in the South, serving a culture that

[87] M. Noll, *Princeton and the Republic 1768–1822*, (Princeton, 1989), 290–6.

[88] In Federalist New England, 'the mark of a wise and good man was that he abhorred the French Revolution and believed democracy to be its cause', H. Adams, *History of the United States in the Administrations of Madison and Monroe* (Boston, 1891), vol. 1, 33.

[89] Lieber, a German emigre and a Francophobe, writing in 1837, wrote three volumes essentially defining classical civic virtue in the contemporary American context, without ever using the term 'virtue'. He wrote about 'patriotism'. See n. 74 above; for comment see Carrington, n. 8 above.

[90] *The Spirit of Laws*, Bk XV, ch. 1, s. 3.

[91] *A Dissertation on Slavery with a Proposal for the Gradual Abolition of it in the State of Virginia* (Philadelphia, 1796).

[92] Too much can be made of this enactment; one of its effects was to enhance the value of slaves already in America. It was for this reason that opposition was slight among slave-owners. See D. Davis, *The Problem of Slavery in the Age of Revolution* (Ithaca, 1975), 324–5.

was increasingly aggressive in its demands for approval as well as legal protection? Lieber, the ablest antebellum scholar of American law and politics, despised slavery,[93] but was daunted; not until he moved from South Carolina to New York in 1858 did he dare publicize his views.[94] Others were similarly cautious.

Most of those teaching law in antebellum America, North or South, were staunch unionists who identified the preservation of the nation as the primary moral aim. They became increasingly embattled on both sides as abolitionists denounced the provisions of the Constitution and as the South increasingly favored dissolution. It became at last apparent that there was no balanced, disinterested position to maintain with respect to the central legal and political issue of the time.

One casualty of the resulting stress was the Translyvania Law Department, which closed its doors in 1858. Another was the substantive legal method employed by antebellum American courts in the disposition of most matters. Most judges, perhaps especially the unionists, recoiled from a substantive analysis of the legal status of slaves, and were driven by events to adopt a sterile formalism in the disposition of fugitive slave cases.[95]

The impact of slavery on American law by no means ended with the then-unprecedented carnage that was the Civil War,[96] or with the ensuing period of Reconstruction. Among the enduring legacies of that war was a time, decades in length, when Americans endured a general anxiety about disorder; an eminent historian of the time has described post-Reconstruction America as engaged in a consuming 'search for order'.[97] An effect of that social condition on the law was described by Grant Gilmore as the 'law's black night',[98] by which term he referred to a failure of the judicial heart for the Grand Manner that had previously characterized American judicial law-making. The American judiciary seemingly feared to exercise its accustomed political responsibility and took refuge in formalism.[99] A formal style was manifested by the

[93] He concluded a letter to Senator John C. Calhoun: 'It is not the *North* that is against you. It is mankind, it is the world, it is civilization, it is history, it is reason, it is God, that against slavery.' *The Life and Letters of Francis Lieber* ed. T. Perry (Boston, 1882).

[94] F. Freidel, *Francis Lieber, Nineteenth-Century Liberal* (New York, 1947), 305 ff.

[95] W. Nelson, 'The Impact of the Anti-Slavery Movement upon Styles of Judicial Reasoning in Nineteenth Century America' (1974), 87 *Harv. LR* 513.

[96] At least 640,000 men, perhaps as much as 25 per cent of the male population of the United States of military age, were killed and many more maimed. The casualties exceeded those in all other American military ventures to date combined. Trench warfare in 1916 is England's only experience with such devastation.

[97] R. Wiebe, *The Search for Order, 1877–1920* (New York, 1967).

[98] *The Ages of American Law* (New Haven, 1977), 4.

[99] *Form and Substance*, 248–9. For discussion of the effect of this period on the structure and administration of the federal courts, see P. D. Carrington, 'The Function of the Civil Appeal: A Late-Century View' (1987), 38 *S. Car. LR* 411.

Supreme Court of the United States in the late nineteenth century, and was for a time the dominant style of state courts dealing with private law questions.[100]

This lingering effect of the Civil War coalesced with a third, and perhaps still more powerful, challenge to the efforts of universities to teach law as preparation for the moral exercise of public responsibility. That third external challenge came when America, with much of the world, grasped the ideas of division of labour and technology as the promise of release from all human bondages.[101] In medicine, engineering, law, economics, and a dozen new fields, many of them serving to facilitate the entry of American women into public and professional life, such as education, nursing, social work, and librarianship, there was a contagion of interest in technocratic professionalism, in the development of almost any kind of skill that could be said to have roots in what was loosely called science.

In hindsight, we can now see that the movement towards meritocratic professionalism was very powerful. It may simply have throttled Marxism as an American political force in its infancy. Widespread land-ownership and the frontier had, with the very important exception of slavery, prevented the development of a substantial underclass until the urban laborers appeared in force in mid-century. But even then, there was no serious prospect of class war in a society dominated by landowners and providing substantial social mobility through open professions. The urban middle class was emerging, and hope, if not prosperity, was offered to almost all.

Manifestly, the contagion of technocracy was destined to have major impact on higher education and on all the professions, including law. Thus, it reinforced the shift in American legal method and theory, sustaining the moment of formalism. To seem a technocrat, not a politician, was an ambition widely shared among judges and lawyers.[102] This ambition fed the aspiration to decide legal matters on the basis of internal logic divorced from social context or political responsibility. That moment of formalism cut deeply against the grain of American political arrangements, and hence was doomed to be short lived, but it survived for long enough seriously to affect legal education in America.

The impulse to technocratic professionalism and the moment of

[100] K. Llewellyn, n. 4 above, at 41 ff. Llewellyn reports that the Formal Style was still evident in Maryland and Massachusetts as late as 1939.

[101] See *M. Larson, The Rise of Professionalism* (Berkeley, 1977). For the special effect on law see Ibid. 166–76.

[102] There was also an increase in the rigid formalism of the judicial method in England in the last four decades of the nineteenth century: see *The Oracles of the Law*, 90–1.

formalism in American law provided just the right environment to reward the initiative of Christopher Columbus Langdell. Seeking the approval of a generation of technocrats, as well as to sell his wares to students otherwise likely to train for legal careers as apprentices, Langdell's eye hit upon the ore of case law enbodied in currently reported opinions of American courts, that manifestation of post-Revolutionary politics. He was able soon to devise a process of refinement of this ore that borrowed heavily from judicial formalism and that could, with some success, be passed off as a new science of law.[103]

Langdell and his academic heir, James Barr Ames, made little effort to extend this pseudo-science to the study of constitutional or other public law. Private law could often be examined 'scientifically', in accordance with its presumed internal symmetry and in disregard of its social and political consequences,[104] where public law seldom could. Langdell, Ames, and their adherents therefore demoted constitutional law in their curriculum and left the writing of it largely to Thomas McIntyre Cooley of Michigan,[105] and others not averse to the soil of politics.[106]

An adverse consequence of this technocratic emphasis was isolation of law study from broader intellectual efforts directed at other social phenomena bearing on the law.[107] Similar isolation befell other fields of academic endeavour, but it was especially unfortunate for a profession trained as a political élite. The admirable intellectual breadth brought to their work by educated antebellum lawyers trained by men such as Wythe, Tucker, Hoffman, Kent, the Transylvanians, or Lieber was treated as a lesser attainment, or at least separate from the goal of the professional lawyer-technocrat.

Partly, no doubt, to emphasize the elevated status of the professionals trained at Harvard, Dean Langdell's school increased

[103] Romans had so spoken of law, and Blackstone claimed no less for the law of his kingdom that that it was rooted in scientific verity: D. Boorstin n. 60 above, at 11–31.

[104] E.g., C. Langdell, *A Summary of the Law of Contracts* 2d edn., (Boston, 1880); see T. C. Gray, 'Langdell's Orthodoxy' (1983) 45 *U. Pitt. LR* 1.

[105] *A Treatise on the Constitutional Limitations which Rest upon the Legislative Power of the States of the American Union*, 4 vols., (Boston, 1868); *Commentaries on the Constitution* (Boston, 1873); *General Principles of Constitutional Law* (Boston, 1880). See B. Jacobs, *Law Writers and the Courts: The Influence of Thomas M. Cooley, Christopher G. Tiedeman and John F. Dillon upon American Constitutional Law* (Berkeley, 1954). Cooley was also the architect of the Sherman Act and first chair of the Interstate Commerce Commission.

[106] These included James Bradley Thayer of Harvard; see e.g., 'The Origin and Scope of the American Doctrine of Constitutional Law' (1894) 7 *Harv. LR* 129, although Thayer's view of the role of the judiciary was decidedly cautious.

[107] P. D. Carrington, *'Book review'* (1984) 72 *Calif. LR* 477, 485–89; cf. C. Woodard, 'Progress and Poverty in American Law and Legal Education' (1986) 37 Syra. L. Rev. 795, 806–812.

admission requirements to admit only college graduates.[108] This allowed the school to assume that its students had already been taught what they needed to know of the classics and political economy and to concentrate on law as technocracy, thereby increasing the isolation. In this respect, the Harvard educational style widely used in the late nineteenth century threatened to unfit law graduates for public service, by imparting to them 'the ability to think of a thing that is inextricably related to something else without thinking about the something else'.[109] By creating a demand for a vast range of professional services and professional training, the impulse to technocracy transformed American universities. Universities became in part what we now recognize as the factories of human capital run by educational entrepreneurs.[110]

With respect to law, the technocratic impulse set in motion a still-growing demand for legal services that has attracted into law study many whose career aims are directed chiefly at the private-sector law firms and corporate offices responding to that demand. Technocratic law-teaching thus sold well because America wanted and perhaps needed a technocratic legal profession, one that would seem in its intellectual substructure respectable in comparison to the other rising professions. That profession, as all can observe, emerged in the century following 1890, when the boom commenced, to become a significant component of the American national economy.

By extending the course of academic law study to three years,[111] Dean Langdell ingeniously, or perhaps even unwittingly, conformed to the growing ambition of students to enhance the value of their services by investing in exclusive professional training. Thus, élite university legal education has in recent decades been seen, at least in important part, as an investment by students on which they expect a handsome return.[112] Most borrow heavily to finance their costly professional

[108] The requirement was first proposed by Langdell in 1875, but not fully implemented until 1909: C. Warren, *History of the Harvard Law School and of Early Legal Conditions in America* (New York, 1908), 39–8; J. Seligman, *The High Citadel* (Boston, 1978), 41–2.

[109] The quoted description has been widely attributed to Professor Thomas Reed Powell. I have not been able to find a source for it; I can attest only that it was part of the lore of the Harvard Law School in 1954. There is no doubt that Powell himself found the teaching at Harvard to be an impediment to sound thinking on public issues: see Chase, n. 10 above, at 118–19.

[110] For a description and a defense of the American 'multi-versity' as it had become by mid-century, see C. Kerr, *The Uses of the University* (Cambridge, 1963). Kerr wrote as the President of the University of California on the eve of substantial disorder from which his institution may yet be convalescing.

[111] R. Stevens, *Law School: Legal Education in America from the 1850s to the 1980s* (Chapel Hill, 1982), 36–7.

[112] J. R. Kramer, 'Will Legal Education Remain Affordable? By Whom? How?' [1987] *Duke L. J.* 240.

training. Relative incomes of many American professions have risen steadily over the last century, but none perhaps more than law.

Within the legal profession, a disparity in income-expectations of those who serve the public and those who serve private interests has grown apace, perhaps particularly in the last two decades.[113] As a result, students thinking of themselves as prospective public servants and leaders are a declining portion of those studying law in America, and are less influential in setting the tone of the American law-school environment.

This acquisition of human capital by financial investment in professional training can dilute the impact of moral education. At best, financial motives are a distraction. No one who has been in a contemporary American law school during the placement season can doubt the powerful short-term effect of that process on the moral values and sensibilities of the students. That effect may well dwarf the efforts of teachers to inculcate appropriate expectations as to how lawyers and judges think and behave in their professional roles.[114] It assuredly weakens, at least for an important time, the students' shared sense of public purpose if most hope and expect to do corporate mergers or other highly remunerative work involving little or no service or perhaps even requiring disservice to the public interest. Partly for this reason, some of the opportunity for moral education has passed from the law schools to the law firms who initiate students into the profession while they perform summer or part-time employment, for it is there that students are more likely to meet 'real lawyers' engaged in the careers to which they aspire. This is so despite Bar-imposed requirements that law schools teach the law governing lawyer conduct.[115]

Nevertheless, treating professional education as a financial investment is not wholly at odds with the aims of moral education as practiced by persons such as Wythe or Lieber. It is certainly not demonstrable that lawyers in the past were more honourable in their participation in public affairs than they are today as a result of the

[113] At the time of the 1990 enactment to increase federal judicial salaries, it was widely observed that the young law clerks working at the elbows of Supreme Court justices would in their second or third year in the private sector earn more than the Chief Justice of the United States.

[114] See R. C. Cramton, 'Change and Continuity in Legal Education' (1981) 79 *Mich. LR* 460, 462. The effort to establish clinical legal education that appeared in the early 1970s was in some degree a response to this problem. See *Clinical Legal Education (Council on Legal Education for Professional Responsibility* (1973) and D. R. Barnhizer, 'The University Ideal and Clinical Legal Education' (1990) 35 *NYLSLR* 1.

[115] A requirement enforced by a national multiple-choice test. For a brief description, see F. Morrissey, 'The Origins and Usefullness of the Multi-State Professional Responsibility Examination' (1981) 50 *The Bar Examiner* 24.

malign influence of the market-place. Even lawyers seeking wealth are unlikely to find it if they do not understand the moral premisses of the legal tradition in which they work. Most contemporary American law students are, therefore, generally willing to accept as part of their professional training the discipline of disinterested thinking about specific and important public issues. Moreover, teachers of public virtue are necessarily preoccupied with issues of contemporary significance, so their interests must sometimes coincide with those of even the most narrowly careerist students. In addition, even the most technocratic students may in time find themselves in public careers, and those who do may be influenced in their public morality by their experience in the university.

Finally, it was no aim of Langdell or Ames to forsake moral education. There is no reason to believe that their own aims were to advance the financial well-being of their students or of the legal profession; on the contrary, their own aspirations appear to have been simply to improve the law by separating it from politics. While their efforts on that score were at best only partly successful, the systematic study of reported cases advocated by them as a teaching device was and is a premier method for the inculcation of public virtue. This is so because case discussion forces the impersonal weighing and balancing of competing values to resolve particular problems.[116] It develops reasoning to persuade a public audience and habits of analysis rooted in the general public interest. Rewarded is the ability to think disinterestedly about highly contentious matters; punished is the passionate insistence on one's own idiosyncratic values or interests, or adherence to abstract theory yielding unwelcome results in application. Students experiencing a heavy dose of such instruction are changed by it, and in some ways, they are made more fit for public responsibility. This is more likely to be true if the judicial opinions that are the grist of discussion reflect the American judicial tradition, or the Grand Manner, that displays balanced consideration of first principles; it may be less true as the opinions are seen as the work-product of youthful law clerks working in the chambers of a judge applying her or his trademark to the thoughts of others.[117]

The fourth external force to challenge law-teaching as preparation for public responsibility derives from the third. As technocratic professionalism engulfed modern society, there developed in the

[116] For a review of the costs and benefits of this mode of teaching, see P. D. Carrington, 'Book Review' (1984) 72 *Calif LR* 477, 489–91.

[117] On the continuing importance of the 'unity of discourse' between law teachers and judges, see E. Rubin, 'The Practice and Discourse of Legal Scholarship (1987–8) 86 *Mich LR* 1835, 1859–1865. For a brief critique of the role of law clerks, see P. Carrington, D. Meador, and M. Rosenberg, *Justice on Appeal* (St Paul, 1977), 44–6.

increasingly prosperous universities a meta-profession of those sustaining the learning from which the status of the professions derived. By 1890, the academic profession had taken on an independent life in America.

Much of the modern American university's tradition and ideology has German origins,[118] and is centered on the institutions of the graduate school and the Ph.D. degree. Its emphases are on intellectual specialization, pursuit of abstraction, and withdrawal from concerns with the practical applications of learning. There is indeed a tendency of the academic profession to glory in the worldly irrelevance of its deepest insights.[119] In this, the American academic profession (and perhaps the English, too) would be an almost perfect complement to the English legal profession, which is said to glory in its aversion to theory.[120]

An effect of the rising status of the academic profession on law has been to socialize law teachers to these, and perhaps other, academic values. Truth sometimes competes with virtue. By 1920 it was already questionable whether some law professors were indeed lawyers or not. By 1900 that is no longer a question, for it is clear that many are not: they have opted for a different professional identity.. As Francis Allen has put it,[121] the academically élite law schools is increasingly a colonial outpost of the graduate school, dominated by persons whose primary interests are in almost any other discipline than law.

The effect of this academization of law faculties on the influence of the schools on public life is not clear.[122] It relieves the intellectual isolation created by the technocratic impulse that immediately preceded it and provides an opportunity for the rediscovery of the relationship of law to all learning that bears on the culture of which it is a part. Such broader learning is the proper domain of public persons. It may be, however, that the tensions between academization and the

[118] German ideas about higher education arrived in Cambridge with the return of George Ticknor and Edward Everett in 1819: V. Brooks, *The Flowering of New England, 1815–1865*, (New York, 1936), 73–110. But the academic profession first gained its distinct identity with the establishment of the Graduate School and the Ph.D. degree at Johns Hopkins University in 1879: see H. Hawkins, *Pioneer: A History of the Johns Hopkins University, 1874–1899* (Ithaca, 1960). These innovations appeared at the University of Berlin in the post-Napoleonic era.

[119] For an expression by an American lawyer that 'metaphysics' is 'the highest wisdom', and therefore the first aim of higher education, see R. Hutchins, *The Higher Learning in America* (New Haven, 1936), 98.

[120] P. Atiyah, *Pragmatism and Theory* (London, 1987), 3.

[121] P. Hay and M. Hoeflich (eds.), *Property Law and Legal Education: Essays in Honor of John E. Cribbet* (Champaign, 1988).

[122] For other assessments, see F. A. Allen, 'Legal Scholarship: Present Status and Future Prospects' (1983) 33 *J. Leg. Ed.* 403; D. R. Barnhizer, 'The University Ideal and the American Law School' (1989) 42 *Rutgers LR* 109; P. C. Kissam, 'The Decline of Law School Professionalism' (1986) 134 *U Pa. LR* 251; and Rubin, n. 117 above.

moral education that American law-teaching was contrived to provide are even greater than those created by the pursuit and acquisition of human capital in the law school. The academic pursuit of abstraction may sometimes be associated with a tendency to intellectual effort that is ideological or dogmatic. Ideology and dogmatism can result from inattention to the messy details that so often distress theory. Alas, republican virtue, like God, is in the details; sweeping statements like some of those made here are seldom the means for finding the common ground that saves the whole by setting our differences aside for another day. Disinterested discourse regarding a public issue is impeded if it is to be resolved at a level of abstractions reaching into many or all aspects of our public life. Where the line of American law teachers following Wythe have taught pragmatism, those recently following intellectual trails into economics or the humanities seem often to manifest a disinclination to that mode of thought. The dogmatic law-teaching that sometimes results puts the teacher at risk of the overheated condemnation of Voltaire: as a public person, he is 'a traitor, because he subject[s] his country to his own opinions'.[123] Partisan political dogmatism corrosive of republican virtue is evident in the American academy today,[124] and may now be infecting law schools.[125]

Moreover, especially over the longer term, the academic withdrawal from practical concerns can endanger the relation between law teacher and law student. A teacher who is seen by students to be disengaged from political reality and not a professional in law is disadvantaged in the effort to inculcate moral standards applicable to professional thinking and conduct in public roles. A professor of literary or economic theory, however able, will not be a professional role-model for novice lawyers.

Despite these travails, it is at least possible that American university education in law is still performing the mission assigned to it by Thomas Jefferson and others, and that was performed by George Wythe, his students at Transylvania, Thomas Cooley, and now countless others. If so, these institutions may yet be influential as they were intended originally to be, although this was not the way that Atiyah and Summers seemed to have had chiefly in mind in proclaiming their influence.

I turn, then, to the other two possibilities that are incidental to the law teacher's role as guide to a public morality appropriate to American democratic government.

[123] *The Philosophy of History* (1767), 314.

[124] For a brief description of the phenomenon, see J. Searle, 'The Battle over the University' (6 Dec. 1990), 37 *The New York Review of Books* 34.

[125] P. D. Carrington, *Law Teaching in a Time of Moral Excess* (forthcoming, 1991).

The Law Teachers as Public Person

The second means of influence of American law schools is harbouring the public activities of a law faculty. In their public activities, law professors act as individual citizens. The means to influence open to law professors are mostly the same as those open to non-academic layers or, in some cases, laymen; in some circumstances, law teachers may have an edge derived from their professional status and from the 'contacts' acquired through their alumni and former students, but this is not always so, for in some circumstances to be an academic is an impediment to gaining attention. These opportunities for service include political activity at the local, state, and federal levels; work with the organized bar or other organizations having a stake and an active programme of involvement in public affairs; consultation with local, state, and federal legislative bodies; and professional service advocating causes before all manner of forums. An appointment to an American law faculty is a licence to engage in all of these activities on one's own terms.

There are disincentives to participation in such activities. To be useful, one must associate with persons who are not always members of an élite. One must go to meetings and not only talk, but also listen politely, often more than once to the same bad idea. One must study and think about issues and problems that are of immediate concern to others, and not only those issues most attractive to one's own interests. The issues to be addressed are often distastefully narrow. To be effective, one must compromise and accommodate. One must repeat oneself. One must risk the sting of visible defeat. To secure the best opportunities, one must sometimes first win trust by bearing the most unwelcome burdens, performing prosaic tasks that do less honour to one's talents than one might wish, for, alas, to be an admiral in law and politics, one must generally spend some time in the boiler-rooms of legal and political institutions.

For the most part, however, those individual American law professors who have in the twentieth century influenced the development of American law have not been daunted by these disincentives, and have achieved influence at least partly by these conventional means open to all. By such common means more than a few law professors in America have effected change in the law. Others have secured high judicial or other public office. By their labours, they may also incidentally have transmitted to other lawyers and to their students the moral message that the concerned revolutionaries of the eighteenth century would have us learn regarding the need for disinterested public service. Many have taught public morality by example.

I suppose that similar avenues to influence are open to law professors everywhere. I note that a former law professor, the Rt Hon Geoffrey Palmer, who once plied his academic trade in Iowa, was recently prime minister of New Zealand. He presumably achieved considerable genuine influence on the law and legal institutions of New Zealand. Within narrow limits, he could effect change in New Zealand law, and for good or ill, his demeanour in office was an example to New Zealand lawyers. Perhaps he is also a model for others elsewhere: if there are too few English law professors being appointed to high public office or consulted by those who are, perhaps some might put themselves in line to stand for Parliament. A few law professors in the Cabinet would make a difference to the shape and condition of English law.[126] Or perhaps English universities might follow for a while the example of nineteenth-century American colleges and appoint some public men and women as professors of law.

This source of influence of American legal education on the law has been significant. It is, however, threatened by both late nineteenth-century pursuits, of the investor's human capital and of the scholar's truth. The financial rewards associated with large investments in professional education can be a threat to the participation of law teachers in public affairs, if professors, like some students, become chiefly engaged in maximizing their marginal revenue in lieu of pursuing the common good as private ministers without portfolio. Endangered in American universities is the example of Louis Pasteur, who applied his science to a series of public problems without leaving the main themes of his work or becoming 'consultant to silk-worm growers, wine-makers, brewers, or poultry-men'.[127] Income-maximization by law professors may also infect the public with mistrust of motives: law professors who sell the trade-mark of their universities to express in a court or other forums professional opinions agreeable to those who pay for them endanger both the repute and the reality of academic disinterest. Those academic lawyers who establish regular relations with clients or firms sacrifice disinterest and thereby diminish their ability to perform the public mission to which Jefferson and Wythe called them.[128]

Academization threatens the public role of the law teacher in quite different ways. Involvement in public affairs fits poorly with the reward-systems of the academic profession. It is at least possible (I have no means of knowing) that one reason for a lack of public status of the English legal academy is that law professors have been socialized

[126] BBC's *Yes, Minister* to the contrary notwithstanding.
[127] A. Flexner, *Universities: American, English, German* (London, 1930), 132.
[128] Cf. Ackerman, '*The Marketplace of Ideas*' (1981) 90 *Yale LJ* 1131.

by their academic colleagues to devalue the prosaic efforts required to achieve status as a public person. The disincentives to public involvement that I enumerated may be especially unattractive to genuinely academic persons. It is also possible that persons who select themselves to be fully committed to the more purely academic profession and its values are less suited to public activities and thus unlikely to enjoy much success in any event. There does seem at times to be, as Woodrow Wilson observed, a 'perennial misunderstanding between men who write and men who act'.[129]

For these reasons, it is not certain that the influence achieved by American law schools by means of the public activities of their faculties can be maintained, or that it could be replicated in England.

The Influence of Academic Literature on American Law

The third possibility for influence, and the one of greatest interest to Atiyah and Summers, is through authorship.

Academic literature played a very small role indeed in the formative first century of American law. William Blackstone had an influence on the American legal profession almost contrary to his purpose in writing, for his work was used chiefly to enable untrained persons to perform legal services.[130] St George Tucker's contribution in editing Blackstone was substantial. James Kent's *Commentaries on American Law*[131] were undeniably influential, at least in the formation of American property law. Parts of the extended work of Justice Joseph Story[132] may have influenced his brethren on the Court. George Sharswood of the University of Pennsylvania wrote a widely read work on professional ethics.[133] Simon Greenleaf's *Evidence*[134] was read by lawyers and judges across the country, and was cited by more than a few courts. Of these authors, only Tucker and Greenleaf can be counted as genuine academics. While writing at Columbia, Kent's relation to the university was nominal, and the impact of his work derived largely from his decades-long role as the intellectual leader of the highest court in the most important state, New York. The work of Justice Story, although written at Harvard while Story was lecturing

[129] N. Demerath, R. Stephens, and R Taylor, *Power, Presidents and Professors* (1967), 27.

[130] See D. R. Nolan, 'Sir William Blackstone and the New American Republic: A Study of Intellectual Impact' (1976) 51 *NYULR* 731; W. Hurst, *The Growth of American Law: The Law-Makers* (Boston, 1950), 256–7.

[131] See n. 70 above.

[132] *Commentaries*, 9 vols., (Boston, 1832–45).

[133] *Professional Ethics* (Philadelphia, 1854).

[134] *Treatise on Evidence* (Boston, 1848). The 13th edition of this work appeared in 1876. It was also published in London.

regularly, can also be largely discounted for similar reasons. The authority of Sharswood's work derived largely from his prominence as a judge and public figure. Any of these works, if written by a genuinely academic author, might well have achieved unmarked obscurity.

George Wythe, the greatest teacher, made no contribution at all to academic literature. George Robertson, the most important teacher at Transylvania, wrote little[135] other than judicial opinions, and his work is now long forgotten. Professor Timothy Walker of the University Cincinnati wrote an excellent one-volume work on American law that saw six antebellum editions.[136] It was addressed to a lay audience, and while useful probably had no influence on the development of the law. The most intellectually ambitious body of work on American law in the era before the Civil War was the work of Francis Lieber. While much of his work was widely read and admired by men such as Kent and Story, it is difficult to trace any consequence to his work until he served actively in the War Department during the Civil War. There, he was the sole author of General Order 100 controlling the conduct of Union troops in occupied territory, an order adopted *in haec verba* by the Prussian army in 1870, and adopted in 1907 by a Hague Convention as the international law of war.[137]

One academic author possibly having a material influence on legal thought in antebellum America was a sometime law professor, Thomas Cooper, sometime president of the University of South Carolina.[138] Cooper was in his youth 'an English Jacobin'. After coming to America, he served a prison term for sedition against President Adams, published books on chemistry, bankruptcy law, libel law, and political economy, and edited the American edition of Justinian. He also earned the condemnation of Daniel Webster as the 'Schoolmaster of Slavery', for he was thought to be the author or chief propogator of the rationalization that slavery is a necessary condition of a free society.[139] Cooper's theory (if indeed it was his) was that an underclass is inevitable, and the preservation of republican freedom for the overclass depends on effective control and nurture of the underclass, a condition maintainable over time only by means of the institution of slavery. This thesis was assuredly heard on the lips of many an antebellum politician. Cooper's possible importance as a source of this theory

[135] *Scrap Book on Law and Politics, Men and Times* (Lexington, 1855).

[136] *Introduction to American Law* (1st ed., Philadelphia, 1837, 11th edn., 1907).

[137] See generally F. Friedel, n. 94 above; E. Root, *Addresses on International Subjects* (Cambridge, 1916), 89–103.

[138] See generally D. Malone, n. 73 above.

[139] The idea had solid English origins dating from 1701: L. Tise, *Proslavery: A History of the Defense of Slavery in America, 1701–1840*, (Athens, 1987), 97–123.

illustrates how academic authors can be 'influential' by uttering theory that is congenial to their cultures.

As noted, there was at the outset of the second century of American law a major shift in theory and method animated by both the post-war search for order and the global impulse to technocracy. To attribute that moment of formalism to the efforts of positivist legal theoreticians[140] such as Ames would deny the effects of the overwhelming cultural force that underlay the development. The most that might be conceded is that the moment was a bit longer on account of their efforts.

Indeed, the Langdell 'scientific' tbeory of law was never accepted by thoughtful contemporaties.[141] Not even Ames's, colleagues at Harvard, James Bradley Thayer[142] and especially John Chipman Gray,[143] were seriously infected by the momentary spirit of formalism. Formalism was bitterly denounced by Oliver Wendell Holmes, Jun., in 1897.[144] It seems not to have impeded the avowedly politicized efforts of Cooley at the University of Michigan, a judge-professor cut in the antebellum mould, whose work on American Constitutional Law was widely cited by the Supreme Court,[145] albeit at times in support of decisions in which he might not have concurred. And assuredly the moment did not control the early twentieth-century teaching of Eugene Gilmore at the University of Wisconsin, a committed political Progressive,[146] whose ideas became the Legal Realism of Columbia and Yale a few decades later.[147] By the time of Roscoe Pound's deanship in 1915, the

[140] The authors of *Form and Substance* stop just short of doing so: see p. 246–8.

[141] See e.g. 'Report of Committee on Legal Education' (1892) 15 *ABA Proceedings* 317.

[142] See e.g. his 'Law and Logic' (1900) 14 *Harv. LR* 139.

[143] See his *The Nature and Sources of Law* (Boston, 1910).

[144] 'The Path of the Law' (1897) 10 *Harv. LR* 457.

[145] American academics have seldom been subject to the monstrous discourtesy of being treated as unworthy of judicial attention. One never needed to die to be cited: *The Oracles of the Law*, 97. One might also be invited to speak to an audience of judges. As one who has done a share of such speaking, I can attest that the judicial audience is always courteous to academics. That this courtesy could extend so far as to result in official action taken in response to an academic presentation cannot be confirmed by this author.

[146] For a chronicle of Progressivism and the politics of the times, see R. Hofstedter, *The Age of Reform* (New York, 1965). The Progressive Movement was in some respects a renewal of the democratic impulse, an effort to engage the people actively in governing at all levels.

[147] Gilmore's interests spanned environmental law, criminology, and law and economics. For an expression of his views, see his 'Some Criticisms of Legal Education' (1921) 7 *ABAJ* 227, 231. For an account of his role in the founding of the American Law Institute, see N. E. H. Hull, 'Restatement and Reform: A New Perspective on the Origins of the American Law Institute' (1990) 8 *Law and Hist. Rev.* 55, 67–70. Underhill Moore, Ernest Lorenzen, and Walter Wheeler Cook were junior associates of Gilmore's at Wisconsin. On the subsequent careers of this trio at Yale, see L. Kalman, *Legal Realism at Yale, 1927–1960* (Chapel Hill, 1986) and J. H. Schlegel, 'American Legal Realism and

moment of formalism was in full retreat.[148] He was appointed as dean despite sentiments about his colleagues' teaching that would do honor to contemporary radicals, and incidentally reflected an exaggerated conception of the influence of American law-teaching: 'The conflict between our law and those who are working for social progress has its roots in our teaching of the law . . . It is not the recall of judges or the recall of judicial decisions that should be invoked, but rather the recall of law teachers, or at least the recall of a great deal of law teaching.'[149]

The moment of formalism probably gave heart to the efforts of great academic treatise writers: Wigmore, Williston, Scott, and a few others. But even these worthy scholars were seldom deceived by antiseptic formalism. Their work was, as it was intended, useful to courts and lawyers in comprehending whole fields of American private law that had never before been synthesized. Some judicial users of such works may have treated them in a formal way, much as an English court might have treated a parliamentary enactment. But the authors were not so innocent as to suppose an absence of political content in their work, except in so far as they, as virtuous citizens of the republic, eschewed partisanship.

Just as Langdell and Ames can scarcely be credited or blamed for the moment of formalism, so its demise can scarcely be attributed to the literary efforts of Pound, Karl Llewellyn, and other academics.[150] It was only a moment, a mere sand-bar in the course of a great river, destined to be swept downstream at the next rising of the current. Pound and Llewellyn, however they may have seen themselves, were less the cause than the manifestation of its disappearance.

As it happens, both Pound and Llewellyn had more consequential work to perform, Pound as one of the most influential judicial law-reformers of the twentieth century, and Llewellyn as the draftsman of the Uniform Commercial Code. While each produced academic literature associated with his reform endeavours, much of it could have been regarded by the most élite academic standards as more pedestrian

Empirical Social Science: From the Yale Experience' (1979) 28 *Buffalo L. Rev.* 459. For an account of the movement in which they had earlier engaged at Columbia, see B. Currie, 'The Materials of Law Study (II)' (1955) 8 *J. Leg. Ed.* 1.

148 In retreat, it may have attracted some overreactions, exemplified by the expression of radical 'realist' views such as those suggesting that judges stop publishing opinions: see e.g. J. W. Bingham, 'What is the Law?' (1912) 11 *Mich. LR*; and see E. Purcell, 'American Jurisprudence Between the Wars: Legal Realism and the Crisis of Democratic Theory' (1969) 75 *Am. Hist. Rev.* 424.

149 [1912] *Proceedings of the Association of American Law Schools* 55, 60.

150 Atiyah and Summers are cautious, but seem to attach more consequence to the corrective writing of the Realists than circumstances warrant: see *Form and Substance*, 251–2.

than Pound's writings on Sociological Jurisprudence[151] or Llewellyn's on Legal Realism.[152] On the other hand, Llewellyn especially came to see his own legal theory as essentially anti-general, anti-ideological, even anti-theoretical.[153] In this, he manifested a kinship with earlier American legal pragmatists such as Jefferson and the antebellum law teachers.

No sooner did legal academic writing appear in America than it became an additional source of authority for judicial decisions that needed to be explained to a doubting public. But such citation was often use, not influence.[154] One must generally express thoughts agreeable to authority, as Cooley, for example, often did, in order to merit frequent citation. American courts had long cited almost anything to justify their decisions, and social-science data were soon to be used in the same way.[155] But academic argument or analysis, or even stubborn data,[158] leading to an unwelcome conclusion are likely to be ignored by judges when engaged in self-justification. Legislative committees and administrative agencies often use academic work in much the same way.

Still influential are treatise-writers who provide structure for the thinking of lawyers and judges about legal doctrine. The structure they provide is reinforced by formal law-teaching, and enables legal discourse to proceed more effectively. But many, perhaps most, contemporary treatises are written by lawyers, not academics. Unlike the classical private-law treatises, most find their subject and their structure in legislation, and serve to synthesize judicial exegesis of legislation. This is very useful work, and the person who does it earns and receives a measure of influence with judges and lawyers. Seldom is such work now done by the academic élite.[157]

An example of academic influence in America is provided by

[151] E.g., E. Pound, 'Common Law and Legislation' (1908) 21 *Harv. LR* 383 and *An Introduction to the Philosophy of Law* (New Haven, 1922).

[152] See especially K. Llewellyn, 'Some Realism about Realism' (1931) 44 *Harv. LR* 1222.

[153] *Jurisprudence* (Boston, 1970).

[154] E.g., D. Owen, 'Punitive Damages in Product Liability Litigation' (1976) 74 *Mich. LR* 1257, cited in *Form and Substance* at 402 n.

[155] Louis Brandeis filed his historic data-filled brief in *Muller v. Oregon*, 208 US 412 (1908). This way be taken as a sign that in that year Brandeis believed that the sitting justices recognized their political responsibility, and were interested in the social consequences of their decisions.

[156] D. Horowitz, *Courts and Social Policy* (Washington, DC, 1977) *passim*. See also P. D. Carrington, 'Foreword: Empirical Studies of Civil Procedure' (1989) 51–3 *Law and Contemp. Prob.* 1.

[157] A. W. B. Simpson, 'The Rise and Fall of the Legal Treatise: Legal principles and the Forms of Legal Literature' (1981) 48 U. Chi. LR 632. Excellent counterexamples are G. Palmer, *Restitution*, 4 vols. (Indianapolis, 1980); C. Wright and A. Miller, *treatise on Federal Practice and Procedure*, 2d edn., 27 vols, (St Paul, 1983–90); A. Larson, *Workmen's Compensation for Occupational Injuries and Death* (New York, 1972–90). There are others.

American tort law. There has been much academic writing on the subject in the twentieth century, and tort law has evolved substantially over that time. Whether the change in the law is the consequence of the excellent academic writing done by persons such as Leon Green[158] seems doubtful.[159] Surely a bigger factor has been the political activity of labour unions, trial lawyers, and others amplifying the stark fact that American law was appallingly inconsiderate of accident victims. One did not need to read Green to see that something had to be done. On the other hand, in order to *do* something about the law of torts, it helped for the professor to become a Justice, as Professor Roger Traynor did.[160]

What was in fact done to the law of torts may be no credit to anyone, for we have designed for America a monstrously expensive system of compensation that benefits lawyers more than victims. Professors Robert Keeton and Jeffrey O'Connell have, as academic ministers without portfolios, led the assault on the system.[161] To the extent that they have been effective, it has been because they have worked within the political system. Their academic literary product was an expression of direct political initiatives and seldom burdened their readers with theoretical exegesis.

It is for legal academics in America an unwelcome reality that there is often a choice to be made between work that can and may be applied usefully to current public issues and work that is intellectually more ambitious, more personally gratifying, and more likely to win recognition among academics. For scholars, American or English, who write literature not confronting in practical terms issues of current concern to persons making decisions, their certain fate is to be ignored by those whom they ignore.

While the relationship is far from exact, it is probably true within the operative limits that intellectual ambition and public service are negative correlates. This is so because persons making public decisions often welcome authoritative advice on narrower issues that can be resolved with little concern for broad social and political values, but are

158 See e.g. *Judge and Jury* (New Haven, 1930); *Proximate Cause* (New Haven, 1934); *Traffic Victims, Tort Law and Insurance* (Chicago, 1958). Cf. G. E. White, 'The Impact of Legal Science on Tort Law 1890–1910' (1978) 78 *Colum. LR* 213.

159 But see C. Priest, 'The Invention of Enterprise Liability: A Critical History of the Intellectual Foundations of Modern Tort Law' (1985) 14 *J. Leg. St.* 461. Cf. G. Calabresi, *The Costs of Accidents* (New Haven, 1970).

160 As a justice of the Supreme Court of Califormia, Roger Traynor played a significant role in the transformation of American tort law. It is perverse to contend that Traynor's judicial efforts are a manifestation of academic influence. See *Form and Substance*, 402 n.

161 See e.g. *Basic Protection for the Traffic Victim: A Blueprint for Reforming Automobile Insurance* (Boston, 1965). Cf. S. D. Sugarman, 'Doing Away with Tort Law' (1985) 73 *Calif. LR* 555.

seldom influenced by the politics or philosophies of academics, or even of their law clerks fresh from the academy. The possibility that much academically fashionable interdisciplinary legal scholarship will ever find application seems remote. Those working in the stratosphere of economic theories of law, or who debate the congruence of constitutional doctrine with classical political theory, or who deconstruct such discourses, have made a choice to remove themselves for at least a time from the arena in which direct influence on real events is possible. As Tocqueville observed in this very context: 'The world is not led by long or learned demonstrations: a rapid glance at particular incidents, the daily study of the fleeting passions of the multitude, the accidents of time, and the art of turning them to account, decide all its affairs.'[162]

For this reason, theorizing about law is perhaps the activity of law professors least likely to bear on the course of events; abstraction is often the enemy of influence.[163] Perhaps this is the nature of all philosophy. Perhaps this trait of political and judicial pragmatism is partly inherited from the English.[164] But it is probably especially true in America that large public decisions are seldom influenced by legal theory, for these are almost always subordinated to the practical considerations that control decision-making in a democracy constrained in part by an élite judiciary.[165] In the American condition, much public decision-making must inevitably be fact-bound and compromised. Theoretical coherence is not a plausible expectation.

American legal theory is therefore primarily for legal theoreticians.[166] This being so, real 'influence' may be moving away from members of élite law faculties with the greatest status within the academic profession to those with lesser pretensions to theory and closer acquaintance with reality, who may be more willing to do the world's legal work.[167] On the other hand, American law may be due for a

[162] *Democracy in America*, vol. 2, 43 (n. 48 above).

[163] Cf. H. F. Jolowicz, 'Utility and Elegance in Civil Law Studies' (1949) 65 *LQR* 322; D. A. Farber, 'The Case Against Brilliance' (1986) 70 *Minn. LR* 917.

[164] See generally Atiyah, n. 118 above.

[165] Tocqueville observed Americans to be generally preoccupied with instances and averse to theory. *Democracy in America*, vol. 2, 41 ff (n. 48 above).

[166] I emphasize 'primary'. Legal theory is not 'the mere plaything of academic scribblers'. R. Summers, n. 36 above, at 34.

[167] This means of influence on American law is widely shared among American law teachers; it is by no means limited to those who teach at schools that attain the critics' list of the top 25. For such a list, see *US News and World Report*, 6 Apr. 1990. Atiyah and Summers draw too sharp a distinction between the élite American law schools and others. If the frame of reference is influence, genuine influence on the development of legal institutions, there are many law professors at lower-status institutions whose careers are far more influential than many law professors at prestige schools who could be named.

modification of its sights not unlike that which has overtaken some American science, science that is now preoccupied with a reconsideration of many seemingly small problems previously overlooked by scientists seeking to synthesize too much.[168] Until recently, the badge of sovereignty in the hierarchy of science (like that of academic law) has been work presenting transcendent abstraction. Such work is now less likely to be regarded as 'cutting edge' stuff. Rising in science is an appreciation of work that rediscovers reality in the homely details of familiar natural occurrences. I would encourage such a movement in legal scholarship. The question is whether law teachers could return to the farm of prosaic legal problems after seeing the vast city of philosophy.

Whichever of the three means a law teacher may employ to influence the law and the culture that created him or her, the enterprise is highly speculative. The work resembles that of the forester whose plantings will become trees or not largely as a consequence of forces and events completely beyond her control, most of them occurring long after she has retired from the scene. Perhaps that is well. Whether the world would be improved if law professors really were effecting many results may itself be a large question. Would there be credit received or blame borne? It is comforting that even Nietzsche bears neither credit nor blame for the twentieth century, but was merely a product of his time and place.

[168] See generally J. Gleick, *Chaos: Making a New Science* (New York, 1987). A founder of the new science of 'chaology', Edward Lorenz, is known, among other things, for his discovery of the Butterfly Effect, so named for the butterfly in China who may, by beating his wings, set off a chain of causation resulting in a material shift in the weather across the southern hemisphere (ibid, 20–3). Lorenz teaches that long-range weather prophecy is impossible, that vast theoretical hypotheses intended for use in weather prediction are probably vain, and that truth, at least in his field, is more effectively pursued at a lower altitude of generalization, with humbler pretensions are expectations. I have, echoing Lorenz, uttered a similar challenge to the federal judiciary. 'Courts of Appeals—District Court Relations', in *The Federal Courts in the Twenty-First Century* (Washington, 1990).

7

The Role of the Judiciary: Lessons from the End of Empire

ROBERT STEVENS[1]

This paper is an attempt to analyse the relationship between, on the one hand, the role of courts as governmental institutions; and, on the other, the way and the grounds on which judges are selected to hear particular cases, and the views and attitudes of judges concerning the political significance of their decisions. This issue will be approached through a study of the work of the Judicial Committee of the Privy Council over the last one hundred years. Among other things, the study will bear out Patrick Atiyah's view[2] that there is an 'English belief that it is largely immaterial which judges hear which appeals', which leads to a failure to appreciate that the composition of a court can determine in advance the outcome of cases of political significance.

The Privy Council entered the twentieth century as the final appeal court for the Dominions and colonies, and it laboured under a heavy appellate burden. The make-up of the Privy Council was purposely casual; Lord Chancellors—or their Permanent Secretaries—frequently gave qualified persons 'interesting cases'.[3] English examinations and discussions of the Committee's work started from the premiss of the 'excellence' and quality of the English judiciary. Yet, looking back over the decades at a court which was entrusted with the interpretation—for instance—of those forty-seven documents that go to make up the Constitution of Canada, one is surprised by the ignorance of many of

[1] The author wishes to thank the following for constructive comments: Jill Cottrell, Christopher McCrudden, Katherine Booth Stevens, William Twining, Edward Veitch, Catherine Walsh, and Robin Winks. Defects, of course, are his own. He also wishes to thank Judi Tessier and Mara van der Pas of his staff for support; as well as the staff of the libraries of the University of California, Santa Cruz and the Law School of the University of New Brunswick. Part of the history in Section (3) relies on *Law and Politics*. Part of this article comes from his inaugural lecture as professor of history at the University of California, Santa Cruz, in January 1990, and this paper was the basis of a faculty seminar at University College, London, in June, 1990.

[2] P. S. Atiyah and R. S. Summers, *Form and Substance in Anglo-American Law* (Oxford 1987), 269.

[3] Ibid., *passim*. See also A. Paterson, *The Law Lords* (Oxford, 1982), 87–9.

the English Law Lords about the nature of a federal constitution and the concept of judicial review.[4]

In the light of English attitudes to the judicial role, denials by judges that their decisions might be of any political importance are not surprising; nor is the remarkable claim that, since appeal courts applied only pre-existing law and did not make political decisions, there was no reason why the Judicial Committee should not be manipulated *qua* court for political purposes, especially for strengthening the Empire and later the Commonwealth. As the declaratory theory of the judicial role in the appellate process and the tradition of substantive formalism hardened in the late nineteenth and early twentieth centuries, politicians engaged in a series of strange political contortions in their dealings over the Privy Council. Just as the apolitical appearance of the English judges allowed them to be siphoned off for apparently non-political purposes, such as the chairing of Royal Commissions, so the Judicial Committee became a strange—apparently apolitical—subject for Imperial and later Commonwealth political concerns.

1. A Case Study of Canada

The British North America Act of 1867 (now known in Canada as the Constitution Act) was held to have left in place the appeal to the Judicial Committee of the Privy Council, an appeal which survived until 1949. One has to be aware of the danger, in looking at the broad sweep of the intervening years, of simplifying what the Privy Council wrought. The Canadian constitution, like the US Constitution, has more than its share of subtleties and nuances in the forty-seven documents that go to make it up. Criticism of the Privy Council's handling of Canadian cases in those early years was based on competing notions of what might now be called 'original intent' in the United States; or, looked at in the context of English legal culture, different approaches to statutory interpretation.[5] Most commentators felt the Privy Council had distorted the centralist intention of the

[4] See, for instance, Lord Halsbury's observation that, 'I do not know what an unconstitutional act means'. Halsbury apparently believed the Royal assent ousted judicial review: quoted in M. Ollivier, *Le Canada, Pays Souverain?* (Montreal, 1936), 176. The position was most strenuously argued in *Webb* v. *Outrim* [1907] AC 81 (PC), where Halsbury refused to follow the American cases used by the High Court of Ausralia. The *Law Quarterly Review* described the Halsbury view as 'illusory as it is obscure': note (1907), 23 *LQR* 130. The decision was therefore ignored in Australia. With respect to Canada, the most that might be said for Halsbury was that the Constitution Act, 1867, in its preamble, said that Canada had adopted a constitution 'similar in principle to that of the United Kingdom'.

[5] Alan C. Cairns, 'The Judicial Committee and Its Critics', (1971) 4 *Canadian Journal of Political Science* 301.

confederators.[6] A later burst of criticism—from a group known as the Constitutionists—felt that the Privy Council had failed in its Canadian mission because it had failed to treat the British legislation as a Constitution and insisted on treating it as any other statute.[7] While these 'schools' of criticism often overlapped, each reflected important and different jurisprudential approaches.

While the Law Lords, sitting informally as the Judicial Committee of the Privy Council in a room off Downing Street and applying the formalistic and declaratory approach to law, settled the great crises of constitutional law in the Dominion of Canada, there is little reason to believe that this group of men knew much about the political disputes they were settling. Indeed, they probably knew little of Canadian politics—few members of the British Establishment did. British judges had generally not visited Canada and had a patronizing view of Canadian judges and lawyers.[8] The English legal culture, however, revolving around the mechanistic implications of the declaratory theory, regarded all that as irrelevant.

In this context, it is worth noting that by the mid-seventies of the last century, there were already efforts being made to end the appeal to London.[9] Looked at purely from a political point of view, what probably saved the appeal in these early years was an apparent change in the interpretation of the 1867 Act by the Privy Council. For the first dozen years of appeals, the Act was generally regarded as having been interpreted in a 'balanced' or 'neutral' way, but by the 1880s and 1890s, under the influence of Lord Watson,[10] there was a move perceived by many critics as being designed to protect Provincial powers at the expense of Dominion ones.[11] The Watson approach was continued by

[6] Ibid. 302.

[7] Ibid. 307.

[8] See, for instance, Sir Almeric Fitzroy's (Clerk of the Privy Council) surprised description of the Canadian Chief Justice, Sir Charles Fitzpatrick: 'Fitzpatrick is much above the usual type of colonial lawyer, a man of polished manners, intelligent address and not without distinct judicial virtue.' Sir Almeric Fitzroy, *Memoirs* (New York, 1925), ii. 490. In turn, Fitzpatrick had an appropriately deferential approach to the 'mother country's' judiciary. He claimed that 'amongst lawyers and Judges competent to speak on the subject there is but one voice, that where constitutional questions are concerned, an appeal to the Judicial Committee must be retained'. Fitzpatrick, 'The Constitution of Canada' (1914), 34 *Canadian LR* 1031.

[9] Coen G. Pierson, *Canada and the Privy Council* (London, 1960), 16–21.

[10] Stevens, *Law and Politics* (London, 1979), 179–80.

[11] David B. Swinfen, *Imperial Appeal: The Debate On The Appeal to the Privy Council, 1833–1986* (Manchester, 1987), 28–9. On this, see generaly W. I. Jennings, 'Constitutional Interpretation: The Experience of Canada' (1937) 51 *Harv. LR*, 1. The harshest criticism of Watson's contributions probably come in the O'Connor Report in 1939, published by the Federal Senate, (the 'Fatal Error in Construction'). For a critique of the O'Connor Committee's positions, see G. P. Browne, *The Judicial Committee and The British North America Act* (Toronto, 1967), 58 ff.

his disciple, Lord Haldane.[12] This trend meant that, in the future, any tampering with the Judicial Committee immediately involved the spectre of the politics of Federal-Provincial relations.

Of a significantly different stripe was Viscount Sankey—the English judge who was to become the favourite of the Constitutionists. Sankey, who became Lord Chancellor in 1929, did make a limited effort to return some power to the Dominion government, but, more importantly, unlike Watson and Haldane, Sankey broadened Loreburn's view that a constitution was not just another statute. In reversing the Supreme Court of Canada and holding that women could be appointed to the Canadian Senate, Sankey noted that

> the British North America Act planted in Canada a living tree capable of growth and expansion within its natural limits . . . Their Lordships do not conceive it to be the duty of this Board—it is certainly not their desire—to cut down the provisions of the Act by a narrow and technical construction, but rather to give it a large and liberal interpretation.[13]

Thus, Sankey was prepared to do what Haldane was not, and in the context of the Statute of Westminster of 1931, which was largely his creation, he allowed Canada to abolish criminal appeals. Sankey also presided in the decision that held air navigation to be exclusively within the power of the Dominion, and shortly thereafter broadcasting was held to be exclusively a federal matter.[14]

The work—both in substance and style—of Watson and Haldane was, however, strongly ingrained. When Ramsey MacDonald lost the premiership in 1935, and Sankey, much to his discomfort,[15] ceased to be Lord Chancellor, there was a move back towards a more formalistic approach to the interpretation of the 1867 legislation. That, in a system of *stare decisis* and conventional statutory construction, inevitably meant deferring to the pro-provincial slant of Watson and Haldane. Moreover, the new Chancellor, Lord Hailsham (the father of the recent Lord Chancellor), was not above packing the Judicial Committee to ensure that there was no 'law making', something which, because the pre-

[12] Stevens, n. 10 above, 200 n. Indeed, Haldane went further than Watson and developed the theory that trade and commerce power was available to the Dominion only in an emergency. Ibid.

[13] *Edwards* v. *Attorney-General for Canada* [1930] AC 124, 136 (PC).

[14] *British Coal Corporation* v. *The King* [1935] AC 500 (PC); *In re Regulations and Control of Aeronautics in Canada* [1932] AC 54 (PC); *In re Regulation and Control of Radio Communications in Canada* [1932] AC 304 (PC).

[15] Stevens, n. 10 above, 227. As part of the political settlement in 1935, Ramsey MacDonald was replaced by Stanley Baldwin. MacDonald might have negotiated the continuance of Sankey as Lord Chancellor, 'but in fact MacDonald was anxious to secure a Cabinet post for his son, Malcolm. So he jettisoned Sankey.' R. F. V. Heuston, *Lives of the Lord Chancellors, 1885–1940* (London, 1969), 527.

vailing legal culture denied the relevance of judicial predispositions, was made all too easy.[16]

The results were almost inevitable.

It is possible, though it cannot be proved, that the desire of Mr Ramsey MacDonald in 1935 to safeguard his son's political career, and the anxiety of Lord Hailsham to leave the lower office for the more exalted and better paid position on the Woolsack—circumstances which sent Lord Sankey into retirement—invalidated a large part of the Canadian 'New Deal'.[17]

Thus, when Canadian Prime Minister Bennett's Conservative government passed its 'New Deal' legislation in 1934 and 1935, the Privy Council solemnly struck down vital parts of it. During November 1936, the Judicial Committee heard five related appeals and gave judgment on them in 1937. Lord Atkin, who presided, and who was not an admirer of the Statute of Westminster,[18] announced that, unlike Sankey's 'living tree', '[w]hile the ship of state now sails on longer ventures and into foreign waters she still retains the watertight compartments which are an essential part of her original structure'. The result of the 'watertight compartments' was that, in a single day, the Judicial Committee struck down the efforts of the Ottawa government to implement the International Labour Organization conventions by providing a minimum-wage law and by limiting hours of work,[19] the unemployment and social-insurance legislation,[20] and federal marketing boards.[21] Only the relatively unimportant provisions with respect to unfair trade-practices survived.[22] It is probable that Lord Wright dissented in some of these cases,[23] and some believe the swing vote was an English tax judge, Rowlatt J, who was sitting to make up the quorum. While some writers have recently sought to take a more sympathetic view of the decisions on the ground that the Privy Council, in general, was merely following decisions of the Supreme Court of Canada,[24] the dispatches from the High Commission in Ottawa made it clear that the political outrage was widespread.

16 Ibid. 531.

17 Jennings, n. 10 above, 36.

18 Geoffrey Lewis, *Lord Atkin*, (London, 1983), 110. Hailsham reported that he had originally invited Sankey to preside: ibid. 100.

19 *Attorney-General for Canada* v. *Attorney-General for Ontario* [1937] AC 326, 354 (PC).

20 Ibid.

21 *Attorney-General for British Columbia* v. *Attorney-General for Canada* [1937] AC 405 (PC).

22 *Attorney-General for Ontario* v. *Attorney-General for Canada* [1937] AC 405 (PC).

23 Jennings, n. 10 above, 36.

24 Browne, *Judicial Committee*; Swinfen, *Imperial Appeal*, 152: 'In retrospect, it is difficult to understand why the Committee's decision with respect to these acts aroused so much ill feeling in Canada.' C. G. Pierson, *Canada and the Privy Council* (London, 1960), 68: 'Their rulings were not only good law, but they were made impartially in the light of constitutional history.' For a balanced view, see Paul Freund, *The Supreme Court of the United States* (New York, 1961), 107–8.

The decisions were given in January 1937. The High Commissioner in Ottawa sent to the Dominions Office in London, in April, a report read carefully by the Lord Chancellor's Office, that there was a 'growing body of opinion in favour of the abolition of appeals to the Privy Council'. The most outspoken critic was M. C. H. Cahan, a former Secretary of State in the Bennett Cabinet who referred, in the Canadian House of Commons debate, 'to futile efforts of this Committee of the Privy Council of the United Kingdom to revive and reassert reactionary policies'.[25] By 1939, Cahan had introduced a Bill to abolish appeals to London, and his career was watched carefully in the Lord Chancellor's Office. Even in the grimmest days of 1940, the Permanent Secretary in the Lord Chancellor's Office, Sir George Schuster, took a healthy interest in the Canadian election returns, writing to a London solicitor: 'I had also noted that Mr Cahan had been defeated. I hope I am not committing an indiscretion when I say that the news gave me a considerable amount of pleasure.'[26]

The reprieve was, however, a temporary one. The O'Connor Report of 1939, commissioned by the Canadian Senate and concluding that the Privy Council had turned a primarily centralized constitution into a strongly federal one, led to a reference to the Supreme Court of Canada with respect to the power of the Dominion to abolish all appeals to the Privy Council. In January 1940, the Supreme Court held that Canada had such power under the Statute of Westminster.[27] During the Second World War, the domestic pressure in Canada to abolish appeals was reduced, but few thought the arrangement would survive the post-war period, and in 1947 the Privy Council in London confirmed the opinion of the Supreme Court of Canada that the right to abolish existed.[28] Lord Chancellor Jowitt, even though he presided in that appeal to the Privy Council, still had a faint hope that the Canadians might keep their appeals.

It was not a totally unrealistic hope. Many of the provinces were reluctant to see the appeal go. In a *Canadian Bar Review* symposium, for instance, it was argued that the Privy Council, 'in its anxiety to disclaim imperialistic tendencies offensive to the *zeitgeist*, proved its generosity at the expense of the provinces'. The Dominion, the argument went, could not abolish appeals with respect to provincial powers, despite the Statute of Westminster.[29] Moreover, Mackenzie

[25] F. L. C. Flood to Malcolm MacDonald (Secretary for Dominion Affairs), 21 Apr. 1937 (LCO 2/3456).

[26] Schuster to Quintin Iwi, 1 Apr. 1940 (ibid).

[27] Stevens, n. 10 above, 202. For a study of the reference process, see John McElroy, 'Separation of Powers and the Reference Power: Is there a right to refuse?' (1988), 10 *Supreme Court LR* 429.

[28] *Attorney-Gereral for Ontario* v. *Attorney-General for Canada* [1947] AC 127.

[29] 'Abolition of Appeals to the Privy Council: A Symposium' (1947) 25 *Can. B. R.* 557. S. M. Gordon at 558.

King, by then Prime Minister, always concerned about 'the British vote', had doubts about whether appeals to London should be abolished.[30]

Jowitt was anxious to save the system. As Labour Attorney-Gerneral in the 1929–31 administration, he had fought tenaciously to keep the Irish Free State from abolishing appeals. Now, in the post-war period, he visited Canada and then persuaded Attlee, the Prime Minister, to appoint Rinfret,[31] the Canadian Chief Justice, as one of the Commonwealth judges entitled to sit in the Privy Council, hoping this might undermine the Canadian enthusiasm for abolishing appeals to the Privy Council.[32] The ruse did not work, and appeals to London were abolished in 1949.[33]

2. And who, pray shall sit?

The politics of the Rinfret experience, however, raised an important constitutional point. Since 1895, so-called Colonial judges could be appointed as members of the Privy Council; but which ones should be? The assumption was that, if the judges were 'good', it mattered not at all the political or social background of the judge, let alone his nationality. During the Second World War, Watermeyer, the newly appointed South African Chief Justice, was made a member of the Privy Council. Since South African appeals were in the process of

[30] James G. Snell and Frederick Vaughan, *The Supreme Court of Canada: History of the Institution* (Toronto, 1985), 190.

[31] Rinfret, who has been educated both at Laval and McGill and had been appointed to the Supreme Court of Canada in 1924. Ignace-J. DeLauriers, *La Cour superieure du Quebec et ses juges, 1849–1980*, (Qvebec, 1980), 221. By 1950, he 'tended to show his impatience in court': Snell and Vaughan, n. 30 above, 197. He did not have a good reputation in civil-liberties cases: Paul Weiler, *In The Last Resort: A Critical Study of the Supreme Court of Canada* (Toronto, 1974), 187–8.

[32] 'I was myself responsible for suggesting the appointment of Chief Justice Rinfret, and my reason for making the suggestion was that I hoped—rather against hope—that the fact that the Canadian Chief Justice was so appointed might influence the Canadian Government against the abolition of the appeal.' Jowitt to Gordon Walker, 7 Feb. 1951 (LCO 2/5227).

[33] The British High Commissioner in Ottawa reported on the dinner to celebrate the confirmation of the Supreme Court of Canada as the final court of appeal: 'From the standpoint of the UK, the proceedings could not have been happier or more gratifying. Every speaker was at pains to make it clear that there was nothing but the highest admiration and respect in Canada for the Judicial Committee of the Privy Council and for the work which it had done for Canada over the years. The change now being made had certainly not come about from any sense of dissatisfaction; on the contrary, there was no Court in the world which had a higher standing than the Judicial Committee and no Court in the world which surpassed it in wisdom, integrity and professional competence; the present chage had merely arisen, as it was bound to do in time, in the course of Canada's natural evolution and development.' Sir Alexander Clutterbuck to Dominions Office, 12 Oct. 1950 (LCO 2/5227).

ending,[34] the appointment may be thought to have been made more in the cause of the war, than the jurisprudential, effort.

The civil servants were somewhat skeptical of these efforts. Rinfret had been an idea of Jowitt's when he had been visiting Canada, and his appointment had been cleared by both Attlee and the Governor-General.[35] Yet, when the Dominions Office started pressing for the appointment of the New Zealand Chief Justice, Sir Humphrey O'Leary, in 1947, Napier (then Permanent Secretary of the Lord Chancellor's Department) was cool. He wrote to du Parcq LJ and Dallas Waters in the Privy Council Office to see whether O'Leary was 'up' to the Privy Council standard. Eventually, Dominions Office pressure won out, and O'Leary was appointed.[36]

At home, meanwhile, there was a shortage of Law Lords. By 1946, the clerks of the Privy Council were complaining. It was not so much that there were more cases, but that they were taking much longer. With only one ex-Lord Chancellor available, the Judicial Committee had been borrowing from the Court of Appeal, and for six weeks in 1945 the House of Lords had to suspend sittings. The only area where the clerks felt comfortable was in Indian appeals where there were still two salaried ex-Indian Judges available.[37] The hearing of Indian appeals with only three judges, however—the two 'Indian' judges and one other—was an anathema to the India Office, because it strengthened the hostility to appeals to London. If respect for appeals was to be maintained, the India Office demanded that 'real' Law Lords had to outnumber the salaried judges.[38]

The Prime Minister agreed to two additional Law Lords with surprisingly little fuss, although the Treasury insisted on a certificate of need before anyone was actually named.[39] Filling the positions proved to be treacherous, since Thankerton had resigned, and du Parcq was openly upset about weakening the Court of Appeal by raiding it for Law Lords,[40] but in March 1947, Oaksey, Morton, and MacDermott were appointed. The Commonwealth problem, however, would not go away.

In August 1949, Jowitt was writing to Attlee, complaining that he was having trouble staffing both the Privy Council and the House of Lords: 'Maugham, Roche, and I regret to add, Wright, have become too old, too deaf or too garrulous. The other judges are now objecting

[34] Finally abolished in 1950: Swinfen, n. 11 above, 157–61.
[35] LCO 2/3453.
[36] 17 Sept. 1947 (ibid).
[37] Memorandum from Clerks of the Privy Council and House of Lords, 26 Nov. 1946 (LCO 2/3461).
[38] Kemp to Napier, 30 Nov. 1946 (ibid).
[39] Ibid.
[40] Waters (Privy Council) to Jowitt, 16 Jan. 1947 (ibid).

to sit with the latter. Simon still helps from time to time but is getting very slow and whenever he presides the case takes far longer than it should if properly handled'.[41] Jowitt was anxious that Canadian and Indian cases be well heard; and he still harboured the hope that both would retain appeals to the Privy Council.[42] One of the problems with Indian appeals was that Sir Madharam Nair, one of the two paid Indian judges, was 'rather a broken reed'[43] It was becoming clear, moreover, that once India proclaimed itself a republic, appeals from that quarter would end.[44] By January 1950, the era was all over and the Republic declared. The High Commissioner in New Delhi reported that 'nothing has impressed the people of India more than the high sense of detachment, independence and impartiality which have invariably governed the deliberations and decisions of the Privy Council'.[45]

As the Labour administration drew to a close in 1951, Patrick Gordon Walker, the Commonwealth Relations Secretary, wrote to Jowitt about membership of the Judicial Committee of the Privy Council. He thought that, although Canada had abolished appeals, the tradition of appointing its Chief Justice should be continued.[46] He also thought it important that the Chief Justice of Ceylon, a country which had continued appeals, should be appointed. Although South Africa had abolished appeals and Prime Minister Malan had turned down a Privy Councillorship for himself, perhaps he would let his Chief Justice take one. India and Pakistan presented a special problem. By this time both

41 Jowitt to Attlee, 5 Aug. 1949 (LCO 2/4506).

42 The Canadian Bar was arguing that the date of abolition be delayed. Memo, 8 Sept. 1949 (ibid).

43 Jowitt to Attlee, 5 Aug. 1949 (ibid.).

44 How to staff Indian appeals was a problem all year. Napier was concerned to know what would happen when Beaumont, one of the two paid Indian judges, retired. Could they use Sir Lionel Leach, a former Chief Justice of Madras, by then an Official Referee. Leach refused to give up the Official Referee's job unless he was paid for his work on the Privy Council (Napier to Waters (Clerk or Privy Council), 26 May 1949). Waters thought an 'iron curtain' on the appeals would come down on Republic Day, but suggested that India be asked to pay the £2,000—part of a judicial salary—to see whether it was 'serious'. Independence (Republic) Day was postponed from 15 August 1949 to 26 January 1950. All appeals were to cease then (F. F. Turnbull (Commonwealth Relations Office) to Napier, 28 June 1949). Jowitt advised Attlee in the 'interests of economy' that Leach be appointed in the interim (Jowitt to Attlee, 5 Aug. 1949). Herbert Morrison, Lord President of the Council, agreed, '. . . although it seems a pity to make a man a Privy Councillor only when a limited period of judicial work is required' (Ibid). Leach was appointed and sat for a number of years in the Privy Council, as needed, frequently undermining his work as Official Referee (Gardiner to Coldstream, 21 Nov. 1952; Coldstream to Gardiner, 21 Nov. 1952. LCO 2/5950). Originally, it looked as if India wanted all cases in the list as of October heard, but the Privy Council argued that it had 'constitutional grounds' for not hearing cases after 26 January. It therefore 'ordered out' all Indian appeals (LCO 2/4506).

45 High Commissioner to Noel Baker, 25 Jan. 1950 (LCO 2/4507).

46 The UK High Commissioner in Ottawa was also lobbying for Canadian Chief Justices to be allowed to sit (Clutterbuck to Leisching, 12 Oct. 1950 LCO 2/5227).

had abolished appeals, and India, as has been seen, had become a Republic. Prime Minister Nehru of India was not offered a Privy Councillorship, and Liaquat Ali Khan of Pakistan had turned his down. 'Nevertheless, you may think it desirable (if India and Pakistan agree) to make an effort to have their Chief Justices available for the Judicial Committee. This might serve, apart from anything else, as a valuable Commonwealth link with the two countries.'[47]

Napier drafted Jowitt's response. It might be a 'good Commonwealth policy' to appoint the Chief Justice of Canada to the Privy Council, but it would be of little help in the work. It was possible that Australia and New Zealand might allow the Chief Justice of Canada to sit in its appeals, but 'neither would tolerate the presence on the Board of the Chief Justice of any other Dominion'. To this, Jowitt added: 'It has always been interesting to me to observe how insistent they all are, as was Canada herself in the old days, that appeals should not be heard before a Board comprising judges from other Dominions.' Napier and Jowitt were, moreover, unimpresed with the arguments in favor of keeping the Indian and Pakistan Chief Justices: 'Many Colonies might resent the presence of either of them on the Board.' In addition to race, there was always the problem of the oath of allegiance as India became a Republic and Pakistan contemplated such a move.[48]

Australia and New Zealand presented rather different problems. During 1951, Jowitt toured the Antipodes and frightened many lawyers there by his narrow, mechanistic approach to the judicial process:

> It is our duty to expound what we believe the law to be . . . do not get yourself into the frame of mind of entrusting to the judges the working out of a whole new set of principles which does accord with the requirements of modern conditions. Leave that to the legislature, and leave us to confine ourselves to trying to find our what the law is.[49]

What Jowitt noticed, however, was that the bars in these two countries were upset that English appeal courts did not refer to Australian and New Zealand precedents, and they were apparently unimpressed by Jowitt's explanation that they could not be referred to by the judges unless they had been referred to by counsel. Jowitt's solution was to encourage the Chief Justices of Australia and New Zealand to sit in the Privy Council, especially in colonial cases.

The problem was that everyone wanted to use the Judicial Committee of the Privy Council to help keep the Commonwealth together—but it would cost money. Jowitt was horrified at the cost of bringing the judges over. Prime Minister Robert Menzies thought some Aus-

[47] Gordon Walker to Jowitt, 15 Jan. 1951 (ibid).
[48] Jowitt to Gordon Walker, 7 Feb. 1951 (ibid).
[49] Stevens, n. 10 above, 338–9.

tralian money would be available, and the New Zealand judges had sabbaticals.[50] It was agreed that Jowitt would talk to Prime Minister Attlee after the election.[51] The election, of course, produced a different Prime Minister and a different Lord Chancellor, but the deed of appointing an Australian judge as a member of the Privy Council was soon done. The UK High Commissioner in Canberra, E. J. Williams, talked to Menzies, who reported that Sir John Latham was 'getting a little past his prime . . . [and] had become exceedingly garrulous'. Sir Owen Dixon was appointed.[52]

Even with such help, there was a shortage of Law Lords. While both the House of Lords and the Judicial Committee were hearing fewer cases, they were taking far longer. Indeed, by 1954, it took on average twice as long to hear an appeal as it had in 1939.[53] More care was being taken with appeals. Lord Reid urged on Kilmuir the importance of having especially good panels in Australian appeals, as criticism of the Judicial Committee increased in Australia.[54] Reid thought, as Simonds had, that five Lords of Appeal in Ordinary should always sit in Australian appeals: 'Their Lordships are all exceedingly anxious to meet Australian opinion in connection with appeals to the Judicial Committee.' Indeed, he thought that, if necessary, hearings in the Lords should be aborted to meet personnel needs in Australian cases.[55]

3. And why not an Imperial Court?

It is a monument to the English belief in a mechanistic view of the role of the judiciary, and to the declaratory theory of law—often, it is true, mixed with a dated view of Empire—that English politicians remained so deaf to the oft-repeated views and advice of the old Dominions. From the turn of the century, the older Dominions had made it clear that, while at some time the final appeal to the Judicial Committee might go, in the meantime they would rather have their appeals heard by English Law Lords than by judges from other colonies or Dominions. English politicians had to be reminded of this with some regu-

[50] Jowitt to Gordon Walker, 28 Sept. 1951 (LCO 2/5227).

[51] Gordon Walker to Jowitt, 12 Oct. 1951 (Ibid).

[52] Williams to Leisching, 16 Jan. 1952 (ibid). Ismay, the new Secretary for Commonwealth Relations confirmed that Simonds did not want New Zealand judges sitting in rotation—the wish of their government (Ismay to Simonds, 18 Dec. 1951; Simonds to Ismay, 20 Dec. 1951, ibid).

[53] Stevens, n. 10 above, 324.

[54] Coldstream to Kilmuir, 31 Oct. 1955 (LCO 2/5234).

[55] Memo., 5 Nov. 1955. Kilmuir minuted 'Thank you for drawing to my attention the real difficulty. Nonetheless I think the reasons advanced by Lord Reid and accepted by Lord Simonds should prevail and we must do our best to minimize the resultant troubles.' (ibid).

larity, as they also had to be remined that, unless England, Scotland, and Ireland (later Northern Ireland) were prepared to have their appeals go to the Privy Council rather than the House of Lords, the final appeal would look increasingly as if it were discriminating against overseas territories.

As the independent Dominions grew in numbers—Australia was added in 1900, New Zealand in 1907, South Africa in 1909—they became more articulate and made greater use of, and more demands on, the Privy Council.[56] Once Cairns had destroyed the idea that, after the Canadian Supreme Court had been established in 1875, there should be no further appeals to London,[57] the various Imperial Conferences, beginning in 1887, put pressure on the British government to ensure an adequate judiciary in the Privy Council. The first major public criticism of the Judicial Committee had been heard in Canada in the 1880s.[58] When Chamberlain, at the 1897 conference, broached the idea of economic union, if not of federation, the role of the courts took on added significance. In this atmosphere the first arrangements were made in 1895 to have 'Dominion' judges as opposed to ex-colonial judges sit with the Law Lords in the Privy Council,[59] and before long more dramatic gestures were being considered.

By 1900 the Dominions and colonies were expressing considerable dissatisfaction about the somewhat random arrangements for staffing the Judicial Committee: the four Lords of Appeal and six judges of the Court of Appeal, various other English privy councillors who had held

[56] In 1900 the Privy Council received 16 appeals from Canada, 27 from Australia, 11 from South Africa, and 6 from New Zealand: *Civil Judicial Statistics 1900*, at 53. In 1910 the figures were Canada, 38; Australia, 16; South Africa, 8; New Zealand, 5: *Civil Judicial Statistics, 1910*, at 24.

[57] Coen G. Pierson, *Canada and the Privy Council* (Toronto, 1960) 16–21.

[58] One of the first problems was the relationship between the Judicial Committee of the Privy Council and Canadian criminal appeals. In the *Connors* case, 1885, an attempted appeal by a convicted murderer, the Attorney- and Solicitor-General (Webster and Gorst) advised the English Cabinet that, while the 1867 Act allowed Canada to abolish appeals in criminal cases, until the Canadian Parliament legislated, the right to appeal survived. Unfortunately, acting on the advice of the Canadian ministers, the Governor-General (the Marquis of Lansdowne) had refused Connors a stay of execution (LCO 1/2). It was also at this point that the Judicial Committee, after an initial decision in *Russell* v. *The Queen* (1882) 7 App. Cas. 829 (PC), favouring the broad federal powers intended by the 1867 Act, decided *Hodge* v. *The Queen* (1883) 9 App. Cas. 117 (PC), which appeared to espouse Mowat's theory of the co-ordinate relationship of the federal and provincial governments: Donald Creighton, *Canada's First Century 1867–1967* (Toronto, 1970), p. 49.

[59] The 1833 Act had provided for the appointment of two former colonial judges as members of the Council and two former Indian judges to be paid £400 per year. The 1871 Act allowed four paid members to be chosen from among the judges of the English Superior Courts or from among the Chief Justices in Bengal, Madras, or Bombay. The 1887 Act reduced to one the former Indian salaried judge under the 1833 Act (and fixed his salary at £800). The 1895 Act allowed up to five Canadian, Australian, and South African judges to be appointed as members of the Judicial Committee.

'high judicial office', two appointments under the 1933 act,[60] together with an Indian judge under the 1895 act. Although by this time the urge to merge the House of Lords and Privy Council—touted by Selborne in the 1860s and 1870s—had largely evaporated, by 1900 a plan was developed to add four more Lords of Appeal to satisfy the demands of the self-governing colonies. Behind the scenes, Joseph Chamberlain, Lord Halsbury, and Sir Courtenay Ilbert (former Law Member of the Governor's Council in India and by then Parliamentary Draftsman) worked out a compromise. Ilbert drafted a bill to add four more Law Lords, appointed for seven-year terms,[61] and it was assumed that overseas judges appointed under the 1895 act would become the new Lords of Appeal.[62].

In July 1901, the Conference on the Final Court of Appeal met, chaired by David Mills, Minister of Justice in Canada. From the outset, the inherent absurdity of achieving agreement among such a heterogeneous group of emerging nations was plain. Mr Justice Hughes of the Supreme Court of Victoria insisted on pushing the merger of the Privy Council and the House of Lords, a suggestion that Chamberlain thought 'quite futile'[63] An unseemly debate ensued about who would pay for any new judges.[64] It soon became clear that, while there was dissatisfaction in the colonies and especially in the Dominions, any new imperial court was liable to cause even more dissension than the Privy Council.[65] The Colonial Office, not surprisingly, reported that the views expressed at the conference were 'too diverse' for any action to be taken. While reform of the Judicial Committee remained a perpetual agenda item at Imperial Conferences, its fate was uniform. Whatever the failings of the Privy Council, the

[60] At that time Hobhouse and James.

[61] 'Its object was probably to secure the existence of colonial Lords of Appeal who should be not too much out of touch with the course of law and justice in the colonies which they were to represent.' (LCO 2/179).

[62] With some horror, Ilbert reported, '[T]here would at least be a risk that a strong self-governing colony would claim a substantial voice in the appointment of a Lord of Appeal.' (ibid).

[63] 'To attempt a change of that kind, with all the difficulties attending it, when we are under the impression that a majority of the Colonies would object to the change, would be, of course, quite futile.' (ibid, Conference Report at 24).

[64] Chamberlain noted, 'I thought that possibly they might think it was a little *infra dig*, that a Judge appointed specially as the representative of a Colony should be paid for by the Mother-country.' (*Conference Report* at 25).

[65] The Canadian Privy Council had already resolved that 'with the information they at present possess the creation of the four Colonial Law Lords suggested would not inspire any additional confidence in the Judicial Committee'; and the New Zealand representative announced at the conference: 'In my opinion a Member or Members appointed from the Dominion of Canada or the Commonwealth of Australia or from South Africa would afford no better guarantee nor bring any further satisfaction to the Colony of New Zealand than is afforded by the presence of Great Britain or others under the existing laws at the hearing of appeals from New Zealand.' (ibid).

powerful Dominions were not prepared to risk the alternatives. At the 1907 Imperial Conference, for instance, Canada once more defended the Judicial Committee.[66] At the 1911 Conference, there was further talk of an 'Imperial Court of Appeal'.[67] Once again, however, although the project was by then being pushed by Australia and New Zealand, Canada opposed it. The British government made firm commitments to improve arrangements for hearing appeals in the Privy Council by creating two additional Lords of Appeal.[68] After some delay a bill was introduced to allow an increase in the number of 'colonial' judicial members of the Council, under the 1895 Act, from five to seven, and to increase the number of Lords of Appeal from four to six. Yet even these additions were not sufficient to assuage growing doubts in the Dominions. In Canada further rumblings were being heard that the right to appeal to London was an extravagance, coupled with irritation at any suggestion that the Dominion was not free to end appeals. The Lord Chancellor's Office was uncomfortable.[69]

The appeals, however, still flooded in. In 1913 the House of Lords sat for 115 days hearing sixty-four appeals, and the Privy Council for 124 days to hear ninety-two cases. Far from having the same panel sitting alternately in Lords and Privy Council as he had hoped,[70]

[66] Prime Minister Laurier said: 'So far as Canada has any concern, we have an appeal to the Judicial Committee of the Privy Council; and it has, as a general rule, given very great satisfaction.' (*Proceedings of the Imperial Conference*, Cd. 3524 (1907, at 210).

[67] Haldane followed the Lord Chancellor's remarks with the observation that '[i]t is understood that this final Court of Appeal for the whole Empire is not merely to be of the strength of the existing one. We have agreed to strengthen it, and propose to add to it, as the Lord Chancellor said, two hand-picked lawyers.' (*Proceedings of the Imperial Conference*, Cd. 5745 (1911, at 244).

[68] '[T]hat they should add to the highest court of appeal, both for the United Kingdom, and the Dominions and Colonies, by selecting two English judges of the finest quality; that the quorum should be fixed at, say, five, and that the court should sit successively in the House of Lords for United Kingdom appeals and in the Privy Council for appeal from the Dominions and Colonies.' (ibid. at 222–23).

[69] The *Montreal Star* (7 Mar. 1913) upset Sir Kenneth Muir Mackenzie by arguing that while 'the right appeal to an impartial tribunal has been of the greatest value to us in delicate constitutional questions—especially those in which race and religion are involved', it was inappropriate in cases where corporations were involved. (It may not be irrelevant that Loreburn's decisions upholding federal power under s. 91 had been largely corporation cases). The *Star* also dismissed the argument that it was not open to Canada to abolish appeals: '[T]his sort of talk, leaving the impression that Canadian law for Canadians is made by somebody outside of Canada, is more mischievous when forced upon a democratic community such as ours.' (LCO) 2/287).

[70] The Clerk of the Privy Council, after noting that Australia and New Zealand were more reasonable at the 1911 Imperial Conference than they had been in 1907 in their demands for merging the Privy Council and the House of Lords, recorded that Loreburn agreed to 'the introduction of a more flexible system in the distribution of the judicial power available, to create what will be in effect one Supreme Court sitting in two divisions. No doubt his concessions in form had been brought about by the influence of Haldane and Asquith (both being present), who have on different occasions subscribed to the principle.' (Fitzroy, *Memoirs*, vol. 2, 448–9). The Imperial Conference of 1917 once

Haldane was faced with such a backlog of cases that he reconciled himself to having the Privy Council sit in two panels or divisions. The law officers gave their opinions that this might not be done without legislation;[71] an act legitimating the arrangement was pushed through in 1915.[72] By 1916, the Lords of Appeal were often staffing three appellate panels. In the Lords, the panel was supplemented by other Law Lords, while in the Privy Council the Law Lords manned panels helped by those appointed under the 1833, 1884, 1895, and 1913 Acts.[73] The arrangement was, perhaps, not the ideal setting for distinguished contributions.[74].

With the increasing independence of the Dominions, reflected politically in the 1931 Statute of Westminster, the preferred solution became not to cut back on Privy Council appeals, many of which already came only with leave, but rather to abolish the absolute right, in all cases, of appeal to the Lords. It was the Statute of Westminister's legitimation of the right of abolition of appeals from the Dominions, however, that was to dominate the *ethos* of the Judicial Committee of the Privy Council in the 1930s. The Irish Free State had chafed under the requirement in the 1922 Treaty that its appeals be heard by the Judicial Committee. The Irish demanded the right to abolish such appeals at the 1926 Imperial Conference, but eventually agreed to a plan by Birkenhead to put their demand off until the next conference. At the 1930 Conference, the Irish Free State was supported by South Africa and ultimately by Canada.[75] It was in this context that Sankey had piloted through the Statute of Westminster (1931), and that

more took up the issue of judicial appeals. Fitzroy summarized the situation in the following terms: 'On Hughes' (Australia) resolution on the subject of a Supreme Court of Appeal . . . everyone subscribed to the theory of such a court, but with no concrete expression of the idea before then, they declined to commit themselves to its urgency. The only fruitful result of the discussion was the testimony elicited from the representatives of Canada, New Zealand, South Africa and India to the extremely satisfactory way in which the Judicial Committee did its work . . . The two obstacles to the realization of Mr Hughes' dream of one Supreme Tribunal for all Appellants resident within the Empire, however attractive in appearance are (1) a matter of finance—will the Dominions contribute to its cost on an adequate scale?—and (2) a matter of repute—will a court largely recruited from Dominion Judges enjoy the confidence of British litigants either at home or beyond the seas?' (ibid, 679).

[71] Sir Rufus Isaacs (Attorney-General) and Sir John Simon (Solicitor-General), LCO 2/287. Two years later (5 Dec. 1915) Loreburn wrote to Buckmaster saying that he could see no reason, in law or practice, why the Judicial Committee should not sit in two divisions (LCO 2/292).

[72] Judicial Committee Act of 1915 (LCO 2/292). The Committee began sitting in two divisions on 14 Feb. 1916. The second division began by hearing prize cases.

[73] See Louis Blom-Cooper and Gavin Drewry, *The Final Appeal* (London, 1972), ch. 6.

[74] W. I. Jennings, 'Appeals to the Privy Council and the Statute of Westminster' (1936), 52 *L. Q. R.* 173.

[75] D. W. Harkness, *The Restless Dominion* (1970), 112–14, 138–89, 165–6, 203–7, 251–72.

Canada abolished criminal appeals[76] and the Irish Free State all appeals.[77] This had been the background for the striking down of the Bennett Social Insurance legislation, and this was the situation at the outbreak of the Second World War in 1939—a war in which the British needed the strongest political unity in Commonwealth and Empire.

4. Well, perhaps, a Commonwealth Court

In the middle of the war, in 1943, Sir Wilfred Greene, MR, in many ways the high priest of the formalistic approach to law,[78] turned his attention to the Judicial Committee of the Privy Council. He concluded that, 'unless steps are taken to place the Judicial Committee in a position of authority which will be accepted by the Dominions, the disappearance of its jurisdiction in Appeals from the Dominions in a comparatively short time is inevitable'.[79] He saw the Judicial Committee 'as a most valuable Imperial link' and 'as a means of ensuring uniformity of legal principle throughout the Empire'. Greene's solution involved turning the Judicial Committee into a peripatetic court.

While Viscount Simon, the wartime Lord Chancellor, did not feel in a position to run with the idea, he certainly saw that, unless something were done, the Privy Council 'will peter out in a generation or less'. Simon also saw that nothing would work unless English appeals, instead of going to the House of Lords, went to the Judicial Committee.

> I can quite see that such a change might draw many protests from those who cling to the existing order, and I do not at all believe that the decisions of what is now called the House of Lords would as a matter of law be necessarily improved by introducing a new element. But neither do I think they would be rendered any worse.[80]

[76] *British Coal Corp.* v. *The King* [1935] AC 500 (PC). See Blom-Cooper and Drewry, n. 73 above, 82–3.

[77] *Moore* v. *Attorney-General of the Irish Free State* [1935] AC 484 (PC).

[78] See e.g. the remarks in his Haldane Lecture: '. . . the function of the judiciary is to interpret and enforce the law. The judiciary is not concerned with policy. It is not for the judiciary to decide what is in the public interest. Those are the tasks of the legislature, which is put there for the purpose . . .', Wilfred Greene, 'Law and Progress' (1944), 94 *L. J.* 349, 351.

[79] 23 Nov. 1963 (LCO 2/7233).

[80] Memo. 11 Dec. 1943 (LCO 2/7233). Simon had received some support for a peripatetic court from Vincent Massey, then serving as High Commissioner for Canada in London: 'The more I thought about this imaginative idea, the more I like it . . . [it] would remove most of the serious objections [in Canada].' (Massey to Simon, 11 Dec. 1943, ibid). The problem was that anglophilia was Massey's Achilles' tendon: Claude Bissell, *The Imperial Canadian* (Buffalo, NY, 1986) vol. 2, ch. I. Simon also noted: 'is it not

With respect to the peripatetic aspect of the court, the biggest issue turned out to be the racial one. Sir David Monteith wrote to Simon from the India Office explaining the danger of embarrassment:

It is almost certain that South Africa and quite likely that Canada and Australia would decline to allow an Indian judge to be eligible to hear appeals in South Africa, Canada and Australia. (It is equally likely that for some time to come India would object to allowing South African Judges to sit on the Board in India.) But if Indian judges are to be ineligible to sit elsewhere than in India, would it not be embarrassing to prescribe that a Dominion judge should be eligible to sit elsewhere than in his own Dominion?[81]

Embarrassment was, in fact, spared by Churchill's decision. He told Simon that: 'Though the idea, as you expound it, is an attractive one, I do not myself think that the present time is a suitable one in which to raise a question of this kind.'[82]

The issue was rapidly revived in 1945 when Jowitt became Lord Chancellor after the Labour election landslide. Jowitt, like some other Lord Chancellors with a liberal reputation, in fact had a surprisingly traditional view of Empire. As MacDonald's Attorney-General he had not shared Sankey's enthusiasm for the Statute of Westminster, and his efforts to keep the Canadian connection have already been described. Indeed, this episode was part of his effort to keep the Commonwealth together by resuscitating the Judicial Committee of the Privy Council. In November of 1945, he was writing to Lord Addison at the Commonwealth Office:

I always like to think that one of the ties which binds Canada to us is the Privy Council Appeal. Of course, there are those in Canada who may think it is rather derogatory . . . Supposing we were to send a really strong Court to Canada to sit in Ottawa, might it not appeal to the Canadian imagination[?] . . . I am doubtful of the wisdom of bringing any of the other Dominions in to sit. I think Canada might not like this, but I wish there were more distinguished Commonwealth judges who could sit with us if we do go to Ottawa.[83]

Addison, in fact, preferred a wider orbit, arguing that all the Dominions should be brought in and that English and Scottish appeals should go to the Privy Council. Once again, however, Addison warned about 'the problem of India'.[84] Goddard, a Conservative whom Jowitt

probable that after Australia and New Zealand have helped defeat Japan by driving the Japanese out of our Colonial Empire, they will expect to have more to say in respect of those areas than at present?' (Memo., 11 Dec. 1943, LCO 2/7233).

81 Monteith to Simon, 12 Jan. 1944 (ibid).

82 Churchill to Simon, 2 Feb. 1944 (ibid).

83 Jowitt to Addison, 2 Nov. 1945 (ibid).

84 Addison to Jowitt, 22 Nov. 1945. (ibid).

had appointed as Lord Chief Justice, egged the Lord Chancellor on, reporting that when he was in Canada, 'Opinion (was) by no means unanimously in favor of abolition'. Indeed, 'several people' had said that if the Privy Council were to sit in Ottawa, 'abolition would be dead'.[85]

Jowitt was captivated by the scheme; his civil servants were not. George Coldstream, then Deputy Permanent Secretary, wrote to Lord Schuster—the former Permanent Secretary—noting that 'the Lord Chancellor has become enamoured of the old scheme to send the Judicial Committee on circuit', reporting that he was preparing a memorandum for Cabinet. 'There is, as I believe, no reason to suppose that a peripatetic body would be particularly welcome in the Dominions.'[86]

The Cabinet Memorandum was, however, drafted with a bullish tone. Most of the earlier objections in Imperial Conferences were ignored or played down. India again loomed large in the thinking:

> It is doubtful whether an Indian judge would be welcomed as a member of this court (say) in Australia or Canada. If, on the other hand, Indian judges are not to be eligible to sit in a court outside India, an embarrassing situation would arise. Moreover, there may be difficulties in finding Indian judges of sufficient eminence to become members of the panel.[87]

Rather lukewarmly, the memorandum suggested that English and Scottish appeals should go to the new body.[88] As a fall-back position, the Cabinet was urged to consider a limited scheme with just Canada.[89] It was, however, Canada that administered the *coup de grace*.

[85] Goddard to Jowitt, 2 Nov. 1945 (ibid). This approach ignored the many signs in the wind, indicating a contrary view. For instance. on 5 December 1945, Mr Justice Barlow (Ontario) wrote to Goddard: 'psychologically it would lose its appeal if the Throne came to the litigants. The tradition, the ceremonial, the distance, the fact that the court sits in the centre of the Empire would all be lost. The august, learned, elevated Judicial Committee would lose all its mystery if it came to sit in the Dominions.' (reported, Goddard to Jowitt, 7 Dec. 1945, ibid).

[86] The most Coldstream thought might fly was a Canadian Privy Council with one or two Law Lords added (Coldstream to Schuster, 21 Dec. 1945, ibid).

[87] *Judicial Committee of the Privy Council: Proposals for an Itinerant Board: Memorandum by the Lord Chancellor*, (Dec. 1945), 9. (Another draft is dated Jan. 1946). Ibid.

[88] 'Whatever the reaction to this proposal may be from English and Scottish critics, I cannot but think that the proposal for reciprocal action as regards English and Scottish appeals might have a considerable effect in assuring the Dominions that the scheme for an itinerant Board was a good one.' ibid.

[89] 'If it proved impracticable to secure general Dominion agreement to the idea of an itinerant Board, I think it would be well worth considering inviting Canada to participate in some modified scheme. The English and Scottish members of the Board might be made members of the Canadian Privy Council, and would sit in Canada as members of the Dominion Privy Council, together with Canadian Judges who are Privy Councillors of that Dominion. This would not be an itinerant Board in the sense of a single corpus of Judges (though of varying membership) traveling from Dominion to Dominion. The

The following month, January 1946, Jowitt reported to Addison that Louis St Laurent, the Canadian Minister of Justice, had been 'most interested and most helpful, but expressed the very clear view that as a matter of timing now was not the time to raise the question'.[90] Addison urged Jowitt, in the light of St Laurent's views, not to send the memorandum to Cabinet.[91]

Another decade passed. Indian and Pakistani appeals were abolished in 1950; Canadian in 1949; South African in 1950.[92] In 1954, Churchill replaced Simonds with Kilmuir as Lord Chancellor and by the end of the year the new Chancellor was making noises about a peripatetic Privy Council. Alex Lennox Boyd, the Colonial Secretary, by then wrestling with a rather different problem—vigorous political-independence movements in most of Britain's colonies—liked what he heard.[93] Sir Charles Dix, the Commonwealth Office Constitutional Adviser, reminded the Lord Chancellor that no scheme would work unless English and Scottish appeals went to the new court—and even then that there was little enthusiasm in the Commonwealth for any such scheme.[94] Sir George Coldstream, by then the Permanent Secretary to the Lord Chancellor's Office, produced a tired response to the Lord Chancellor, worthy of *Yes Minister*: '(you) still think there is something to be said for the simple solution of sitting in places other than London.'[95]

relative ease of travel between this country and Canada, and the particularly strong ties formed during the war between that Dominion and this country make the scheme, *prima facie*, really practicable in the case of Canada. Although the Canadian Bill to abolish the right of appeal to the Privy Council received a very fair measure of support in the Canadian Parliament in 1938, it is doubtful whether the situation is not now rather different. In any event, it is questionable whether all the Provinces of the Dominion are really in favour of abolition. If this view of the probable Canadian re-action is right it would surely be worth making soundings in Canada, whatever may be the outcome of the appeal to the Privy Council which will probably not be heard before the late summer of 1946.' (ibid).

90 Jowitt to Addison, 9 Jan. 1946 (ibid). See also Coldstream to Sir Arthur Dawe at the Colonial Office: 'Perhaps I should tell you in confidence that in taking this course, Lord Jowitt and Lord Addison were much influenced by the informal expression of opinion which had been given to Lord Jowitt by Mr St Laurent, the Canadian Minister of Justice, who is at present in this country. St Laurent suggests that the Canadian appeal to the Privy Council which will be heard this summer might well result in a decision that Canada is perfectly free to abolish the right of appeal to the Privy Council by Canadian legislation. That being so, a proposal along the lines suggested, would, if made to the Dominion now, give the impression that it was a last minute effort by the UK to retain some sort of superior right.' (ibid).

91 Addison to Jowitt, 21 Jan. 1946 (ibid).

92 Swinfen, n. 11 above, ch. 6. The last Canadian appeal was not heard until 1959. *Ponoka-Calmar Oils Ltd.* v. *Earl F. Wakefield Co.* [1960] AC 18. See W. G. Morrow, 'The Last Case' (1978) 16 *Alberta L. R.* 1.

93 Lenox-Boyd to Kilmuir, 7 Dec. 1945 (LCO 2/7233).

94 Memo. Dix, 20 Dec. 1954 (ibid).

95 19 January 1955 (ibid).

In December, Coldstream produced a memorandum for Kilmuir warning that the peripatetic court was an 'old issue'. The history of the early decades of this century were rehearsed, and then of the twenties and thirties:

> The question was raised, somewhat half-heartedly, from time to time in the 1920s and 1930s, but never got anywhere. Lord Schuster (who understood so well the art of the practicably possible) told me in 1945 that he had become convinced that the proposals for an itinerant Board would be unlikely to find favour with the Dominions and were very likely to raise dissensions that were then at rest.

He then retraced the Simon resuscitation and the Jowitt resuscitation, and pointed out that, whereas 'the accent at that time was upon the maintenance of this link between the Mother Country and what I may term the old Dominions', the problem had changed. What Coldstream did endorse was the suggestion that

> the project of an Itinerant Board is well worth considering in relation to Colonial Appeals and probably to appeals from the Supreme Courts of Federations within the Commonwealth which have not achieved Dominion status, and even those which may not achieve independent status for many years to come. It is for those members that the maintenance of an effective right of appeal to the Privy Council is likely to prove such a valuable constitutional link.[96]

Africa was an obvious candidate within the Coldstream guide-lines. Sir Barclay Nihill, President of the Court of Appeal for Eastern Africa, lobbied hard for a member of his court to be appointed on terms similar to those which Mr L. M. de Silva, the Ceylanese (Sri Lankan) judge, had been given.[97] Kilmuir, however, still hankered for a peripatetic court. He called a ministerial meeting in March 1955 to assess the situation. In addition to the civil servants, the Lord Chancellor, the Lord President, the Dominion Secretary, and the Colonial Secretary were there. Kilmuir opened the discussions, arguing

[96] Memo., Coldstream to Kilmuir, 16 Dec. 1954 (LCO 2/7237).

[97] 'I have hesitated to put forward this matter before for a personal reason. I am approaching the age of retirement and as the senior Appellate Judge in East Africa, I should naturally be disappointed if my name were not considered for appointment.' (Nihill memo., Nairobi, 7 Jan. 1955, LCO 2/7233). Nihill suggested that, following the Ceylon model, the East African governments pay £2,500 per annum to support such a judge. Nihill had actually been recommended for such an appointment by Jowitt in a letter to Napier (at that time Permanent Secretary of the Lord Chancellor's Office), 25 Mar. 1954 (LCO 2/5788). The Attorney-General of Kenya, Sir John Wyatt, preferred a peripatetic Privy Council. He wrote a highly articulate letter to the Governor of Kenya—for transmission to London—dated 21 Feb. 1955 (LCO 2/7233).

that Simon and Jowitt had failed but that, 'he considered that the importance of this proposal lay not in the relationship to the old Dominions so much as the new territories which would shortly be achieving independence—the Central African Federation, Nigeria, and the Gold Coast (Ghana)'.

The discussion was, in its own way, fascinating. The Commonwealth Secretary, for instance, noted that 'the members of the Judicial Committee were not young and it would be a strain for them to travel long distances by air to countries where the climate was bad'. Delay, the quality of counsel, the quality of colonial judges, and the absence of good libraries were all noted. The Colonial Secretary was the strongest supporter, arguing that 'there are some African Judges who are good enough to be members of the Privy Council'. The Lord President was doubtful: 'He though that any advantage that might be conferred upon Colonial territories would not be worth while if the prestige of the court was lowered in the eyes of the older Commonwealth countries'.

To today's observer, the discussion emphasized both the unreality of the Commonwealth and of the attempt to apply the simplistic, mechanistic English approach to judicial decision-making to societies with very different political environments. One of those at the meeting noted that, 'some Commonwealth countries could be relied upon to propose good men, but others could not'. Another noted: 'The standard of the local Bar would present a great difficulty: the standard varied in different Colonial territories, and in West Africa it was so low that there was not one single competent advocate.' Another emphasized the racial problem. If 'colonials' were appointed to the Privy Council, 'this would not be liked by the older Commonwealth countries'.[98]

After the somewhat abortive discussion, C. W. B. Rankin, Private Secretary to the Lord Chancellor, was instructed to produce a paper. This was a more realistic assessment than the politicians and lawyers were capable of:

> Modern Colonial policy, as I understand it, is not to meet nationalism head on, but to try to deflect it into productive channels useful to us. This means that we must avoid appearing in any way to derogate from the grant of self-government within the Commonwealth; and I think that this proposal if put into effect would have that appearance . . . However welcome to the judiciary and the legal profession the extension of the jurisdiction of the Judicial Committee might be, it would be regarded by politicians and administrators in the new countries with impatience . . . It seems to me that an itinerant Board, instead of increasing the influence of the Judicial Committee, might just as

98 *The Peripatetic Privy Council*, 25 Mar. 1955 (ibid).

easily provoke premature demands for the abolition of the right of appeal altogether.[99]

While Coldstream purported to add a more balanced comment before the paper went to Kilmuir, he did not believe that the peripatetic scheme would help with 'links' to the older Commonwealth. Indeed, 'short of some whole-hearted expression of desire from Australia, the practical effect might be to cause resentment rather than gratitude'. On the other hand, and perhaps coming as a surprise to those who have questioned the English judiciary's competence in matters of constitutional law,[100] Coldstream argued for

> the value of a great, authoritative Supreme Judiciary in the formative years of a new constitution . . . It should be represented as a contribution which the British Government would be ready and willing to make towards the younger but nevertheless independent, members of the Commonwealth fellowship. It would be a real and significant contribution, because no one doubts that the quality of British justice is the best in the world, and young nations are doubtless as anxious as young persons to have the best of anything.[101]

Kilmuir, it seems, got the message from Rankin rather than Coldstream. He commented on the paper: 'I am grateful—if slightly depressed—for this very clear statement of the arguments . . . It may be that we have missed the bus.' Indeed, the reactions were to be expected. The fear of the insertion of colonial judges into the Privy Council was enough for Australia to insist later in that year that its appeals always be heard by five English Law Lords. Kilmuir made that commitment.[102] Indeed, when the following year a Conservative MP was planning to revive the issue of a Commonwealth Court in the House of Commons, he was warned behind the scenes that Australia and New Zealand 'would not be amused' to have their cases heard by colonial judges.[103] Even the Duke of Edinburgh, who inquired about a Commonwealth Court that same year, got a bland response. The Duke was warned that it was 'a controversial issue'; the best judges were not

[99] *Proposal for an Itinerant Board of the Judicial Committee*, Rankin to Coldstream, 5 Apr. 1955 (ibid).

[100] Some, for instance, would argue that the Privy Council decisions in *Adegbenro* v. *Akintola* [1963] AC 614 (PC, Nigeria) helped precipitate the Biafran War. For other comments on the Board's later constitutional work, see Stevens, n. 10 above, 608 n.

[101] Ibid.

[102] The decision was the result of discussions between Kilmuir and Lord Reid. Simonds was also involved (Coldstream to Kilmuir, 31 Oct. 1955, LCO 2/5234). See also Coldstream to file, 31 Oct. 1955 (ibid). Sir Owen Dixon had made it clear that Australia would not allow an African to sit on Australian appeals (memo. from Lord Kilmuir, 21 Nov. 1958, LCO 2/7236).

[103] Coldstream to Theisiger, 28 June 1956 (LCO 2/5237).

easy to get; and in some colonies, the standards of bench and bar were not high.[104]

Still Kilmuir could not let the idea of a peripatetic Privy Council drop. In late 1958, the Lord Chancellor once again floated the scheme, sending a memorandum to all the Law Lords about his idea—apparently resuscitated by a discussion with Sir Owen Dixon, the Chief Justice of Australia, although the latter was not in fact in favour of such a system. The idea floated was for one Division of the Privy Council to sit in London while the other went on circuit, although Kilmuir insisted that the 'touring side' would have to be as good as the 'home team'. The Lord Chancellor, for instance, thought that in Year I, the touring side might go to the Federations of Rhodesia and Nyasaland, East Africa, West Africa, and Ghana. In Year II it might be the Caribbean Federation and British Honduras; and in Year III, Australia, New Zealand, and Hong Kong. The rhetoric was familiar:

> The common law constitutes a bond between the countries of the Commonwealth which should be strengthened to bring them together . . . (and to ensure the) uniform development of law throughout the Commonwealth . . . As new Commonwealth countries achieve independence, political control over them is lost; but the Judicial Committee provides an opportunity to exercise control of a different kind and to guide development indirectly by the exercise of a jurisdiction which commands universal respect . . . everything must be done to keep the jurisdiction alive and apeals should be encouraged . . . the inhabitants of the territories visited by the Committee would get to know and respect its members personally and would be able to observe themselves the virtues of the Court . . . the reproach would be removed that the decisions of the Judicial Committee taken in the remote calm of Downing Street are based upon no direct experience or knowledge of the conditions existing in distant territories . . . The ease and comfort of air travel now make it possible for the first time in history for the Court to go on circuit, and such discomforts as there may be are nothing compared to what the Judges of Assize had to put up with until comparatively recent times.

Kilmuir also saw the arguments against such a circuit system:

> The arguments for an itinerant Court do not take sufficient account of the nature and vigor of nationalism in the Commonwealth . . . In all cases where the right of appeal has been abandoned, it has not been because of complaints about the working of the court . . . but for purely nationalistic reasons . . . far from being a link, it is argued, the jurisdiction of the Judicial Committee in these circumstances is a chain which, if past experience is a guide, is likely to chafe against nationalist sentiment and irritate it . . . The political process in Canada was not lessened by the fact that Canadian Privy Councillors sat to hear appeals in London . . . We may well be thankful for example that the

[104] Kilmuir to Commander Parker, 13 July 1956 (LCO 2/5238).

relations of the United Kingdom with South Africa and Pakistan have not been put to what might have been a fatal strain if an appeal had been brought to the Judicial Committee on the question of the entrenched clauses in the South Africa Act or the constitutional validity of the recent actions of the Governor-General in Pakistan . . . Remoteness is not necessarily a weakness, and it is debatable whether the physical presence of the members of the Judicial Committee in Commonwealth countries would increase the attraction of the Court. Their aloofness from local politics would certainly be less, if only through unavoidable social contacts.

For Kilmuir, however, the advantages outweighed the disadvantages. 'I consider that from the standpoint of the Commonwealth policy at large, the arguments in favour of the Judicial Committee sitting in certain Commonwealth countries outweighs the objections . . . Lawyers everywhere regard London as the Centre of the Legal World.'[105]

Only Lord Denning among the Law Lords was enthusiastic about the scheme:

The only hope of restoring the Judicial Committee to something like its former glory is to turn it into the Supreme Court of the Commonwealth . . . Just as Henry II revolutionalized the administration of justice in England by sending his judges round the country on circuit, so I think the administration of justice in the Commonwealth can be revolutionalized by sending the Privy Council round the countries which acknowledge its jurisdiction.

Indeed, Denning was in favour of including South Africa, Canada and India—and he thought it important to have the Law Lords wear robes. Yet only Lord Reid offered Denning any support: 'unless we go forward we may slip back and more Commonwealth countries may stop appeals to London. While certainly Australia would not want its constitutional cases adjudicated, other countries might want this, [and that] might lessen fears of minorities.'

The basic case against was argued by Kilmuir's predecessor—Viscount Simonds.[106] The proposal, while having 'superficial attraction', has been 'so often made and been so often dropped upon examination . . . its advantages are speculative and uncertain, its disadvantages certain, patent and overwhelming'. Simonds did not take the common-law argument seriously, since most new Commonwealth countries did not have 'real' common law but basically customary law and ordinances. Moreover, he was aware that the Privy Council was not at its best in constitutional issues. 'I have often been painfully aware how inadequate has been my own training in the very special field of legal problems which arise out of a federal constitution.'

On Simonds went. 'Some will remember the row there was when

105 Kilmuir, Memo., no date (LCO 2/7236).
106 Memo., 2 Nov. 1958 (ibid).

the late Sir John Rowlatt (Rowlatt of all people!) sat to hear some Australian appeals. A Chief Justice of Nigeria or the Caribbean would not be more favorably received.' The notion of a peripatetic Privy Council was a 'wholly disadvantageous idea with respect to Australia and New Zealand'. Moreover, some Law Lords would never have accepted the job if they had known they were required to go on circuit.

> A Board sitting in Downing Street at a distance of some thousands of miles is more likely to inspire and retain the respect of the natives of Ghana than is a body of old gentlemen visiting the territory . . . it is, in my opinion, a matter not for reproach but for congratulation that the decisions of the Committee are taken 'in the remote calm of Downing Street'.

Simonds finished with three final thoughts: What about wives?[107] What about expense? Finally: 'The quality of the native counsel may not be such as to give the Bench the assistance which they surely need.'

The other Law Lords concurred with Simonds. Lord Morton noted,

> I have grave doubts that the scheme would achieve the good results mentioned . . . Eleven-and-a-half years of sitting in the Judicial Committee lead me to the belief that it is not well suited to go on circuit . . . I think that the Africans, who love pomp and circumstance and are (or used to be) inclined to judge a man's importance from appearance, might feel rather 'let down' when five old men in ordinary clothes appeared.

Lord Tucker announced: 'This is a political and not strictly a judicial question and is therefore one upon which my opinion is not of much value, but I feel bound to say I am sceptical with regard to the anticipated results and am inclined to the view that the consequences would be more likely to be detrimental than beneficial.' Tucker had been reluctant to come to the Lords because 'Law Lords are so often expected to take on jobs of a non-judicial nature, a practice of which I disapprove and for which I do not consider myself qualified'. Going on circuit would be worse.

Lord Somervell did not approve of second appeals; thought local appeal courts 'not bad'; thought a peripatetic Privy Council would not strengthen the Commonwealth and would just send up costs. Lord Keith did not think the proposal 'expedient'. Lord Cohen admitted he used to be in favour and had once thought that a peripatetic court would have discouraged Canada from abolishing appeals. He no longer thought that. Lord Radcliffe opposed the scheme because it would expose the Committee's ignorance of local conditions, although he

[107] Wives loomed large in all the law lords' thinking. This may have been a dig at Kilmuir, whose wife lived openly with Earl De la Warr, (A. Horne, *Macmillan* (London, 1988), vol. 2 346.)

shared the view that a Commonwealth Constitutional Court might be of some value.[108]When the meeting of Law Lords was finally held on 1 December 1958, six of the nine said bluntly they would not go on circuit. Many felt, with Lord Cohen, that it would do more harm than good. Kilmuir accepted that 'clearly the proposal could go no further at present'.[109]

Although we now know that Harold Macmillan thought Kilmuir a lightweight,[110] he has on balance been treated generously by commentators and historians.[111] Certainly Kilmuir's encounter with a peripatetic Privy Council or a Commonwealth Court might well be assumed to have been the end of the story. Strangely enough, it was not. The mechanistic approach to law was so heavily ingrained in English legal thinking, especially on the so-called political left, and political unreality was so elusive to the legal mind, that there was to be one last canter through the process. It was a strange tale.

During the late fifties and early sixties, it looked as if the Commonwealth might break up over South Africa. What the Commonwealth represented was less and less clear. Even the Conservatives finally thought Britain's future lay with the European Community. In 1964, however, the Labour Party was returned, and Harold Wilson chose as his Lord Chancellor Gerald Gardiner. Gardiner thought of himself as a radical of the left; yet he was remarkably conservative on very many issues. Few Chancellors have been so conservative with respect to the profession (indeed, it was Mrs Thatcher's current 'Conservative' Chancellor, Lord Mackay, who proved to be the radical). Gardiner, however, saw the Commonwealth through the eyes of a lawyer's lawyer, tainted with the bourgeois hue of the Society of Labour Lawyers and the élitist Marxism of the Haldane Society.[112]

Gardiner's rather strange position was that the judicial role of the House of Lords should be abolished to save litigants' money, but a peripatetic Commonwealth Court should be established (which would substitute for the House the Lords and be the only appeal court for the Court of Appeal, the Court of Criminal Appeal, the Court of Session, and the Court of Appeal for Northern Ireland) to save the Commonwealth.[113] Moreover, he saw all members of the Commonwealth participating. In May 1965, Gardiner proceeded to float the idea in Parlia-

[108] Coldstream memo. of Radcliffe visit, 15 Oct. 1958 (LCO 2/7236).

[109] Minutes of 1 Dec. 1958 meeting (ibid).

[110] Macmillan wrote, 'He was always a "beta minus"; the stupidest Lord Chancellor . . . hopeless in Cabinet—that's why I got rid of him . . .' (Horne, n. 107 above, 316).

[111] Stevens, n. 10 above, 420–5; Heuston, *Lives of the Lord Chancellors 1940–1970* (London, 1987). 181–204.

[112] Heuston, previous notes, 207–43; Stevens, n. 10 above, 431–6.

[113] Gerald Gardiner and Andrew Martin, *Law Reform—NOW* (1963), 16.

ment and received support primarily from a group of Conservative MP's who had been playing with the idea for the previous couple of years.[114] The next month—June 1965—the Commonwealth Conference turned a largely deaf ear to the idea. The older Dominions took their traditional position of severe scepticism, while the new African countries had adopted a form of African Socialism that owed little to Gardiner's intellectual concerns. Only Malaysia, which had worked out a special relationship with the Privy Council, was supportive.[115] There was, however, to be one last public appearance of the idea—the Commonwealth and Empire Law Conference in Sydney in September. While the English Attorney-General felt 'confident' that the Conference would endorse the idea of a Commonwealth Court, and while Gardiner thought he had the support of the Indian Chief Justice, it proved an embarrassing non-starter.[116] The Commonwealth Court was dead; the Judicial Committee of the Privy Council was on the way to extinction.[117]

5. Conclusion

Such an ignominious end must have seemed inevitable to anyone sensitive to the unreality of the mechanistic view of the judicial appellate function. A mechanistic jurisprudence is pretence. A declaratory theory of law, ill suited to constitutional issues, cannot be applied in supra-national situations. Whatever the pressures that sustain it in a single jurisdiction, they are inconsistent with the politics of reality that inevitably impinge in a broader context. For the older Dominions, abolition was closely related to political maturity. Some Third World countries abolished appeals because they feared the Privy Council might undermine their economic goals—and more sinisterly—their increasingly repressive regimes. The Canadian courts have wrestled more effectively with constitutional issues since the abolition of appeals to London in 1949 and the patriation of the Constitution in 1982. Some of the former colonies have thrived legally; others have not. In the last thirty years the English too have veered away somewhat from the mystical view of judicial formalism, the irrelevance

[114] The support in Parliament was based on a group of Tory MPs, Graham Page, Derek Walker-Smith, and Edward Gardner. Swinfen, n. 11 above, 185. Chapter 7 of this book ('The Commonwealth Court Revisited') is based on interviews with members of the Lord Chancellor's Office about this last foray into a Commonwealth Court.

[115] Stevens, n. 10 above, 415–6.

[116] For details, see Swinfen, n. 11 above, 211–16.

[117] Australian appeals were abolished by the Australia Act, 1986, and the last case was heard in 1987: *Austin* v. *Keele*. (1987) 61 *ALJR*. 585.

of the judge—both politically and personally—and the primacy of logic.[118] The collapse of the Privy Council jurisdiction, strangely enough, coincided with the decline of substantive formalism in the English legal process.

118 See e.g. Lord Mackay, 'Can Judges change the Law?' (1988) LXXII *Proceedings of the British Academy*, 285.

8

The Origins of Futures Trading in the Liverpool Cotton Market

A. W. B. SIMPSON

The Case of the Ships *Peerless*

I first became interested in the origins of futures trading through investigating the historical background to the contract case, *Raffles* v. *Wichelhaus and Busch* (1864).[1] This case was first seriously discussed by an American exile to the English bar, Judah P. Benjamin, in his treatise on the law of sale.[2] The story of the two ships forms the basis for arguments about the principles of contract formation.[3] The form of contract, known as a contract 'to arrive', or an 'arrival' contract,[4] out of which the litigation arose, evolved, somehow, into the form used for futures trading in cotton; Liverpool was one of the places where a large, organized futures market developed in the nineteenth century.[5]

[1] 2 H & C 906, 33 LJ Exch. 160. For a full account of the historical context see my 'Contracts for Cotton to Arrive: The Case of the Two Ships *Peerless*' (1989), 11 *Cardozo LR* 287.

[2] *A Treatise on the Sale of Personal Property with reference to the American Decisions and the French Code and Civil Law* (1868), 37, 149–150. He practised on the Northern Circuit, which included Liverpool.

[3] See e.g. R. L. Birmingham, 'Holmes on Peerless: *Raffles* v. *Wichelhaus* and the Objective Theory of Contract', (1985) 47 *Univ. of Pittsburg LR* 183.

[4] Such contracts were also called 'time contracts'. They were not invented in the nineteenth century. For example, the early *assumpsit* case of *Pykeryng* v. *Thurgoode* (1532) involved such a contract and a claim for the difference between the contract and market price. See for the text J. H. Baker and S. F. C. Milsom, *Sources of English Legal History* (London, 1986), at 411. Benjamin (n. 2 above, 497 ff.) discusses the law governing them.

[5] See below text to n. 102 ff. for Chicago and New York. Futures trading also developed in New Orleans, but did not originate there. A deliberate decision to introduce such trading there in 1871 was not successful; this was probably imitative of New York, where the market was organized for the practice in 1869. A second attempt in 1879 was more successful. In 1882, Julius Aroni of the New Orleans bar published the first book on the subject, *Futures*. This book discusses in some detail the legality of the practice.

Characteristics of Futures Trading

The dating of this development is not easy to establish, and there are problems in defining what is meant by an organized futures market. But there was certainly a time—say before the 1860s—when no such markets existed anywhere. By 1870, or a little later, they did, notably in Chicago, Liverpool, and New York. In such markets what is traded is contracts, not commodities—cotton, pork-bellies, orange-juice, or whatever—in an ordinary sense.[6] Futures trading seems, to some, to represent the very worst expression of the philosophy of the free market; to others, its most flamboyant celebration.

Certain characteristics of an organized futures market serve to define such institutions; they draw a line between forward-delivery contracts for commodities, and transactions associated with them, on the one hand, and dealing in futures on the other, though drawing a *sharp* line is not really possible.

First, futures markets are places[7] where trading is conducted on a considerable scale, typically in a pit, and only at particular hours. This permits rapid trading, and everyone is in a good position to know what everyone else is doing.

Secondly, although what is bought and sold is a contract for future delivery of a commodity rather than the commodity itself, yet such futures contracts are conceived of as entitling the parties to tender and receive actual delivery of the commodity. The seller may tender delivery within the contractual period, and if tender is refused his obligations (but not the buyer's) are at an end. If the market price has fallen he can claim compensation. As for the buyer, if delivery is not tendered he is entitled to compensation if the market price has risen.[8]

[6] The following literature seems particularly useful: J. G. Smith, *Organised Produce Markets* (London, 1922); G. L. Rees, *Britain's Commodity Markets* (London, 1972); J. C. Williams, 'The Origin of Futures Markets' (1982) 56 *Supp. to Agric. Hist.* 306; J. Williams, *The Economic Function of Futures Markets* (Cambridge, 1986); A. R. Marsh, 'Cotton Exchanges and Their Economic Functions' (1911) 38 *Annals of the American As. of Pol. and Soc. Science* 571; F. Hyde, B. B. Parkinson, and S. Marriner, 'The Cotton Broker and the Rise of the Liverpool Cotton Market' (1955–6) VIII *Ec. Hist. Rev.* 75; S. Dumbell, 'The Origin of Cotton Futures' (1926–9) 1 *Ec. Journal, Supp. Ec. Hist. Ser.* 259 (May 1927); A. C. Stevens 'Futures in the Wheat Market' (1887) II *Quarterly Journal of Economics* 37; K. J. Lipartito, 'The New York Cotton Exchange and the Development of the Cotton Futures Market' (1983) LVII *Business Hist. Rev.* 50; R. Bouilly, 'The Development of American Cotton Exchanges, 1870–1916', unpublished dissertation, University of Missouri (1975); C. H. Taylor, *History of the Board of Trade of the City of Chicago*, 3 vol. (Chicago, 1917).

[7] Modern methods of communication are perhaps in the course of changing this.

[8] The compensation may mean the difference between the contract price and a 'market price', or the buyer may be entitled to buy equivalent commodities in the market (that is, at a real market price) on the account of the seller, he remaining liable to pay the contract price. This is really an alternative way of settling differences. The 'market' price of a commodity may be a notional average price related in some way to trades taking place

Hence a seller can, in effect, buy back the contract by tendering compensation at the last moment for delivery, or earlier if the buyer agrees. Similarly, the buyer can discharge his liability by payment of a 'difference', that is, a difference between contract and market price and, depending on the movement of the market, only one party will be liable to the other. Although delivery is possible, it does not normally happen, and stories are told of the consternation caused when a trader has inadvertently failed to close a contract, and has truck-loads of pork-bellies delivered to him. The operation of futures markets would collapse if delivery regularly occurred; typically a trader has no organization for handling the commodity.[9]

Thirdly, futures contracts are standardized as to quantity and quality or grade, and only vary in relation to price and delivery dates. Delivery dates, called positions, are also partially standardized, and are periods: months, or pairs of months. Only a limited range of positions are traded. The seller can select the moment for delivery but has to deliver, or settle, at the end of the month.

Fourthly, the traders are organized with rules and customs which enable them to control trading-practices, discipline deviant members, and resolve disputes without recourse to the courts. Trading-rules are codified and all contracts between members are treated as being subject to these standardized rules, which are regularly amended and modified in the light of experience.

Fifthly, the organization of the market will include arrangements which simplify the process of balancing accounts between traders, typically through some form of clearing-house.

Sixthly, the traders' organization will provide traders with information both as to trades in the market, and as to external factors affecting the state of supply and demand—stock sizes, crop size, weather reports, and so on. The organization will spend money on collecting statistics, providing telegraph services, and the like.

The Liverpool Cotton Brokers Association

In the nineteenth century, Liverpool was the port through which cotton was imported for the Lancashire processing industry. The trade

about the same time, or it may be an actual price at which a particular contract is made in the market.

[9] In the Chicago wheat market it appears that identical contracts are used for trading in 'futures' and 'actuals', and hence delivery does occur. The reason is that wheat is not a very variable commodity, and those who want it find the stereotyped form of contract used by 'futures' traders convenient. In the case of cotton, which is very variable, spinners need to tailor contracts to the specific type for which they have a use, and stereotyped contracts are not appropriate.

in cotton was then the greatest British import trade. According to Ellison,[10] in the early part of the century the trade was conducted by merchants who, having imported cotton from around the world, particularly the southern states of the USA, Egypt, and India,[11] sold through selling-brokers to cotton spinners, who employed buying-brokers.[12] Cotton varies much in type and quality, and is extraordinarily difficult to grade objectively.[13] Bales may be damaged in transit, be fraudulently[14] or negligently packed, or be stored so as to increase moisture content. No two bales were ever identical. Hence, sampling and pricing cotton was a specialism. Expert brokers, particularly buying-brokers, acted as agents for spinners and protected their interests.

The trade was long administered under unwritten custom, operated by members of the Liverpool Cotton Brokers Association, formed on 2 April 1841.[15] Its principal original function was to provide statistical information related to the size of the cotton stock in Liverpool at any particular time. It is, as I have said, a typical feature of futures markets and of the 'spot' markets which preceded them that much information is shared, though individuals attempt to outsmart others by possessing additional information or by making better use of shared information.

[10] Thomas Ellison (1833–30 May 1904) was fascinated by the trade, and wrote extensively about it. He had been apprenticed in the cotton trade to a well-known broker, Maurice Williams, probably in about 1851. He entered business on his own account in 1864 as partner to G. H. Haywood. In 1858 he published *A Handbook of the Cotton Trade*, and in 1886 a history of the trade, cited below. There is an obituary in *The Times* on 31 May 1904. His *Gleanings and Reminiscences* was apparently published in Liverpool in 1905, but I have not seen a copy.

[11] Called at the time the East Indian trade. Indian cotton was in general of much lower quality than American or Egyptian.

[12] T. Ellison, *The Cotton Trade of Great Britain* (Liverpool and London, 1886). On the history of the trade generally see W. O. Henderson, *The Lancashire Cotton Famine 1861–5* (Manchester, 1969); J. Watts, *The Facts of the Cotton Famine* (first edn. Manchester, 1865, repr. 1968), M. Williams, *Seven Years History of the Cotton Trade* (Liverpool 1868), D. A. Farnie, *The English Cotton Industry and the World Market 1815–1896* (Oxford, 1979). I am indebted to Dr Farnie for help in locating material, and indeed generally.

[13] At this time three grades were normally quoted on the Liverpool market in East Indian cotton—'Fair', 'Middling', and 'Ordinary'. There could also be half-grades, such as 'Middling Fair', and quarter-grades. Grades could elaborate and change over time and differed between markets, extreme difficulty existing in translating a New Orleans grade into a Liverpool grade.

[14] For example by putting stones in the middle.

[15] Primarily an association of buying brokers, at least in origin. Some records survive in the Liverpool City Record Office (class MS 380 COT). Those used in this piece comprise: 1/1 (22 Jan. 1842–21 Feb. 1851, memoranda of weekly meetings of all members); 1/2 (Apr. 1864–Dec. 1866, weekly meetings); 1/4 (Feb. 1868–Aug. 1870, weekly meetings); 1/5 (2 Sept. 1870–Apr. 1871, weekly meetings); 1/6 (May 1871–May 1872, weekly meetings); 1/7 (May 1872–Mar. 1873, weekly meetings); 1/8 (Apr. 1873–Sept. 1874, weekly meetings); 1/9 (Sept. 1875–Nov. 1876, weekly meetings); 3/1 (13 Nov. 1871–16 Dec. 1873, meetings of general committee). These records are laconic working-notes.

The association organized the rapid arbitration of disputes between principals, the arbitrators being brokers not directly involved.[16] These disputes principally concerned grade and quality, and were inescapable, given the nature of the product. All commodity markets employ systems of this kind: traders cannot wait for the courts to settle disputes. And the more difficult it is to establish objective systems of grading and quality control, based upon definitions or standard samples, the more necessary becomes the use of trusted experts who decide the matter cheaply.[17] Brokers took turns to act as arbitrators, an arrangement which encouraged good-faith decisions.

The use of arbitration[18] explains the relative rarity of reported legal cases dealing with the vast cotton trade.[19] An early resolution of the association read thus: 'that the custom amongst cotton brokers of submitting disputes to arbitration, is one firmly established in the cotton trade, and has hitherto been found to give general satisfaction . . .'[20] Until 1863 recourse to arbitration rested solely upon custom. The form of contract introduced late that year for contracts for cotton 'to arrive' provided explicitly for arbitration of disputes as to quality, but did not regulate the practice. Later the association regularly published a code of general trading-rules; the earliest set of general rules I have located dates from 1871, though texts of the rules governing 'arrival' contracts have been found for 1863 and 1867. The rules of 1871 provided that all disputes should be arbitrated.[21]

16 The formation of the association is described by Ellison, n. 12 above, at 174–86 and 272–7.

17 A modern illustration is the dog-show; there is no conceivable mechanism for selecting the dog of the show except that of entrusting a power of decision to a supposed expert.

18 For an account of the legal status of arbitration clauses at this period see my 'Contracts for Cotton to Arrive: The Case of the Two Ships *Peerless*' n. 1 above, at 322, n. 165.

19 An example is *Neill* v. *Whitworth* (1865) 18 CB (NS) 433, LR 1 CP 684. The case concerned a contract made on 2 Oct. 1863, and involved litigation between a London merchant and a Manchester merchant arising out of the standard form then in use. The form of contract employed provided for arbitration; however, the provision for arbitration then in use only covered disputes over quality, and at the time the law was such that arbitration was essentially voluntary. Other reported cases from this period are *Campbell* v. *Mersey Dock Co.* (1865) VIII LT (NS) 245; *Williams* v. *Reynolds* (1865) XII LT (NS) 729; *Morgan* v. *Gath* (1865) XIII LT (NS) 96; *Thorburn* v. *Barnes* (1867) XVI LT (NS) 10; *Azemer* v. *Casella* XVI LT (NS) 14, 571; *Re an Arbitration between Rouse and Co. and Meier and Co.* 23 LT (NS) 865.

20 MS 380 COT 1/1, resolution of 23 Dec. 1842. This arose out of a particular dispute in which litigation seems to have been threatened. The resolution noted that there was no precedent for recourse to the courts. MS 380 COT 1/1 contains notes of resolutions between 22 Jan. 1842 and 21 Feb. 1851.

21 *Constitution, Laws and Usages of the Liverpool Cotton Broker's Association 1871*, para. 19 (dealing with disputes over sales of cotton after arrival) and para. 54 (10). In the former case the arbitrators did not have to be members of the association. There had been a dispute over the system of arbitration between the brokers and the Cotton Spinners Association in 1864–5, which may be followed in MS 380 COT 1/2.

Originally arbitrations not relating to quality were conducted by the president, vice-president, and an umpire appointed by the parties.[22] Disputes over quality were handled by two brokers, with a third as umpire if needed. The system became more complex with an appeal to the committee. By 1865 a fee of one guinea had been established for an arbitration, and ten for an appeal.[23] Appeals were unusual; for example, in 1864 there were only four. The committee sometimes arbitrated disputes over London contracts; this was stopped in 1870.[24] By determining appeals the committee created a case law, and the president would answer formal questions on the custom of the trade at the weekly meetings of the brokers.

There could be friction between the brokers, the cotton merchants, and the spinners over this system. Thus, in 1865 there was disagreement with the spinners, and a broker called James Pitcairn Campbell became involved in litigation with Messrs Topp and Coupland, who had repudiated a contract, apparently an 'arrival' contract. At the assizes the judge ruled that neither the arbitration clause nor trade custom applied. This alarmed the association, which communicated its view that the repudiation was unjustified to Topp and Coupland, who, not being brokers, were not members of the association. Eventually the dispute was amicably settled in Campbell's favour.[25] At this date a new form of contract was coming into use, and this was submitted to counsel, no doubt in the hope of preventing any repetition of recourse to the courts. In 1870 another dispute broke out when Messrs Taylor and Greg, members of the association, refused to accept an arbitrator's decision; notice was given of a motion to expel them from the association, but in the end the matter was again settled amicably.[26] Considerable efforts were made by officers of the association to encourage negotiated settlements. The association also tried to establish uniformity of grades by adopting standard samples,[27]

[22] See records for 7 Oct. 1842.

[23] MS 380 COT 1/2, 10 Feb. 1865.

[24] MS 380 COT 1/5, 7 Oct. 1870.

[25] See MS 380 COT 1/2 for 1864–5 for the dispute, the full details of which do not appear from the records. I have not yet traced the litigation in local newspapers.

[26] MS 380 COT 1/5, entries for 14 Oct. and following. The dispute arose because they had a contract for Dhollerah cotton, and delivery was tendered of cotton which they thought was Mangarole, a different 'growth' of Surat cotton. Their position was that if this was so, no question of adjusting the price could arise; the sellers had simply failed to make a valid tender at all. There was, however, considerable difference of opinion as to which growth the cotton was, or whether it was some sort of mixture. The arbitrators ruled the buyers should accept, subject to a reduction in price, the cotton being adjuged Dhollerah. The principle that price-adjustment was only proper for variations in quality, but not growth, was not challenged.

[27] Thus on 30 Dec. 1842 standard samples of 'Fair' were agreed; these could be borrowed.

and it arranged a uniform scheme of fire insurance.[28] It also assumed the power to expel members for misconduct, the first recorded case occurring in 1843.[29] Expulsion for misconduct,[30] for bankruptcy, and for reaching an accomodation with creditors, was regulated in December of 1870.[31] Expelled members could be readmitted.

The association also modified trade customs by what amounted to legislation. Thus, in 1842 it settled the fee of 1½ per cent due to a broker for sampling and reporting on a bale, and on 3 April 1843 resolved:

> it is recommended as a rule for the future that all cotton shall be sold with a warranty that it is equal to sample, and that any claim for damaged or unmerchantable cotton be allowed, if such claim, properly authenticated, is made within twelve months from the date of purchase, and that a clause to this effect be inserted in every invoice as part of the contract.[32]

This recomendation involved the standardization of printed contractual documents. Although no records of the association exist from 1851 until April of 1864,[33] we can guess that other similar matters of contract were clarified or regulated, and we know from a correspondence in *The Times*[34] that in late 1863 the association settled a standardized printed form of contracts for cotton 'to arrive', though members were not apparently required to use this form.[35]

[28] See 23 June 1843.

[29] MS 380 COT 1/1. On 21 Oct. 1843 Messrs Wood and Briddon were thus expelled. Their crime was that of buying cotton in the name of principals without actual authorization, a practice regarded as dishonourable.

[30] MS 380 COT 1/5. The Committee had to propose expulsion and the proposal be accepted by two-thirds of those present and voting at the weekly meeting. The rules of 1871 include this arrangement in Rule 31.

[31] No date, but late 1870; there is a gap in the records.

[32] This was merely a recommendation, and a committee was set up to discuss the matter with all interested parties. The plan was adopted on 26 Apr. 1843, invoices thereafter having the provision 'Warranted free from damage and false packing provided the claim be made in twelve months'. This provision does not go to grade; it relates to defects only becoming apparent when the bales are unwrapped. There had been litigation on the matter in a case in 1796, and it was then argued that there existed a custom in the Liverpool market that in the absence of fraud no claim of this kind was allowed unless objection was made at the time of sale. The King's Bench had rejected this argument.

[33] When MS 380 COT 1/1 begins, intervening records having been lost.

[34] See 12 Nov. 6, col.4. Correspondence followed on Dec. 11, 14, and 17.

[35] The full text was as follows: 'FORM OF CONTRACT FOR COTTON TO ARRIVE. / Liverpool——186— / M.—We have this day——to arrive ex——from——Guaranteed ——. In case of dispute arising out of this contract the matter to be referred to two respectable brokers for settlement, who shall decide as to quality and the allowance, if any, to be made. / The cotton to be taken from the——with customary allowance of tare and draft and the invoice to be dated from the delivery of the last bale from the——or——. / To be delivered in merchantable condition to the buyer, the damaged, if any, to be rejected, provided it cannot be made merchantable. / Should, however, the vessel or

Arrival Contracts: The 'Shipment' Form

Dealings might respond to specific orders from spinners, be for re-export, or be 'on speculation', when the cotton would form part of the available cotton stock. Market reports from 1816 use these three categories; large quantities might be bought 'on speculation'.[36] For example, in 1825 purchases for consumption totalled 622,106 bales, and of these 302,000 had been purchased 'on speculation'. 'Bull' speculation was involved, based on the belief that the price would rise so that it was worth holding cotton against this possibility. Most of the speculative transactions were probably in cotton 'on the spot', available in the market for inspection and delivery. Until reasonably reliable systems of sampling, grading, and arbitration were developed, there were obvious risks in buying cotton without an opportunity to inspect.[37]

Even in the eighteenth century there was trading in cotton afloat, but this was not common until the 1850s.[38] By the 1860s, market reports often mention such trading. The contracts were called 'contracts to arrive',[39] and there is some evidence that before the 1850s they were commonly made only after the vessel was reported off Point Lynas, about fifty miles from the port, where there was a signal station. They might also be made later, but before unloading had begun. In the mid-nineteenth century it became common to make them when the vessel was still on the high seas, or even before it had sailed.

The explanation for this development is that information could now travel more rapidly than cargoes. Cotton continued to be normally carried by sailing vessels long after the invention of steamships, because the capacity of the latter was limited; engines and coal occupied much space, and the coal had to be carried to coaling stations

vessels be lost, the contract to be void; but should the cotton be transhipped to other vessels arriving at the port, the contract for such portion to hold good. / Payment within ten days from date of invoice or before delivery, if required, equal to ten days and six months.' (It will be seen that the trading-rules are here inserted into the text of the contract. As the rules became more complex they were codified in a separate document, to which all contracts referred.)

[36] See E. J. Donnell, *Chronological and Statistical History of Cotton* (New York, 1872), 84. Donnell gives figures for speculative purchases from 1821. Ellison takes them back to 1816. Early figures are taken from circulars issued by brokers for the information of their clients.

[37] It was not the normal practice to unpack bales; they were inspected and samples removed with a tool rather similar to an apple-corer. The process of evaluating a parcel of cotton must have inevitably involved an element of averaging. The point of the warranty, discussed above, was to cope with defects which only became known when the bales were unpacked for actual use.

[38] See e.g. *The Economist*, 29 Nov. 1851, 1,333; 6 Dec., 1,356.

[39] See *The Economist*, 4 Oct. 1862, 1,115; 18 Oct., 1,170; 25 Oct., 1,198; 8 Nov., 1,252.

by sailing vessels. One writer[40] has, indeed, connected the trade in cotton in transit with the introduction of steamships carrying mails on the Atlantic route in the 1840s; by the 1850s steamships were crossing in about ten days, sailing vessels in up to two months. In fact, 'arrival' contracts were at first most common in the East Indian trade where the time difference between the arrival of information and the arrival of cargo was much more considerable.[41] Cotton went round the Cape of Good Hope long after the Suez Canal opened in 1869; sailing vessels could not use the canal because of the lack of reliable wind systems and the high cost of towage.[42] The voyage, a minimum of 11,000 miles, took around four months.[43] But as early as 1849, mail from India would regularly reach England in around a month; cables were faster still, though expensive and unreliable.[44] Until 1869 mail travelled from India by the 'overland' route, being trans-shipped and carried across the isthmus. The system was extremely reliable; mail-ships were subsidized, punctuality being encouraged by penalties. Furthermore, an elaborate system of reporting, organized by Lloyd's of London, purveyed information on the movements of vessels, published in *Lloyd's List*.

The American Civil War further encouraged trading in cotton 'to arrive'. It caused the Lancashire Cotton Famine, and greatly increased trade in cotton from India, now the principal source of supply. The price of East Indian cotton rose to unprecedented heights and became very volatile; any rumour of peace would cause a drop. It was believed, wrongly, that a vast stock of American cotton, held up by the blockade, might come on to the market and collapse the price of East Indian cotton. So, during the war, there was immense speculation in cotton, huge fortunes being made and lost in Liverpool. Published

[40] J. H. Todd, *The Marketing of Cotton* (London, 1934). On the rise of the steamship, see D. B. Tyler, *Steam Conquers the Atlantic* (New York and London, 1931). Steamships could maintain a steady speed and constant track; this enabled them by 1838 to establish crossing-times as low as sixteen days, *The Great Western* establishing this record.

[41] This is suggested by the market reports published regularly in *The Economist* in the 1850s and 1860s.

[42] Some cotton did, however, come through the canal: *The Times* reported this on 31 May 1870, one of the first vessels involved being *The Bywell Castle*, known to students of British Admiralty law from 'the rule in the *Bywell Castle*'. I assume such vessels carried other higher-value merchandise too, and were not simply cotton-carriers.

[43] The October vessel in the *Raffles* case left Bombay on 20 Oct. 1862 and arrived in the Mersey on 14 Feb. 1863. The second vessel left Bombay on Christmas Eve of 1862 and arrived in the Mersey on 19 Apr. 1863, after calling at Queenstown (now Cobh).

[44] Although a cable service covering the whole distance was not established until 1865, much of the distance was covered before this. See F. J. Goldsmid, *Telegraph and Travel: A narrative of the Formation and Development of Telegraphic Communications between England and India* (London 1974); J. Kieve, *The Electric Telegraph. A Social and Economic History* (Newton Abbot, 1973). There is an excellent article by J. A. Fleming in the 11th edition of the *Encyclopedia Britannica* (1911). Commercial documents had of course to be sent by mail.

market reports for 1862 and 1863 contain many references to arrival contracts for Indian cotton, some for cotton which would not arrive for very considerable periods, up to four or five months ahead. Probably these were what was known as 'ship-named' and 'port-named' contracts, specifying both the vessel and the port of shipment, as did the contract in the *Raffles* case. Some appear to have been made even before the vessel sailed from India.

These early 'arrival' contracts did not attempt to specify the date of arrival, even approximately.[45] They were called 'shipments', and usually, though not always, specified the vessel and of course the quantity of cotton, together with its type and quality.[46] Some such contracts, unlike that used in the *Raffles* case, specified approximate sailing dates (for example, 'October shipment').[47] Even where no month of shipment was specified it would normally be known to the parties. Market reports of such contracts commonly mention a month or a pair of coupled months of shipment.[48] Sailing vessels did not put to sea on a predetermined day but when conditions seemed appropriate, so this was as precise as one could expect to be. It was

[45] Actual notes or bills of sale have usually not survived; some examples may lurk in libraries or private collections of documents, but I have not located any early examples. Consequently one has to deduce their contents from the form of market reports. The earliest-known text of such a contract, so far as I am aware, is provided in the law reports of the case of *Neill* v. *Whitworth* (n. 19 above), the contract dating from 2 Oct. 1863. This followed the standard form settled by the Cotton Brokers' Association and read as follows: 'Bought for account of Messrs. Neill, Brothers, of B. Whitworth & Brothers Manchester, 500 bales of cotton, at 15 1/8d. per 1b., guarranteed October shipment, to arrive in Liverpool per ship or ships from Calcutta. / The cotton guaranteed fair Bengal. Any slight variation in mark not to vitiate this contract. In case of dispute arising out of this contract, the matter to be referred to two respectable brokers, who shall decide as to quality, and the allowance, if any, to be made. / The cotton to be taken from the quay: customary allowance for tare and draft; and the invoice to be dated from date of delivery of last bale. / To be in merchantable condition; the damaged, if any, to be rejected, provided it cannot be made merchantable. Should the cotton be transhipped into other vessels arriving, the contract to hold good; but if any of the vessels be lost, the contract to be void, so far as regards such ships only. / Payment, cash within ten days, made equal to ten days and three months. Cash on account, before delivery, if required. TRUEMAN AND ROUSE.' On 8 Jan. 1864 the vendors declared the ships by which the cotton was to arrive as the *Talavera* and *Fort George*. This declaration would include the marks. The former vessel arrived on 3 Feb., but the latter ran aground on the Welsh coast, and half the cotton was taken from her and arrived by rail to be warehoused in the wreck-transit sheds. The issue in the case was whether delivery could be tendered from the warehouse.

[46] Type or growth differs from grade (essentially quality). But cotton of a given type and grade might still be defective, for example through sea-water damage, and this might make it unmerchantable. Grades did not depend upon staple.

[47] See n. 45 above for an 1863 example specifying the month of shipment.

[48] Market reports probably reproduced what was included in the contract, but may sometimes have conflated what was specified in the contract itself with information on ship-movements which was known and formed the basis of contracting. There is no way of being certain in any particular case.

necessarily up to the parties to form their own estimate of a vessel's likely time of arrival and discharge, based on such information as came to hand.

These 'shipment' contracts, it must be emphasized, were for specific lots of cotton, identified by the marks on the bales which, before tender, the seller had to supply to the purchaser, together of course with the name of the ship if this had not been specified in the contract.[49] Normally this information would arrive in the mails. The process was called 'the declaration'. P. J. Hemelryk, who had experience of the trade as a broker from 1870, and indirect knowledge from 1859,[50] wrote of the period 1864–70, a little later: 'With regard to shipments, originally between 1864 and about 1870, the cotton was sold, the ship named, the quality guarranteed, and after a little while the marks were given.' This describes the nature of the transaction which *Raffles* v. *Wichelhaus* entered into a little before Hemelryk became a broker, probably in January 1863.[51]

Arrival Contracts: The 'Delivery' Form

During the 1860s—the first example I know of is in 1862[52]—a new and significantly different form of arrival contract appears. This was called a 'delivery', as opposed to a 'shipment'.[53] 'Deliveries' were radically different from 'shipments', in which the time for performance—which, in a volatile market, was commercially very important—was only fixed indirectly by the contract, being the date at which the carrying vessel happened to arrive.[54] In 'deliveries' the time for performance was fixed in the contract itself by reference to calendar months. Hence the period for delivery, and the last moment at which it could be tendered, was

[49] The trading-rules of Aug. 1867 specify, by rule 2, that in arrival contracts which name either the ship or ships, or the time of shipment, the declaration must be made within a specified period, which differs according to the origin of the cotton.

[50] He had been a Liverpool general merchant between 1859 and 1870. His *Forty Years Reminiscences of the Cotton Market*, a lecture of 1899, was published in 1916.

[51] See for fuller discussion my article cited above, n. 1.

[52] The reference is in *The Economist*, 29 Nov. 1862, 1,333; the contract was for new (that is, new crop) Dhollerah.

[53] There is a reference to such a contract in MS 380 COT 1/2 on 16 Sept. 1864. A contract had been made for Fair Egyptian cotton for August delivery; a declaration (of the marks) was made on 30 Aug. and some of the cotton was below standard when sampled. The seller then purported to amend the declaration, that is by specifying other bales. It was ruled that no amendment was possible after the last date fixed for delivery (that is, 31 Aug.). Another example of such a contract made on 1 Apr. 1864 was the subject of litigation in *Williams* v. *Reynolds* (above, n. 19).

[54] And be unloaded in the dock; there could be some time between arriving off the port, finding a berth, and completing the discharge of cargo.

now directly specified. For East Indian cotton coupled months were used, such as March-April. The same practice is found in contracts after the Civil War relating to American cotton, though eventually one month becomes more usual in that trade. This form of arrival contract, unlike the earlier form, resembles a modern futures contract, where each contract states a calendar month, a 'position'; on its last day settlement becomes finally due. Plainly this change from 'shipments' to 'deliveries' is quite critical to the evolution of organized futures trading.

'Deliveries' came into use because the passage-times of sailing vessels had become more predictable. There was better route-planning, related to knowledge of wind systems; vessels became stronger, with better sail-carrying powers.[55] Furthermore, although sailing vessels did not themselves carry auxiliary engines, they now regularly used steam tugs, often over very considerable distances, to reduce the delays and dangers inherent in navigating square-rigged vessels in crowded waters.[56]

Although 'deliveries' became increasingly common, it was a long time before they wholly supplanted 'shipments'; in the 1870s both forms are regularly quoted in market reports. Indeed, a considerable variety of contractual forms continued in use much later than this. Some 'shipments' specified shipment months. Some named the port of shipment, some the ship, some both. Similarly, 'deliveries' might vary in detail, being 'port-named' or whatever. Different merchants followed their own inclinations.

It is a curious fact that the contract form later used in Liverpool for fully developed futures trading specified a two-month period for East Indian cotton, and one month for American, periods selected not because they had some special relevance to price movements but because of their relationship to the predictability of the passage-times of square-rigged sailing vessels. They persisted into a world in which the sailing vessels, as cotton carriers, had long become obsolete, and powered vessels came to be able to operate to time-tables.

Assignment of Rights in Arrival Contracts

During the Civil War there developed an extensive speculative business in assigning rights in 'arrival' contracts. No doubt this had

[55] Hemp standing rigging was replaced by wire. This enabled a heavier press of sail to be carried.

[56] Although square-rigged vessels can and regularly are tacked, they can, in the absence of a favourable current, make virtually no headway directly against the wind. Fore-and-aft rigged vessels can.

always been possible, but the scale and frequency of this practice increased at this time. This provoked a controversy which was aired in *The Times* in 1863.[57] One point raised was that a speculator needed no capital; he could buy cotton, and by assignment sell on if the price moved, collecting the difference. Thus, 'without a sixpence outlay [he could] realise a handsome profit on a quantity of cotton he could not have provided had he purchased it on the spot'. A consequential anxiety was the risk of the buyer's default if the price moved the wrong way; one suggestion was that a purchaser of cotton 'to arrive' should be required to deposit 25 per cent of the price with a bank by way of security—a system which, in the form of 'margins', was to be adopted in 1865 in the Chicago Board of Trade and in 1871 in the New York Cotton Exchange.[58] The correspondence suggests that a typical feature of futures markets is evolving; traders are simply speculating in price-fluctuations. Such traders, when engaged in speculation, are not in any real sense acting as cotton merchants, since they do not pay for and take possession of cotton, nor are they acting as brokers, exercising skill in inspecting and grading cotton as agents for others. They deal in 'differences', in gaps between the contract and market price, and not in cotton. For the practice of assigning rights in contracts down a chain of intermediaries, though it may operate to transfer actual cotton to the last purchaser, necessarily entails the settling of differences between the intermediaries. The prices at which the intermediate deals are made reflect shifting estimations of what the market price is likely to be when the cotton in which the dealers are speculating actually arrives.

At this early period there probably existed no distinct class of traders whose business was primarily or exclusively confined to dealing in differences. Speculators would normally also actually deal with the commodity itself and, if they were brokers, be specially skilled in sampling and grading the material, as well as being skilled in predicting movements in the market—the specialism of the pure speculator. Eventually, however, a class of pure speculators emerged who had no direct relationship with the commodity whatsoever. The modern futures trader would, I suppose, be quite horrified if he ever actually had to lay hands upon a pork-belly, or plunge a sampling tool into a dirty bale of cotton. He is quite remote from such sordid things.

A problem, well attested for the 1860s, is the complexity involved where rights had been assigned down a long chain of assignees. Ellison instanced a 'delivery' contract of cotton for a particular month. By the time the cotton arrived the chain might include as many as thirty persons. The first seller formally tenders delivery to the first

[57] See n. 34 above.
[58] See below, n. 104.

purchaser; the document declaring the marks is passed, by endorsement, down the chain from office to office. Further documents, and eventually cash, pass up the chain, until after a period varying between ten days and six weeks, the matter is concluded. The process was described by Ellison in his book *The Cotton Trade of Great Britain* (1886):

> There were delays at every stage; delays in passing on the declaration: delays in sampling the cotton; delays in the appointment of arbitrators; delays in forwarding of weighing over notices; delays in making out of invoices; delays in passing through payments on account and payments for final settlement. (p. 282)

One can imagine the scene as clerks and messengers scurried about in a world which possessed no telephones, and in which accounts were eventually settled in cash. To facilitate rapid and frequent trades—and it is high velocity which enables a market to be finely tuned to changing estimations of price-movements—the complexities must be reduced by rationalizing the mechanics of the system. The lower the transaction-costs can be made, the finer the differences which can be made the subject of speculation; conversely, when transaction-costs are high, dealings will take place only if there are considerable price fluctuations. No doubt it was the large fluctuations during the unsettled period of the Civil War which then encouraged speculative assignments, in spite of the high transaction-costs which were then involved.

Though very inconvenient, the practice I have described made possible an extensive trade in differences. Traders could also use the system in order to 'hedge' against price-fluctuations, but only imperfectly. For example, if a spinner has, in March, entered into a contract to buy 100 bales of June cotton, at 10*d*.a pound, this will protect him against any price-rise between March and June. But his contract does not protect against the risk of a fall. Conversely, the contract protects the seller only against a fall in the price; if the price rises he loses out. The hedging is thus imperfect. Between March and June the buyer could choose to assign his rights at the going market-rate for June deliveries, in reliance on his own view as to what is going to happen. Thus, if he decided that the June price was going to be below 10*d*., whereas traders generally continued to think 10*d*. to be right, he could assign at this figure, and rely on buying in June at a lower price. But in doing so he would not be hedging (that is, protecting himself against a price-fluctuation which went against him), but himself assuming the risk. So the system enables speculation to take place, but provides only imperfectly for risk-transfer from merchants to speculators.

Now the practices described, common during and just after the Civil War,[59] normally start with someone selling a parcel of real cotton, which is (or is believed to be) either on a vessel or about to be loaded on to one. Certain consequences follow. The first is that the contracts, dealing as they do with different quantities, growths, and grades of cotton, and with different vessels and ports of origin, are extremely varied in all respects, and not just in price and delivery-period. The contractual obligations could be standardized in codified trade customs, and their interpretation made predictable by the practice of arbitration and appeal. But the contracts themselves were quite unlike the contracts traded in a modern futures market. There the contracts are all for a standardized quantity of the commodity, or a multiple of that quantity, and (subject to qualifications to be explained) for one standard quality or grade; they differ only in price and delivery-period ('positions'). In a sense the contracts are fungible.

A second characteristic of the system described is that short selling, selling cotton you neither possess nor have a contractual right to receive, does not seem to have been involved to any significant extent, much less short selling of cotton between parties neither of whom intended that delivery of the cotton should ever be made. No doubt instances of short selling must always have occurred, either through error or deliberately during times of heavy speculation, sellers intending to purchase cotton of the appropriate quantity and grade in the market at below the contract price when delivery fell due. In 'arrival' contracts there was an interval between the date of contracting and the date at which specific cotton was identified by the 'declaration' as being the cotton sold, and a further interval between 'declaration' and actual tender. The existence of these intervals helped a 'short' seller. Furthermore, there would be users of cotton who, especially in times of dearth, would be happy (subject to price-adjustment) to accept usable cotton tendered even if it did not correspond to the cotton identified in the declaration.[60] There is evidence that short selling, regarded as disreputable ('most reprehensible and painful') by the older generation of brokers, was going on to a certain extent in 1863, as appears from the correspondence in *The Times*. The records of the brokers also contain a reference in 1865 to a variant form of short selling which was condemned as improper. One Mr Bird has sold to a second individual bales of cotton he had already earlier sold to a first person, and done so before the first contract had been cancelled. No

[59] And no doubt on a smaller scale well before.

[60] Importers may have made arrival contracts on the basis of imperfect information of precisely how much cotton their foreign agents had acquired in the port of loading; they might sell cotton in excess of what had been loaded.

doubt there were others who engaged in such practices and got away with it; we cannot tell how frequently this would happen.

The report of *Williams* v. *Reynolds* (1865)[61] provides evidence of a speculative practice involving a form of short selling which appears to have been viewed as respectable enough. There had been a 'forward-delivery' contract of 1 April 1864 for about 500 piculs of China cotton, at 16¾*d*. per pound, guaranteed fair, to be delivered in August 1864. Given the nature of cotton, the quantity contracted for was always to some degree uncertain. This contract seems to have made in the bona fide belief that about this amount would arrive. In the event it did not, and only 181 piculs were delivered. The litigation reveals a trading practice, apparently then in use, under which purchasers, instead of assigning their rights to a second purchaser, would make a distinct new contract to sell the same amount and type of cotton to a second purchaser, relying on performance of the first contract to enable delivery to be made. This is not short selling as I have defined it, though it does involve selling cotton which the seller does not yet possess, and which he may not be able to acquire in time, as here happened. The new contract made on 25 May was at 19¾*d*. per pound, and the case turned on assessment of damages: should the first vendor pay the difference between the contract price of 1 April and the market price on the date of the second contract—25 May—or the difference between the contract price of 1 April and the market price on the last day permissible for delivery under that contract, which was 31 August? Had this trading practice been established for some time the point would surely have been settled by custom.[62] Conducting speculation by making distinct new contracts, as opposed to merely assigning rights in existing contracts, was to become a standard feature of futures trading, and may have derived from this trade practice. It is essential to any system of 'bear' speculation.

Short Selling and the Basis Middling Contract

Short selling, regularly practised on a large scale, is necessarily hazardous if the type and grade of cotton is precisely specified in the contract, since that particular grade may be in short supply at the time fixed for delivery. Indeed, it is quite possible, given too great an enthusiasm for short selling, for more cotton of a particular grade to be sold, for example for October delivery, than exists in a deliverable state

[61] Cited above, n. 19. A picul is a man's load.

[62] The court ruled that the second solution was correct. This meant that the plaintiffs received £515. 19*s*. 0*d*. rather than £257. 19*s*. 6*d*.

in the Liverpool stock, or even the whole world, at the appropriate time. The more precisely the quality and type is specified, the greater the risk of this happening.[63] Clearly, a modification either of custom or contractual form which widened the class of deliverable cotton will facilitate and encourage the practice of short selling. It is with the rise in short selling that trading in forward-delivery contracts, soon to be called 'futures', comes to acquire its strikingly fictitious character.

Persons who have neither cotton nor contractual rights to cotton, and no intention of obtaining any, sell quantities of the commodity for forward delivery to other persons who have no wish to acquire the stuff, the joint intention being that the parties should, when delivery falls due, or earlier, simply settle differences between the contract price and the market price. P. E. J. Hemelryk, who was in business in Liverpool as a general merchant from 1859, and in 1870 became a cotton broker, recorded his recollection of the development:

> I believe a firm in Manchester was the first to discover it would sometimes be profitable to sell what one has not got, and what eventually might not be needed. In 1864 the first transaction of that kind in Surats[64] took place. Later on, between 1864 and 1870, it was done continually.

The critical innovation which facilitated short selling was, so tradition has it, the brain-child of one John Rew, who entered the cotton business in 1863. Rew's contracts fixed a price related to one grade of cotton, but allowed other cotton, down to a specified lower grade, to be delivered, subject to a price-adjustment, settled if need be by arbitration.

Rew's device builds from the practice enshrined in the 1863 form of contract, which permitted arbitrators to make an 'allowance'—an adjustment of the price to reflect some defect in quality. Probably arbitrators could not do this if the difference was as significant as a whole grade.[65] There is, indeed, a ruling of the committee of the association on 27 July 1865 on this point: that in a sale of Egyptian cotton 'Fair Quality', to arrive, any cotton below 'Mid-Fair', a half-grade, is to be rejected.[66] Rew's contracts extended this power, broadening thereby the class of deliverable cotton.

Rew's contract came to be called a 'basis middling' contract—the contract price was fixed on the basis of delivery of 'middling'-grade

[63] *Morgan* v. *Gath* (above, n. 19), illustrates this problem.

[64] Surat is the name of a port from which cotton was shipped; the name came to be applied to all types of cotton shipped from Bombay, that is to say coming from the hinterland of that port.

[65] A grade of cotton is a relatively crude subdivision. The material can be graded into half- and quarter-grades.

[66] MS 380 COT 1/2.

cotton. The tradition is that Rew, after the Atlantic cable had come into operation in 1866, facilitating transactions in cotton to arrive, employed his form of contract to enter into hedging transactions in American cotton. He would buy American cotton by cable, for forward delivery, and hedge by selling equivalent quantities, 'basis middling', for the same position. Any price-movement would thus be offset, the two transactions, as it were, cancelling each other out. The tradition is wrong: I have in fact found reference to 'basis middling' contracts well before the cable was in operation.[67] John Rew probably used a contract form already in use—it would be convenient sometimes in situations where neither short selling nor hedging was involved—to develop his system of offsetting transactions, and prospered in consequence.

Before the invention of the 'basis middling' contract it was possible, as I have explaind, for a person engaged in selling actual cotton to protect himself against a fall in price by making a contract for forward delivery, and a buyer (say a spinner) could similarly protect himself against a rise. The use of offsetting contracts enabled both buyer and seller to protect themselves against the risk of any movement in price. The risk does not, of course, disappear; it is transferred to speculators who are willing to enter into such offsetting contracts. Since this system entails the making of contracts simply to transfer risk, rather than transfer lots of cotton, it inevitably goes hand in hand with a regular practice of closing or cancelling such contracts by settling differences.

References to 'basis middling' or similar contracts[68] are common in the American trade from 1868, and in the East Indian trade in the early 1870s. They could hardly pass into common use unless the market was organized so as to establish, reasonably objectively, notional market prices for grades, with imperfections papered over by arbitration.[69]

The Birth of Futures Trading

Futures trading in cotton has become established when trades in fictitious contracts for cotton 'to arrive', that is short sales, employing

[67] Thus *The Economist*, 6 Jan. 1863, 17, mentions a contract for 'upland, on a basis of middling'.

[68] The rules of the Liverpool market for 1871 have a provision (54(1)) which permits cotton lots which 'average the quality denominated in the contract' to be considered 'equal to contract'. This is not unlike Rew's device, and widens the class of deliverable cotton.

[69] The notional 'market price' of a commodity must be based upon some form of averaging-out of actual trades over a particular period of time, or estimate as to what traders at a particular time will be willing to pay. Thus the opening price in the New York cotton market is announced by an official when trading begins; when I visited this

'delivery' contracts rather than 'shipments', are being conducted on a considerable scale, and are being employed as a medium for speculation which has replaced the earlier practice of trading in assignments of non-fictitious contracts for cotton 'to arrive'. Historians are naturally much preoccupied with chronology, and have tried to place fairly precise date on the birth of futures trading. Thus, S. Dumbell argued that futures trading existed in the Liverpool market before the Civil War. But he did not differentiate the use of contracts for forward delivery, which have existed in one form or another since the Middle Ages and indeed before, from organized fictitious trading in contracts. He also did not attempt to analyse the transition from one system to the other.[70] Again, Arthur Marsh, writing in 1911, dated the development to 1868 or 1869. He had no direct experience of the Liverpool market, but had been Chairman of the New York Exchange, and would have had contacts with Liverpool traders.[71] Other writers with more direct knowledge, whilst being vague about dates, suggest a development in the period after the Civil War, and one related to improvements in telegraphic communications.[72] This vagueness is justified: what is involved is that a few innovative traders make use of contractual forms, originally evolved for trading in real cotton, for the purpose of speculation and risk transfer, and by degrees the practice becomes increasingly common, and more acceptable. In response, the market practices become organized to facilitate the practice. Hence, precise dates are not to be found. What is originally involved is, in a sense, an abuse of contractual forms, and this tends to conceal what is happening from us. Thus, such of the early records of the Cotton Brokers Association as deal with contractual practices, and such early trading-rules and contract forms as have survived, all appear on the surface to be related to non-fictitious trading in actual cotton. It was for such trading that they had been evolved. The records are, in any event, difficult to interpret without direct knowledge of current trading-practices. These they do not record; they were not compiled for historians.

market the official became increasingly visibly agitated as the moment for trading approached, presumably because of fear lest his estimate should prove gravely erroneous. During trading, computers purportedly average trades conducted in the ring, but since the officials are unable to report all of these accurately, the process is defective. When I visited the exchange one of the officials was elderly and a little deaf.

[70] See Dumbell, n. 6 above.

[71] See Marsh, n. 6 above, 592. Marsh is here quoting from Thomas Ellison.

[72] August F. Weiner, who had been engaged in the cotton trade from 1857 to about 1884, said that futures trading was unknown before the Civil War, and was grafted on to the practice of trading in East Indian cotton to arrive developed during the war, being encouraged by improved telegraphs. See LXIX *The Journal of the Royal Statistical Soc.*, at 365–6. He was commenting on a paper by S. T. Chapman and D. Knoop. Thomas Ellison's account is similar.

I have already referred to the codification of trading-custom in the text of the standard-form arrivals contract of 1863.[73] The later practice was to shorten the text and incorporate trading-rules by reference to a separate printed code, revised from time to time, all contracts being subject to the code. This practice appears to date from 1864; the code of this year (and associated standard-form contract) only related to 'arrival' contracts.[74] These rules became more elaborate with the passage of time. There were certainly revisions in 1864, 1865, 1866, 1867, and 1869,[75] and perhaps in other years, but the earliest complete code of rules which I have located, apart from those of 1863, dates from August 1867, and comprises ten rules dealing exclusively with 'arrival' contracts.[76] The next is a general code of all the rules governing the association, dating from January 1871, a copy having been found, in response to my request, in the current offices of the Cotton Association in Liverpool.

The 1867 rules, printed on one sheet of paper and presumably intended to be pinned up on an office wall, make no explicit reference to fictitious trading. They simply regulate, rather more minutely than had been the case in 1863, delivery, declarations, disputes over defects in quality, and arbitration. Any fictitious trading at this date took place, as it were, in spite of the rules, which were not adapted to facilitate the practice. Nor does this code refer explicitly to any distinction between 'shipments' and 'deliveries', though there is implicit reference in Rule 2. This provides that for 'ship-named' contracts, or contracts for shipment before a certain date, a declaration must be made within a set period; by implication no such requirement applied to 'deliveries' where the ship was not specified.[77] Another provision in Rule 2 dealing with last minute tender reads:

That in cases where Cotton is *tendered* on the last day of the month, the seller shall be in possession of a warehouse delivery order, to enable the buyer at

[73] See above, n. 35. Regulation comes earlier. Thus, on 3 Apr. 1843 a recommendation that sales be subject to warranty was made; on 28 Jan. 1845 rules were made for sampling; on 12 Mar. 1847 a rule was laid down as to the time for tendering cash payments—half-an-hour before the banks shut. But no codes were produced at this early period. See MS 380 COT 1/1.

[74] See MS 380 COT 1/2, resolution of 17 June 1864. I have not located a text of the 1864 code.

[75] S. Dumbell, n. 6 above, refers to these and no doubt had access to texts. There are also references in MS 380 COT 1/2 and 1/3

[76] Text in MS 380 COT 1/4. These rules incorporate additions made between 1863 and 1867; e.g. the provision in Rule 1 on falsely packed bales was added on 20 Aug. 1867. The provision on arbitration in Rule 7 probably dates from 1864, and the provisions as to declarations to Aug. 1866. The code of Aug. 1867 was again amended on 6 Dec. 1867 to enable a 'ship and port named' contract to be cancelled by the buyer if the ship, at the time of contracting, had not yet reached the port of shipment.

[77] The point of the distinction seems to me to be obscure.

once to take delivery of the Cotton. In default the buyer shall have the option either of declaring the contract cancelled, so far as regards any undeclared number of bales, or of claiming from the seller the difference in the market price of the Cotton undeclared, or of purchasing similar Cotton against the seller, who shall forthwith make good to the buyer the loss (if any) on such repurchase.

This rule was plainly designed to favour buyers who actually want to receive cotton; it insisted, when tender was made at the last permissible moment, upon ability to deliver immediately. For 'shipments' at least this rule, and indeed the rules in general, were if anything hostile to short sellers.

An aspect of the rules of 1867 which might be expected to throw light on the rise of fictitious trading is the regulation of 'declarations'. When an arrival contract, relating to real cotton in transit, was made, the cotton was identified by what was known as a declaration, made in writing, which named the ship or ships[78] on which the cotton was to arrive, and the marks on the bales. The declaration tied together the contract and the cotton, and presumably would normally be based on information sent by mail. So far as I can tell the custom was to make the declaration as soon as the information became available.[79] Now in fictitious trading there is no cotton, so there could be no declaration. One might expect the rules to respond to this fact if fictitious trading was then common, but there is nothing in the 1867 rules which seems to do so. They do indeed regulate the practice of making declarations.[80] In the case of an arrival contract from an East Indian, Chinese, or Japanese port, the declaration was to be made within two months,[81] and shorter times were fixed for European or American ports. This requirement must have had the effect of discouraging the use of 'shipment' contracts by short sellers, and this may have been the point of the regulation. Information identifying the cotton would not have been of any practical use to a buyer before the ship arrived, but an obligation to declare in good time would discourage short selling and other dubious practices.[82] Declarations on delivery contracts were not regulated, perhaps because the practice was to declare at the time of tender and not earlier, and the buyer was adequately protected against short sellers by the rule as to tender. The lack of regulation

[78] Even in 'ship-named' contracts there could be trans-shipment in some situations, as provided in the rules of 1863.

[79] In the case of cotton shipped from India about a month after the ship sailed.

[80] By clause 2.

[81] Or three if the mails did not arrive as expected.

[82] If a seller was able to delay a declaration identifying the cotton by ship and marks there would be some scope for a seller who had rights in various parcels of similar cotton afloat to earmark parcels to a particular contract in response to the state of the market.

may, however, have incidentally encouraged the use of this type of contract by short sellers.

All in all it looks very much as if in 1867 fictitious trading was not sufficiently common, or perhaps sufficiently respectable, for the rules to be adapted to the practice. However, the absence of any requirement of early declaration in 'delivery' contracts was bound to facilitate 'bear' transactions employing this form of contract; so long as the seller could obtain suitable cotton by the last delivery-day he was safe. Conceivably this was intended, and there is evidence that short selling occurred. Thus, on 23 October 1868 Messrs Comer and Charlton Jones proposed tightening up the rules governing the time of declaration with the aim of discouraging the use of arrival contracts for 'bear' transactions.[83]

The 1871 'Rules Relating to Cotton Sold to Arrive', collected as sub-clauses of Rule 54 of the *Constitution, Laws and Usages of the Liverpool Cotton Brokers' Association*,[84] again do not seem to be adapted to fictitious trading. It is plain from them that a wide variety of contract forms were then being used, principally 'shipment'; contracts. All were lumped together as arrival contracts. One provision did, however, deal expressly with 'deliveries', which had not been specifically mentioned in the 1867 rules; this provision indicates their rising importance.[85] Although at this date trading in contracts which did not relate to identifiable parcels of cotton, and which were in that sense fictitious, may well have existed on an increasing scale, the rules, on their face, seem entirely adapted to trading in real cotton—in 'actuals'—the form of trade around which arrival contracts had developed.[86]

Unfortunately the next set of trading-rules which I have located dates from 1878.[87] Between 1867 and 1878 a major change has taken place. There is now one set of trading *Rules Relating to Cotton Sold To Arrive* and an entirely separate set of *Rules Relating to Cotton Sold For Delivery*. Under both, delivery of cotton is possible, and the rules governing the former are still largely appropriate to the sale of

[83] See MS 380 COT 1/4.

[84] Arbitration is covered in part by para. 19.

[85] Rule 54(2): 'In cases where Cotton shall be tendered under a contract for delivery on or before a given date, the seller must, at the time of the tender, be able to give the buyer immediate delivery of the Cotton.' This slightly modifies the rule of 1867 by explicitly limiting in to deliveries.

[86] The provision in the rules of 1867 which I presented as protective of the buyer is still there, but with a change. The rights it gives to the buyer only arise when, in a 'shipment' contract, the seller fails, *after a formal request*, to identify the cotton by declaring the name of the vessel and the marks. Possibly the point was to prevent contracts being cancelled when the seller, by some oversight, failed to make the declaration in time. In the case of a delivery, the only specified obligation is that the seller who tenders must be able to give immediate delivery.

[87] MS 380 COT 4/30. The rules referred to are of July 1878.

identifiable lots of specific cotton. But both sets of rules explicitly provide for the practice of closing contracts[88] and settling differences. Even more significantly, the standard contract forms, which accompany the rules, envisage contracts being made not for real lots of cotton, which would come in various quantities, but for standard 'parcels' of cotton of a notional character, each weighing 43,200 lbs. By this date the delivery form is regularly used for futures trading.[89]

The change in trading-practice between 1871 and 1878, which involved a sharp separation between 'shipments' and 'deliveries', and the rules governing them, appears to have occurred in mid-November 1873. The date can indeed be deduced from the appearance in the press of market reports in a new form, one which reflects this separation. Thus, a report in *The Economist* late in 1873 contains quotations, presumably derived from the Liverpool Exchange, in the following form:

Delivery, American, any port, L.M.C., October–November $8\frac{1}{4}$.
Shipment, American, any port, G.O.C., October–November $8\frac{3}{4}$.

The initials refer to versions of the 'basis middling' contract: L.M.C. means 'not below low middling' ('Low Middling Clause') and G.O.C. means 'not below good ordinary' ('Good Ordinary Clause'). It was the delivery form, which defined the last moment for delivery or settlement in the contract, which came to be used for futures trading. It will be seen that the contracts being quoted are stereotyped, and have no reference to any particular lot of cotton. Some revision of standard contract forms to produce these two types of stereotyped contracts must have come into use in mid-November. It is significant that Alfred B. Shepperson, a knowledgeable American writer on *Cotton Futures*, writing in 1911, claimed that the Liverpool futures market began in 1873; I take it he refers to the changes reflected in the market reports.

The records of the association also confirm that an important change took place in 1873. There are some references in the reports of the management committee to the new forms of contract[90] and much fuller accounts of the discussions which took place at the weekly meetings of the brokers.[91] From these it appears that an entirely new set of rules was passed by the association in June of 1873—they came into force in mid-November—and two new standard forms of contract, one for

88 For arrival contracts they provide a way of fixing the date at which the contract may be closed.

89 Presumably because of the conservatism of the trade. Delivery contracts adapted to specific parcels of cotton may also have been coming into use.

90 380 COT 3/1 July 29 1873, 27 Sept. 1873.

91 380 COT 1/8.

arrivals, and one for deliveries, were settled at the same time, after legal advice had been taken. Unfortunately the records do not include texts of the new rules or the new contracts.

The Problem of Cancellation of Contracts

The discussions which led to this change began in April of 1873. They centred on a problem caused by cancellation of contracts. It was not new, for back in 1870 a special committee had proposed the resolution: 'That means ought to be adopted to avoid the cancelling of contracts.'[92] As we have seen, the system of speculation which became prevalent in the Civil War period involved assigning the buyer's rights down a chain of assignees. These rights normally related to identifiable parcels of cotton. The first buyer in the chain and his assignees were apparently entitled to cancel the contract (cancel, that is, without paying differences) on a variety of grounds—if the seller did not make the declaration in due time; if the contract time for shipment in a shipment contract was not observed; if the cotton, when sampled, was below the permissible grade as specified in the contract, or if it was of a different growth. All this made good sense in a system of transactions adapted for persons who actually wanted cotton, but no sense for speculators in price-differences, since if the first buyer or an assignee cancelled, the entire chain collapsed, and with it all the speculative transactions involved. What speculators in price-movements needed was contracts which were incapable of cancellation, contracts which permitted the parties only the choice between delivery or the payment of differences.

A long discussion of the problem at a meeting of brokers on 2 April produced no solution. On 3 April 1873 a Mr P. S. Boult proposed by way of solution that for arrival and future-delivery contracts there should in future be no right to cancel whatever. The last buyer in the chain should have the choice of taking whatever was tendered, with price-adjustment, or of returning the cotton to the seller at the market value of the day, his decision binding all intermediate parties. In the course of further discussions it was also proposed that in future all contracts should be for standard units of weight. Approving reference was made to the system in the New York Cotton Exchange:

> Mr Boult said the suggestion . . . of a specific weight might be good—such as in New York where he was informed by Mr Marsh the system had been in use three years and had worked well settling deliveries. First seller invoiced to last buyer at price of day—differences actually ascertained, weights fixed at 450

[92] MS 380 COT 1/5, 30 Sept. 1870.

pounds—binding intermediate parties and the loss ascertained on each transaction.[93]

Clearly some brokers, Mr Boult being an example, wanted to facilitate speculative fictitious trading. The mention of New York provoked Mr Morgan, reflecting the conservative nature of the older brokers, to say that he 'thought a fictitious business would be introduced—it should be as bona fide as possible'. Mr Hobson thought that they should adopt (I take it, for speculative purposes) deliveries rather than shipments, and on fixed weights, 'on a different system from Shipments'. The suggestion fastens on the root of the difficulty—the use of one set of contractual practices (the rules for arrival contracts) to serve two quite different functions (speculation and the acquisition of cotton). This discussion suggests that in 1873 futures trading was still not really established, and was more fully developed in New York; some brokers wished to develop such trading, perhaps envying the system across the Atlantic. In the event, the whole matter was referred to a special committee. At the same time a more efficient system was evolved for making declarations; all were to be made in one place, the rooms of the association, which was to be deemed the office of the buying broker.[94]

Out of this committee emerged the new trading-rules of 1873 and the two new contract forms, one for 'shipments', one for 'deliveries'. The former, the older form, was now alone called an 'arrival' contract. The earliest located text of the new rules come from 1878, being an amended version of the 1873 text. The 'delivery' rules still, of course, make provision for actual delivery of cotton, but express provision is made for the practice of closing contracts, and there is no right whatever to cancel such a contract: 'No contract shall be cancelled on any ground.'[95] In various traditional variant forms, 'delivery' arrival contracts remained in use in the 1870s and 1880s—for example 'port-named' contracts—and apparently long after. I presume they were used by cotton merchants engaged in the trade in actuals.[96] 'Deliveries' became the form of contract commonly quoted, since they were the

[93] Meeting of 7 Apr. 1873.

[94] This was first done on 1 May, with complete success. The idea of a clearing-house was discussed, and for declarations, this was a sort of clearing-house.

[95] Rule 9. I assume this dates from 1873. The terminology of the New York market used the terms 'close' and 'cancel' as synonymous, so that a contract could be closed or cancelled but on payment of differences. In Liverpool, if a contract was 'cancelled' this meant that the deal was avoided.

[96] I must concede that it is obscure from the sources I have consulted how this trade was normally conducted. What I suspect happened was that importers made forward-delivery contracts, and the practice of assigning rights in such contracts passed out of use; speculative and hedging transactions were conducted through the vehicle of distinct 'futures' contracts.

medium of price-speculation. In a typical market report they are are referred to as follows: 'Delivery: American, any port, L.M.C. July $6\frac{3}{4}$, July–August $6\frac{22}{32}$, Aug.–September $6\frac{11}{16}$, Sept.–October $6\frac{17}{32}$, Nov.–Dec. $7\frac{7}{32}$.'

It will be seen that all references to a specific lot of cotton of a particular type on a particular ship sailing from a particular port has been excised, so that each contract for American cotton for a particular position is identical with any other contract except as to price. This stereotyping is assisted by the adoption of a standard unit of quantity of 43,200 pounds[97] in about 100 bales. Delivery contracts have now become fungible, and have themselves become the subject-matter of the trade.[98] Although I cannot document this, it is likely that soon after 1873 traders abandoned the earlier practice of conducting speculation by assigning rights in existing contracts down a chain, and adopted instead the practice of intervening in the market by making new contracts,[99] a practice which, as we have seen, had been used by some traders since the mid-1860s.

In the East Indian cotton trade the process of standardization took longer, and considerable lack of uniformity is reflected in market reports well into the 1880s; my impression is that the older forms of contract remained in common use there. The 'arrival' contract lingered on into this century; the *Cotton Yearbook* for 1921 gives a form settled in 1914, noting that it is practically obsolete. It came to be called 'the Arrival Spot Contract', the curious hybrid title reflecting the fact that it was used for dealings in real ('spot') cotton, and not for fictitious trades.

Institutional Sophistication

Other developments took place in the 1870s and early 1880s. The term 'futures' was first used in *The Economist* in 1875; by 1876 it is commonplace. The elaborate chain-and-ring transactions required to balance accounts (originally by actual cash transfer) were superseded in 1876 by bookkeeping through the establishment of the Cotton Clearing House. The system of payment was further simplified when the Cotton Bank was set up in 1878. These developments greatly reduced transaction-costs, but another problem proved more intractable. If

97 Later changed to 44,800 lbs., as appears from the rules of 1881.

98 It will be noticed, too, that the trading is now being carried on not in quarter-pennies, the finest tuning achieved in the period of the early Civil War, but in thirty-seconds of a penny.

99 Existing contracts might be left open or closed; I have no information as to the normal practice.

contracts are to be rapidly traded without undue risk, then all traders must be credit-worthy; there is no time for credit enquiries. To put the same point differently, contracts will not all be as good as each other if some traders are unable to satisfy their obligations.

In the Chicago commodity market this problem had been addressed in 1865 by requiring the deposit of margins, which provided some degree of security. This system was copied by the New York Cotton Exchange in 1871. An incidental benefit was that it tended to prevent cornering of the market. A speculator attempting a corner would need to find, in addition to sums for brokerage and regular running-expenses, cash sums to deposit; this restricted his activities. The Liverpool brokers were not much concerned over corners; it was thought that the size of the cotton market was so vast that a corner was not possible. But there was nervousness over insolvency. In September of 1870 it was first provided that a trader declared bankrupt, or one who made an arrangement with his creditors, was to be expelled, subject to readmission if obligations were eventually met. A system of margins (called deposits) was also then proposed, but remained optional.[100] As we have seen, a margin system had been suggested in correspondence in *The Times* back in 1863.[101]

The Liverpool brokers were too complacent. One Morris Ranger, an American trader of German origin, noting the favourable arrangements in Liverpool, set about achieving a corner in 1879. The mood of the market was bearish, anticipating a fall in price, and there had been heavy selling for the September–October position, a point at which the cotton stock fell to its lowest between crops. The bears did not, of course, possess the cotton they had sold. Ranger bought for the same position until considerably more cotton had been sold to him than existed in a deliverable state when the final-delivery date came at the end of October. He had, as they say, squeezed the bears, and could dictate terms of settlement to them. He was generous to them, and the clerks were so impressed by his achievement that they left their desks and cheered him to the echo for his feat in achieving the impossible. In 1881 he nearly succeeded again. In response, some traders set up a system of settling differences at fortnightly intervals, to restrain traders from going deeper and deeper into the market when it turned against them, in the hope that it would all come right in the end. In 1883 Ranger attempted a bear corner and failed; with assets of only £8,000 he faced liability to pay differences of over three-quarters of a million. Ever popular, he, 'the Napoleon of Cotton', was with reluctance expelled. His Waterloo behind him, he retired to his St Helena, 80 East

[100] MS 380 COT 1/5. See 23 and 30 Sept.
[101] See above, text to n. 58.

Fifty-Sixth Street, New York City. There he died, in suitably modest circumstances, in 1887. Payment of periodic differences at once became the rule in Liverpool.

This was the last major development. Thereafter the system of trading was endlessly modified in detail, but apparently no major change took place. The Exchange was suspended during the war of 1939–45, and revived after an interval when a Conservative government returned to power; to socialists futures trading is of course supposed to be evil. But by then the Lancashire cotton industry was in fatal decline, and trading in cotton futures was soon abandoned.

The Priority of the Liverpool Market

If I am correct in assessing the significance of the changes made in 1873, and it must be conceded that many details of the history seem to me to be obscure, the Liverpool market was organized to facilitate futures trading later than the New York Cotton Exchange. However, two historians have taken the contrary view.[102] The New York cotton spot market had existed early in the nineteenth century; statistics exist from 1817 of sales. The Exchange was incorporated in 1871, but it is clear from the writings of E. J. Donnell, who was active in the matter, that organized futures trading had been in operation from January of 1869.[103] Statistics he quotes clearly distinguish spot transactions from futures. The latter vastly exceeded spot trades. For example, for 1872–3, 552,340 bales were sold in the spot market, and 5,306,010 in the fictitious futures market. In 1881 the figures were 198,500 and 26,721,800. Donnell, writing in 1872, claimed that futures trading began in the Civil War:

> Some of our manufacturers entered into large contracts with the government and covered themselves by purchasing the raw materials for delivery at some future date. The price, within certain wide limits, was then of much less importance than the certainty of getting cotton when needed.

This explanation in terms of the desire to have access to commodities essentially explains the reason for making contracts for forward

[102] K. J. Lipartito, 'The New York Cotton Exchange and the Development of the Cotton Futures Market' (1983), LVII *Business Hist. Rev.* 30, 52 n. 4, relying on R. Bouilly, n. 6 above. Bouilly follows Dumbell in putting an early date on 'futures' trading, but in reality is talking about forward-delivery contracts.

[103] I have built up a set of copies of early trading-rules from 1871, principally from holdings of the New York Public Library. The rules were frequently changed in the early period, and I have been unable to locate the very earliest rules. Unlike the early Liverpool rules, on their face they provide for futures trading.

delivery, rather than the development of the purchase and sale of contracts as a mechanism for speculation in the future price, the latter being in a sense parasitic upon the former.

There is evidence, though it is not of a very satisfactory character, of futures trading in the Chicago Board of Trade in wheat rather earlier, and the system of margins was introduced there in 1865.[104] It seems quite possible that Chicago, rather than Liverpool or New York, was the original home of organized futures trading, though whether the idea was borrowed by the cotton dealers, or developed independently, is another matter.

The Contribution of the Common Law of Contract

The development of futures trading took place outside the regular law; the traders organized and policed the system themselves. In Britain, unlike America, there was no active hostility to futures trading, expressed through the regular law. Such hostility may be expressed in moral terms, but commonly reflects a supposed conflict of interest between the producers of a commodity and the traders, viewed by the producers as harmful parasites. Such a conflict did not emerge in Britain, where there were no cotton producers. The common law made its modest contribution by accomodating the system, although it would have made little practical difference if it had not. A wagering contract was bad at common law; surely a system of speculating on price fluctuations must count as a wagering contract? This was got around by a fiction. A futures contract did, of course, give a right to tender and to require delivery, though these obligations were not specifically enforceable. These obligations tie the practice to reality, the reality being the market price of spot cotton at the moment of delivery,

[104] Margins were introduced on 20 May 1865. Various accounts are given of the origin of futures in Chicago. The development is linked in most accounts to the rise in short selling on a large scale. On suggestion relates this to a government practice of entering into forward-delivery contracts for mess pork in the Civil War; this led to extensive short selling. Another explanation links the evolution to the use of elevator receipts for grain, and the practice of borrowing such receipts and repaying borrowings in other receipts. Thus, suppose that A thinks the market will fall over the next three months. He sells grain (say 10,000 bushels) now, and delivers to B by handing over a receipt for this quantity, a receipt he has borrowed for three months from C, who receives a fee or a loan of money in return. In effect A is a short seller. When the time comes to return the receipt he can buy a receipt for 10,000, which will, if the market has fallen, cost less, and return that, or he can borrow another receipt and continue his 'bear' speculation. If all that happened was that individuals bought warehouse receipts the trading would be limited by the quantity of grain held against receipts in the grain elevators. But the practice of *borrowing* receipts, if I understand the system, means that one receipt for 10,000 bushels can, through its being lent, be used to satisfy a considerable number of contracts.

though in practice, as we have seen, delivery virtually never takes place. The common law by fiction equated the obligations of the parties with their 'intentions'. So long as there was an 'intention' to tender and take delivery, the contract was good; only if there was an 'intention' merely to pay differences was the contract to be viewed as a bet on the future price of cotton. All that was then needed was to say, in defiance of the truth, that there always was such an intention, and the system was, doctrinally, home and dry.[105]

[105] Drafts of this essay have been in existence for many years and many friends have helped with comments. I must particularly mention D. Farnie, D. Baird, M. Becker, M. Fox, J. Langbein, D. Hutchinson, F. Schauer, S. Shavell, B. Baker, and W. Gray. I am also grateful to the Nuffield Trust for a grant which was given me to inquire into Victorian leading cases.

9

Abstract Payment Undertakings

Roy Goode

I. Introduction

This essay is concerned with a particular form of undertaking which appears to break every principle of law governing the formation of contracts. I refer to the abstract payment undertaking, a money promise which is independent of the transaction that gives it birth and which is considered binding when received by the beneficiary (or sometimes even when issued by the promisor) without acceptance, consideration, reliance, or execution in solemn form. The type of contract (if it be such) generated by an abstract payment undertaking fits neither the bilateral nor the unilateral model. It is not bilateral, for no promise is given in exchange; nor is it unilateral in the ordinary sense, for its irrevocability does not depend on the performance, or even the commencement of performance, of a designated act or forbearance.

Since such a promise is not required to be supported by consideration there can be no question of recovery of the payment on the ground of failure of consideration. On the other hand, the promise cannot be treated as a gift promise; to the contrary, those who issue such promises are hard-headed financiers who do so for that most sound of commercial reasons, profit. The promise is therefore not gratuitous in the commercial sense; the position is simply that the promisor looks for his reward from a party other than the promisee.

The purpose of this essay is threefold: to explain the phenomenon by which the law has come to recognize the binding force of such a promise; to identify, if possible, the conditions which must be satisfied in order for the promise to become irrevocable and subsequently to be enforceable; and to test the limits of the autonomy of the promise by examining the impact of a variety of fact situations on the promisee's right to collect payment.

These issues will be examined in the context, first, of the medieval bond and, secondly, of three modern forms of payment undertaking: the documentary credit; the documentary bond or guarantee, otherwise known as the stand-by credit;[1] and the non-documentary inter-bank payment order. The negotiable instrument will also be discussed, but only briefly, for though it involves the insulation of the payment undertaking from the underlying contract it is not truly abstract in character.[2]

II. The Traditional Bases of Liability on a Promise

What gives binding force to a promise? Every legal system has had to grapple with this fundamental problem, so brilliantly analysed in the writings of my distinguished predecessor, Professor Patrick Atiyah. The significance of promise as a foundation of liability has varied from place to place and from age to age. There are, of course, non-delictual forms of liability which do not depend on a promise at all, but with these I am not concerned. Where promise features as an ingredient of the plaintiff's claim, what criteria should be applied to determine its legal validity? No legal system makes *all* promises binding. To start with, there are many promises which no one could suppose were intended to attract legal consequences, for example, acceptance of an invitation to dinner or to a friendly game of tennis. Then there are promises which by their terms are revocable until acted upon, such as the revocable letter of credit.

If we ignore these cases and confine ourselves to a promise which, objectively viewed, is seen as intended to attract an immediate legal commitment, what further element beyond the promise itself is needed to give it validity in law? One possibility is to say that the promise by itself is sufficient, that it is open to a person by a unilateral declaration of will to commit himself to another irrespective of that other's action or assent. But even in jurisdictions where the promise by itself is treated as a juristic act it is not by itself considered sufficient to commit the promisor. Some further element is said to be necessary, such as the promisee's knowledge of the promise, his assent to it, the *cause* of French law,[3] consideration, benefit, reliance, or solemnity of form. The second and third of these can scarcely be said to be positive prerequisites of a binding promise; rather, it is the rejection of a promise or the existence of a factor vitiating *cause* which operates negatively to destroy the legal effect of the promise. Thus in both French and German law the promisee's assent may be tacit, with the

[1] See below, 220.
[2] See below, 217.
[3] Which may be loosely defined as a legitimate motivation for the promise. This includes a desire to make a gift.

normal effect that the promise is binding unless rejected. So whatever the legal theory, the assent of the promisee is not in a practical sense a condition precedent to the legal force of the promise; it is the rejection of the promise which constitutes a condition subsequent destroying its legal effect. Similarly the fourth element, the French *cause*, which is often depicted as an essential element of binding promise, seems more accurately described as the absence of a legally vitiating factor, such as defect of will or contravention of positive law. By contrast, the fulfilment of a requirement of knowledge, consideration, reliance, or solemnity of form is a condition precedent to the existence of a legally operative promise.

III. The Insulation of the Payment Undertaking

For centuries creditors entitled to a money sum have sought ways to detach the debtor's payment undertaking from the contract as a whole and give it autonomous status, that is, to make it abstract by divorcing it from the underlying contractual consideration. Two distinct but related objectives have motivated these efforts: to avoid defences by the debtor based on the underlying transaction; and to facilitate the marketing of the money claim by the creditor as an unconditional entitlement to payment free of equities. The principal method of achieving the first objective has been to embody a parallel payment undertaking in a separate document, such as a bond, bill of exchange, or letter of credit, the dishonour of which provides the creditor with a distinct cause of action not deriving from the underlying contract.[4] The second objective is achieved by the use of a bill of exchange or other negotiable instrument.

The essence of the abstract payment undertaking is that it is conditioned only by the terms of the document in which it is contained. If the obligation is tailored to that of the underlying contract there is no insulation against defences arising under the latter and the obligation is no longer abstract. Thus a guarantee[5] or suretyship bond would be useless as an insulator, for the surety is answerable only on the default of the principal debtor and can thus avail himself of any defences available to the principal debtor.

[4] Insulation can also be provided in the same contract by a clause providing that the debtor shall pay irrespective of any breach by the creditor of his own obligations. Such a clause may be stipulated in favour of the original creditor or may be limited in its effect to preclusion of the assertion of defences against the creditor's assignee—commonly termed a 'cut-off' clause. These methods will not be discussed.

[5] The word 'guarantee' is here used in its strict sense to denote a secondary obligation, as distinct from the on-demand performance guarantee discussed below.

IV. Classifications of Abstract Payment Undertakings

Abstract payment undertakings may be classified in various ways, in particular according to whether:

1. they are issued by the debtor himself or a third party;
2. they secure money obligations, non-money obligations or both;
3. they are intended as the primary source of payment or only as the secondary source.

Each of these classifications has some legal significance, but in practice it tends to be marginal.

Where the payment undertaking is given by the debtor himself it will be obvious that its insulation from the underlying transaction is likely to be somewhat less effective than where it is given by a third party, if only because in the former case the mutuality of parties allows of set-off of a liquidated cross-claim arising under the underlying transaction whereas the lack of mutuality precludes such a set-off where the undertaking is given by a third party.[6]

Independent payment undertakings may also be classified by reference to the nature of the underlying obligation they are intended to secure. Some payment undertakings, such as documentary credits, secure exclusively money obligations; others, such as performance guarantees, secure exclusively non-money obligations (typically the construction of buildings and other works under a construction contract); yet other undertakings, such as bills of exchange and stand-by credits, are general-purpose instruments which can be used to secure any kind of obligation, money or non-money. This is significant only in that payment undertakings securing non-money obligations are necessarily secondary in intent, if not in form, and in so far as the question of default in the underlying transaction is capable of becoming an issue[7] it may be harder to prove or disprove than default in performance of a money obligation.

This brings us to the third classification, which has been the source of much confusion because of failure to distinguish the intent of the undertaking from its form. Where the parties have agreed that the promisee's first port of call for payment is to be by recourse to the separate abstract payment undertaking, not by reliance on the payment obligation in the underlying contract, the creditor is not entitled to resort to the underlying contract unless the parallel payment undertaking is dishonoured. Into this class of undertaking fall bills of

[6] The third party promisor may, of course, have a set-off in respect of his own cross-claim against the promisee, but in practice this will arise only from the coincidence of prior dealings between them. See below, 234.

[7] This is usually the case only where it is asserted that the claim for payment is fraudulent. See below, 234.

exchange given as conditional payment and documentary credits. But there are undertakings which, though unconditional in form, are intended as a fall-back (or in convenient American terminology, 'stand-by'), to be invoked only where there has been default in performance of the underlying contract. Examples of this second category are bills of exchange taken as collateral security and documentary guarantees.[8] The characteristic of these documents is that there is nothing on their face to indicate that they are not primary payment instruments, and they have to be treated as such unless it can be shown that the call on them was fraudulent in that the beneficiary knew full well that there had been no default by the other party to the underlying contract. In short, though they are secondary in intent they are primary in form, so that breach or performance of the underlying contract[9] is not a defence to a claim for payment in the absence of fraud.[10]

I have not referred to banknotes in this section as they are a special case. In form a banknote is a promise by the Chief Cashier of the Bank of England to pay the bearer the face value of the note on demand, and as such it constitutes a promissory note for the purpose of the Bills of Exchange Act 1882. But since the banknote itself constitutes both money and legal tender the promise to pay has no legal significance. A person presenting the note to the Bank of England will get at most another note in exchange; and since money is a fungible he is not even entitled to that, for what he already has is as good in law as anything he might seek by way of exchange. If follows that the holder of a banknote cannot sue on it, so that the promise to pay, historically significant in that the bearer could at one time demand gold or silver, is now a legal fiction.

V. The Different Forms of Payment Undertaking

1. THE MEDIEVAL BOND

The earliest insulation device was the single (or simple) money bond, an unconditional acknowledgment of indebtedness or payment undertaking under seal.[11]

[8] The term 'documentary guarantee' is here used to cover any form of written payment undertaking which, though intended to be called only on default by the debtor in the underlying transaction, is triggered purely by a written demand and such other documents (if any) as may be specified in it, regardless whether there has in fact been default. The label covers various types of bond (bid bond, advance-payment bond, performance bond, etc.) and stand-by credits.

[9] Breach in the case of a primary undertaking such as a documentary credit, performance in the case of an undertaking which is secondary in intent, such as a performance bond, etc.), on-demand guarantees and stand-by credits.

[10] See below, 233.

[11] Otherwise known as an obligation or writing obligatory. See generally A. W. B. Simpson, *A History of the Common Law of Contract* (Oxford, 1975), 88 ff. J. Milnes Holden, *The History of Negotiable Instruments in English Law* (London, 1955).

The mere issue of the bond committed the issuer to payment. The bond was intentionally penal in character, being customarily fixed at double the amount of the debt due from the issuer. The court was not concerned with the underlying transaction which gave rise to the bond and would not entertain a defence that the issuer never owed the money or that he had performed the contract in respect of which the bond was given. More usual, if less insulating in its effect, was the double (or conditional) bond, which was indorsed with a condition of defeasance rendering it void upon the fulfilment by the issuer of specified acts or of covenants set out in a separate indenture. The bond, being given under seal, was actionable as such, but the obligee's claim could be defeated by proof that the stated condition had been fulfilled.[12] Where the bond was given to secure the payment of money it was termed a common money bond. All bonds were required to be in solemn form, that is, contained in a document both sealed and delivered.

Both forms of bond had the great advantage that the court would not inquire into the reason for the obligor's failure to pay. It may have been due to a breach of contract by the obligee, but with this the court had no concern, even if the effect of the breach was totally to deprive the obligor of the benefit for which he had undertaken to make his payment. The bond thus provided a high degree of insulation from the underlying transaction. Indeed, in the case of the single bond this was almost total, since the absence of any condition of defeasance meant that even if the debtor had paid what was due he had no defence. He was considered the author of his own misfortune, for when tendering payment he should have insisted upon the bond being cancelled or handed over or a receipt given under seal.[13] As Professor Simpson has rightly observed, in terms which are equally true of the modern performance bond: 'The law governing bonds is tough law, inspired by the general philosophy it is not the business of the courts to remake private contracts; having made their bed the contracting parties must lie in it.'[14] In the case of the single bond this was carried to remarkable

[12] Why creditors did not insist on simple bonds is unclear. Professor Simpson merely observes that the conditional bond was more usual, 'for it was by the use of conditioned bonds that important agreements were made actionable in the days when the bond was the basic contractual institution' (n. 11 above, 90). This is understandable in cases where the parties were of equal bargaining power, but in many loan transactions the borrower had little freedom to negotiate and it is hard to see what advantage the creditor could derive from being subjected to a condition of defeasance, particularly since simple bonds were construed in favour of the obligee, whereas conditional bonds were construed in favour of the obligor (William Sheppard, *Touchstone of Common Assurances* 7th edn, (London, 1820), ii. 367).

[13] Simpson, n. 11 above, 100.

[14] Ibid. 113.

lengths in that at law even fraud was not a defence.[15] But equity adopted a different rule; and in the case of the conditional bond the creditor's insulation from the underlying transaction was steadily eroded as courts of equity began to grant relief against forfeiture of the penalty fixed by the bond. Eventually it became settled, both in equity and at law, that penalties as such were unenforceable; the creditor was entitled to his debt and no more, or in the case of a breach of contract, to compensation for his actual loss in the form of damages.

The modern suretyship bond, which in form is little different from the old-style conditional bond, is widely used but much attenuated in force compared with its forebear. It differs from an ordinary guarantee under seal only in that, instead of default being a condition precedent to its operation, performance is a condition subsequent which defeats the bond. The onus thus lies on the debtor to prove performance, not on the creditor to prove default. Suretyship bonds have thus lost much of their abstract character and will not be considered further.

2. THE NEGOTIABLE INSTRUMENT

Where a bill of exchange or other negotiable instrument is given as 'conditional payment' of a sum payable under a contract, as where the buyer draws or accepts a bill in favour of his seller for the price, the engagement of the signatories to the bill generates one or more contracts (one contract for each signatory) separate from the underlying transaction. The phrase 'conditional payment', though commonly used, is misleading, for it confuses a commitment to pay with payment itself. The effect of a bill given, say, in respect of the price of goods is that the promise of payment embodied, expressly or by implication, in the contract of sale is conditionally replaced by a new promise on the part of the buyer, namely to pay the amount of the bill, if he is himself the acceptor, or if not then to procure its acceptance[16] and payment by the drawee. The replacement of the price obligation is conditional in that if the bill is dishonoured the seller is given the option of suing on the instrument or on the original consideration. Given the semi-atonomous character of the instrument it will rarely be to his advantage to sue on the original contract.

English law divides contracts into simple contracts and specialties. A specialty contract is one which takes effect by the mere fact of its formal execution, without any additional requirement such as consideration. The status of specialty may be conferred either by the

[15] J. B. Ames, 'Specialty Contracts and Equitable Defences' (1895) 9 *Harv. LR* 49, 51.

[16] If the bill is a term bill. Sight bills are not accepted; the drawee either pays them or declines to pay.

common law, as in the case of an instrument under seal,[17] or by mercantile usage. The negotiable instrument was at one time considered a type of mercantile specialty, on the theory that it was enforceable without consideration.[18] But the theory was always erroneous and eventually vanished from sight.[19] It would be entirely misleading to equate the status of a negotiable instrument with that of a deed. A negotiable instrument does not enjoy the same degree of immunity from the consideration doctrine. In particular, it has no legal effect unless value has been given by someone. Its special status in relation to consideration lies in the fact that consideration is presumed unless the contrary is shown and need not move from the promisee. It suffices that the acceptor received value for his acceptance or that value was furnished by some party in the chain between the holder and the defendant.[20] But assuming that the plaintiff is a holder for value, his rights on the instrument are autonomous to the extent that they are unaffected by a breach of the underlying contract except so far as this produces a total or partial failure of consideration,[21] and if he is a holder in due course (which broadly means a bona fide purchaser for value without notice of any defect in his transferor's title) he enjoys almost total insulation not only from the underlying contract but from defects in title and other defences that would be available on the bill itself against other categories of holder.[22]

Where the acceptor receives value for his acceptance, so that there is a valid contract between him and the payee, there is nothing very remarkable in the fact that a transferee from the payee taking as a holder in due course can sue the acceptor without having himself furnished value to the acceptor. The bill is a reification of the contract debt, a negotiable chattel which passes as a matter of property to the holder in due course, so that his rights are those of a transferee of the debt, and the direct contractual relationship which in the theory of negotiable instruments law exists between the acceptor and any holder for value is in a sense as irrelevant to the acceptor's liability as is that of a debtor to the assignee of the debt, between whom there is no contractual relationship at all.

What is more significant is the way in which a holder in due course can succeed to a *non-existent* contract and sue upon it as if it did exist.

[17] The requirement of a seal has now been abolished; instead the instrument must show on its face that it is intended to be a deed and must be attested (Law of Property (Miscellaneous Provisions) Act 1989, s. 1).

[18] T. A. Street, *The Foundations of Legal Liability* (Long Island, 1906), ii. 381.

[19] Ibid. 381–3, 387–9.

[20] Bills of Exchange Act 1882, s. 27.

[21] See R. M. Goode, *Commercial Law* (Harmondsworth, 1982), 467, 475.

[22] Ibid. 445–6, 467, 475.

The promise of payment embodied in a bill of exchange reaches its highest level of abstraction when the instrument is in the hands of a holder in due course and the acceptance of the bill was entirely gratuitous and was not by way of accommodation.[23] For example, A, as a twenty-first birthday present to his son, B, accepts a bill of exchange drawn on him by B in his own favour which B then negotiates to H, who takes for value as a holder in due course. In this case we cannot explain H's right to sue A as that of a transferee of a true contract right created by the issue of the bill, for no contract ever came into existence. B, the original payee, could not have sued A, whose commitment was purely voluntary. The apparent contract created by the issue of the bill was a *nudum pactum*. How is it possible for H to purchase a non-existent contract and sue on it as transferee?

We could in fact fit A's liability to H within the framework of traditional contract law—albeit by doing some violence to the concept of negotiation as a *transfer* of the right to payment—by treating H not as the transferee of an existing contract right but as a party to a unilateral contract concluded directly between A and H. By accepting the bill, A is in effect undertaking to any future holder for value, H, that in consideration of H buying from B what is in law a worthless piece of paper A will pay the face value of the paper to H.

An alternative solution, based on a legal fiction but more compatible with the concept of transfer, is that A is estopped as against a holder in due course from disputing that he received value for his acceptance; in short, the presumption of value becomes conclusive. This, indeed, seems to have been the theoretical basis of liability prior to the enactment of the Bills of Exchange Act.

The status of the holder for value as transferee of a contract right deemed in his favour to have been created by the issue of the bill means that, like other forms of negotiable instrument, it ceases to be interesting for our purposes, since the payment undertaking, though insulated from the underlying transaction, is not abstract. The holder for value succeeds to the rights of the original payee under a notional bilateral contract. Accordingly, negotiable instruments will not be further discussed.

3. THE DOCUMENTARY CREDIT

If the right of a holder in due course to sue a party to a bill of exchange to whom he provided no consideration is explicable on the basis that

[23] The liability of an accommodation party can be attributed to his function as a surety for the drawer, the consideration for the guarantee being the purchase of the bill by the holder for value.

he is a transferee and thus, like an assignee of a debt, need not have furnished consideration himself, no such explanation accounts for the phenomenon of the binding force of a documentary credit which is expressed to be irrevocable. The bank's undertaking to the beneficiary to pay[24] against designated shipping documents is generally assumed to commit the bank to the beneficiary as soon as the latter receives it.

Various ingenious theories have been advanced to reconcile the binding effect of a documentary credit with traditional concepts of contract law, for example, that the credit is a guarantee; that the bank issues the credit as agent of the buyer; that the consideration for the credit is the beneficiary's agreement to present the shipping documents, or alternatively is the actual presentation of the documents; that the credit becomes binding as the result of the buyer's reliance on it, such reliance either constituting acceptance of an offer giving rise to a unilateral contract or making the bank's undertaking binding by estoppel; that the credit is a form of negotiable instrument.

All these theories, and others besides, fall to the ground as being inconsistent with the practice and understanding of the parties. It is clear that the credit is not a guarantee, for the bank's payment obligation is primary, not secondary; it is the first port of call for payment. Nor does the bank issue the credit as agent of the buyer; it acts as principal on its own behalf, and though it does so on a mandate from the buyer the agency relationship between bank and buyer is purely internal.[25] The notion that the payment undertaking is supported by consideration is equally untenable, for the beneficiary makes no promise to the bank to present the documents, presentation being merely a non-promissory condition of his right to be paid, and the treatment of the act of presentation as consideration is inconsistent with the fundamental purpose of the credit, which is to give the beneficiary an assurance of payment in advance of performance. Again, the proposition that it is the beneficiary's reliance on the bank's promise which gives it binding force is irreconcilable with the commercial understanding of the credit as irrevocable from the moment of receipt by the beneficiary. Similarly, a letter of credit is not a negotiable instrument, for it is not transferable except with the assent of the bank, and in any event its production is not a condition of payment, the essential hallmark of a negotiable instrument.

The state of English jurisprudence on letters of credit is rather curious. It is well over two hundred years since Lord Mansfield's valiant attempt in *Pillans* v. *Van Mierop*[26] (a case involving what was in

[24] The term 'pay' is used here as shorthand to cover acceptance and payment.
[25] R. M. Goode, n. 21 above, 661, 671.
[26] (1756) 3 Burr. 1663.

essence a letter of credit) to demonstrate that contracts were enforceable without consideration was defeated by the House of Lords in *Rann* v. *Hughes*;[27] and to this day there is no reported English case which directly holds that a letter of credit becomes binding on receipt despite the want of consideration in the ordinary contract sense. This is scarcely surprising, for any bank which sought to take the consideration point would destroy its commercial reputation overnight. Only the liquidator of a failed bank is likely to put the point in issue, and happily bank failures in this country are rare. But there are dicta in several cases in which the courts have taken it for granted that letters of credit are enforceable undertakings,[28] and any argument to the contrary would be likely to receive short shrift at the hands of the judiciary.

Still, we need some legal basis for the binding force of the credit. We can, of course, content ourselves with saying that it is a contract *sui generis* or (a view preferred by American writers) a *sui generis* non-contractual 'engagement', but these formulations do not assist in identifying the badges of enforceability of the bank's undertaking.[29] The question arises in still starker form in relation to documentary guarantees, where the level of abstraction is even higher.[30] The basis of the binding nature of the abstract promise will be considered in detail in Section VI.[31] Suffice to say at this stage that it is now accepted around the world that the letter of credit constitutes an autonomous undertaking distinct from and independent of the underlying contract of sale and, in the absence of fraud, enforceable by the beneficiary even where he has failed to perform his part of the contract. This is logical enough, for the parties to the letter of the credit are not the same as the parties to the contract of sale, so that there is no good reason why the issuing bank should be entitled to invoke the protection of the sale contract, to which it is a stranger.

Thus the letter of credit provides the beneficiary with much the same degree of insulation from the related contract as that enjoyed by the holder in due course of a negotiable instrument. The factors which are admissible to defeat a claim on a credit are few in number compared with ordinary contracts,[32] for in the typical case there is no prior

[27] (1788) 7 Term Rep. 350 n.

[28] See e.g. *Hamzeh Malas & Sons* v. *British Imex Industries Ltd.* [1958] 2 QB 127, 129 *per* Jenkins LJ; *United City Merchants (Investments) Ltd.* v. *Royal Bank of Canada* [1983] AC 168, 184, *per* Lord Diplock.

[29] In the United States the search for such criteria has been rendered unnecessary by legislative adoption of Article 5 of the Uniform Commercial Code.

[30] See 220.

[31] See below, 222.

[32] See B. Kozolchyk, *Letters of Credit* (1980) 9 IECL, ch. 5, s. XI, and below, 227.

contact between bank and beneficiary and the letter of credit results not from negotiations between them but from the instructions given by the bank's own customer, the applicant for the credit.

4. THE DOCUMENTARY GUARANTEE

The documentary credit is a primary payment instrument, both in form and in intent; the issue of the credit and its payment by the bank against specified documents constitute the mode of payment of the price agreed between seller and buyer as a term of the underlying contract of sale. By contrast the documentary guarantee, as pointed out earlier, is primary in form only; in intent it is a back-up, to be resorted to only if the account party (that is, the counter-party to the party for whose benefit the guarantee was issued) defaults in performance.

The documentary guarantee of the kind used in this country and in continental Europe is designed to secure performance of a non-monetary obligation, a further point of distinction from the documentary credit. The American stand-by credit is a member of the same legal species,[33] but its use has diversified to the point where it has become a general financial back-up facility available to secure monetary as well as non-monetary obligations, and in more recent times it has been used additionally as a form of credit enhancement to reinforce the rating of securities issues. Moreover, leaving on one side their intended secondary character, stand-by credits are operated by banks in much the same way as documentary credits, so that, in contrast to performance guarantees, they may be issued for the issuer's own account as well as for that of another party; they may be reinforced by the confirmation of another bank; and they may provide for payment at the counters of a bank other than the issuing bank. But these are differences of scope and practice. In business terminology, stand-by credits are differentiated from demand guarantees as having certain distinctive characteristics, in much the same way as lessors of vehicles and equipment distinguish between lease, rental, and contract hire, but just as the three latter terms are legally synonymous so also in law there is no distinction between a stand-by credit and any other form of documentary guarantee.

By far the most common form of documentary guarantee is the

[33] The stand-by credit evolved in the United States because of the fear that the label 'guarantee' might lead courts to think of it as a suretyship bond, which most American banks are prohibited from issuing. Hence the desire to have it equated as far as possible with the documentary credit, and the successful pressure to have it included in the 1983 revision of the Uniform Customs and Practice for Documentary Credits (UCP). See further John F. Dolan, 'Efforts at International Standardization of Bank Guarantees' (1989) 4 *BFLR* 237, and Boris Kozolchyk, 'The Emerging Law of Standby Letters of Credit and Bank Guarantees' (1982) 24 *Ariz. LR* 319.

simple on-demand bond or guarantee.[34] This is one of the most abstract forms of payment undertaking, for the stipulated sum is payable on first written demand without the need for production of any additional documents or the fulfilment of any other express conditions whatsoever. It is not even necessary for the demand to contain or be accompanied by a statement that the account party has defaulted in performance of his obligations under the underlying contract.[35] Again, despite the theoretical problems the documentary guarantee is accepted both in England[36] and elsewhere[37] as binding on receipt by the beneficiary.

5. THE NON-DOCUMENTARY INTER-BANK PAYMENT ORDER

The documentary credit and the documentary guarantee share the characteristic that, while both are abstract payment undertakings divorced from the underlying transaction, the beneficiary's right to payment is dependent on fulfilment of a non-promissory condition, namely the presentation of one or more specified documents.[38] But this does not exhaust the field. A still more abstract type of undertaking arises from the inter-bank payment order, which by the custom of bankers may commit one bank to put another in funds without the presentation of documents, and indeed without the fulfilment of any condition precedent whatsoever other than the arrival of the specified payment date.

[34] The form of this varies according to the obligation secured. For example, the bid (or tender) bond is designed to ensure that a person whose tender for a contract is successful will in fact enter into the contract, failing which the bond can be called. The advance-payment bond protects the beneficiary against the contractor's failure to repay an advance payment made for work he does not carry out. The performance bond secures the due performance of the contract up to completion; the maintenance bond, the execution of remedial works necessary to put right defects arising during the defects liability period.

[35] However, the latest draft to the new *Uniform Rules for Demand Guarantees* in course of completion by the International Chamber of Commerce provides, in Article 20, that unless that Article is specifically excluded every demand guarantee shall include or be accompanied by a written statement that, and in what respect, the principal (the acount party) has committed a breach of his obligations. The new Rules will replace the 1978 *Uniform Rules for Guarantees* (ICC Document No. 325) which, in requiring the production of a judgment or arbitral award, deviated so substantially from normal commercial practice that the Rules did not gain general acceptance. The draft new Rules are intended to reflect market practice more accurately while providing at least some safeguard against improper calling of demand bonds and guarantees.

[36] See *Edward Owen Engineering Ltd.* v. *Barclays Bank Ltd.* [1978] 1 All ER 976, 981 *per* Lord Denning M. R.

[37] See N. Horn and E. Wymeersch, *Bank-Guarantees, Standby Letters of Credit and Performance Bonds in International Trade* (Deventer, 1990); Roeland F. Bertrams, *Bank Guarantees in International Trade* (Deventer, 1990), ch. 12. 2.

[38] In the case of a documentary guarantee the requirement may be no more than the making of a written demand.

For example, D owes money to C. D intructs his bank, DB, to transfer funds to C's bank, CB, for the account of C. DB sends a payment order to CB instructing CB to credit C's account with the required payment. Under the rules or usages of some clearing systems, acceptance of this order by CB (or deemed acceptance through failure to make a timely rejection) has two consequences. First, it commits CB to pay the specified amount to C on the stipulated payment date. Secondly, it commits DB to put CB in funds by that date.[39]

It is not entirely clear how far an inter-bank payment order does create an abstract payment undertaking. The irrevocability of the payment instruction, and thus of the obligation to put the receiving bank in funds, derives in many cases from clearing-house rules to which all members of the clearing are required to adhere as a condition of membership. Where this is so, the payment undertaking is not in truth an abstract undertaking at all, it merely forms part of the set of obligations created by the clearing-house rules and binding on members by virtue of the multilateral contractual relationships established by membership of the clearing. But in cases not governed by clearing-house rules the custom of bankers may establish the irrevocability of the payment instruction;[40] indeed, the clearing-house rules may constitute evidence of the previously uncodified custom of bankers.

VI. The Binding Force of Abstract Payment Undertakings

In considering the enforceability of abstract payment undertakings it is important to separate three steps in the enquiry that are all-too commonly confused. The first question is what makes the undertaking binding in the first place, given the absence of positive vitiating factors. In other words, what does the promisee have to show in order to establish the irrevocability of the undertaking? It is this question which is addressed in the present section. The second question is when an apparently valid and irrevocable undertaking is of no effect, or

[39] This is the position under the CHAPS rules governing the London automated clearing. The new Article 4A of the Uniform Commercial Code takes a similar position, though allowing revocation after acceptance in certain exceptional cases (s. 4A-211). Under some systems, such as the New York CHIPS, a payment order becomes irrevocable at the time of issue, so that the sending bank's commitment does not depent on the receiving bank's assent or even on its receipt of the order. By contrast, the UNCITRAL *Draft Model Law on International Credit Transfers* would allow the sending bank to revoke the payment order even after the receiving bank's acceptance if the receiving bank has not acted on the order.

[40] Assuming, of course, that this suffices in law, a question which will shortly be addressed.

subsequently becomes void *ab initio*, as a result of a vitiating factor present at the time the undertaking is given. This question, which like the first is to be tested in the light of circumstances existing at the time the undertaking would otherwise have become irrevocable, will be examined in Section VII. The third question, analysed in section VIII, is what defences are available to negative the promisor's duty to pay pursuant to a promise which has continued to have legal effect up to the point when payment is claimed by the beneficiary.

In deciding what types of payment undertaking have legal effect by virtue solely of their communication to the beneficiary, one approach might be to identify the characteristics which the various forms of payment undertaking described above have in common and to say that an undertaking which lacks one or more of these characteristics does not enjoy the privileged status of an abstract payment undertaking. Proceeding on this basis we can identify the following characteristics which a payment undertaking would need to possess to qualify as abstract:

1. It is issued by a bank or similar financial instition.
2. The issuer is a stranger to the underlying transaction.[41]
3. The undertaking is of a kind that is widely used.
4. It conforms to normal banking practice.
5. It is undertaken for a commercial purpose, rather than gratuitously. In particular, the issuer receives remuneration for giving the undertaking, though from the account party, not from the beneficiary, whilst the beneficiary has a contractual right to receive the undertaking, though the right is against the account party, not against the issuer.
6. The undertaking is expressed to mature on a specified date or on presentation of specified documents without reference to performance of the underlying transaction.
7. The undertaking is recognized by mercantile usage as irrevocable on receipt by the beneficiary.[42]

The problem with this approach is that it freezes the categories of abstract payment undertaking by reference to existing mercantile usage and makes no allowance for new forms of instrument that may evolve.

An alternative approach is to rely exclusively on the last item in the list and to make prevailing mercantile usage the sole criterion for the

[41] However, this is not always the case. For example, a bank may issue a stand-by credit for its own account rather than for the account of a customer.

[42] In the case of a documentary credit governed by the UCP, this is the case only where the credit is expressed to be irrevocable (Art. 7(c)). This rule is likely to be changed in the revision of the UCP which is now under way.

enforceability of an undertaking as an abstract payment undertaking. Subject to the overriding requirement of reasonableness by which every mercantile usage has to be tested, this approach is undoubtedly to be preferred. It avoids forcing abstract payment undertakings into the strait-jacket of existing practice and allows maximum flexibility for the development of new payment instruments. Moreover, there can be no serious doctrinal objection. If the common law was prepared to recognize the law merchant, and thus to accept the enforceability of a bill of exchange despite the absence of consideration moving from the promisee, why should it baulk at recognition of a mercantile usage which makes a payment undertaking binding solely by virtue of its communication to the beneficiary?[43]

What, then, is the commercial *raison d'être* of the abstract payment undertaking? Why should a usage which regards the promisor as bound solely by virtue of communication of the promise be upheld as reasonable? As a preliminary point, since there is no means of inventing consideration in this situation the only alternatives to communication as the committing element are solemnity of form and reliance. To require every payment undertaking to be by deed (which now requires attestation)[44] would be impracticable.

This leaves reliance. There are compelling reasons why a requirement of reliance is equally impracticable. First, a beneficiary who intends to act in reliance on the undertaking, as by manufacturing, purchasing or dispatching goods to the account party, needs the assurance of the undertaking without anxiety as to whether he will be able to establish reliance. It is not always easy to show the causal connection between a promise and the act said to constitute reliance on the promise, and this is particularly difficult where reliance takes the form of inactivity, as where the beneficiary decides not to halt a shipment to the account party when he still has the opportunity to do so. Secondly, a reliance requirement would make it virtually impossible for the issuer to know whether and when he had become committed; and issuers need to know this as soon as possible in order to make provision for their prospective liability. Thirdly, the payment process can involve a lengthy chain of participants, particularly in the case of international funds transfers. A payment order emanating from the debtor's bank

[43] In legal systems which do not have the requirement of consideration the theoretical problem is less acute but may arise in different form. Thus, there has been much debate among French legal scholars whether the documentary guarantee is exempt from the normal requirement of *cause* or whether the *cause* is the issuer's legitimate desire to commit himself to the payment, so that the law gives effect to the autonomy of he will. See M. Cabrillac and C. Mouly, *Droit des sûretés* (Paris, 1990), title II, ch. II; and Michel Vasseur, 'Dix ans de jurisprudence française relative aux garanties independantes' (1990), *RDAI/IBLJ* no. 3, 357; Bertrams, n. 37 above, 179.

[44] Law of Property (Miscellaneous Provisions) Act 1989, s. 1.

may pass through a number of intermediary banks before reaching the creditor's bank. If the commitment of each bank in the chain is to be dependent on an act of reliance by its receiving bank, then the first bank will not be committed until the last bank has acted in reliance on the payment order. The consequent delay and uncertainty as to the time of commitment could seriously impede the smooth functioning of the payment arrangements. Finally, the speed and volume of business transacted through modern electronic clearing-systems and the networking effect of the systems themselves make it imperative to crystallize the payment commitment at the earliest possible moment and to restrict 'unwinds' to extreme cases, such as failure of a settlement banks,[45] in order to avoid the chaos that would result from the knock-on effects of an unwind.

We may conclude, then, that any payment undertaking of a kind which by mercantile usage is treated as binding on receipt by the beneficiary will be so treated in English law where it conforms to the requirements for such usage and the usage can be shown to be reasonable in the sense of having a commercial purpose which is not objectionable in terms of legal policy. I now turn to the second stage of the enquiry.

VII. *Ab Initio* Vitiation of the Payment Undertaking

The question to be considered here is not whether the beneficiary has fulfilled the conditions which entitle him to receive payment under the terms of the payment undertaking, nor whether any other event has occurred since issue of the undertaking which constitutes a defecne to a claim for payment, but whether the undertaking itself was devoid of legal effect at the time of its issue or became nullified *ab initio* as the result of a vitiating factor present at that time. This is an issue which has remained curiously unexplored in legal literature, possibly because the presence of vitiating factors at the time of issue of an abstract payment undertaking is a relatively infrequent occurrence.

There is no good reason why the same factors which vitiate an ordinary contractual promise should not operate with equal force to invalidate an abstract payment undertaking. It is worth emphasizing that we are not here concerned with performance of the underlying transaction, which in general is irrelevant to the promisor's liability and in any event comes into consideration only at the point when payment

[45] Even this degree of conditionality, provided for by the New York CHIPS rules but never yet invoked, is controversial, and is not permitted by the comparable London CHAPS rules. The CHIPS rules were amended in 1990 with a view to providing a greater assurance of settlement finality.

is claimed, but rather with factors present at the time the undertaking is given which have an invalidating effect, either automatically by force of law or as the result of exercise by the promisor of a right to rescind his promise or have it set aside.

1. MISTAKE

Certain types of mistake render a contract wholly void, for example, a mistake as to the existence of the subject-matter, or a mistake as to identity which is known to the promisee and which goes to the root of the undertaking, because the promisor did not intent to enter into a contract with anyone other than the person with whom he thought he was contracting. Though there is no English authority on the point, we can reasonably conclude that letter of credit contracts enjoy no special immunity from avoidance where the payment undertaking itself is vitiated by mistake. Consider the following cases involving the issue of an irrevocable credit:

1. The issuing bank is instructed by its customer to issue a letter of credit to A but by mistake issues it to B, who is aware of the mistake. The purported contract generated by the letter of credit is void.

2. The contract of sale calls for the issue of a letter of credit to the seller, A, but by mistake the buyer instructs his bank to issue it to B, who is aware of the mistake. The letter of credit contract is void.

3. A letter of credit is issued pursuant to a supposed contract of sale which, unbeknown to the parties, is void.[46] This case is more debatable. There is no English authority and the case law in other jurisdictions is divided.[47] In principle the mutual mistake of the parties to the underlying contract of sale is irrelevant; in order to vitiate the letter of credit the mistake must arise in the relationship between bank and beneficiary. But this test would seem to be satisfied on the facts given. Though the bank will typically have neither an involvement in nor a knowledge of the supposed underlying contract, its letter of credit is issued, and is received by the beneficiary, on the basis that there is an agreement between account party and beneficiary whereby the former is to procure and the latter to accept the issue and subsequent payment of the letter of credit by the bank. If it transpires that the agreement was from the outset null and void, so that in law the parties are taken never to have effectively assented to the issue of

[46] E.g. because it is void (as opposed to merely unenforeable) by statute or because it relates to specific goods which had perished before the making of the contract.

[47] See B. Kozolchyk, *Letters of Credit* (1980) 9 IECL, ch. 5, para. 215 and, in relation to documentary guarantees, Horn and Wymeersch, n. 37 above, 34, 45, 49, 53; Bertrams, n. 37 above, 178 ff.

the credit, then issuer and beneficiary were at the time of issue under a mutual mistake as to a matter fundamental to the letter-of-credit contract and therefore rendering it void. The same result would seem to follow if the contract of sale were avoided (for example for misrepresentation) before the issue of the letter of credit. The position would be otherwise if the contract of sale were not void but merely unenforceable, for example, for illegality,[48] for the right to payment still exists even where there is no remedy for its infringement. Again, rescission or termination of the sale contract *after* issue of the letter of credit would have no impact on the credit, for the latter was not subject to any vitiating factor at the time of issue and the principle of the autonomy of the credit[49] insulates it from subsequent events affecting the underlying contract of sale.

2. MISREPRESENTATION, DURESS, UNDUE INFLUENCE

Where the letter of credit is procured by a misrepresentation on the part of the beneficiary, then in accordance with general principles of contract law the bank may rescind the credit *ab initio*. Cases of misrepresentation will occur even more infrequently than those previously described, for there is no pre-existing relationship between issuer and beneficiary (except by coincidence) and usually no communication between them prior to the opening of the credit. Similar considerations apply in the case of duress or undue influence.

3. UNENFORCEABILITY OF THE CREDIT

There may be factors rendering the credit itself (as opposed to the underlying contract) unenforceable, as where the opening of the credit is unlawful by the law of the place where payment under it is to be made[50] or constitutes an exchange contract which is contrary to the exchange-control regulations of a state which is a member of the IMF Fund.[51] But the credit is not vitiated by factors applicable solely to the relationship between the account party (the applicant for the credit)

[48] In general, illegality does not nullify a contract under English law, it merely renders it unenforceable. The position is otherwise where the provisions of a statute expressly or by implication impose the sanction of total nullity of the infringing contract.

[49] See below, 233.

[50] *Toprak Mahsulleri Ofisi* v. *Finagrain Compagnie Commerciale Agricole et Financiere SA* [1979] 2 Lloyd's Rep. 98; *Power-Curber International* v. *National Bank of Kuwait S.A.* [1981] 1 WLR 1233. In both cases the plea of illegality failed on the ground that the law under which the credit would be illegal was not the applicable law.

[51] IMF Agreement (the Bretton Woods Agreement), Art. VIII (2)(b), incorporated into English law by the Bretton Woods Agreement Order 1946, SR & O 1946, No. 36; *United City Merchants (Investments) Ltd.* v. *Royal Bank of Canada (The American Accord)* [1983] 1 AC 168, discussed on a separate issue below, 228.

and the issuer of the credit, for example fraud, dishonour of a bill of exchange intended to put the bank in funds before issue of the credit.

VIII. Conditions of the Right to Payment

As stated earlier, it is necessary to distinguish conditions which the promisee must satisfy in order to earn payment from events which may negative the promisor's duty to pay even where those conditions are fulfilled. The former constitute an essential prerequisite of the promisee's right of action; the latter, defences which it is for the promisor to establish. The failure to draw this distinction has led to some confusion both in case law and in legal literature. This section is concerned only with the former; the latter are examined in the next section.

Let us begin with the documentary credit. The beneficiary of a credit is not entitled to payment unless he fulfils the conditions specified in the credit, by tendering within the stipulated time documents conforming in all respects to the terms of the credit. English law adopts the principle of strict compliance: the documents must be presented by the (or a) beneficiary designated in the credit and must conform strictly to its terms. Even a minor deviation from the terms of the credit having no commercial significance disentitles the beneficiary to payment except where it falls within the limits of tolerance provided by the UCP as incorporated in the credit.[52]

All this is elementary documentary credits law and would have required no further analysis in this essay but for some passages in the speech of Lord Diplock in *The American Accord*.[53] In that case goods were shipped under a bill of lading on which the date of shipment had been falsely inserted as 15 December, the last permitted date for shipment under the contract of sale, when in fact they had been shipped on 16 December. The beneficiary in good faith tendered documents purporting to show shipment on 15 December but the confirming bank, which had discovered the true facts, rejected them.

At first instance[54] Mocatta J held that the fraud had been committed by the ship's loading broker and that as he was not the beneficiary's agent and the beneficiary had acted in good faith he was entitled to payment. On appeal[55] the Court of Appeal correctly identified the issue as being whether the documents presented to the bank conformed to the credit and, having held that by reason of the falsity of

[52] See Art. 43.
[53] Above, n. 51.
[54] [1979] 1 Lloyd's Rep. 267.
[55] [1981] 3 WLR 242.

the statement of the shipping-date they did not conform to the credit, allowed the appeal and gave judgment for the bank. This decision was reversed by the House of Lords,[56] not on the ground that the false statement in the bill of lading did not render it a non-conforming document, but on the ground that the bank's duty to pay arose on the tender of documents which *appeared on their face* to conform to the credit. The leading speech was delivered by Lord Diplock and is remarkable not so much for the result reached as for the process of reasoning which led to the upholding of the appeal.

It has, so far as I know, never been disputed that as between confirming bank and issuing bank and as between issuing bank and the buyer the contractual duty of each bank under a confirmed irrevocable credit is to examine with reasonable care all documents presented in order to ascertain that they appear on their face to be in accordance with the terms and conditions of the credit, and if they do so appear, to pay to the seller/beneficiary by whom the documents have been presented the sum stipulated by the credit, or to accept or negotiate without recourse to drawer drafts drawn by the seller/beneficiary if the credit so provides. It is so stated in the latest edition of the Uniform Customs.[57]

The statement that banks owe a duty to examine documents with reasonable care is, of course, entirely correct. The further proposition, that if the documents *appear* to conform to the credit the bank is not merely entitled to pay but obliged to pay is wholly erroneous and finds no warrant whatsoever in either the 1974 edition of the UCP or its 1983 successor. The primary source of the bank's payment obligation is to be found in the letter of credit itself. This provides for payment[58] against specified documents covering goods of a stated description and showing shipment by a stipulated date. Nothing in the letter of credit entitles the beneficiary to payment by tendering documents which appear to conform to the credit when they do not do so in fact. General provision (c.) of the general provisions and definitions of the 1974 UCP provides in terms that payment, and so on, is to be made: 'against stipulated documents, provided that the terms and conditions of the credit *are* [not 'appear to be'] complied with.' [emphasis added].

This is reinforced by Article 3(a): 'An irrevocable credit constitutes a definite undertaking of the issuing bank, *provided that the terms and conditions of the credit are complied with*: i. to pay . . .' [emphasis added]. By Article 9: 'Banks assume no liability or responsibility for the form, sufficiency, accuracy, genuineness, falsification or legal effect of any documents . . .'. This is quite obviously a rule for the protection of

[56] [1983] 1 AC 168.
[57] Ibid. 184.
[58] Or acceptance or negotiation.

banks; it *entitles* them to pay against documents which, on a reasonable examination, appear to conform to the credit, but it certainly does not *oblige* them to do so if they know the true facts. The stated condition of the beneficiary's right to payment is presentation of documents which in fact conform to the credit, not those which merely appear to do so.

Still more remarkable are Lord Diplock's observations on the effect not merely of false statements in a document but of forgery of the document.

> It would be strange from the commercial point of view, although not theoretically impossible in law, if *the contractual duty owed by confirming and issuing banks to the buyer to honour the credit on presentation of apparently conforming documents despite the fact that they contain inaccuracies or are even forged* were not matched by a corresponding contractual liability of the confirming bank to the seller/beneficiary (in the absence, of course, of any fraud on his part) to pay the sum stipulated in the credit on presentation of apparently conforming documents[59] [emphasis added].

The notion that a bank owes its own customer a duty to allow him to be defrauded by forged documents is surely bizarre! Nor is this all.

> I would not wish to be taken as accepting that the premiss as to forged documents [i.e. that a bank could decline to pay against a forged document even if the seller had no knowledge of the forgery] is correct, *even where the fact that the document is forged deprives it of all legal effect and makes it a nullity, and so worthless to the confirming bank as security for its advances to the buyer. This is certainly not so under the Uniform Commercial Code as against a person who has taken a draft drawn under the credit in circumstances that would make him a holder in due course, and I see no reason why, and there is nothing in the Uniform Commercial Code to suggest that, a seller/beneficiary who is ignorant of the forgery should be in any worse position because he has not negotiated the draft before presentation*[60] [emphasis added].

The fundamental errors contained in this passage are quite uncharacteristic of the late Lord Diplock, who was noted both for his learning and for his lucidity. Yet his observations do not withstand the most cursory examination.

In the first place, a document which by reason of forgery is a nullity cannot by any stretch of imagination be described as conforming to the credit. What the buyer bargains for in his contract of sale and the bank requires as a condition of payment are documents which are genuine, not worthless pieces of paper conferring no rights of any kind. The UCP certainly protects the bank against paying in good faith against forged documents which appear on their face to be genuine after

[59] Ibid. 184–5.
[60] Ibid. 187–8.

reasonable examination; it is quite another thing to say that the beneficiary who in good faith tenders, say, a bill of lading not issued by the shipping company by which it purports to be issued or a certificate of insurance which purports to incorporate the conditions of a non-existent policy tenders conforming documents. Such a proposition extends the autonomy of a credit *ad absurdum* and reduces letter of credit law to a mockery.

Secondly, it is trite learning that the holder in due course of a bill of exchange is insulated from defences arising under the underlying transaction, including a letter of credit transaction. The beneficiary who is able to negotiate a draft to a holder in due course before presentation gains an advantage for the obvious reason that it then becomes unnecessary for him to look to the issuer for payment; and the holder in due course has no need of recourse for his status entitles him to payment from the issuing or confirming bank regardless of the circumstances. It is hard to follow the logic of the proposition that a beneficiary who has not negotiated the draft should be allowed to claim from the *issuer* on the ground that if he *had* negotiated the draft he would have collected payment from the *new holder*.

Finally, it is simply not correct to say that the Uniform Commercial Code protects the beneficiary before he has negotiated the draft. The fact is that Section 5-114(2) of the Code denies him protection, even after negotiation, by providing no fewer than four distinct, though overlapping, exceptions to the autonomy of the credit,[61] at least three of which apply to the situation discussed by Lord Diplock. Under the first exception the issuer may dishonour the credit if a document does not conform to the warranties which the law infers from its presentation; and Section 7-507 implies a warranty on the part of a person presenting a document of title that the document is genuine. The second exception entitles the issuer of the credit to refuse payment where any of the documents presented is forged. The third exception absolves the issuer from the duty to pay against documents that are fraudulent. The fourth exception covers 'fraud in the transaction' a phrase of somewhat uncertain meaning.

So far as English law is concerned, the ruling by the House of Lords in *The American Accord* might just possibly be sustainable on the ground that the insertion of a false shipping date in the bill of lading did not prevent it from being what it purported to be, so that it could be validly tendered by a beneficiary in good faith. But the reasoning which led to the ruling is manifestly untenable. Moreover, it cannot be justified in terms of the commercial need to protect banks in their

[61] For a detailed analysis, see John F. Dolan, *The Law of Letters of Credit*, 2nd edn., (Boston and New York, 1991), 7–38 ff.

handling of documents presented under letters of credit, for it was the bank's choice not to pay. It would almost certainly have been within its rights if it had made payment, in reliance on Article 9, in the absence of an injunction restraining it from doing so.[62] The proposition contended for here, that the beneficiary who presents non-conforming documents is not entitled to payment even if they appear on their face to be in order, does not carry with it the implication that the bank must therefore withhold payment, nor does it imply any duty on the bank to make enquiry. It means merely that the bank is not *obliged* to pay.

I venture to suggest that the root of the difficulty underlying Lord Diplock's reasoning lies in the conflation of two distinct principles of documentary credit law. The first is that the documents must conform to the credit; the second, that fraud on the part of the beneficiary or his agent absolves the bank of its duty to pay. Where a document is forged, the fraud involved is potentially relevant not only *qua* fraud but as rendering the document non-conforming. Forgery as fraud is not a defence within the second principle unless perpetrated by the beneficiary or his agent. What was overlooked by the House of Lords in *The American Accord* is that the selfsame forgery also means that the document is not genuine and cannot, therefore, be a conforming document. For this purpose it is irrelevant who committed the fraud and whether the beneficiary knew of it or not. The position is simply that he has failed to fulfil the essential condition of payment under the credit. Thus, what should have been the threshold question, namely conformity with the credit, was submerged beneath what should have been the second-stage question, the defence of fraud.

So far I have confined the discussion to the documentary credit, for it is this form of payment undertaking which gives rise to the most difficulties. The same considerations apply in principle to the documentary guarantee but in practice arise relatively infrequently, for most such guarantees require no more than a simple written demand to trigger the payment obligation, so that unless the demand itself fails to conform to the guarantee[63] the only defence to payment is fraud. This is difficult to establish, particularly where, as is common, the primary guarantee has been issued by the beneficiary's local bank against a counter-indemnity by the account party's bank. If in such a case the account party wishes to obtain an injunction to restrain

[62] See p. 234.

[63] As was held to be the case in *I.E. Contractors Ltd.* v. *Lloyds Bank plc*, Financial Times, 8 Aug. 1990, where the Court of Appeal held that on a proper construction of the counter-indemnity issued by the account party's bank in favour of the local bank, the demand had to include a statement that the local bank, the issuer of the guarantee, had incurred an obligation to pay the beneficiary, and that the absence of this statement invalidated the demand.

payment under the counter-indemnity, and consequent debit to his account, what he has to show is not fraud on the part of the beneficiary but fraud by the local bank, for example, in paying a claim it knows to be false or in making a claim when it has not itself received a demand for payment.

The inter-bank payment order is a special case, for assuming the receiving bank to have accepted the order, the sending bank's duty to put the receiving bank in funds arises automatically on the stipulated pay-date without the need for presentation of documents or, indeed, the fulfilment of any conditions by the receiving bank.[64] The inter-bank payment order can therefore properly be described as the most abstract of all payment undertakings, other than those embodied in money itself.

IX. The Autonomy Principle and its Limits: Defences to a Payment Claim

Assuming that the letter of credit, documentary guarantee, or other abstract payment undertaking is not affected by any vitiating factor in existence at the time of its making,[65] then once the beneficiary has passed the threshold test by presenting documents which do in fact conform to the undertaking, he is in a strong position, for it is well established that the contract engendered by the undertaking is independent of the underlying transaction.

The beneficiary's right to payment is, therefore, quite unaffected by the fact that he has committed a breach of the underlying contract or that this is unenforceable by reason of illegality[66] or has been terminated by the other party or has come to an end by frustration. Even a total failure of consideration does not affect the beneficiary's entitlement to payment, for since an abstract payment undertaking needs to consideration, no question of failure of consideration can arise. The position would, of course, be otherwise if the contract of sale had come to an end before issue of the payment undertaking,[67] but once it has been issued the account party's obligation under the underlying contract to procure the issue of the undertaking becomes executed, so that the question of withholding performance of it because of the beneficiary's breach cannot arise.[68]

64 Unless, of course, the order itself specifies conditions of payment.
65 See above, 225.
66 But see p. 227, text and n. 48.
67 See above, p. 227.
68 See R. M. Goode, 'Unconditional bonds: the common law', in Humphrey Lloyd (ed.), *The Liability of Contractors* (London, 1986), 99 at 105–6.

But the autonomy principle is not absolute. The beneficiary is not entitled to payment where he or his agent have been guilty of fraud in relation to the documents or where, though the fraud is that of a third party, the beneficiary or his agent is aware of the fraud at the time the documents are presented or the fraud is one which renders the documents non-conforming.[69] Other exceptions to the autonomy principle are initial illegality of the payment undertaking, frustration or suspension of the duty to pay through supervening illegality or governmental action, and exercise of a right of set-off by the promisor in those unusual cases where, by coincidence, he has had previously dealings with the beneficiary giving rise to a cross-claim.[70]

There remain at least two unresolved problems. First, does fraud by the beneficiary which does not affect the documents but relates only to the underlying transaction—for example a fraudulent misrepresentation which induced the account party's entry into the contract—affect his right to payment under the credit? Probably not, but the position is unclear. Secondly, if the issuing bank, prior to payment, receives compelling evidence of the beneficiary's fraud in the presentation of documents, is the bank still entitled to pay if the documents appear on their face to conform to the credit? Plainly it is not obliged to do so; the question whether it is entitled to do so remains unsettled. There is an argument for saying it has a choice, to pay or not to pay. A bank which has to decide whether the evidence of fraud *is* compelling is placed in a difficult position, for if its assessment is wrong it not only breaches its duty to the beneficiary but damages its commercial reputation. Accordingly, to require the bank to withhold payment in the absence of an injunction may expose it to the very form of assessment and inquiry which the courts have made clear cannot reasonably be expected of banks. All that can reasonably be expected of the bank is that it should act in good faith.[71]

X. Conclusions

An abstract payment undertaking becomes irrevocable on communication to the beneficiary, or even on transmission and prior to its receipt, where there is a mercantile usage to that effect as regards undertakings of that kind, the usage serves a legitimate commercial

[69] See above, 230.

[70] For an example, see *Hongkong and Shanghai Banking Corp.* v. *Kloeckner & Co. AG* [1989] 3 All ER 513.

[71] The prudent course for the bank to adopt is to notify its customer of the presentation of the documents and the bank's concern about fraud and allow the customer a short time to apply for an injunction to restrain payment. If the customer takes no action or the application for the injunction is made and dismissed, then the bank should have little to fear in making payment.

purpose, and the undertaking is made in conformity with the usage. The undertaking will be void, voidable, or unenforceable in the same conditions as apply to contracts generally where a vitiating factor is present at the time of issue of the undertaking. Where this is not the case, the undertaking is irrevocable but the promisor is not obliged to pay until fulfilment of the conditions specified in the undertaking, and even then will be entitled to refuse payment on the ground of fraud in the documents committed by or to the knowledge of the beneficiary or his agent, supervening illegality or other frustrating event, or exercise of a right of set-off. Fraud in the underlying transaction which does not manifest itself in the documents presented in accordance with the terms of the undertaking is probably not a ground for withholding payment.

In the absence of an injunction to restrain the promisor is entitled to pay against apparently conforming documents, even if it has compelling evidence of fraud, so long as it acts in good faith.

The abstract payment undertaking has become a necessary phenomenon of commercial life. Its boundaries and limitations have yet to be fully worked out, particularly in the context of international inter-bank electronic payment orders, on which there may soon be an UNCITRAL Model Law. The mysteries of a promise which defies all known rules of contract formation remain to tantalize us for the foreseeable future. But the future derives its strength from the ideas and traditions of the past; and the evolution of English commercial law, particularly under the influence of the greatest of our commercial lawyers, Lord Mansfield, has shown the responsiveness of the courts to the needs of the commercial community, a responsiveness made all the more necessary in a country whose capital is the world's leading financial centre.

The last word on the development of the abstract payment undertaking, as on so many other aspects of contract law, may be left to Patrick Atiyah when commenting, in his classic work *The Rise and Fall of Freedom of Contract*, on the famous judgment of Lord Mansfield in *Miller* v. *Race*:[72]

> Thus there became apparent the immense value of separating a promise from the transaction to which it was attached, and treating it as a distinct and independent source of liability. It was also a signal victory for the growing importance of contractual expectations; the mere expectations of the bona fide holder of a banknote now served to defeat the property rights of the original owner. Promises and the expectations generated by them were thus becoming themselves an important form of property.[73]

[72] (1758) 1 Burr. 452.
[73] At p. 138.

10

Pre-contractual Duties of Disclosure

S. M. WADDAMS

In 1871 Chief Justice Cockburn, considering a hypothetical case of a sale of land under which were valuable mineral deposits known to the purchaser but not to the vendor, said that it was a case in which 'a man of tender conscience and high honour would be unwilling to take advantage of the ignorance of the seller; but there can be no doubt that the contract . . . would be binding'.[1] On the basis of this statement, and many others to similar effect, it is usually asserted that there is, in English law, no general duty in one party to disclose material facts to the other party to a proposed contract. This legal position is sometimes referred to by the latin expression *caveat emptor*,[2] but the principle is not confined to buyers, nor to contracts of sale. The principle is also often referred to by saying that silence is not equivalent to a misrepresentation, and that there is no general duty of good faith in pre-contractual negotiations. Another way of putting it is that the law permits one party to take advantage of another's unilateral mistake. All these formulations point in the same direction, but as will be seen, there are significant differences among them.

It will be suggested in this essay that the present state of the law is more complex: duties of disclosure are in practice imposed by a variety of judicial techniques, some of which are not usually thought of in this context. Arguments have been adduced in favour of open acceptance of a general duty to disclose material facts. My own view, as will appear, is that such a general rule would not be desirable, but that there is room for enlargement of the duty of disclosure in some cases by the development of existing techniques.

There are to be found, in old as well as in modern cases, a number of assertions inconsistent with the view that there is no duty of

[1] *Smith* v. *Hughes* (1871) LR 6 QB 597, 604.

[2] For the significance of this concept more generally in nineteenth-century thought, see P. S. Atiyah, *The Rise and Fall of Freedom of Contract* (Oxford, 1979), 464–79.

disclosure, or of good faith. Thus, in *Mellish* v. *Motteux*,[3] Lord Kenyon said: 'In contracts of all kinds, it is of the highest importance that courts of law should compel the observance of honesty and good faith.' In *Phillips* v. *Homfray*, Lord Hatherley LC said, in a case where a purchaser of land failed to disclose, on buying from a neighbouring landowner, that the purchaser had already taken coal from the land without permission: 'This court requires the utmost good faith between buyer and seller, and will not specifically enforce a contract which is not entirely according to good faith.'[4] In Kerr's treatise on Fraud (1883 edition)[5] it is stated that concealment of a fact 'is as much a fraud as if the existence of such fact were expressly denied or the reverse of it expressly stated',[6] though this proposition was severely qualified in the following pages of the treatise.[7] Some modern Canadian cases have asserted a duty upon a vendor of a house to reveal material facts, at any rate if dangerous to the purchaser's health.[8] A recent English case makes reference to a duty of good faith.[9] Several cases have suggested that an offeree may not 'snap at' an offer known to have been made under a mistake.[10] Despite these suggestions, however, the general position against a duty of disclosure has been reaffirmed in recent English and Commonwealth cases.[11]

Instinctively, one is inclined to feel that there are many cases in which disclosure ought not to be required. A prospective employee,

[3] (1792) Peake 156. Similar dicta can be found in *Blisset* v. *Daniel* (1853) 10 Hare 493, 522 (Turner V-C), and *British Equitable Insurance Co.* v. *Great Western Railway Co.* (1868) 38 LJ Ch. 132, 135 (Malins V-C).

[4] (1871) LR 6 Ch. App. 770, 778. But this statement leaves open the possibility of damages at common law.

[5] W. W. Kerr, *A Treatise on the Law of Fraud and Mistake*, 2nd edn. (London, 1883). See also G. Spencer Bower, *The Law Relating to Actionable Non-disclosure* (London, 1915), 1–4.

[6] Kerr, n. 5 above, 58.

[7] See pp. 58–9, 59, 60, 63. Possibly by 'concealment' Kerr meant to imply active deception.

[8] *Rowley* v. *Isley* (1951) 3 DLR 766; *McGrath* v. *McLean* (1979) 95 DLR (3d) 144, 151 (leave to appeal to SCC refused); *Sevidal* v. *Chopra* (1987) 64 OR (2d) 169. It seems anomalous, however, to base liability for economic loss on failure to warn of a danger to health that has never materialized, and where injury to health is not complained of.

[9] *Interfoto Picture Library Ltd* v. *Stiletto Visual Programmes Ltd* [1989] QB 433, 445 (Bingham LJ). The question in issue was the somewhat different one of incorporation of contract terms.

[10] *Magee* v. *Pennine Insurance Co.* [1969] 2 QB 507 (CA); *Belle River Community Arena Inc.* v. *W. J. C. Kaufmann Co Ltd.* (1978) 87 DLR (3d) 761 (Ont. CA). Where the offeree knows that the terms of the offer are mistaken, it is well established that the offer cannot be accepted: *Smith* v. *Hughes* (1871) LR 6 QB 597, *Taylor* v. *Johnson* (1983) 151 CLR 422.

[11] *Stephenson* v. *Toronto-Dominion Bank* (1989) 68 OR (2d) 118 (CA); *Banque Keyser Ullmann S.A.* v. *Skandia (UK) Ins. Co. Ltd.* [1990] 3 WLR 364 (HL); *Queen* v. *Cognos* (1990) 69 DLR (4th) 288 (Ont. CA); *Royal Bank of Canada* v. *Hislop* (BCCA, 1989). Contrast the position in French law: P. Legrand, 'Pre-contractual disclosure and information: English and French Law Compared' (1986) 6 O.J.L.S. 322; J. Ghestin, 'The obligation to disclose information', in D. Harris and D. Tallon (eds.) *Contract Law Today* (Oxford, 1989), 157–66.

most people would say, should not be expected to disclose that he resigned from a former position without notice, or that he had a disagreement with a former employer. If the employer wishes to know, she can ask for information; if she does not ask, she takes the risk of the adverse fact.[12] Similarly, a buyer in a second-hand bookshop is not bound to disclose that a book is underpriced,[13] nor is a buyer at an auction bound to disclose that a lot is more valuable than its description suggests, nor is a borrower bound to disclose that she has defaulted in repayment of former loans, or that she has been refused credit by other lenders. A buyer of land does not usually disclose facts suggesting that the land is underpriced. A lawyer, in settling a case on behalf of a client, does not usually feel bound to disclose all the weaknesses of his case, and, in fact, he is bound by his duty to his client not to do so.[14]

On the other hand, no one doubts that a researcher, conducting a medical experiment, is bound to disclose the risks to a prospective subject.[15] This result can be supported in several ways: it might be said that the patient does not truly consent unless she is fully informed; it might be said that the researcher, in asking for consent, gives an implicit assurance that risks known to her have been disclosed; it might be said that, in the circumstances, the researcher's silence amounts to an assertion that she knows of no significant risks that have not been disclosed. It will be apparent that, as is usual in legal reasoning, the deployment of these formulations announces a conclusion that disclosure is required, whereas the assertion that the risk is cast upon the ignorant party announces the opposite conclusion. Legal results can thus usually be made to conform with instinctive feelings, but instinct is a very uncertain guide on this issue which, since ancient times, has been perceived as posing difficult moral questions.[16]

Misleading Conduct

Many cases can be found where, by a variety of techniques, a contracting party has been prevented from taking advantage of

[12] But see *Fuller* v. *De Paul University* 293 Ill. App. 261, 12 NE 2d 213 (1938) (applicant to Catholic institution bound to disclose degradation from priesthood); *Courtright* v. *Canadian Pacific Ltd*. (1985) 18 DLR (4th) 639 (Ont. CA) (prospective employee—a solicitor—bound to disclose pending criminal charges).

[13] See illustration 6 to s. 551 of the *Restatement of Torts (second)* (1977).

[14] *Turner* v. *Green* [1895] 2 Ch. 205. But in *Mackenzie* v. *Carroll* (1974) 53 DLR (3d) 699 (Ont. HC) a solicitor was held to be bound to disclose a material change in circumstances.

[15] See *Halushka* v. *University of Saskatchewan* (1965) 53 DLR (2d) 436 (Sask. CA).

[16] The duty of disclosure was discussed by Cicero as a disputed philosophical question. See B. Nicholas, 'The Obligation to Disclose Information', in Harris and Tallon, n. 11 above, 167–8.

superior knowledge. First, inquiries may be made by the less-knowledgeable party, and any misleading response will be a legally significant misrepresentation. Though mere silence is not equivalent to a misrepresentation, a half-truth[17] or a nod or a wink or a shake of the head or a smile[18] or a tone of voice or any sort of conduct,[19] if deceptive, can amount to misrepresentations. A statement that is true when made but that becomes false in the light of altered circumstances is treated as a misrepresentation.[20] Since, in negotiating a contract, the parties almost always say something, there is very often scope for a finding that the conduct of the knowledgeable party, taken as a whole and in its context, was misleading. This may be an explanation of the duty of disclosure on entering into a partnership.[21] A prospective partner who gives an incomplete statement of his financial circumstances makes a misleading statement.

Silence Equivalent to Assertion

A related concept is that silence may, in its context, amount to an assertion that there is nothing of significance to reveal. In *Brownlie* v. *Campbell*, Lord Blackburn said:

> Where there is a duty or an obligation to speak, and a man in breach of that duty or obligation holds his tongue and does not speak, and does not say the thing he was bound to say, if that was done with the intention of inducing the other party to act upon the belief that the reason why he did not speak was because he had nothing to say, I should be inclined myself to hold that that was fraud . . .[22]

It is not entirely clear what Lord Blackburn meant by a duty to speak. The statement, however, suggests that in some circumstances silence may amount to an assertion that there is nothing of significance to reveal. The same judge said, in another case, 'the fact not

[17] See *Arkwright* v. *Newbould* (1880) 17 Ch. D. 301, 318, per James LJ; *Nottinghamshire Patent Brick & Tile Co.* v. *Butler* (1886) 16 QBD 778; *Olsen* v. *Poirier* (1978) 91 DLR (3d) 123 (Ont. HC) aff'd CA 111 DLR (3d) 512n.

[18] These expressions are from *Walters* v. *Morgan* (1861) 3 DF & J 718, 724, *per* Lord Campbell.

[19] *Gronau* v. *Schlamp Investments Ltd.* (1974) 52 DLR (3d) 631 (Man. QB) (concealment by vendor of crack in wall).

[20] At least if the change in circumstances is known to the person making the statement. See A. H. Hudson, 'Making Misrepresentations' (1969) 85 *LQR* 524.

[21] See *Bell* v. *Lever Bros. Ltd.* [1932] AC 161, 227, *per* Lord Atkin; *Lindley on Partnership*, 12th edn., E. M. Scamell (London, 1962) 342.

[22] (1880) 5 App. Cas. 925, 950. See also *Bodger* v. *Nicholls* (1873) 28 LT 441, 445 (Blackburn J). Tending in the opposite direction is *Ward* v. *Hobbs* (1878) 4 App. Cas. 13 (HL).

disclosed . . . is impliedly represented not to exist'.[23] Kerr made the same point in his treatise, saying that 'a man may by mere silence, without active concealment, produce a false impression on the mind of another'.[24] On the same principle, silence may constitute a representation for the purposes of estoppel.[25]

Guarantees

In contracts of guarantee, it is very commonly the case that the creditor knows facts about the financial affairs of the principal debtor that are material to the guarantor. A general duty to disclose has been denied,[26] but in some cases it has been held that silence may give a misleading impression. Thus, in *London General Omnibus Co. Ltd.* v. *Holloway*,[27] an employer failed to reveal, when applying for a fidelity bond for an employee, that the employee in question had previously been found guilty of dishonesty. It was held that the bond was unenforceable. Vaughan Williams LJ said that there was a duty to disclose when 'the non-disclosure constitutes a misrepresentation', because both parties contracted on the assumption that 'the clerk whose fidelity . . . is the subject of the security has not, to the knowledge of the person taking such guarantee, been guilty of a breach of honesty in the performance of the duties of the very office . . . fidelity and honesty in which is guaranteed'. In such circumstances he thought that 'the omission to mention that such a fact does exist is an implied representation that it does not'.[28] Again the result rests on the proposition that silence may amount to a positive assertion that the facts in question do not exist.

This approach is not always available, however, because a failure to disclose material facts is not always equivalent to a false assertion, nor does it always produce a false impression. This proposition can be tested by contemplating the not uncommon case where the knowledgeable party expressly states that she is not willing to make disclosure. A case may be supposed of a negotiation between business competitors for the lease from one to the other of equipment. If the lessor should inquire about the lessee's intended use of the equipment,

[23] *Lee* v. *Jones* (1864) 17 CBNS 482, 501.
[24] Kerr, n. 5 above, 63–4.
[25] G. Spencer Bower and A. K. Turner, *The Law Relating to Estoppel by Representation*, 2d edn. (London, 1966) 45–59.
[26] *Hamilton* v. *Watson* (1845) 12 C.&F. 109, *North British Ins. Co.* v. *Lloyd* (1854) 10 Ex. 523, *Royal Bank of Canada* v. *Hislop* (BCCA, 1989). But *Railton* v. *Mathews* (1844) 10 C.&F. 934 appears to suggest a duty to disclose material facts.
[27] [1912] 2 KB 72.
[28] Ibid., at 77, 79.

and the lessee should reply: 'You can hardly expect me to tell you that', there would (if the lessee had an unusual use in mind) be a deliberate concealment, and perhaps a deliberate taking advantage of the lessor's ignorance, and yet no misrepresentation. Often an enquiry is answered by the words 'satisfy yourself'. What can be said expressly can usually also be said by implication, and there are many cases equivalent to the examples just given, where it is fully expected by both parties that relevant facts will be withheld. In such cases, though there may be advantage to one party and mistake by the other, the knowledgeable party's conduct can scarcely be said to be deceptive, still less dishonest or dishonourable.

Contracts of Utmost Good Faith

Insurance contracts are usually said to be contracts of utmost good faith, in which disclosure, on both sides, is required.[29] The rule requiring disclosure by the insured has, however, sometimes been supported on the basis of definition of the risk undertaken by the insurer rather than on any principle of honesty as such. In the leading case, in 1766, it was said that 'although the suppression [of facts] should happen through *mistake*, without any fraudulent intention; yet still the indemnitor is *deceived*, and the policy is *void*; because the risque run is really different from the risque understood and intended to be run . . .'[30] Perhaps it is on this principle that the Marine Insurance Act requires disclosure not only of what is known to the insured, but of what ought 'in the ordinary course of business' to be known.[31] The insurer, however, takes the risk of facts of which the insured is justifiably ignorant.

The line between insurance contracts and contracts of guarantee is indistinct, and some nineteenth-century cases suggest that the latter might also, in some circumstances, be contracts of utmost good faith.[32] The prevailing view is now, as has been seen, that liability for non-disclosure rests on proof that the non-disclosure amounts to a misleading assertion, and that a contract of guarantee is not a contract of utmost good faith.

This category of contracts of 'utmost good faith' is surprisingly

[29] *Banque Keyser Ullman SA* v. *Skandia (UK) Ins. Co. Ltd.* [1990] 3 WLR 364, 369, 380.

[30] *Carter* v. *Boehm* (1766) 3 Burr. 1905, 1909.

[31] Marine Insurance Act, 1906, s. 18(1) (UK), Marine Insurance Act RSO 1980, c. 255, s. 19(1). See E. J. MacGillivray and M. Parkington, *Insurance Law*, 7th edn. (London, 1981) 619–20, 815.

[32] *Owen* v. *Homan* (1851) 3 Mar. & G. 378, 397; *Seaton* v. *Heath* [1899] 1 QB 782, 793. See Halsbury's *Laws of England* (London, 1911) xv, 539, notes m and q.

inexact. In 1932 Lord Atkin said that, 'apart from special fiduciary relationships', contracts for partnership and contracts of insurance were 'the leading instances'.[33] A third class of cases, generally said to be of utmost good faith, is rather vaguely designated 'family settlements',[34] or 'family arrangements',[35] where it has been said that 'full and complete communication of all material circumstances is what the court must insist on'.[36] Again, in this kind of case, the honest intention of the knowledgeable party is no defence, if the court later determines that relevant information was withheld.[37]

It becomes apparent on an examination of these cases that their scope and underlying principle are quite uncertain. Are fiduciaries to be included, or should they be treated as a separate category? Do the cases rest on a requirement of honesty, or on the notion that the less-knowledgeable party only agrees to what is described? Are these cases in which silence is found to be actually deceptive? Are the categories of utmost good faith closed? If the underlying principle is that 'one party is likely to have the command of means of knowledge not available to the other',[38] it is plain that there is no reason to limit its operation to a few classes of contract.[39]

Maritime Salvage

Salvage cases have imposed a duty upon the master of a ship calling for assistance to disclose the extent of any damage that the ship had suffered. English admiralty law was civil law, and the Admiralty Court was not bound to follow English common law on matters within its own jurisdiction. In 1854 Dr Lushington, the Admiralty Court Judge, said:

[33] *Bell* v. *Lever Bros. Ltd.* [1932] AC 161, 227. *Chitty on Contracts*, 26th edn. (London, 1989), 481 includes also, in some of their aspects, contracts to subscribe for corporate shares, contracts for the sale of land, and suretyship contracts.

[34] *Pollock on Contracts*, 11th edn. (London, 1942) 453.

[35] *Halsbury's Laws of England*, 4th edn., vol. 18, discussed in *Wales* v. *Wadham* [1977] 1 WLR 199, 216 ff.

[36] *Gordon* v. *Gordon* (1819) 3 Swan 400, 473 (Eldon LC).

[37] Ibid. 477.

[38] *Banque Keyser Ullman SA* v. *Skandia (UK) Ins. Co.* [1990] 1 QB 665, 769. See also *Pollock on Contract*, 11th edn., 437: 'within the peculiar knowledge of one party, and the other has to rely, in the first instance at all events, on the correctness of the statements made by him'; G. Spencer Bower, n. 5 above, 58.

[39] See K. L. Scheppele, *Legal Secrets* (Chicago, 1988), 136, 178, suggesting requirement of disclosure by party having superior means of knowledge. In *Courtright* v. *Canadian Pacific Ltd.*, n. 12 above, it was held that a solicitor was bound to disclose to a prospective employer that criminal charges were pending against him. The trial judge (5 DLR 4th 488) treated the case as one requiring utmost good faith. The Court of Appeal simply said that 'in the circumstances' good faith was required.

An agreement to bind two parties must be made with the full knowledge of all the facts necessary to be known by both parties; and if any fact which, if known, could have had an operation on the agreement about to be entered into is kept back, or not disclosed to either of the contracting parties, that would vitiate the agreement itself. It is not necessary, in order to vitiate an agreement, that there should be moral fraud; it is not necessary, in order to make it not binding, that one of the parties should keep back any fact or circumstance of importance, if there should be misapprehension, accidentally or by carelessness; we all know that there may be what, in the eye of the law, is termed equitable fraud.[40]

In another salvage case the same judge said: 'If, though unintentionally, there was a concealment of a fact so material that it ought to invalidate the agreement, I should not enforce it.'[41] This indicates a striking contrast to the common law of the time. It is notable, however, that Dr Lushington did not rest the obligation on honesty or morality. Interestingly, also, he did not require disclosure of all material facts. For example, in one case he held that it was not necessary for the master of a ship in distress to disclose the value of the cargo being carried, although this was a most material fact to the potental salvor because a salvage award in the Admiralty Court was based directly on the value salved.[42] The distinction may be that, where the master fails to disclose that his ship is taking on water, he impliedly states that it is not: his request for assistance carries with it an assertion that the ship is in no greater danger than it appears to be. On the other hand, a request for assistance says nothing about the value of the cargo.[43]

The salvage cases, though not usually called contracts 'of utmost good faith',[44] are like the insurance cases in that the material facts, known to be of vital importance to one party, are peculiarly within the knowledge of the other, and where an independent inspection by the less-knowledgeable party is impracticable. An analogy might be drawn also with the modern statutory provisions on insider-trading of shares.[45] There, facts are within the knowledge of the insider, and the outsider has no practicable means of ascertaining them.

[40] *The Kingalock* (1854) 1 Sp. 263, 265.

[41] *The Canora* (1866) LR 1 A.&E. 54, 56.

[42] *The Henry* (1851) 15 Jur. 183.

[43] The distinction is reminiscent of that sometimes proposed between 'intrinsic' and 'extrinsic' qualities in goods sold, but this distinction is difficult to apply to non-sale contracts. See Nicholas, 'The Obligation to Disclose', n. 16 above, 184.

[44] But they are so categorized by Goff and Jones, *Law of Restitution*, 3rd edn (London, 1986), 162.

[45] E.g. *Corporations Act*, RSO 1980, c. 95, s. 76.

Tort Law

Some cases have approached the problem by way of the tort of negligence. Where the facts indicate that one party is relying on the other to tell him all relevant facts, the other may be liable if, withholding relevant facts, she does not warn him to take independent advice.[46] These cases, again, do not support a universal duty of disclosure. They assert, rather, that conduct in certain circumstances may be misleading. Generally speaking, tort liability for economic loss seems, in English law, to be in a period of retreat, and so it is not altogether surprising that tort actions for non-disclosure were rejected in the insurance context in two recent English cases.[47] Nevertheless, the door is not closed to liability on this basis. It has not been doubted that economic loss is recoverable where caused by reliance on misrepresentation, where there is breach of a duty of care. Parties in contractual negotiation will usually be in a sufficiently close relationship to give rise to a duty of care. The principle remains intact, therefore, that misleading conduct in the course of negotiation may give rise to tortious liability.[48]

Warranty

Many problems of the kind under discussion have been resolved, not by imposing a duty of honesty, or of care, upon the knowledgeable party, but by imposing an absolute obligation by means of warranty or its equivalent.[49] At one time, a seller of goods was entitled to enforce the sale even though she did not own the goods sold. No one would now suggest that the proper solution to this problem is to impose upon the seller a duty of disclosure. The implied warranty of title avoids the necessity of inquiry into what the seller knew or ought to have known, and is altogether a more effective legal device for protecting the reasonable expectations of the buyer.[50] So accustomed are we to it that

[46] *Tracy* v. *Atkins* (1979) 105 DLR (3d) 632. P. D. Finn, 'Good Faith and Nondisclosure', in *Essays on Torts* (Sydney, 1989).

[47] *Bank of Nova Scotia* v. *Hellenic Mutual War Risks Assn. (Bermuda) Ltd.* [1990] 1 QB 818, rev'd on other grounds [1991] 2 WLR 1279; *Banque Keyser Ullmann SA* v. *Skandia (UK) Insurance Co. Ltd.* [1990] 1 QB 665 (CA), affd. on other grounds, [1990] 3 WLR 364 (HL).

[48] Tortious liability may be imposed when no contract is reached between the parties. The concept of a duty in tort to disclose, therefore, might be very far-reaching, for example, where one intending vendor fails to disclose to a potential purchaser a material fact affecting the value of land in a district, who then buys from another vendor in the same district.

[49] See P. S. Atiyah, 'Judicial techniques and the law of contract', in *Essays on Contract* (Oxford, 1986), 265.

[50] *Sale of Goods Act*, RSO 1980, c. 462, s. 13.

we do not think of it as related to a duty of disclosure, but the effect of the implied warranty is that if a seller wishes to enforce a sale of goods to which she has no title, she must, in effect, disclose the defect in title or the risk of it. A similar device has evolved recently by private contract in the Ontario real property market. A certain kind of insulation (urea formaldehyde foam insulation) after quite extensive use, was found to be potentially dangerous, and buyers of houses were understandably anxious on the subject. The standard form of contract was amended to include a warranty that urea formaldehyde foam insulation had not been used. This is, again, a much better device for protecting the purchaser than an obligation upon the vendor to disclose if he knew or ought to have known of the insulation. A practical effect certainly is that the seller of a house containing the insulation has to disclose the fact to the purchaser, but the effect has been attained more effectively by the evolution of the standard contract form than it could have been by imposition of a duty of disclosure. From the buyer's point of view, the state of the seller's mind—still more of the seller's conscience—is irrelevant. The buyer's disappointment and loss are the same whether or not the seller knew or could have known the true facts. The warranty approach, therefore, may, if the scope of the warranty is clear, lead to greater certainty and greater simplicity of application, and may match the buyer's expectation more exactly.

Mistake

All cases under consideration are cases of mistake. To the extent, therefore, that relief is available for mistake there is a practical duty of disclosure. That is to say, if the presence of a mistake will in itself relieve the mistaken party, the knowledgeable party who wishes to enforce the contract will only be able to do so by removing the other's mistake. The scope of relief for mistaken assumptions is rather uncertain; probably relief is available only when the mistake is of a fundamental or basic nature. If relief is available for a mistake that is shared by both parties, is the case for relief made stronger or weaker where the mistake is not shared? From one point of view, knowledge by the party who benefits tends to show that he has an expectation of profiting, and this has sometimes been adduced as a reason for enforcing the contract.[51] But more significant than the knowledge of

[51] In *Sherwood* v. *Walker* (1887) 66 Mich 568, 33 NW 919, a cow thought by the seller to be infertile was sold at beef prices and turned out to be worth ten times the price when she proved fertile. On one view of the facts, the buyer expected, if he did not know, that she could be made to breed. G. E. Palmer, *Mistake and Unjust Enrichment* (Ohio, 1962), 16,

the non-mistaken party, I would suggest, is whether the mistaken party knows of the former's expectation. Where he does know, there is a strong case for enforcement, for the mistaken party can then be said to have taken the risk of the mistake. The question of whether the contract allocates the risk of the mistake in question[52] must depend on surrounding circumstances. In the case of the underpriced book in a second-hand bookshop, the seller can be taken to know that the buyers will include bargain-hunters: the nature of the business invites them. From the point of view of encouraging honesty, however, knowledge of the true facts by the party benefitted tends to strengthen the case for relief. A sale by an ignorant seller of books believed to be of low value but in fact containing a valuable first edition might not be enforced if both parties were mistaken (this is a difficult question that would depend on whether the mistake was sufficiently fundamental); an expert buyer who knew the fact and deliberately concealed it could hardly claim to occupy a stronger position than the mistaken buyer.[53]

Unjust Enrichment

These examples lead us to the question of unjust enrichment, closely associated with relief for mistake in contracts.[54] Where, as is usual in the cases under consideration, mistake affects value, the non-mistaken party will be enriched by the contract. Whether or not the enrichment is to be called 'unjust' depends on (or is the same question as) whether the contract is enforceable. It should be noted, however, that an enrichment in such cases is just the same whether or not the party benefitted knew, or ought to have known, of the true facts. Imposition of a duty of disclosure, therefore, will not always prevent enrichment by mistake.

Unconscionability

Unconscionability is distinguishable from mistake as a ground for relief from contractual obligations. A person of superior bargaining power

adduces this as a point in favour of enforcing the contract. It is pointed out by Nicholas, 'The Obligation to Disclose' (n. 16 above, 185), that knowledge of facts in cases of sales at under value tends to merge into belief, expectation, and judgement. The case of the buyer acting on private knowledge is often indistinguishable from the case of the buyer perceiving the significance of facts known to both parties.

52 This is a crucial factor in the rules on mistake in the *Restatement (Second) of Contracts* (1981). See ss. 153, 154.

53 The expertise of the buyer in this example may be significant. French law imposes a duty of disclosure on 'professionels' in dealings with non-professionals, or 'profanes': Legrand, n. 11 above, 330–41; Ghestin, n. 11 above, 164.

54 See G. E. Palmer, *Mistake and Unjust Enrichment* (Ohio, 1962); *Restatement (Second) of Contracts*, s. 152(1).

may be mistaken and will not be denied relief merely because the party benefitting by the mistake lacks bargaining power. However, the boundaries are not watertight. If unconscionability is defined (as it often is) as taking undue advantage of inequality of bargaining power, one might quite plausibly say that superior knowledge is itself a form of superior bargaining power, and that one who fails to disclose material facts gains an advantage from it. Whether it is an undue or improper advantage, however, still remains to be determined. In the case of the buyer in the bookshop it would seem odd to describe the contract as unconscionable. On the other hand, the sale of land at an under value has been one of the paradigm cases of unconscionability, and the effect of granting relief is that the buyer is prevented from taking advantage of her superior knowledge.[55]

In some cases, called cases of 'undue influence', the relationship between the parties is so unequal that one is wholly prohibited from bargaining for an advantage at the expense of the other. In these cases, also, one of the incidental effects is that a party with superior knowledge may not take advantage of it.

Fiduciary Relationships

Where a relationship of trust exists between parties there is, again, a general prohibition on one party bargaining at the other's expense. One effect is that a party may not take advantage of superior knowledge, and it has often been said, on this account, that there is a duty of disclosure.[56] It would seem, however, that as in the cases of undue influence, the duty of disclosure is an incidental consequence of the wider principle. The party in whom trust is reposed is equally prevented from profiting, at the other's expense, by superior judgement or by mere good chance. To put the point another way: even full disclosure by a trustee would not necessarily enable her to enforce an advantageous contract against a trust beneficiary. It has been said that the categories of fiduciary relationship are never closed,[57] and the possibility therefore is always open of seeking so to classify a relationship. It has been pointed out, however, that if courts become so ready to find fiduciary relationships that they find them

[55] The crucial factor, however, from the point of view of unconscionability, is not the knowledge of the buyer, but the ignorance of the seller.

[56] See e.g. Lord Atkin in *Bell* v. *Lever Bros. Ltd.* [1932] AC 161, 227; *Hayward* v. *Bank of Nova Scotia* (1985) 19 DLR (4th) 758 (Ont. CA); *Standard Investment Ltd* v. *Canadian Imperial Bank of Commerce* (1985) 22 DLR (4th) 410 (Ont. CA).

[57] *Laskin* v. *Bache & Co Inc* (1971) 23 DLR (3d) 385 (Ont. CA); *Guerin* v. *The Queen* (1985) 13 DLR (4th) 321, 341 (SCC).

wherever they think a remedy is appropriate, the concept will lose all defining and predictive power. A recent decision of the Supreme Court of Canada suggests that the courts will hesitate before imposing fiduciary duties in ordinary contractual relationships.[58]

Proposed Reforms

It has been suggested in the preceding pages that duties of disclosure are more commonly imposed than is generally supposed. Nevertheless, there remain a substantial number of situations in which it is reasonably clear that there is no such duty, and where it can truly be said that the law permits one party to take advantage of another's mistake. Is this state of the law defensible? Reform of the law has been recently proposed on moral and on economic grounds, the two, on this occasion, operating in uncharacteristic harmony with each other. Morally, it has been suggested, the present law is undesirable because it protects dishonesty and sharp parctice.[59] Judicial assertions of the existing rule are often accompanied by apologetic expressions suggesting that the knowledgeable party, who fails to disclose, acts immorally,[60] or at least distastefully.[61] But is this so clear? There is certainly a relationship between contract law and morality, but it is not a simple one.[62] One may legitimately take advantage of the existing state of the law, even if it is imperfect. An agent commissioned to buy at the lowest price would not be morally bound to disclose to a vendor that higher prices might be obtainable from other buyers—indeed he would be bound (by his duties to his principal) not to do so. Though this does not settle the question of the principal's contractual rights, it is difficult to maintain that the morality of the principal's conduct depends on whether or not an agent is employed.

It may be said that though the individual may legitimately take advantage of existing law, the law itself would be better, and community standards higher, if disclosure were required. But is it clear that we would benefit from an actual legal rule to this effect? A rule

[58] *Lac Minerals Ltd.* v. *International Corona Resources Ltd.* (1989) 61 DLR (4th) 14 (SCC); cf. *Hospital Products Ltd.* v. *United States Surgical Corp.* (1984) 55 ALR 417, 454 (Austr. HC).

[59] See *Caveat Emptor in Sales of land*, and the companion *Honesty or Suspicion in Conveyancing*, consultation papers of the English Law Commission (1988). C. Fried, *Contract as Promise*, (Harvard, 1981), 78–83, though generally sympathetic to moral arguments, regards non-disclosure as a difficult case. See also F. A. Trindade, 'Note' (1989) 105 *LQR* 191.

[60] *Smith* v. *Hughes* (1871) LR & QB 597; *Fox* v. *Mackreth* (1788) 2 Cox 320; *Walters* v. *Morgan* (1861) 3 De GF & J 715, 723–4; *Horsfall* v. *Thomas* (1862) 1 H & C 90, 99–100.

[61] *Stephenson* v. *Toronto Dominion Bank* (1989) 68 OR (2d) 118, 120.

[62] See P. S. Atiyah, *Promises, Morals, and Law*, (Oxford, 1981).

requiring parties to disclose material facts of which they knew would introduce much uncertainty, especially if transactions could be reopened after substantial lapses of time. One probable effect would be that, in some transactions, notably sales of land, parties would attempt to restore finality by a contractual provision removing the legal effect of non-disclosure. Those who favour reform of the existing law are bound to consider their attitude to such provisions. If they accept them as legitimate, it is difficult to maintain that the existing law is itself immoral. Moreover, any departure from the present legal position could be readily reversed by contractual provisions, express or implied.[63] On the other hand, arguments against the validity of such provisions are difficult to maintain; few would argue for a rule that prevented parties from agreeing that their transactions should be final.[64]

From an economic perspective, the case for reform initially looks compelling: it is desirable that contracting parties should have full information, and this can be achieved at minimal cost by requiring all parties to disclose everything they know. If the objective is to avoid mistakes, the knowledgeable party is certainly the 'least cost avoider'. But some have objected that a rule requiring disclosure would operate as a disincentive to the acquisition of information,[65] and this consideration has led Professor Kronman to suggest that in cases where resources have been invested for this purpose no disclosure should be required. But, recognizing the difficulty of distinguishing such cases individually, Kronman goes on to suggest that disclosure should not be required in transactions of a type that generally involve the use of resources for the acquisition of information, but that otherwise disclosure should be required.[66] Classification of contracts in these terms would not always be a simple task,[67] and it is doubtful whether the proposed classifications would correspond to decided American cases.[68] Moreover, the effect would be to allow the knowledgeable party to retain the benefit of the contract in the case of the expert buyer from an inexpert seller, the very case that seems closest to unconscionability and moral fraud. Kronman's test would

[63] In some circumstances the presence of a contractual exclusion might have the effect of putting the mistaken party on notice that there might be non-disclosure, but this effect would be minimal where the exclusion was part of a standard form.

[64] At least if the agreement was fair and reasonable. See Misrepresentation Act 1967 (UK), s. 3.

[65] See 4. Spencer Bower and A.K. Turner, *Law of Actionable Misrepresentation*, 3d edn. (London 1974), 105–6.

[66] A. T. Kronman, 'Mistake, Disclosure, Information and the Law of Contracts', in A. T. Kronman and R. A. Posner (eds.), *The Economics of Contract Law* (Boston, 1979).

[67] See Nicholas, n. 16 above, 186.

[68] See Scheppele, n. 39 above, 111–26.

also apparently require prospective employees to reveal negative aspects of employment history, an instance where, in general, disclosure is not thought to be required, morally or legally.

Proponents of reform generally extend their proposals not only to facts actually known, but to facts that a reasonable person ought to know.[69] The attraction of this extension is clear, for it is always difficult to determine the state of a person's actual knowledge and it would seem anomalous to give an advantage to the carelessly ignorant. But it should be noted that several consequences follow upon the extension. First, the basis for the duty of disclosure is moved away from a principle of honesty, for a person would be responsible for an honest (but unreasonable) non-disclosure. Secondly, the requirement of disclosure ceases to be costless, for a party required to disclose what he reasonably ought to know may be obliged to make costly inquiries. The Law Commission proposed in 1988 in a consultation paper, that a vendor of land should be required to disclose all material facts about the property of which he knew or ought to have known at the time of the sale.[70] The Commission then contemplated with equanimity the prospect that, if its proposal were adopted, all vendors would be obliged in practice to commission structural surveys. This idea causes further difficulties, for the vendor's interest in commissioning the survey would be quite different from the purchaser's. Surveys are of almost infinite variety. The vendor would want, and would pay for, a superficial survey to give his house a clean bill of health; the purchaser would want a thorough survey backed up by a responsible surveyor. If the surveyor were paid by the vendor, but potentially liable to the purchaser, she would protect herself, so far as possible,[71] by disclaimer, and the purchaser who desired full protection would still have to commission his own survey. These measures would impose costs on both parties. A third point is that making the criterion what the vendor ought to have known would introduce a new question of law often itself difficult, and hence costly, to determine. Moreover, from the purchaser's point of view, a requirement of disclosure, even in its extended form, still would fall far short of the protection given by a warranty, such as the warranty against use of urea formaldehyde foam insulation mentioned above. All the changes contemplated would tend to increase the cost of transactions. Most purchasers of houses are, at some other times, vendors. It is not obvious that imposing costs on vendors is advantageous to purchasers in the long run. Costs caused by uncertainty will fall on both parties. In the face of a hostile

[69] See Law Commission papers, n. 59 above.
[70] See n. 59 above.
[71] See *Smith* v. *Bush* [1990] 1 AC 831 (HL).

response, based in part on these considerations, the Law Commission withdrew its proposal.[72]

Finality of transactions is probably the strongest argument in favour of the existing law, and this raises further economic questions. Under the present law, despite some uncertainties, the sale of a residential house is treated (with few exceptions) as final. This has the merit of giving security to both parties, who are free to act on the basis that, after completion (and perhaps from the date of the contract) the price is the vendor's, and the land is the purchaser's, with all the advantages and disadvantages of ownership. Would it be an improvement in the law if house sales could be rescinded years after completion on the ground that material facts had not been disclosed at the time of the contract? If this were the law, whenever either party had reason to regret the transaction (and there would be many such cases), there would be a powerful incentive to assert that the other party knew, at the time of the sale, of a material fact that was not disclosed. Material facts relating to land sales include not only facts relating to physical condition, but such matters as the price at which neighbouring land has been sold, permissible uses of the land, and facts that are likely to affect the anticipated uses of neighbouring land. Both parties to a sale of land commonly make judgements on the basis of many facts, real and supposed, only a few of which turn out to be relevant. It would be impossible, in many cases, to draw a clear line between facts and conclusions drawn from facts. It is scarcely feasible for the parties to declare every fact that, in the judgement of each, might possibly make the proposed contract disadvantageous to the other. There would be uncertainty in every element required to be proved by a party seeking rescission for non-disclosure, particularly if the dispute arose many years after completion of the sale. It would not usually be clear what facts were to be treated as material, which of them were known at the time of the agreement, and which ought to have been known. Measurement of the pecuniary consequences of default would often itself be costly when rescission was sought by a purchaser in possession of the property, who would have an incentive to magnify those consequences, the vendor having no opportunity of alleviating them. The Law Commission, in its 1988 paper, had expressed the hope that its proposal (of a duty upon the vendor to disclose) would lead to the replacement of what it considered the present adversarial atmosphere in contractual relations by a 'more co-operative climate',[73] but the introduction of legal uncertainties that are costly to resolve is

[72] *Let the buyer be well informed*, Conveyancing Standing Committee, Law Commission (1989).

[73] *Honesty or Suspicion in Conveyancing*, 3.

more likely to multiply disputes, to impair the security of ownership,[74] and to impose costs on vendors and purchasers alike.

Good Faith

The *Second Restatement of Contracts* makes liability for failure to disclose dependent upon 'failure to act in good faith and in accordance with reasonable standards of fair dealing'.[75] This formulation certainly has the merit of flexibility, but it provides little guidance for the disposition of actual disputes. It has often been suggested, as in the example used at the beginning of this essay, that a buyer of land knowing of valuable mineral deposits there is morally (though not legally) bound to disclose the fact. It might have been supposed then that this would be a case where good faith and reasonable standards of fair dealing would require disclosure, but one of the illustrations to the text of the *Restatement* indicates that the drafters did not intend to require disclosure in that case,[76] presumably because they thought that good faith and fair dealing permitted a purchaser to profit in that way. The effect is to import a duty of good faith into pre-contractual negotiations, but then to alter what is usually taken to be the meaning of good faith in this context by announcing that it does not always require disclosure, even of facts known to be material. There is, perhaps, a warning here that the adoption of broad legal principles does not always produce the expected results,[77] though it may certainly alter the framework of discussion.

At first sight, it seems attractive to embrace concepts of good faith and fair dealing. Pollock summarized the whole object of contract law in rather similar language, saying that it was 'to establish a positive sanction for the expectation of good faith which has grown up in the mutual dealings of men of average right mindedness'.[78] The Law Commission entitled its summary paper on the duty of discosure in land sales, 'Honesty or Suspicion in Conveyancing', inviting the inference that those who would dissent from its views were no friends to honesty. Story wrote that 'the principles of natural justice and sound morals . . . require the most scrupulous good faith, candor, and truth in

[74] It should be pointed out that the Law Commission was proposing a duty that would apply to vendors only, not purchasers.

[75] s. 161(b).

[76] Illustration 10. It is otherwise if the knowledge is acquired by trespass: Illustration 11.

[77] Formerly a distinction was drawn between a duty of 'utmost good faith' (*uberrima fides*—disclosure required), and a mere duty of 'good faith' (*bona fides*—disclosure not required). See Spencer Bower, n. 5 above, 1–2.

[78] F. Pollock, *Principles of Contract*, 4th edn. (London 1885), 9.

all dealings whatsoever'.[79] It is true that the law, in its general objectives, represents a community sense of morality, but actual legal rules must also be fair and workable in practice with a reasonable degree of regularity, and reasonably inexpensive to apply. Justice is the general objective of law, but the search for justice is not advanced by the adoption of rules that are so expensive to apply that they put its attainment out of practical reach. A nineteenth-century judge made the distinction, saying that, 'though truth and justice are the aim and end of all courts, still they must not be sought through the aid of too expensive machinery. The true principle is . . . to choose the course which, on the whole, will best administer justice with a due regard to the means of those who seek it'.[80] Rules that increase the amount and the extent of litigation likely to arise from transactions make the transactions themselves potentially more costly, and so less useful to the community. On the other hand, there are many illustrations in contract law of the danger of pursuing certainty at all costs. The single-minded pursuit of certainty and finality defeats its own object by inviting the use of tortuous escapes. What is needed is a set of rules sufficiently in conformity with the community sense of morality not to produce results perceived as outrageous, while at the same time preserving sufficient content to be workable and reasonably inexpensive of regular application, and maintaining a fair degree of security of property transfers.

There are many examples in law demonstrating that social and moral objectives can sometimes be better attained indirectly than directly. There is always a gap between the general objective of the law, or of any part of it, and its actual working rules. In the present context I would suggest that, accepting the ultimate desirability of 'the most scrupulous good faith, candor, and truth in all dealings whatsoever', and the promotion of good faith as a general object of contract law, it would nevertheless not be desirable to turn these propositions into actual rules of law.[81] A more effective way of producing honest behaviour is likely to be the adoption of specific rules that, in particular contexts, make honesty the best policy.

Conclusion

It is doubtful whether simple rules on this question are attainable or desirable. For example, a rule that a prospective employee is always

[79] J. Story, *Equity Jurisprudence*, 13th edn, (Boston, 1886), 218–19 (para. 194).
[80] *The Resultatet* (1853) 17 Jur 353, 354 (Dr Lushington).
[81] Neither Story nor Pollock made any such suggestion.

bound to disclose damaging employment history is as unsatisfactory as a rule that such a person is never bound to disclose.[82] There must be, also, sufficient flexibility for the law to take account of changing circumstances and of changing expectations. For example, there should be no general rule that applicants for employment must disclose material facts, but if holders of a particular office invariably have certain qualifications, the application may be taken as impliedly carrying an assertion that the applicant is so qualified. The most promising line of thought appears to me to be to anticipate a development of the techniques already in use.

The notion of express and implied warranties lends itself to development. In certain kinds of transactions, patterns of facts and of expectations repeat themselves. Then it is open to a court to say that there is an implied term that the facts conform to the expected pattern, or that the party remaining silent knows of no divergence from it. There is room for movement in this approach, for patterns of facts are of infinite variety, and expectations about them change with time. Despite judicial pronouncements seeking to restrict the power of courts to imply terms, they continue on occasion to do so.[83]

A similar idea, also familiar to our ways of thinking about this subject, relates to the interaction between silence and misrepresentation. In some circumstances, silence taken with the other conduct of a party can, as mentioned earlier, fairly be construed to amount to an assertion that the transaction and the background facts conform to an expected pattern, or that the party remaining silent knows of no divergence from it. Failure to disclose a known divergence from this pattern would then give rise to liability, not on the principle of a general duty of good faith, but on the more limited principle that silence, in particular cases, in fact paints a misleading picture. This approach treats the knowledgeable party's conduct as a misrepresentation, and would not necessarily give rise to the full liability for damages consequent on a breach of an implied term.[84] Factors such as ease of access to the information and general practice in the community,[85] though not themselves determinative, would be highly relevant in concluding whether, in the circumstances, silence gave a misleading impression.

[82] See nn. 11 and 12 above.

[83] *Reigate* v. *Union Manufacturing Co. (Ramsbottom) Ltd.* [1918] 1 KB 592, 605; *Liverpool City Council* v. *Irwin* [1977] AC 239 (HL). For a recent case readily implying a term, see *Bayliss* v *Barnett*, noted (1990) 106 LQR 179.

[84] The distinction was made in *Bank of Nova Scotia* v. *Hellenic Mutual Association Ltd.*, note 47, above [1990] 2 WLR at 589.

[85] These factors are stressed by Scheppele, n. 39 above, and in the *Restatement*, discussed above.

These suggestions are modest compared with proposals to transform the law by the introduction of general standards of honesty, good faith, morality, and fair dealing. But complex problems seldom yield to simple solutions, and I think that this is a case where the incremental approach has more to recommend it than the revolutionary.

11

Three Problems with the New Product Liability

JANE STAPLETON

In *Accidents, Compensation and the Law*, Patrick Atiyah wrote: 'All the disabled are entitled to equal sympathy and equal support from the State and *ad hoc* treatment of special groups can only lead to the abandonment of all rationality in policy.'[1] It was a double-barrelled broadside directed at the then-present system of compensation for personal injuries, both calling for government organization of compensation rather than the existing plethora of systems, and attacking tactics which, on no principled grounds,[2] elevated certain subgroups of the disabled by granting them preferential treatment in either public or private law compensation systems. So withering were the attacks made by Atiyah and others on the systems of personal-injuries compensation that its comprehensive reform by government was widely thought proper and almost inevitable. For a number of reasons this was not to be. The principal subsequent legal reform in the area is Part 1 of the Consumer Protection Act 1987, the domestic adoption of the European Community's 1985 Directive on Product Liability ('the Directive'), which provides for a new, additional remedy for certain victims of injuries caused by certain products.[3] This law offends both parts of Atiyah's principle. First, in response to what were seen as unacceptable anomalies between the remedies of those in a contractual relationship with a member of the chain of commercial manufacture and supply of products and those not in such a relationship, it gave a new remedy to both these subgroups of personal-injuries victims, and in so doing simply shifted the location of the anomaly without a convincing justification. Secondly, the law offends the principle because it probably pre-empts comprehensive reorganization of personal-injury compensation by a reformist UK

[1] P. S. Atiyah, *Accidents, Compensation and the Law*, 3rd edn. (London, 1980), 431.

[2] For rare examples of such grounds, see J. Stapleton, *Disease and the Compensation Debate* (Oxford, 1986), 112.

[3] *OJ* No. L 210, 7.8.1985.

government. This discussion focuses on these and the other, more well-known, problem of the Directive, that of claims for defective design.

What is so special about injuries due to defective products?

The answer to this question does not emerge explicitly from either of the two major UK reports relevant to this piece of law reform—the Law Commissions' report of June 1977 and the Pearson Commission's report of March 1978[4]—or from the memoranda and documents associated with the Directive and its drafts. The focus on products is assumed throughout as self-evidently justified. Moreover, since the considerations of policy spelt out by the Law Commissions, for example, concerned issues of deterrence, insurability, evidentiary problems, and so on, which at first sight apply equally to other claims for injuries caused by commerce, we must look elsewhere to find the implicit assumptions that underlie the preference accorded to victims of the condition of products put into commercial circulation. To do this I will look at the central distinction drawn between defective products and defective services.

Under the Directive and the rule developed by US common law in the early 1960s (hereafter roughly abbreviated as 's. 402A of the *Restatement*'),[5] it is intended that if a car's brakes fail because of, say, a manufacturing flaw, the resultant injuries will fall within the new product-liability rules, but if they fail because they were defectively repaired at the local garage, there is to be no claim thereunder. *A fortiori* injuries caused by pure services, that is not through the medium of a product (such as oral medical advice), are also not to be covered. This is often summarized as follows: defective products ('moveables' under the Directive) are to be covered; defective services are not.[6] Apart from the explicit and unenlightening 'policy concerns' of

[4] The Law Commission and Scottish Law Commission *Liability for Defective Products* (Law Com. No. 82) Cmnd. 6831 (1977), hereafter 'Law Com.' (for 'policy considerations' see para. 23); *Royal Commission on Civil Liability and Compensation for Personal Injury* (Ch. Lord Pearson) Cmnd. 7054-I (1978), hereafter 'Pearson Com'.

[5] It is, of course, a significant generalization to speak of *one* US 'rule'; most jurisdictions have followed variations of the formulation set out in s. 402A of the *Restatement of Torts (Second)*.

[6] It is intended that defective services will be subject to a separate fault-based liability via a separate Directive: see *OJ* No. C 12, 18.1.1991. For other examples of reformers and courts adopting separate strategies for defective goods and defective services see: Pearson Com., chs. 22–3, and the US case law discussed by W. Powers 'Distinguishing between products and services in strict liability' (1984) 62 *NCLR* 415.

reformers, I have identified two sources for the assumption that defective products are sensibly treated differently from defective services: the origin of the product-liability rules in the warranty of merchantability; and the belief that a liability rule for defective products can shift the focus away from human conduct to 'the product itself'.

Both the special products rule developed by the common law in the United States and the EC rule as set out in the Directive grew out of the implied warranty of merchantability (hereafter 'the warranty').[7] Their limitation to moveables and to losses caused once the product had been put into commercial circulation by a defendant in the course of business, both testify to this inheritance. But the justifiability and workability of the warranty has not been inherited by the new product rules, because the sphere of operation of the warranty is defined not in terms of the problematic distinction between defective goods and services but in terms of a distinction between types of contract. This is the distinction between contracts for the sale of goods and other contracts, for example, for work and materials, for services, or for the sale of land. In the nineteenth century there were reasons for distinguishing simple sale-of-goods contracts from other types of contracts. Unlike the latter, the conditions under which contracts for the sale of goods were formed were rapidly changing. In particular, reasonable opportunities for inspection of goods by commercial buyers was becoming less and less feasible for a variety of reasons in an increasing number of sales of new goods. Sometimes the nature of new types of complex good made inspection for quality difficult or impossible, at least without expert technical advice. Even if the intrinsic nature of the good did not produce this situation, the new forms in which it was packaged and delivered often did. But most importantly of all, inspection was often rendered difficult, if not impossible—at least for commercial buyers in a chain of sales—by the increasing numbers of such contracts formed between parties acting at a distance, in some cases before the relevant goods had come into existence, and by the speed at which goods were passed down lengthening commercial chains.

This form of inequality of bargaining power which occurs where there is informational asymmetry because the original seller is typically

[7] In the US this was explicit in a series of cases in which certain indicia of the warranty claim (for example, privity) were abandoned, while others such as the requirement of a product (and a predominance, in the defendant's transaction, of supply rather than of service—see below n. 11) were retained. In the UK, the Law Commission's reference grew out of its discussion of the warranty and its boundaries within a wider enquiry into the supply of goods: Law Commission, *Exemption Clauses in Contracts: Amendments to the Sale of Goods Act 1893* (Law Com. No. 24) (1969), paras. 62–3.

in a better position to gauge quality, is a natural phenomenon of a complex market. It was judicial concern with this type of inequality between commercial entities and the economic loss it could cause such buyers which led to the special treatment of contracts for the sale of goods. It was the incidents which happened to attend such *bargains* which required special treatment, not their subject-matter *per se*. In the twentieth century substantial concern developed about another form of inequality of bargaining power, the inability of individual purchasers of mass-produced goods and mass services (such as carriage by rail, and so on) to renegotiate the terms of standard contracts, in particular standard exemption clauses. The resultant controls[8] gave no extra protection to the consumer-buyer of mass-produced goods over the consumer-buyer of mass services. Similarly, concern that private individuals had difficulty appreciating and resisting attempts to exclude business liability for negligence, the increasing incidence of such attempts, and the particular importance now attached to keeping open avenues of compensation for personal injury, led to contract terms and notices purporting to exclude or restrict liability for such loss being rendered ineffective by statute.[9] Again it was recognized that the causes for concern in such consumer contexts did not differ and required no separate treatment according to the subject-matter of the transaction or the avenue of negligently caused injury.[10]

So although the doctrinal origin of the product rules in the warranty is clear from the record of their evolution (in the US in the relevant case law and in the European discussion papers) and from the scope of their operation, they do not possess the coherence of the warranty rules because the evil allegedly being addressed in the product rules is quite different from the perceived evil which determined the sphere of operation of the warranty. The evil addressed by the product-liability rules was the difficulty allegedly experienced by victims of product-caused injuries in recovering damages for the physical harm they had suffered. Reformers were not concerned with economic loss caused by inequality of bargaining power in certain transactions (sale of goods), but with physical loss to plaintiffs who often had not even a suitable contract on which they could sue. Therefore, provision in the product-

[8] Unfair Contract Terms Act 1977, s. 3.

[9] Ibid., s. 2(1). See also s. 2(2).

[10] Where modern statutory controls do vary according to the subject-matter of the transaction, the explanations given relate not to the subject-matter *per se* but to other considerations. For example, while purported exclusions of the statutory implied terms as to quality and fitness for purpose in consumer transactions were invalidated, the parallel warranty as to the quality of a service is only subject to a requirement of reasonableness, because *inter alia* the Law Commission was not convinced that the latter practice was common: *Implied Terms in Contracts for the Supply of Services* (Law Com. No. 156, 1986), para. 3. 21.

liability rules of a remedy structured crudely along the lines of the warranty's response to a type of inequality of contractual bargaining power, and in particular, the limitation of the remedy to defective products is inappropriate. Simplistic references to the warranty origin of the new rules do not explain why it is sensible to treat product injuries preferentially. If anything, judged from the reformers' perspective of compensation between strangers for physical losses, the retailer's strict obligations to buyers for the latter's physical injuries should have been seen as the anomaly. Nor does it even provide a basis on which to feel confident that the distinction between defective products and defective services will be sustainable. That common-law courts did not, in their response to claims for physical injury, distinguish between the victims of defective goods and defective services, confirms the point that it is an inappropriate distinction to draw in the context of such claims. Will it nevertheless be workable?

The warranty relies on the different and relatively workable distinction between contract types.[11] Can the product rules' distinction between defective goods and defective services be made to work in the context of a consumer remedy for physical loss? The answer is: not very convincingly. If we ignore whether the distinctions are justified, we see that while it makes sense to speak separately of goods and services, and to speak separately of contracts (predominantly) for the sale of goods and contracts (predominantly) for the supply of services, the concepts of defective goods and defective services are not easily separable. This is because the concepts overlap: indeed, in most legal claims the alleged 'defect' in the good, that is the condition in it which is the cause of the injury, will itself be the result of a human act or omission, or, in other words, a service.

Almost[12] all defects in goods can at some level be accurately

[11] There are borderline cases where the transaction involves both a service and a supply element ('hybrid transactions')—when does the service element in a transaction predominate so that it no longer qualifies as a sale of goods?—but troublesome cases here seem to be relatively few. Importantly, the Directive seems to have side-stepped the 'hybrid transaction' pitfall which bedevils the US products rule, which is still generally only applied to those actions which are regarded as predominantly a supply of a defective product. Under the Directive and CPA, liability for injuries due to a defective condition in a product is imposed no matter whether the transaction in which the defendant supplied the product (or in the Directive's words, 'put the product into circulation') was predominantly one of sale or predominantly one of, say, service (see ss. 46(1)(a)(b)). So long as the source of the injury was the condition of the product, it will not matter that the transaction in which the defendant put the product into circulation/supplied the product was hybrid. If, of course, the source of the injury was the service (for example, defective installation of a product) no liability under the Directive or Part I of the CPA can arise (see s. 2(1)). Compare P. S. Atiyah, *The Sale of Goods*, 8th edn. (London, 1990), 245.

[12] It is true that the defective condition in a product may be due to an Act of God before it was supplied by the defendant-producer (and this would give rise to liability

described as attributable to human agency. Often this is not immediately apparent. For example, it may not be obvious that manufacturing defects are traceable to the designer or human operator of the manufacturing process or of its machinery. Similarly, design defects in goods can be traced to the activities of the designer of the goods or the party responsible for the accompanying warnings/instructions/packaging, and the like, neither party necessarily being the producer of the finished product.[13] In some cases the human origin of the defect in a good is clearer to see—as, perhaps, in the case of an incorrectly calibrated ruler,[14] and certainly in the case of a dangerous recipe published in a cookbook. Yet formally in all of these cases, what is defective is the idea or information conveyed, and the origin of the defect is human conduct. This means that attempts[15] to draw an explicit, coherent line between cases such as that of the defective ruler and cookbook are doomed to failure. In this light, even arguments in favour of special protection for the communication of ideas—on the basis of which US courts refuse to impose strict liability for publications—look somewhat incoherent.[16]

An important area illustrating this point is that of utilities. In the case of gas and water the alleged defect may be contamination, which raises the sort of issues familiar from cases such as *Donoghue* v. *Stevenson*. But alternatively the 'defect' in the utility supplied may be that it was supplied at dangerously high or low or fluctuating levels of pressure or voltage. Here the hand of human agency becomes a little clearer. Indeed, in the case of electricity—explicitly included within the

under the Directive), but the typically high standard of care imposed on quality-control practices by the law of negligence (see below) suggests that even under an overtly fault-based regime, most such cases would be ascribed to failures in human conduct either in the design or operation of the quality-control checks. See also G. Schwartz, 'The Vitality of Negligence and the Ethics of Strict Liability' (1981) 15 *Georgia LR* 963, 971.

[13] In which case, the latter's activity can be seen merely as the nondefective service of assembly: this argument was used unsuccessfully to resist imposition of strict liability in *Challonor* v. *Day & Zimmerman & Co.* (1975) 512 F. 2d 77. For example, the producer of the finished product may have followed the explicit instructions or design of an out-of-house designer who may, for example, be a buyer who gives his/her own specifications (see Pearson Com., para. 1248—although here *volenti* would presumably prevent successful claims by the buyer); or a pharmacist may simply follow a formula dictated by a GP. There will also come a point where the activities of a repairer or reconditioner cause such a major reconstruction that such a person qualifies as the 'assembler' or 'producer' of a new product and becomes liable for the workmanship of design which he has built into the object.

[14] Lord Lucas of Chilworth thought a defectively calibrated ruler would be caught by the CPA (as it may well be held to be), *HL Debates*, vol. 483 col. 800 (19.1.1987).

[15] Such as that of the parliamentary drafters in Clause 3(3) and 3(4) Consumer Protection Bill, rejected with uncomprehending disdain by the House of Lords: *HL Debates*, vol. 483, cols. 797–802 (19.1.1987); vol. 485, cols. 847–8 (9.3.1987).

[16] *Cardozo* v. *True* (1977) 342 So. 2d 1053, 1056–7.

definition of a 'product' by the Directive[17]—a little reflection on its nature highlights how artificial it is to describe the utility in such cases as 'defective'. It is a much more accurate description to say that what is defective is the form or way in which it was generated (or the medium through which it was delivered.)[18] This in turn may be due to human agency either directly or indirectly via the design of generating (or transmitting/delivery) equipment.[19] The fact that in relation to electricity it is quite evident that defective services almost always underlie the defective 'product', has created substantial confusion in the United States as courts try to decide if they should describe electricity as a defective product falling within s. 402A. Without directly adknowledging this overlap and how it renders the formal categorization question intractable, US courts have been forced to resolve the cases on other, arbitrary grounds—such as whether the electricity caused injury at a place after a physical point of supply (usually held to be the local meter), in which case electricity tends to be deemed a 'product' and strict liability is imposed accordingly.

If the condition in products which gives rise to complaint is nearly always human conduct, applying product-liability rules draws an odd distinction between some results of human conduct and other results of human conduct. Human conduct which injures but not by the route of the condition of property—for example, 'pure services'—is *not* covered by the US rule or the Directive, but conduct, or 'services', which does result in a relevant condition in a product *may* be covered. Indeed, the latter point reveals a related oddity in the rules: that not all human conduct which results in a relevant condition in a product is covered. First, there are cases where the condition was introduced by what I will call a 'downstream service-giver', such as a garage mechanic who misaligns the brakes he is substituting or repairing in the plaintiff's already-bought car. None of such cases is covered by either the US rule or the Directive. These rules only cover product

[17] EC Directive Article 2; CPA s. 1(2). On who is the 'producer', see discussion in *HL Debates*, vol. 483, col. 868 (20.1.1987).

[18] Under the CPA such defects are excluded by the definition of 'relevant time' at which the defect must exist (time of generation), s. 4(2). *Query*, whether the relevant time under the Directive (the time the defendant 'put the product into circulation', Article 7(a)), will be held to be a later time, for example the time of supply through a local meter (see later text on confusion in US)? *Query*, also whether, if electricity had not been expressly included in the definition of 'product' in the Directive and CPA, it would qualify as a good? What about that form of delivered electricity which drives telephone receivers to provide the 'service' of telephones? Will there be liability under the CPA for power-surges along telephone lines which cause injury to hearing?

[19] Another illustration of the point from the spectrum of electromagnetic radiation would be X-rays (on which the Directive is silent) supplied at too high a wavelength: see *Dubin* v. *Michael Reese Hospital* (1979) 393 NE 2d 588.

injuries arising from conditions already present when the product was put into circulation.

It is difficult to find explicit, let alone detailed, explanations of why injuries caused by the mechanic are excluded from the rule. Apart from the erroneous assumption that the warranty origin of the rule somehow provides an explanation, there seems only an indirect, vague assertion that there is something significantly different in policy terms between cases of defective goods and defective services (and the conduct of the mechanic is characterized as the latter). But whatever the relevant policy concerns are, it is unlikely that they could provide an adequate basis for discriminating between the cases since, as we have seen, in the vast majority of cases actionable defects in products are attributable to human conduct. It follows that, whatever the attributes of the production of products which give rise to those policy concerns, they must be relevant to certain services, since the production of products necessarily involves services.

It may be that these attributes, whatever they are, are less common in cases such as that of the mechanic and of pure-services contexts, so that we could accept as justified rules limited to injuries due to the condition of new products when put into circulation (thereby excluding the case of the mechanic and cases of pure services). But here we find a further problem in understanding what is the key concern of the reform, because the rules focus on the physical production (and supply) of defective products. Yet this can obscure, and indeed pervert, at least one alleged objective of the reform, which is to deter certain forms of *human behaviour*, namely the creation of certain dangerous conditions in goods. For deterrence of this preventative sort to work, liability must usually be directed to the person to whose conduct the injury is principally attributable.[20] Very often, of course, this responsible party also happens to be a party who can be held liable under s. 402A of the *Restatement* or under the Directive, for example, the producer who has used in-house designers or process engineers or who is vicariously liable for its employees' acts in the course of manufacture, or in drafting the accompanying instructions/warnings, and so on. But where the party principally responsible is, for example, an 'upstream out-of-house' designer, that person will escape liability under the regimes contained in the Directive or the *Restatement*. This is because neither regime imposes liability on the person to whose conduct the injury was principally attributable, unless this conduct produces a defective condition in a good *and* that person supplied it. Pure services such as medical advice, map-drawing, and taxi-driving

[20] For this party is usually the party who can best (that is, most cheaply) take preventative action next time.

are, as we have seen, excluded by the first condition; and trade-mark licensers, out-of-house designers, and downstream servicers are excluded by the second.[21] In the former group of cases no remedy is available under the new rule. In the latter a remedy will lie against the producer if the defect existed in the good when it left his hands. Whatever the arguments for holding the producer jointly liable in such cases (and one can mount arguments in favour of the producer of the final product taking some responsibility for its condition *vis-á-vis* the victim's claim), producers will no doubt wonder why their activities are vulnerable to liability under the rules while those of the party principally responsible for the defect in prevention terms is not liable at all.[22] Because the Directive/CPA regime lacks an adequately tight contribution rule, the proper relocation of liability costs on to the service-giver in order to promote prevention is effectively left to turn on the efficiency of private contractual arrangements.

The point I am making here is that if prevention is a goal, its achievement requires that the focus of liability be directed at a type of human behaviour. Even if, for some unexplained reason, we are only interested in injuries caused by the condition of goods as put into commercial circulation, the prevention goal requires that human behaviour be the focus of liability, and it should be human behaviour which produces dangerous conditions in such goods. But the Directive's focus on defective goods *per se* detracts from that goal by obscuring the human origin of the relevant condition and allowing inappropriate parties to be designated the responsible parties.

There is another way in which concentration on the concept of a 'defective product' hinders realization of the policy goals of reformers. The problem here arises out of the concept of 'defect' itself. A robust strict liability rule would be one under which reasonable care by the defendant was no defence and liability was triggered simply by, say, a causal connection between the defendant's conduct and the injury.[23] Neither the common-law rule in the US nor the Directive contain such a simple principle. Under both, liability is only to be imposed if the condition of the product is 'defective'. Thus a producer can escape if it can show that even as assessed at the time of trial, the benefits of the product outweighed its costs. In addition, substantial defences are allowed, including that the relevant risky condition of the product was

[21] With respect to trade-mark licensers, contrast the position in the US: J. Henderson and A. Twerski, *Products Liability* (Boston, 1987), 161.

[22] In this context, the provision of a defence for component manufacturers when the out-of-house defective design happened to emanate from the producer of a subsequent product in which the component was comprised, looks anomalous: Consumer Protection Act, s. 4(1)(f)(ii).

[23] J. Stapleton, 'Products Liability Reform—Real or Illusory?' (1986) 6 *OJLS* 392.

not discoverable / reasonably discoverable given the state of the art at the time of circulation (the development-risk defence).[24] Now it used often to be said that a strength of the product rule was that it shifted the analytical focus from a defendant-producer's behaviour (on which the tort of negligence explicitly focuses) to the quality of the product.[25] But it is slowly being acknowledged that this is only superficially accurate, and therefore could not by itself justify a separate products rule.

The factors relevant to whether a product is defective, under both the US rule and under the Directive (such as the availability of safer substitutes) plus the development-risk defence, demand an evaluation of the quality choices of the producer. It is true that in cases of manufacturing errors (where the production-line fails to produce the thing as intended) this evaluation is, in practice, side-stepped and claims are resolved mechanically in the plaintiff's favour. This is even though theory allows the defendant to argue that, given the available substitutes, his quality-control system was adequate and not defective, and hence that the safety of the product was no less than what 'a person is entitled to expect'.[26] But this side-stepping happens in negligence claims concerning manufacturing errors too, even though in these cases the theory *exlicitly* demands the court to look to the reasonableness of the defendant's conduct. But apart from the special case of manufacturing errors, the implicit requirement of the US product-liability rule that the court evaluate the design and marketing (adequacy of warnings, and so on) choices of the producer has emerged as the centre of dispute in litigation, and it will also under the Directive. Again the textual focus in the rules on defective products obscures this reality: that it is the underlying human activity which is being evaluated.

So the question is: if the separation out for special treatment of injuries caused by defective products cannot be justified by reference to the warranty origin of the product-liability rules, nor because it is possible in this way to shift the enquiry away from human conduct, how did the concept of the defective product become the focus for

[24] In the US a product is often not even defective in such circumstances. The CPA refers to reasonable discoverability in its development risk defence (s. 4(1)(e)), but this must be read (see s. 1) down to refer simply to discoverability as in the Directive (Article 7(e)). Even so, I have argued that the only way the latter test can be operated is with a reasonableness criterion, albeit one which may require a very high level of care: Stapleton, n. 23 above.

[25] See e.g. *Barker* v. *Lull Engineering Co.* (1978) 573 P 2d 443, 447; P. Keeton 'Product Liability and the Meaning of Defect' (1973) 4 *St Mary's LJ* 30, 33; S. Birnbaum, 'Unmasking the Test for Design Defect: From Negligence [to Warranty] to Strict Liability to Negligence' (1980) 33 *Vand. LR* 593, 601.

[26] EC Directive Article 6(1).

reform? Apart from the possibility that this was merely the result of an inappropriate development of the warranty idea, could it also be the result of the different, though illogical, way in which cases of product-caused injury may be perceived: where human conduct results in the defective condition of a good it is possible *to pretend* that we are judging a product rather than human conduct, at least until the realities of the law in operation make the pretence impossible. This would help explain why, for example, the new liability is directed at the producer of the product and not also at the author of the defect (such as an upstream designer). More importantly, it might also help to explain why, initially at least, a separate stricter standard for product cases was acceptable to European reformers.

Strict liability looks at results and ignores the reasonableness of the defendant's conduct. The form of strict liability which UK and European reformers initially recommended was one which judged the costs of the product with hindsight and did not allow a defence of unforeseeable risk.[27] That regime would, for example, have held the drug manufacturer liable for the Thalidomide injuries regardless of whether it could have discovered the risk. Was it that reformers were able initially to recommend a stricter liability for products, despite the general modern hostility of their legal systems to strict liability for physical losses, because in the case of goods / moveables the underlying involvement of human conduct can be masked by concentration on the object and on the concept of 'defect' which is superficially devoid of any reference to human conduct? Certainly it is the case that, in the early development of the US rule, manufacturing errors were the central concern, and here human failing is easily masked: the availability of the production-line norm can be allowed to pre-empt an evaluation of the defectiveness of the product and hence of the defendant's safety choices.[28]

On the other hand, when faced with the question of whether to impose stricter liability—including liability for risks not reasonably discoverable—on defendants expressly for their conduct, as would be necessary in relation, for example, to taxi-driving, engineering, surveying, and so on, US courts and European reformers have baulked. Is this because the connection between the plaintiff's injury and the human conduct which caused it was obvious? Once this connection is out in the open, the commitment to stricter liability is

[27] See Law Com., para. 105; Pearson Com., para. 1259; first draft of the EEC Directive, Article 1 (reproduced in Law Com. at p. 79).

[28] This route around the breach issue even occurs in *negligence* claims (see earlier text), confirming the suggested tendency lawyers may have to replace the costly investigation of behaviour with a mechanical device—even one at odds with the theoretical standard.

severely and directly tested. Compare the following examples of unforeseeable risks. Say a producer, after exhaustive testing, markets a cosmetic consisting of a simple blend of naturally occurring substances (for example, milk and grass) which carries an unforeseeable risk to users of developing cancer ten years after use. According to the initial European reform recommendations, such risks of a defective product were to be sheeted home to the producer as a 'cost of his enterprise'. But reformers baulked at imposing stricter liability in the equivalent situation of a business selling the 'health tip' that such and such a home-made blend of milk and grass was a useful cosmetic. The commitment to stricter liability based on 'enterprise liability' never extended to pure services.

So too it eventually crumbled even within the negotiations for a defective-products rule in Europe when industry opponents of the new law emphasized the unreasonableness of holding liable producers who had used all reasonable care but had failed to discover an undiscoverable risk. The compromise of allowing a development-risk defence leaves the Directive's focus on 'defect' only being significant in practice in providing a device by which importers and others could be made strictly liable for the unreasonable safety choices of others.

Although there was no equivalent initial commitment to a strict liability regime for producers in the US—that is, a commitment for the liability to cover undiscoverable risks—it is significant that the brave attempt by the New Jersey Supreme Court at consistency in the application of its enterprise-liability rationalized product rule in holding[29] a producer liable for an unforeseeable risk was denounced and successfully side-lined[30] by an argument that emphasized the human limitations of producers, the injustice of a law requiring 'omniscience'[31] from defendant-producers. It is interesting to note that after three decades of litigation concerning the US rule, not only is the central concern with the reasonableness of the defendants' conduct now evident, but it is highlighted by the phenomenon that litigated cases (virtually all of which relate to alleged design defects)[32] often include failure-to-warn allegations, complaints clearly directed at behaviour.

My suggestion that the reform focus on defective products may have been strengthened by a doomed attempt to shift attention away from

[29] *Beshada* v. *Johns-Manville Prods. Corp.* (1982) 447 A.2d 539.

[30] On how this and other cases can fail to become settled valid law in the US system, see P. Atiyah and R. Summers, *Form and Substance in Anglo-American Law* (Oxford, 1987), 49–51.

[31] Comment, 'Requiring Omniscience: The Duty to Warn of Scientifically Undiscoverable Product Defects' (1983) 71 *Geo. LJ* 1635.

[32] J. Fleming, *The American Tort Process* (Oxford, 1988), 65.

human conduct and make the imposition of stricter liability more palatable, gains some support from the attitude of reformers to computer software. Some years ago I argued that software, being mere information, is not a 'good' for the purposes of the UK law of supply of goods;[33] and that were defective navigational software to cause a plane to crash or a heart-lung machine to cut out, those thereby injured might at first seem to have problems establishing a cause of action under the CPA which defines 'product' in terms of 'goods'. But the CPA s. 1(1) requires UK courts to construe its provisions to accord with the Directive which defines 'products' in terms of 'moveables'. This might not seem to help much, but some commentators[34] suggest that defective software may fall under the Directive, and that the European Court of Justice might take a 'flexible' attitude to the notion of 'product' which will allow it to be expanded more widely than 'goods' to allow in phenomena which, in policy terms, are 'like' defective goods. But what is it about defective software that suggests it might be like defective goods? Is it like goods because, although it is a service, the human origin of errors in a program is less obvious than the human origin of most pure services? Is their human origin masked in a way that facilitates imposition of liability? Perhaps; but it should be noted that this masking characteristic is a variable. Suppose that the designer (A) of a navigational software program incorrectly enters the height of a mountain, causing a plane to crash. If the software package is to be a 'product' for the purposes of the Directive, is a map incorrectly drawn by B, which carries the identically incorrect information to the pilot, also to be a product?[35] If so, what about where the same information is conveyed to the pilot orally by an on-board navigator (C)—is he the supplier of a 'product'? In all cases, of course, it is the same piece of incorrect information which causes the crash; all that changes is the degree to which the human error is masked by the form in which the information is delivered.

In deciding if 'defective software' is to be a 'defective product' within the Directive, the ECJ has to identify what it is about defective 'goods' which makes claims arising out of the injuries they cause special. The warranty origin of the focus on defective goods does not provide the answer. Nor does the fact that many goods are mass-produced,

[33] J. Stapleton, 'Software, Information and the Concept of Product' (1989) 9 *Tel Aviv Univ. Studies in Law* 147. The fact that information like this can be, and usually is, reduced to hard-copy form for commercial purposes is doctrinally irrelevant.

[34] S. Whittaker, 'European Product Liability and Intellectual Products' (1989) 105 *LQR* 125.

[35] Contrast US cases on advice-givers. Here a number of courts have been prepared to conclude that aeronautical charts are 'products': P. McCowan, 'Liability of the Chartmaker' (1980) *Insurance Counsel J* 359; D. Abney, 'Liability of Defective Aeronautical Charts' (1986) 52 *J. Air Law & Commerce* 323.

because liability under the Directive is not confined to mass-produced goods and, in any case, non-goods such as software and maps can be mass-produced and cause physical injury. For the same reasons, the complexity of some goods and their sophisticated production techniques do not provide the key. Nor can the reason be that the focus on defects in goods in the Directive eliminates the necessity to evaluate conduct: it does not. Nor, in the long term, will it support the pretence that this is so, as the history of litigation on the US rule shows.

It is hard to see what *is* special about defective goods. The above discussion suggests that there is no reason for treating goods differently apart from the very vague (and often contradictory)[36] policy goals mentioned by reformers relating to deterrence, insurability, and so on. If such goals *are* all that is available to guide the ECJ in deciding what are 'products', the concept is doomed to extend well beyond the notion of goods but in an unpreditable way,[37] and this will expose the dearth of any special reasons why a subset of victims of physical injuries caused by commerce were given preferential treatment in law-reform priorities.[38]

When reasonable minds differ . . .

If we move from the question of why (some) product injuries are special to the question of what impact the Directive is likely to have, one common prediction is that most difficulties in practice will be faced in the area of design-defect litigation. Certainly that has been the focus of US lawyers' concern and reform activity, but, as I will argue, the 'solutions' proffered do not meet the challenge of the phenomenon giving rise to their concern because that phenomenon is not sufficiently well understood.

In the US, the initial euphoria which met the adoption of the new

[36] See e.g. the antagonism of deterrence and insurance goals: J. Stapleton, 'Duty of Care and Economic Loss: A Wider Agenda' (1991) 107 *LQR* 249, 271.

[37] Stapleton, n. 33 above, 160–1. This was the fate of the concept of 'product' within the US rule where, for example mass-produced houses have been held to be 'products' by some courts: J. Maloney, 'What is or is Not a Product Within the Meaning of Section 402A' (1974) 57 *Marg. LR* 625, 627: 'the social policy underlying the doctrine has become the definition of a "product"'; J. Wunsch, 'The Definition of a Product for the Purposes of Section 402A' (July, 1983) *Insurance Counsel J*, at 344; G. Walker, 'The Expanding Applicability of Strict Liability Principles: How is a "Product" Defined?' (1986) *Tort & Insur. LJ* 1.

[38] The inadequacy of these other reasons is beyond the scope of this article. For a treatment of this issue in the US context see W. Powers, 'Distinguishing Between Products and Services in Strict Liability' (1984) 62 *NC LR* 415, 434.

product-liability rule in the early 1960s gave way in the 1970s and 1980s to deep anxiety and widespread calls for a statutory narrowing of the rule. The principal cause for this concern was the belated recognition that, although proponents of the rule had been preoccupied with injuries caused by manufacturing errors,[39] the rule as set out in s. 402A of the *Second Restatement* (and the variants adopted in some states), encompassed defects constituted by the condition of the product as designed. The problem here is one of the standard to be applied to the product. I described earlier how, in cases of manufacturing errors, the standard applied under the US product rule is that of the production-line norm, and that although not supported by the theoretical basis of the rule (which would allow defendants to argue, for example, that the cost of a quality-control system sufficiently foolproof to catch the relevant error, was prohibitive),[40] it is an approach followed even in negligence claims arising out of such injuries. This was no doubt why, apart from the tactical advantages in marginal cases of shifts in burdens of proof, the promoters of the rule predicted that the rule would have only a small impact on outcomes—their enthusiasm being for the alleged conceptual rationalization represented by the development.[41] Indeed, George Priest has argued that none of the proponents of the US rule even believed that the problem of consumer product injuries was a significant one for society.[42]

By the 1970s, however, adventurous plaintiffs' lawyers, their claims-consciousness no doubt heightened by the rapidity and acclaim with which the new rule had been adopted, were routinely suing under the rule for alleged defects in design. Occasionally such suits took the form of a complaint about the very marketing of such a design, but for reasons I do not have space here to pursue, the usual substance of the complaint was one of 'failure to warn' of the condition which caused injury. In either case the key issue concerned the standard against which such conditions were to be judged. In some design cases there is no dilemma: where the relevant aspect of the design prevents the product performing the task (or the range of tasks) which all would agree such a product is expected to perform. Here the clear and agreed minimum-performance standard serves to resolve the case. Examples include a chair design not being able to support the weight of a ten-stone adult and a television not being able to be used without

[39] G. Priest, 'The Modern Irony of Civil Law: A Memoir of Strict Products Liability in the United States' (1989) 9 *Tel Aviv Univ. Studs. in Law* 93.

[40] Some manufacturing errors may even be (within reasonable cost) undiscoverable to the producer.

[41] See e.g. W. Prosser, 'The Assault Upon the Citadel (Strict Liability to the Consumer)' (1960) 69 *Yale LJ* 1099, 1114.

[42] Priest, n. 39 above, 109.

short-circuiting. It *is* true that even here design claims can have a particular ramification which manufacturing errors do not. This is that a finding of defectiveness against a *mass-produced* design condemns not just the item involved but the whole line (and this produces severe economic consequences wider than the individual case). But in this group of design cases this is not regarded as a problem. The fact that a producer of chairs which do not hold a ten-stone person is in effect forced by one lawsuit to endure the costs of abandoning an entire product line and (probably) of recalling identical items already sold does not generate criticism.

The problem lies in other design claims where there is no clear or agreed performance standard against which to judge the product. Significantly, but not surprisingly, many of the flood of product complaints in the late 1970s and 1980s were of this type. How 'crash-worthy' must a car design be? That a car's design should, in general, withstand a very mild collision (2 mph?) without crushing its occupants is agreed, but at significantly higher speeds there is no agreement. In designing a car, the design-engineer must trade off certain characteristics: more metal in the car doors to withstand crashes means higher fuel-consumption, lower brake-efficiency, and so on. Different designers might compromise these factors in different ways.[43]

How can the law set a standard by which to evaluate design choices such as this? Some US courts faced problems in such cases by allowing, urging, or demanding plaintiffs to bring evidence of a 'better', 'safer' design. This comes close to undermining the common-sense view that non-defectiveness must be a *minimum* standard which can be satisfied even if the defendant 'could have done better'. A more fundamental question was raised by James Henderson in an important article in 1973.[44] He argued that the conscious[45] design choices of manufacturers typically pose 'polycentric issues' for adjudication; that is, they require the resolution of an issue (defectiveness of design) on which many factors bear—factors, the weight of which may vary according to the

[43] Even the technical basis of these trade-offs may be 'softened' by variations in opinion: technical experts may differ about, say, the inferences to be drawn from experimental data about the stress coefficient of a particular metal.

[44] J. Henderson, 'Judicial Review of Manufacturers' Conscious Design Choices: The Limits of Adjudication' (1973) 73 *Columb. LR* 1531.

[45] Henderson misleadingly confined his analysis to advertent choices. It is possible that the relevant design behaviour being evaluated was inadvertent (for example failing to appreciate the known and agreed stress coefficient of a car door-panel). But, *as in negligence*, the performance standard of the behaviour should in theory be assessed regardless of the advertence or inadvertence of the defendant. Nor does every inadvertent design-choice necessarily bring the design below the legal standard: contrast Henderson, n. 44 above, 1548, 1550–1.

weight ascribed to any one other factor. It is difficult, if not impossible, to reduce polycentric questions to the sort of step-by-step analysis of discreet questions to which the adjudication process is best suited. The more polycentric the question, the less the opportunity available for litigants to participate meaningfully in the decision-making process because of the absence of sufficiently specific rules upon which to focus their arguments. This, Henderson argues, offends the rule of law so that the greater the commitment to adjudicating such issues, the greater the threat to the integrity of the adjudication process itself.[46] He argued that, unless more specific and discreet issues relating to product standards were focused upon, outcomes would remain unpredictable.[47]

Inconsistency and unpredictability of outcome in design-defect cases was certainly coming to be seen as a major problem in the 1970s. Clearly, inconsistency and unpredictability generate confused deterrence incentives, because potential defendants receive conflicting signals about what value to put on design variables in the future. Potential defendants would also find it hard to gauge their need for insurance cover. It was becoming widely feared that this unpredictability was having an unduly chilling effect on research and development of new product designs. It was not surprising, then, that although most commentators and courts seemed to reject Henderson's pessimism, their confidence that the jury system could 'adequately and responsibly perform the necessary balancing test required'[48] by the evaluation of design choices began to be conditional on the formulation of standards 'which identify the proper variables, which are capable of being administered in the civil trial context and which provide the jury with effective, intelligent guidance'.[49] The gathering pressure for reform became focused, *inter alia*, on setting such guide-lines for design cases.[50]

While nearly all reform proposals are successful in making explicit the reasonableness standard by which design defects are to be judged, these proposals fail successfully to address the polycentric potential of the design cases. Even Henderson's own recommended sequence of distinct issues requires the plaintiff to prove that an alternative design

[46] Ibid. 1539.

[47] J. Henderson, 'Renewed Judicial Controversy Over Defective Product Design: Toward the Preservation of an Emerging Consensus' (1979) 63 *Minn. LR* 773, 780.

[48] S. Birnbaum, 'Unmasking the Test for Design Defect: From Negligence [to Warranty] to Strict Liability to Negligence' (1980) 33 *Vand. LR* 593, 638. See also 648–9 on random and unpredictable outcomes in design cases.

[49] G. Schwartz, 'Foreword: Understanding Products Liability' (1979) 67 *Calif. LR* 435, 450–1.

[50] Significantly, virtually all reform proposals retain a strict standard for manufacturing errors confirming the argument in Part 1 of this essay.

was technologically feasible at the time of manufacture, and then that 'it would have enhanced overall product safety and been cost-effective to adopt'.[51] But cost-effectiveness of a design rests on its social costs, and even crude estimates of such figures are generally unavailable to designers and juries. More importantly here, while certain factors related to social costs can appear objective (for example, the anticipated incidence of accidents due to the design and the physical cost of each accident), others are subjective. The degree to which a buyer values cosmetic elements of design[52] varies between buyers, but might it not also vary in relation to other design features: for example, the same buyer may put a different value on cosmetic appeal according to fuel consumption? If judgements of cost-effectiveness themselves raise polycentric issues, even a jury with full information could arrive at different outcomes in evaluating complex design trade-offs.

In any case, what I want to argue is that this and related attempts to control the problem of design standards are misguided, because there is a more fundamental phenomenon they do not address. This phenomenon *is not confined to the evaluation of polycentric questions,*[53] nor to cases arising under the post-war product-liability rules, nor to design-of-product complaints in general. It is not even confined to cases turning upon a reasonable-care standard. The fact that the phenomenon first caused concern in certain defective-design cases arising under the US products-liability rule is an historical accident caused by factors such as claims-consciousness.[54] The challenge thrown out by this phenomenon, therefore, is not one which can be met by reform directed solely at defective-design cases or even at product cases in general.

The phenomenon has two parts, the first of which is that reasonable minds may differ on how to apply a relevant standard to particular facts. We have seen that in a large number of product-defect cases this characteristic is absent because the standard being applied is clear and attracts widespread support; the manufacturing-error cases and the 'below agreed minimum performance' cases of defective design. The same is true in a large number of non-product cases: throwing bricks into a crowded street for fun would clearly be agreed to be a breach of

[51] J. Henderson, 'Why Creative Judging Won't Save the Product Liability System' (1983) 11 *Hofstra. LR* 845, 849 and n. 17a therein.

[52] And if value is to be measured by willingness to pay, cosmetic values must enter into the equation.

[53] Although, as we will see, it may well be compounded in such cases.

[54] And unrelated doctrines, for example the patent danger rule in negligence has been identified as one factor in explaining why so few complaints of negligent product design were made in the pre-s.402A era: G. Robb, 'The Effect of the Proposed Federal Product Liability Act on Current Law Regarding Liability for Defectively Designed Products' (1983) 6 *J Prod. Liab.* 147, 151–2.

the reasonable-care standard in negligence. But in many other situations reasonable minds may differ about the application of a standard.[55] Even here, though, problems of confidence in the legal system often do not arise because the fact that reasonable minds can differ is masked by the actual or apparent uniqueness of the fact situation. Thus, a road accident can be portrayed at some level as unlike any other road accident, so that the fact that the defendant in case A was held negligent but the defendant in (the factually similar) case B was not, will not necessarily be perceived as a failure of consistency in the system. In this way confidence in the system is maintained; so is the pretence that coherent deterrence incentives are possible under the relevant standard.

But greater problems arise in cases where the behaviour being evaluated has been 'frozen' and duplicated in an identical way so that undeniably identical cases may occur in the future. Here, the possibility that reasonable minds may differ in applying the relevant evaluative standard threatens to produce different results on undeniably identical facts. One of the most common ways in which behaviour is 'frozen' in the relevant way is in the creation of *mass-produced* goods. Here the finding that one item's condition falls below the required standard has implications in later cases involving the identical condition in an identical item. Often, as we have seen, this potential multiple flow-on effect poses no threat to confidence in the system, either because the relevant condition was in fact a one-off manufacturing error or because there is an agreed standard which will be applied consistently (for example, repeat manufacturing errors and 'below agreed minimum-performance design defects'). However, in that subset of design complaints where reasonable minds differ, confidence in the adjudicatory system will be shaken as apparently identical design-defect cases are decided differently at different times.

It is important to stress that this problem is not confined to cases raising complex or polycentric issues. It can arise in a simple case. Take the example of the strength of a chair design. While there is no doubt a consensus that a dining-chair should withstand a weight of ten stone, consensus becomes less likely the greater the weight the chair is required to withstand. Reasonable minds might well differ about whether the chair should reasonably be expected to bear a thirty-stone person. This example shows that the problem of inconsistent outcomes in US design cases is not solvable by more finely tuned guide-lines for the fact-finders. What guide-lines would produce consistent answers to

[55] The argument applies not only when conduct is being evaluated under a standard but also where, for example, the adjudicator has to decide if a scenario presented a 'foreseeable' risk.

the question of whether a chair which fails to hold a thirty-stone adult is defective? The process is not fact-finding but opinion-giving. Nor is the problem limited to the special product-liability rules set out in s. 402A of the *Second Restatement on Torts* in the US and the Directive in the EC. It arises equally in common-law claims of negligent design. More importantly, it is *also* present outside the goods area altogether. It would arise, for example, in claims which called for the evaluation of the condition of mass-produced 'frozen' services such as mass-produced software packages and mass-produced realty such as play-ground structures. It also arises outside tort law, for example in the test of merchantable quality in sales law.

To sum up: where reasonable minds can differ on an issue *and* that identical issue can be raised in court again and again in a way that cannot be masked, the potential inconsistency of outcomes threatens both the common assumption that justice requires identical issues to be resolved identically and the assumption of economists that legal standards can—at least in theory—provide coherent economic incentives for future behaviour. Put in this wider context design defect cases are not a special problem. They simply reveal the tip of this larger dilemma for courts and theorists.

EC Directives and Pre-emption of Wider National Reform

Even if we were willing to tolerate the apparently unjustified preference given to victims of certain products in the Directive and could find a way effectively to meet the threats posed by defective-design litigation, the new law would still carry with it another serious problem.

One of the factors used to win domestic electoral support for UK entry into the European Community in 1972 was the Community's consumer-protection programme.[56] Within this programme, initiated by the Heads of Government meeting in Paris in 1972 and set out in a Council of Ministers Resolution in 1975,[57] one of the most attractive features was the harmonization and improvement of avenues to compensation for consumers suffering losses, in particular by moving civil liability for defective goods towards the stricter regime operating

[56] Part of the EC's 'human face': A. Dashwood, 'The EEC Commission's Proposal on Products Liability' [1977] *J Bus. L* 202; G. Borrie, *The Development of Consumer Law and Policy—Bold Spirits and Timorous Souls* (London, 1984), 99, 101–2. On the history of consumer protection in the EC in general see E. Lawlor, *Individual Choice and Higher Growth*, 2nd edn. (Luxemburg, 1989).

[57] *OJ* No. C 92, 25.4.1975. Later consumer protection Council Resolutions are listed in n. 83 below. In general see G. Close, 'The Legal Basis for the Consumer Protection Programme of the EEC and Priorities for Action' (1983) 8 Eur. LR 221.

in the US. A draft Directive on the topic was promptly published in 1976.[58]

There proved to be deep divisions among the Member States on the detail of the new proposed liability. Despite the presentation to the Council of Ministers by the European Commission of a second compromise draft in 1979,[59] the Member States continued to disagree on a common formula. Businesses in some states had already been forced to adapt to tort liability more rigorous than simple fault, as adventurous courts tried to develop better consumer remedies. Examples of such states were France, Belgium, and Luxemburg. In the 'chicken-pest' case of 1968 the West German Supreme Court had reversed the burden of proof of negligence in product cases, while the continued aftermath of the Thalidomide tragedy, which had struck West Germany particularly badly, culminated in 1976 in the statutory subjection of the pharmaceutical industry to strict liability (albeit with financial ceilings on claims in recognition of the potential size of drug disasters).[60] On the other hand, in other Member States such as Italy, Spain, and Portugal business faced a comparatively comfortable fault-based regime. The progress of reform was slowed: by a growing concern that, far from being an enviable model, the US products-liability regime provided strong reasons for caution; by increasing objections from business groups wary of the effects of the economic recession; by the insistence of some Member States that there be financial limits on liability to ensure it could be insured against; and by the fluctuating attitudes of Member States as governments within them changed. The most important example of the latter was the election in 1979 of a Tory government in the UK committed to the inclusion of the development (that is, unforeseeable)-risk defence to protect business.

None the less, the possible domestic political advantage to be gained from consumer-protection measures, and more importantly the internal dynamics of the EC, ensured that negotiations about the draft EC Directive continued. In a quasi-federalized system such as the EC, where central laws predominate over inconsistent 'state' laws, there are, quite apart from legal constraints, political pressures against individual Member States enacting consumer-protection measures.

[58] *OJ* No. C 241, 14.10.1976 (also *Bull. of EC Supp.* 11/79).

[59] *OJ* No. C 271, 26.10.1979. For accompanying memoranda, see Com. of EC, document No. COM (79) 415, itself based on (1979–1980) Europ. Parl, Working Doc. No. 71/79 (1979).

[60] Chicken-pest case: Judgment of Nov. 26, 1968, Fed. SC in Civil Matters (Bundesgerichtshof), W Ger., 51 Official Reporter [BGHZ] 91 (1969); s. 84 of the Drug Act (*Arsneimittelgesetz*), Bundesgesetzb; att, Teil I [BGBI.I] 2445. On domestic Member-State rules relating to manufacturers' (etc.) liability, see N. Reich and H. Michlitz, *Consumer Legislation in the EC Countries* (London, 1980), 94–100; M. Whincup, *Product Liability Law* (London, 1985), 140–151.

These might result in a flight of business to Member States who have not enacted such measures but if the European Community were to act the resultant measures would be effective throughout the EC market and would not generate such a relocation of business. This arrangement, therefore, discourages domestic reform even where centralist measures have not yet been taken.

Events in the negotation period 1979–85 also illustrate a wider problem in the EC politico-legal system, namely that the EC's legislative process is relatively unreceptive to democratic input. Once the second draft Directive entered the maze of European negotiations in 1979, political bargaining, largely behind closed doors, seemed to take over. Very little non-governmental lobbying on issues of principle seemed to occur. Such UK input as there seems to have been came via UK-government representatives and appointees rather than, say, via MEPs, unions, or lobby groups.[61] Similarly, in terms of the reporting back of the progress of the negotiations to interested parties in the Member States who were outside the relevant government circles, I have found very few public documents produced for this purpose over the entire nine-year period from first- to final-draft stages of the Directive. Moreover, it seems to have taken a considerable time for hard-copy notification of the existence of such documents to reach, say, the major law libraries of the UK.[62] This clearly creates a problem in establishing the democratic legitimacy of laws emanating from the EC.

Eventually, by allowing Member States to derogate from the Directive on three issues, a somewhat reluctant consensus was achieved in 1985 and a final Directive was adopted by the Council of Ministers.[63] Now, while it seems at first obvious that, if valid, the Directive prevents the Member States legislating inconsistently with its provisions in regard to civil liability for products (although on this, see below), the wider impact on domestic reforms is little appreciated. I want to argue that the acceptance and implementation by the UK of

[61] A subcommittee of the Economic and Social Committee of the EC, ECSOC, (which consists of about 200 members nominated by Member States made up of representatives of employers, workers, and other interest groups) had reported on the first draft Directive on 3.2.1978, and its later opinion on it dated 13.7.1978 was published *a year later* in *OJ* No. C 114/16 (7.5.1979). However, the origin, size (only 15 members spread across all Member States), and obscurity of this subcommittee suggest that it did not provide anything like as efficient a conduit for the communication of the concerns of domestic-interest groups as the relevant bodies and avenues in the UK law-reform process.

[62] In 1990 the monthly listing of relevant EC documents (including ECSOC Opinions), *Documents* (ISSN 0256–0976) was taking eight months to appear in the Bodleian Library in Oxford. Even at the UK head office of the European Commission, the delay was six months.

[63] *OJ* No. L 210, 7.8.1985, p. 29.

the EC Directive not only defused what little domestic political impetus there was for *comprehensive* personal-injuries reform along the lines of the Woodhouse scheme operating in New Zealand since 1972, but introduced significant new barriers to such change. In their 1977 report the Law Commissions had strongly opposed the draft Directive on the grounds that it might preclude the UK moving to a more broadly based personal-injuries compensation scheme which did away with distinctions based on the cause of injury.[64] The National Consumer Council and Director-General of Fair Trading expressed similar concerns.[65] If such a new scheme were to abolish other forms of redress—as nearly all comprehensive proposals do—it would be incompatible with the UK's apparent obligations to provide the redress established by the Directive, and would expose the UK to infringement proceedings by the European Commission before the European Court of Justice.[66] In other words, a Member State would be prevented from embracing the trade-off, which is the political and financial key to a Woodhouse-type reform, under which future victims are denied the remote chance of tort-level damages in exchange for lower but guaranteed support following disablement. It may well also be that a Member State would be precluded from adopting such a scheme *even if it retained the liability set out in the Directive*, if the European Court of Justice regarded such a move as upsetting the 'level playing-field' of the common market by disturbing the balance of consumer/producer interests struck by the Directive.[67] On this view, then, the Directive if valid would not only freeze domestic action within the apparent scope of its operation (certain product claims), but freeze action throughout a much wider field. The very fact of valid European Community action in the consumer-protection area would legally fetter futher advance in any Member State on the wider front of personal-injuries compensation.

But is there a possibility that a Member State could successfully challenge the Directive as being *ultra vires* and therefore no impediment to later national developments in the products-liability or wider compensation fields? Presumably the 'cleanest' way of making such a challenge would be to repeal Part I of the Consumer Protection Act 1987 and await non-implementation proceedings.[68] An argument

[64] Law Com., para. 138. A result acknowledged by the Europ. Commission: Com. of EC, Answer to Written Question No. 506/77 (from Mr Calewaert), 22.11.77.

[65] Borrie, n. 56 above, 117–8.

[66] Unless there was a political settlement—the other Member States allowing one State to derogate completely and permanently from the Directive.

[67] For example, as a result of producers being levied in order partially to fund the scheme.

[68] Under Article 169 of the EEC Treaty. Direct challenge to the legal basis of the Directive by a Member State under Article 173 is now time-barred (time-limit is two

that the Directive has an insufficient legal basis in the Treaty of Rome could take two forms.[69] The Preamble of the Directive itself refers to Article 100 of the Treaty, which allows the Council of Ministers to issue Directives for the approximation of laws which directly affect the establishment and functioning of the common market. The Preamble then asserts that the Directive is necessary 'because the existing divergences [on producer liability for defective products] may distort competition and affect the movement of goods within the common market and entail a differing degree of protection of the consumer . . .' (bracketed words added).

The first argument is that, since the Directive does not achieve harmonization of laws and actually increases diversity of rules on product liability between Member States, it is *ultra vires*. In the first place, Member States are free to depart from the Directive's rule in three major areas.[70] The European Court of Justice may not regard this as a grave defect since most States are likely not to make any of these departures.[71] Secondly, however, liability under the Directive is in addition to, and not in substitution for, the domestic laws of the Member States, including existing statutory liabilities such as that under the German pharmaceutical legislation of 1976.[72] Provisions such as these allow states, in areas where they are hostile to particular aspects of European Directives, to 'do in practice what they were already doing or perhaps wished to do apart from any European intervention'.[73]

An alternate or additional ground for challenge by a future government is to argue that harmonization of *product liability laws* has itself no legal basis in the Treaty of Rome. The Preamble cited three justifications: competition, free movement of goods, and consumer protection. Let us look at the first two: that 'enhanced competition' and 'free movement of goods' are advantages to the market is clear. That a firm's exposure to local product-liability rules is reflected in its costs is

months), and collateral challenge via Article 177 would be awkward technically if taken by the Member State itself.

[69] There is not a great deal of discussion of the point, but see Close, n. 57 above; S. Whittaker, 'The EEC Directive on Product Liability' (1985) 5 *Yearbook of European Law* 233.

[70] The Directive (see Articles 5, 8, 9, 10) also assigns various issues to be determined according to domestic rules, for example standards of proof/causation; contributory negligence; the compensatability of non-pecuniary losses; rights of contribution and indemnity; rights of surviving dependants; rules regulating suspension or interruption of the limitation period.

[71] By February 1990, of the seven Member States to have implemented the Directive, only one has omitted the development risk defence (Luxemburg), only one has included unprocessed agricultural produce (Luxemburg), while three have set a financial ceiling (Greece, Portugal, West Germany): [Feb. 1990] *Product Liability International*, 30.

[72] See Art. 13.

[73] Whittaker, n. 69 above, 236.

also clear. What is not clear is that variation in these rules between Member States results in significant variation in costs relative to other factors affecting such costs (local taxation or the cost of fuel and insurance, for example), so that as a result competition and free movement of goods within the market is significantly affected. Competition and free movement *could* be affected if, for example, the local liability rules were so onerous that they acted as an informal customs barrier to producers in other Member States, so that they either never entered the local market or felt it necessary to adapt their products and quality-control systems. But was there any evidence that this was happening?

Early questioners of the legal basis of the proposed Directive, including the European Parliament's Legal Affairs Committee, its Committee on Economic and Monetary Affairs, and the UK Parliament's House of Lords Select Committee on the European Communities,[74] noted that in the formulation and text of the Directive it was merely asserted that domestic liability rules relating to products *may* distort competition / free movement. But a nexus to legislative power cannot usually be established by mere assertion or by the mere possibility that the condition giving occasion for the exercise of power exists. Thus, in federal constitutions, it is not sufficient for the federal legislature to assert that a matter comes within its enunciated heads of legislative power. It must actually do so, even if a generous interpretative attitude is otherwise being taken to the limits of central power. This has been, for example, the approach of the European Court of Justice to the interpretation of those Treaty of Rome provisions which define the Community's lawmaking power in terms of subject-matter, such as 'vocational training' under Article 128.[75] The position is different, however, where the lawmaking power is defined[76] in terms of a socio-economic effect. Sometimes here, as in

[74] 1978–9 Eur. Parl. Working Doc. (DOC no 246/78) (1978), paras. 3, 12 (Legal Affairs Committee) and Appendix V, para. 3 (Committee on Economic and Monetary Affairs), but this report was sent back by the European Parliament for reconsideration and a compromise was reached whereby the 'constitutionality' issue was dropped: see 1979–80 Eur. Parl. Doc. (DOC no 71/79) (1979). Even so, some Conservative MEPs continued to raise the legality point: see *Europe*, 27.4.79, 8; 'Liability for Defective Products', House of Lords Select Committee on the European Communities, Session 1979–80, 50th Report, HC para. 10. Similar doubts were raised about the final Directive's legal basis by the Director-General of Fair Trading in the UK: G. Borrie, 'Product Liability in the EEC' (1987) 9 *Dublin ULJ* 82, 89. See also Borrie, n. 56 above, 118–120.

[75] See e.g. *Commission of the European Communities* v. *Council of the European Communities* [1989–5] ECR 1425 (that 'vocational training' does not include 'scientific research').

[76] The same questions arise where the source document states the relevant power in terms of subject-matter but this is then judicially interpreted to authorize not only laws on that subject-matter but laws which affect that subject-matter: a noted example was the United States Supreme Court upholding federal civil-rights laws under the commerce power.

Articles 85 and 86 of the Treaty of Rome (the competition powers), evidence of actual effect is clearly not necessary as the power is couched in terms of provisions which '*may* affect trade between Member States' (emphasis added). In contrast to this, Article 100 authorizes the harmonization of laws which 'directly affect' the common market. Certainly, if the ECJ were to deduce that in the latter case, actual evidence of the relevant effect was needed to establish the legality of the measure, the 1985 Directive would, as critics allege, be vulnerable on these grounds. For there was no evidence adduced that domestic liability rules do *directly* affect the functioning of the market to a significant extent relative to other sources of distortion. There was no evidence adduced, for example, that there had been a flight of players in the pharmaceutical market from Germany after the introduction of strict liability in 1976, nor was there evidence that German pharmaceutical companies had thereafter found it significantly more difficult to compete in other Member States. Nor was there any evidence adduced that the Directive would result in enhancement of competition and the movement of goods.

But such evidence is unlikely to be called for by the ECJ, which would probably (and rightly) perceive the extraordinary difficulties in adjudicating coherently on such issues. If the Directive is to be held *intra vires* the power in Article 100 it will not be, as some optimists suggest, because the European Court of Justice would simply want to uphold the validity of a Council Directive, duly (indeed, unanimously) agreed between Member States.[77] Such optimism overlooks the fact that governments change. There may well be later national governments who will want to do more, for example, to protect consumers than the earlier agreement and more than the majority of Member States will agree to do. If the ECJ is to hold the Directive to be within Article 100, a more likely consideration will be the recognition that the latter provides no obvious avenue by which the court could hold *ultra vires* harmonization measures in fields which conceivably touch on the common market.

The wider the ECJ interprets Community power under Treaty of Rome provisions, such as Article 100, to be, the more limited will be the areas for manœuvre by later dissenting governments where earlier community action is interpreted not as intended to provide a minimum or 'floor' of protection, but as intended to create a level economic playing-field across the market by fixing a mandatory balance of competing interests (see below, p. 285). Since a domestic law which seeks to give more protection upsets this balance, it is vulnerable to attack for disturbing the 'level playing-field' of the Community. The

[77] Whittaker, n. 69 above, 235.

more often earlier Community action is seen as aimed as striking such a mandatory balance, the more often will Member States find that their ability to respond to perceived social evils is fettered. At a political level, it is now becoming appreciated that continued enthusiasm by Member States for the Community depends on the clear designation of secure and generous areas in which national governments are free to act without being tied to the community consensus about how to deal with the particular evil and the social trade-offs attendant on any solution. A weak manifestation of this is the acknowledgement by the European Commission of the importance of the restraining doctrine of 'subsidiarity', that is, the principle that *by internal discipline* binding EC measures should be limited to those which it was agreed were absolutely appropriate or more effective at the Community level. But this doctrine provides no security for a later dissenting government, nor does it in itself generate legal boundaries of lawmaking competence because it is not yet properly set out in the Treaty of Rome (the source of legitimacy of all EC measures).[78]

The stronger manifestation of these concerns is the call for an explicit constitutional settlement by which EC measures would be *legally* confined within designated realms, so that the validity of measures could be judged not by the (temporary) political acceptance by Member State governments at the time of enactment, but by an external, explicit division of powers under which Member States retained substantial and prevailing authority over, for example, social-welfare provision into which a comprehensive approach to personal injuries and disabilities in general would fall. Given these concerns it is not clear that the ECJ will accept that there are no problems in the legal basis of the Products Liability Directive as it is stated in the Preamble, simply because it met with approval by Member State governments at the time. After all—as we have seen—there was a considerable body of contemporary critics of its legal basis both within the European and Westminster parliaments, as well as outside. The ECJ might try to respond to the recent political concern with 'States rights' by developing new doctrines to restrain Community lawmaking. For example, by emphasizing the word 'directly' in Article 100, it might hold that, since liability rules could not have a sufficiently *direct* effect on the common market, the Directive had no legal basis in that Article.

Even if a future dissenting Member State established that the asserted effects on competition and movement of goods provided no legal basis for the Directive, could the measure be supported on a different ground? Could this alternative independent ground of

[78] F. Vibert, 'Europe's Constitutional Deficit', in *Europe's Constitutional Future* (London, 1990), 69, 79–80.

validity be found in the third justification cited in the Preamble to the Directive, the purported consumer-protection goal? Again, 'nationalists' or 'States-rights advocates' would note that the 1957 Treaty of Rome—concluded in an era when commercial rather than consumer concerns were dominant—scarcely mentions the 'consumer' (it does so only twice), let alone a consumer-protection programme or policy. It might be difficult to argue that consumer protection was seen as an essential attribute of the concept of a 'common market', especially one authorizing a harmonization measure consisting of the claimed 'levelling-up' of liability which, if anything, would make the market a more onerous place to carry on business.[79]

Yet in its Explanatory Memorandum to the 1976 draft Directive, the Commission noted that domestic rules offering differing degrees of protection to consumers are 'not compatible with a common market for all consumers'.[80] This idea that the 'common market' had a social dimension underlay the initial political decision to adopt a consumer-protection programme in the EC taken at the Paris meeting of Heads of Government in 1972, where Article 235 of the Treaty of Rome was cited as a possible legal basis for action.[81] That Article allows measures designed to achieve the objects of the Community in cases where the Treaty has not expressly provided the necessary power. But if the concept of the 'common market' cannot legitimately be seen directly to have the type of social dimension required to support consumer-protection measures, consumer protection would not by itself be an object of the Community which could trigger Article 235.

However sound early doubts about the legal basis of the Directive may have been, a development in the late 1980s might frustrate future challenges to its validity. Article 100A of the Treaty of Rome was added by the Single European Act 1986.[82] This provides for the adoption of harmonization measures which have as their object the establishment and functioning of the internal market, and requires the Commission, in its proposals for such measures which concern consumer protection, to take as a base a high level of protection to ensure consumer confidence in the functioning of the market. These references to consumer protection go a considerable way to supporting the view that the Treaty of Rome did—or a least now does—authorize a consumer-protection programme under an independent 'object' of the Treaty,

[79] On the arguments that a free market necessarily requires consumer protection, see Lawlor, n. 56 above, 8–9. But see e.g. criticism by the Danish Government discussed by Close, n. 57 above 222–3, and Borrie, n. 56 above, 104, who seems to regard products-liability as an issue with no real Community dimension.

[80] See Law Com., 82. The 1976 Memo. is reproduced at the end of the Law Com.

[81] Close, n. 57 above, 224.

[82] Suppl. 2/86 of *Bull. of EC*.

and moreover a programme of 'levelling-up' protection. Such a programme was launched in a resultant Council Resolution in November 1989, giving particular prominence to moves on unfair contract terms and access to justice.[83]

But the adoption of this programme presents a tactical dilemma to a future UK government hoping to establish a greater degree of consumer protection than the Community standard, for example by setting up a comprehensive system of personal-injuries compensation. This is because there are now *two* relevant but potentially antagonistic Community objectives and they have different implications for a Member State's ability to legislate in the relevant field. *First*, as we have seen, if the relevant object of the Community is seen as *economic*, an important goal is that the common market be a 'level playing-field' for business. If a Community law is judged to rest on this economic goal of the EC, it will be read as setting *the* appropriate balance between whatever competing interests are involved and departures from that balance by a Member State wanting, say, to give greater protection to one such interest, must be prevented. Sometimes a Community measure makes this explicit: an example is the 1990 Directive setting maximum tar-yields of cigarettes, under Article 7 of which Member States may not, 'for considerations of limitation of the tar yield of cigarettes, prohibit or restrict the sale of products which comply with' the Directive's levels.[84] But even if a Community law does not make this effect explicit, it would be implicit if the object of the law was held to be the creation of the 'level playing-field'.

This enforced uniformity of measures might seem odd to the citizens of the UK, especially in the consumer field. This is because, in areas where the UK might have accorded more protection to the individual (for example, maximum tar-yields lower than that set by the 1990 Directive), membership of the EC has *limited* the protection the citizen might otherwise have had, contrary to the apparent promises on entry to the EC and later of *enhanced* consumer protection. But advocates of community law might argue that this was simply the price to be paid for advances on other fronts. The products-liability Directive itself provides an illustration of this argument: a 'level playing-field' approach would prevent a Member State extending the protection of the new law to the producer's work-force by purporting to abolish the defence in Article 7 that the defendant 'did not put the product into circulation', but it also provides the basis for

[83] *OJ* No. C 294, 22.11.1989, p. 1. For earlier resolutions on the EC consumer-protection programme, see *OJ* No. C 92, 25.4.1975, p. 2 (First Programme): *OJ* No. C 133, 3.6.1981, p. 1 (Second Programme); *OJ* No. C 167, 5.7.1986, p. 1 ('New Impetus').

[84] *OJ* No. L 137/36, 30.5.90. On the general point of level playing-fields, see C of J of the EC, Case 120/78 (1979). [1979] ECR 649 (the 'Cassis de Dijon' case).

the current infringement proceedings brought by the European Commission against the UK for providing in its implementing legislation a development-risk defence wider than that in the 1985 Directive.

If, then, the products-liability Directive is based on the economic goal of a 'level playing-field'—and the Preamble asserts this in referring to distortions in competition and hindrances to the free movement of goods—the only legal[85] tactic a future dissenting Member State could use to overcome the blockage the Directive would thereby represent to comprehensive personal injuries reform would be to argue that it is *ultra vires*. As we saw, this would require the ECJ to develop 'States-rights' controls on the power conferred by Article 100 of the Treaty of Rome, deciding that it did not support the 1985 Directive because, for example, liability rules do not sufficiently *directly* affect the common market. The ECJ would also now have to be persuaded to read down the notion of 'consumer protection' in Article 100A to authorize only those consumer-protection measures—such as regulation of product-safety standards (for example, maximum tar-yields)—which clearly assist the economic aspects of the market such as competition and free movement, and which can be independently validated on these economic grounds.

A *second* competing formal object of the Community is that of a *social union* with explicit emphasis on consumer protection. This means that Community laws purporting to promote such an object may be *intra vires* even though the connection with trade is tenuous. More importantly, if, as it seems to be from provisions such as Article 118A of the Treaty of Rome,[86] the social objective can encompass provisions which provide a floor of protection for citizens, then might not a Member State argue that, even if validated by the social objectives of the Community, the products-liability Directive does not preclude a Member State providing citizens with even better protection? The first problem with this tactic is that the actual wording of the Preamble of the 1985 Directive suggests that it is concerned to *remove* differing degrees of consumer protection in Member States (see above). It is important to emphasize the antagonism here: a goal of providing a minimum floor of protection is inconsistent with a goal of fixing a level playing-field—*the Directive could not be aiming to do both*. Secondly, even if the Directive were interpreted to allow a Member State to provide 'better protection' for its citizens, whether a comprehensive personal-injuries system would be regarded in this way

[85] On the political option see above, n. 66.

[86] Article 118A(3): 'The provisions adopted pursuant to this Article shall not prevent any Member State from maintaining or introducing more stringent measures for the protection of working conditions compatible with this Treaty.'

would depend on the level of benefits it offered relative to the systems it replaced and the weight given to the argument that those (few) at present who have rights to tort-level damages would be worse off under such a system. However these questions are to be resolved in the future, the uncertainties surrounding the legal status and nature of the barrier to domestic reform represented by the products-liability Directive will tend to have a paralysing effect on the political will of reforming governments. The task of comprehensive reform of personal-injury compensation will appear more intractable than ever.

The fact that the products-liability Directive has severely put back the cause of personal-injuries reform is little appreciated. Those few advocates of radical reform of personal-injuries compensation in the UK who remained active in the 1980s failed adequately to grasp the legal and political dangers of European action—even though the parallel problem in the regulatory field was evident[87]—and in some cases actively embraced the Directive on the grounds that some reform is better than none. The principal new lobby-group of the late 1980s—the Citizen Compensation Campaign (Citcom) set up in 1988 under the presidency of Lord Scarman—adopted an agenda of reforms which accepted the basic premiss of liability-based compensation and concentrated on limited substantive and procedural reforms rather than setting its sights on a comprehensive compensation system. Ironically, the more astute UK campaigners, such as the Consumers' Association, actually appreciated that little real expansion of liability was involved, but thought the symbolic recognition of a 'strict' producers' responsibility, plus the potential increase in the claims-consciousness of the public and solicitors, were sufficient reasons to embrace the Directive.[88] Unlike other interest groups,[89] consumer groups failed to ensure that Member States clearly retained the option of providing better protection, be it simply better remedies for product victims (by, for example, the abolition of certain defences) or, more importantly, comprehensive access to compensation regardless of cause of injury. When weighed against the potential long-term pre-emption of substantive product-liability reform and of wider compensation options, support for the Directive may prove to have been a grave strategic mistake.

[87] See the 'regulatory gap' problem, discussed by T. Bourgoignie and D. Trubek, *Consumer Law, Common Markets and Federalism in Europe and the United States* (Berlin, 1987), 3–4, 13–14. See also discussion of the 'Cassis de Dijon' decision of the ECJ in Lawlor, n. 56 above, 17.

[88] See e.g. the views of David Tench of the Consumers' Association reported in (Sept. 1985), *Product Liability International* 139.

[89] For example, those involved in lobbying for Article 118A(3) of the Treaty of Rome; see n. 86 above.

12

Evaluating the Goals of Personal Injury Law: Some Empirical Evidence

DONALD HARRIS

A major justification put forward today for retaining tort liability for personal injuries is that the fear of incurring liability will lead potential defendants to take care to avoid causing accidents. Much of this paper will be devoted to examining, in the light of recent empirical data, both this goal, and that of compensating injured people.[1] But something should be said about the view that tort law is a mode of corrective justice,[2] which requires restoration of the previous balance between the wrongdoer and the victim. This goal is that the wrongdoer should be compelled to restore the victim's previous position: he enjoys individual rights, and if they are violated the wrongdoer is required to reverse the wrong. In the case of unintended harm, corrective justice would require that losses caused by careless action should be shifted from the innocent victim to the careless person.

In respect of carelessness, the criticism of this approach is that the widespread practice of liability insurance (and its compulsion in some activities) prevents any personal reparation from the culpable injurer to the individual victim: indeed, in some situations, such as car driving, the potential victim may have contributed to the same insurance fund in exactly the same way as the potential tortfeasor. Nowadays, tort liability for personal injuries should be treated as the gateway to an insurance pool which has been generated by a large group of premium-payers, whether drivers, employers, occupiers, manufacturers, or providers of services.[3] Tort law selects those injured persons who are

[1] This paper does not attempt to consider all the justifications for tort liability, as does P. Cane in (1982), 2 *OJLS* 30.

[2] E. Weinrib, 'Understanding Tort Law', (1989), 23 *Val. ULR* 485.

[3] This analysis still holds for some large organizations which are self-insured, in the sense that they budget a sum each year to meet tort claims, instead of paying a premium to an insurance company.

entitled to have access to these funds, and determines the amount of the compensation to be paid for their injuries. The concept of corrective justice is not suitable for empirical testing, and will therefore not be considered further in this paper. But it is accepted that it may be a relevant concept when direct action between individuals is the appropriate remedy (for example, an injunction to prevent the continuance of a private nuisance, or an order for the return of a chattel) or where the law forbids liability insurance against potential tort liability.[4]

Deterrence

Deterrence is a simple concept: if I am faced with a choice between alternative courses of action, one of which is antisocial because of the harm it will or might cause to others, my decision is likely to be influenced by any penalty which society will impose on me if I choose the antisocial alternative. The sanction may come from the criminal or the civil law, or may depend on religious belief or social pressure (for example, moral censure and ostracism). In the case of personal injuries (unintended harm in the vast majority of instances), it is claimed that the prospect of having to pay the cost of any losses due to carelessness will act as an incentive to take care. Even if, in the absence of this incentive, I would take some care to avoid accidents, it may induce me to take more care. Tort liability is claimed to be an important financial incentive for preventing those injuries which can be avoided by taking reasonable precautionary action. The corollary of this deterrent principle is that, when care has been taken by the actor, he should not be held liable for any accidental losses caused by him despite his care: to impose liability in this situation would not deter the carelessness of others in the future. Advocates of the deterrent function accept that tort law leaves many injured people without compensation, but argue that this is a price worth paying in order to achieve deterrence.

Theorists[5] have pointed out that tort law does not impose any sanction if the carelessness in question did not cause injury to another; that the level of the sanction is not related to the degree of carelessness but rather to the (sometimes unrelated) extent of the injury caused; and that the widespread use of liability insurance seriously undermines the

[4] Which was the situation in Soviet Russia: see B. Rudden, *Soviet Insurance Law* (Leiden, 1966), ch. 7.

[5] See e.g., H. A. Latin, 'Problem-Solving Behavior and Theories of Tort Liability', (1985) 73 *Calif. LR* 677; M. F. Grady, 'Why are people negligent? Technology, non-durable precautions and the medical malpractice explosion', (1988) 82 *Northwestern ULR* 293.

threat of potential liability upon the insured person for any specific instance of carelessness. (Because of practical difficulties, experience rating of insurance premiums is seldom invoked by liability insurers.) But there may be some deterrent effect which is not financial. Despite the protection of liability insurance, some defendants, such as doctors, still have to face the psychological pressure of being sued, the loss of time involved in defending the claim, and the risk of adverse publicity if found liable in tort.

An Economic Account of Deterrence

The dominant approach of economists to accident law is that it should induce the 'efficient' (or socially desirable) level of precautions against avoidable harm to others.[6] I am free to choose whether I should engage in a particular activity, for example, driving a car, and, if I do, I may choose which level of precautions I should undertake—in the case of car driving, at which speed, with which level of built-in safety devices, with which level of regular maintenance, and so on. When deciding whether to drive at all I shall automatically weigh the benefits against the costs of driving. In estimating costs, I will naturally count those which fall directly on me (internal costs), not only the cost of the car itself and its running costs, but also the risk of injury to myself if I am involved in an accident. My overall expected benefit must exceed my overall expected cost before I will choose to drive at all. The risk of an accident will depend on the probability that it might occur, multiplied by the expected cost, if it did occur. If I can see that some precautionary steps will reduce the risk to myself (for example, driving a more expensive but safer car, or driving at a lower speed), I will balance the extra cost of those steps so that it does not exceed the extra benefit to me, that is, the amount by which the risk to myself is reduced.

The economist argues that the same approach should be used for an external cost, whenever I should see that my proposed activity will create the risk of loss or injury to others. Without some form of pressure, most of us might ignore these external costs. So the law steps in to compel me to take them into account in my cost–benefit analysis in deciding whether to drive, and, if I do, which level of care to adopt

[6] See e.g., S. Shavell, *Economic Analysis of Accident Law* (Cambridge, Mass., 1987); G. Calabresi, *The Costs of Accidents* (New Haven, 1970). This section of this paper does not consider Calabresi's theory of market (or general) deterrence based on the price-mechanism, because it is aimed at ensuring that categories of activities which cause accidents should bear the cost of those accidents rather than at deterring carelessness as such.

to avoid accidents. The law ensures that the expected harm to others (the probability of causing them harm, multiplied by the cost of that harm) is added to the internal costs which I will naturally take into account. (The law compels me to 'internalize' what would otherwise be a cost to others.) The internalization will occur whether the liability rule is based on the negligence standard or on strict liability. Under either regime, I should, as a rational decision-maker, determine the 'efficient' level of care in the same way. The economic approach is easiest to understand when we can think of care as a series of incremental units along an increasing scale of care, as in the example of reducing speed, or of increasing expenditure on safety. (Sometimes it is difficult to conceive of the amount of care in incremental units, for example, where the only relevant care is to take a single precautionary measure, such as switching on a light or a safety device.) The theory is that I should choose the cost-minimizing level of care against accidents: that efficiency is reached when the cost of the last additional unit of care exactly equals the value of the extra saving in expected accident costs. The extra unit of care might reduce the probability of an accident occurring, or might reduce the severity of the expected harm (or both). In theory, there should always be a point at which it is no longer cost-effective to incur the cost of an additional unit of care, because it would produce only a smaller reduction in expected accident costs. At this point, it is cheaper for society as a whole to bear the remaining risk of incurring the expected accident costs than to spend more money on further reductions in the risk. (For the remaining accidents which occur despite the adoption of this 'efficient' level of care, the cost will be borne by victims under a negligence rule, but by actors under a strict liability rule: the cost-justified level of precautions remains the same, despite the different outcome in who bears the cost of any accident not avoided by that level of precautions.)

This economic theory of the deterrence of reasonably avoidable accidents depends on the actor being held liable to pay all the costs of the accidents which he causes by failing to take a cost-justified measure of avoidance. If only some of the external costs are imposed on him, others in a similar position in the future will be tempted to ignore part of the expected costs which they should take into account, and so might take less care than is socially justified. The desirable level of deterrence will not be achieved *either* if the negligent actor can avoid some of the costs he imposes (for example, the cost of medical care for the victim provided by the National Health Service, or the tax which would have been paid on the victim's future earnings), *or* if he can avoid paying any external costs because he escapes paying any damages at all. If an accident victim fails for any reason to recover the full cost from a person who was in fact negligent, the signal to other potential tortfeasors must be weakened. This point is crucially important in evaluating the data presented below.

The economic approach is exclusively forward-looking, in that the purpose of imposing liability on past tortfeasors is simply to deter future tortfeasors. So the goal of deterrence could be achieved without any compensation being paid to the victims of negligence. So long as the cost of negligently-caused accidents is imposed on the negligent injurers, the same deterrent effect would occur no matter who received the transfer—it could benefit the Exchequer, be paid to charity, or go to swell funds to which all accident victims had access on a no-fault basis. From the point of view of potential tortfeasors, negligent actions can have a 'price' attached to them no matter to whom the 'price' is to be paid.

Can Deterrence be Tested?

Until recently, the deterrence justification has rested largely on a priori reasoning or on common-sense intuition. But in the final analysis it is an empirical question whether deterrence actually works in any given activity. Empirical testing as to whether deterrence does or does not work is very difficult to undertake. It is impossible to construct two parallel societies where all circumstances are identical except for the fact that in one negligence liability is imposed, while in the other, no liability is imposed even for negligence. We may attempt to study a single society which has moved from one rule to the other, as in New Zealand, where negligence liability has been replaced by a rule of no liability in tort for causing death or personal injury, in view of the nationally organized, no-fault scheme of social insurance for all accident victims. But the problem here is to hold all other factors constant—the level of activities of all kinds, the level of technological development, the level of public knowledge of risks, and so on. If any of these factors change, as they must in real life, we cannot conclude that any change in the accident-rate was caused solely by the alteration in the liability rule. We are left to best estimates, which will try to take account of relevant changes in other factors.[7] In the context of the

[7] Much of the economic literature on assessing the impact of tort liability relates to road accidents, where both the Oxford and Rand studies (examined below, 294–8) show that tort law operates in a much higher proportion of accidents than in any other category. See C. J. Bruce, 'The Deterrent Effects of Automobile Insurance and Tort Law: A Survey of the Empirical Literature', (1984), 6 *Law and Policy* 67. For an economic assessment of Australasian no-fault schemes, see R. I. McEwin, (1989) 9 *Int. Rev. Law and Economics* 13; and on the New Zealand scheme, C. Brown, (1985) 73 *Calif. LR* 976; and on the no-fault automobile-insurance scheme in Quebec, see R. Devlin, (1990) 10 *Int. Rev. Law and Economics* 193.

debate over capital punishment, for instance, attempts have been made to compare the experience of different jurisdictions in the United States, some with and some without capital punishment. But there is always the serious possibility that any observed differences in the murder-rate may be due to factors other than the penalty for murder.

Deterrence works by preventing carelessness, and so cannot be evaluated simply by studying instances where it has failed to work, that is, where claims for damages are brought. But knowledge of the proportion of accident victims who actually obtain damages will lay a foundation for evaluating the deterrent function of tort law. In recent years, the methodologies of the social sciences have been employed to study the impact of legal rules on ordinary people. This impact can go far beyond the practical experience of any judge or practitioner, who can see only those situations brought to his attention. This has been demonstrated in the most spectacular way by study of the consequences of accidents, which shows that only 14 per cent of accident victims ever consult lawyers about making a claim for damages. The other 86 per cent constitutes the mass of accident victims, whose experiences do not come to the attention of lawyers. These percentages have been discovered through household surveys in which members of the public are interviewed directly, to learn from them what their experiences have been after accidents.

Statistics on Accidents and the Recovery of Damages

There have been a number of social surveys to determine the incidence of accidents and the frequency of the recovery of damages by accident victims. The Royal Commission chaired by Lord Pearson[8] commissioned a large household survey in 1974, which was designed to screen out a nationally representative sample of injured people who had been treated in hospital or by a doctor, and whose injury had led to at least four days' incapacity for work or for other normal activities.[9] This survey found that 6.5 per cent of accident victims recovered some damages: 10.5 per cent of those injured at work, 25 per cent of motor-vehicle injuries, and 1.5 per cent in the case of other injuries.[10]

The Oxford survey, conducted by a multi-disciplinary team of researchers at the Centre for Socio-Legal Studies, was a national household survey in 1976 of the experience of those suffering illness as

[8] The Royal Commission on Civil Liability and Compensation for Personal Injury (1978), 3 vols., Cmnd. 7054.

[9] Vol. 2, paras. 467 ff.

[10] Vol. 1, para. 78.

well as injury.[11] Over 12,000 households (representing over 35,000 people) were screened by personal interview to find a nationally representative sample of people whose normal activities had been interrupted by accident or illness for more than two weeks during the previous year.[12] All accident victims (over 1,200) and a sample of illness victims were later interviewed at length to discover how they coped with their situation, and what compensation and support they received from different sources. Those who had made claims for damages and their solicitors were followed up with further enquiries to discover the outcome of the claims (1976–9).[13] The survey found that, of this sample of victims (those incapacitated for two weeks or longer), 12 per cent had recovered some damages. (This is a higher percentage than found in the Pearson survey, which covered a wider range of the less-serious injuries—see above.)

The success rate in the Oxford survey varied greatly according to the category of accident: fewer than one in three of road accident victims (29 per cent), fewer than one in five of work accident victims (19 per cent), and fewer than one in fifty of all other types of accident victim (2 per cent) obtained any damages at all.

During 1988–90, the Rand Corporation conducted another national study of the legal consequences of accidents.[14] About 26,000 households across the United States were surveyed by telephone to discover a nationally representative sample of those whose injuries 'caused at least one day of restricted activity or one visit to a health care provider or some liability claiming behavior over the previous 12 months' (unlike the Oxford study, this survey excluded illnesses). From the survey, a sub-sample of about 2,800 injured individuals were identified, and later interviewed about their experiences. A picture of the incidence and types of accidents in the US emerged, of the costs to victims and their families, and of the compensation which they received from different sources. This essay will consider only the findings relevant to the role of the tort system.

The vast majority of accident victims do not even consider making a

[11] D. Harris, M. Maclean, H. Genn, S. Lloyd-Bostock, P. Fenn, P. Corfield and Y. Brittan, *Compensation and Support for Illness and Injury* (Oxford, 1984).

[12] The methodology is described in M. Maclean and H. Genn, *Methodological Issues in Social Surveys* (1979).

[13] The Pearson survey (above) found that, at the time of the interviews, just over one-third of the claims for damages were unsettled (vol. 2, para. 393, and Table 86). Unlike the Oxford survey, these pending claims were not followed until their outcome was known, nor were claimants' solicitors surveyed; instead, estimates were made of the expected outcomes (see note 1 to table 87 in vol. 2). The follow-up Oxford survey found a higher proportion of cases being abandoned than the Pearson survey had estimated: see Harris *et al.*, n. 11 above, 135, n. 6.

[14] D. R. Hensler *et al.*, *Compensation for Accidental Injuries in the United States* (Santa Monica, CA, 1991).

TABLE 12.1. *Claims for damages for personal injuries in cases of incapacity for two weeks or more. Comparison between US and UK (England and Wales only)* (%)

	All accidents		Road accidents		Work accidents		Other accidents (non-work, non-road)	
	US	UK	US	UK	US*	UK	US	UK
Considered claiming damages	34	26	72	47	41	46	18	9
Thought a claim possible	26	23	62	40	26	43	14	7
Consulted a lawyer	16	14	46	33	14	25	6	3
Obtained damages†	—	12	—	29	—	19	—	2

Notes: * Work accidents in the US are not a good comparison with the UK because in the US injured employees cannot sue their own employers in tort but are confined to a workers' compensation claim: they can sue defendants other than employers.
† See n. 16.

Sources: US = Rand Survey (1988–9); UK = Oxford Survey (1976–9).

claim for damages against someone else. This was shown by the Oxford study of England and Wales, and, even though the US is widely regarded as the most litigious nation in the industrialised world, the Rand study has subsequently confirmed that the situation is very similar there. It found that, across all accidents in their sample, only 19 per cent of injured Ameicans even considered making a claim for damages; that 10 per cent took some action to claim; that 7 per cent consulted a lawyer, but only 4 per cent actually instructed a lawyer to make a claim.[15]

Table 12.1 attempts to draw together some data from both the Rand and Oxford studies, so that comparisons can be drawn.[16] Although the criteria for the two surveys were not the same (the Rand survey included many less-serious injuries—restricted activities lasting one to thirteen days—which would not have fallen within the Oxford criteria), the Rand researchers drew from their main sample a subset which approximated the Oxford criteria so that comparisons can legitimately be made. And although the samples do not coincide, the 'attrition rate' between the percentages as one reads down each column can validly be compared, that is, the drop-out rates between 'considered claiming' down to 'obtained damages' are comparable.

From this Table, several general conclusions may safely be drawn which apply to both countries. First, over accidents causing two or more weeks' incapacity, only a quarter of victims reached the stage of thinking it might be possible to bring a claim in tort. Secondly, only about half of those who began by considering claiming went on to the stage of consulting a lawyer.[17] Thirdly, claims for damages were heavily concentrated in two categories, road and work accidents;

[15] Hensler *et al.*, Figure 5.2 (p. 122). Many claims for damages in the US are paid directly by the responsible party or his insurance company: ibid., Table 5.7. Table 5.12 reports the outcomes known at the time of the interview. In the case of claimants who (without legal representation) had negotiated directly with the injuror, 58 per cent had received some payment (no claims were still pending); in the case of claimants who (without legal representation) had negotiated directly with the injuror's insurer, 49 per cent had received some payment, but 14 per cent of claims were still pending. The Oxford survey found that in the UK 8 per cent of those obtaining damages had not used a lawyer to make the claim: Harris *et al.*, p. 81.

[16] The Rand report does not include data on the outcome of claims for damages which were pending at the time of the interviews. Although final outcomes are not known, some indication may be given by the figures for 'liability claims attempted' in respect of all accident victims in the Rand sample (that is, the figures are not limited to victims with two or more weeks' incapacity): for all accidents, claims were attempted by 10 per cent of victims; for motor-vehicle accidents 44 per cent; for work accidents 7 per cent; and for other accidents 3 per cent (Table 5.2).

[17] The evidence does not support the hypothesis that damages are more likely to be obtained by those with the more serious injuries, whether seriousness is judged in physical terms or in relation to time taken off work: Harris *et al.*, n. 11 above, 56–58. But the Rand Report (Hensler *et al.*,), Table 5.5, shows that in the US *claims* are more likely to be made by the more severely injured (the outcomes are not yet known).

outside these categories it was rare for the tort system to be invoked. The general picture is one in which tort liability is applied on a significant scale only in road accidents. In the 'Other' category of accidents, where the vast majority of accidents fall (63 per cent of accidents in the US and 86 per cent in the UK—the definitions of the categories vary a little), the tort system operates for only about one accident in fifty.

These surveys did not directly address the issue whether deterrence through tort liability works so as to reduce the number of accidents. But they do raise fundamental questions about the deterrent function of tort law. If in the largest categories of accidents—those at home, on someone else's premises, at sport or leisure, and those suffering an adverse medical outcome or an injury from a defective product (such as a drug or piece of equipment)—tort liability is imposed in only a minute proportion of cases (a finding in both countries), is this because there is little need to deter or because of other reasons? (Both the Rand and Oxford studies record reasons given by those who had considered the possibility of claiming but then had not proceeded with a claim. Among many constraints in the UK, the leading factors were the lack of claims-consciousness, problems about finding sufficient evidence, and fear of the legal costs involved.)[18] Can deterrence in 2 per cent of UK accidents (outside the road and work categories) be more than a symbolic response to the problem of negligence in society? Can even the proportion of successful claims for work accidents (19 per cent in the UK) produce an adequate level of deterrence (in economic terms the optimal or efficient level)? It seems implausible that the fault of someone other than the victim occurs in only one-fifth of work accidents.

The Harvard Medical Practice Study

Neither the Pearson nor the Oxford surveys purported to measure the proportion of accidents which were caused by the negligence of someone other that the victim. Whether the deterrence goal is achieved could be assessed more accurately if all accidents in a given category could be studied, not only to find out how many led to a payment of damages, but also to come to judgements on the presence or absence of negligence in each case. Although such a study would be a formidable undertaking, one has recently been completed in the United States for a category much in the public eye, that of medical mishaps. A large, multi-disciplinary team based at the Harvard School

[18] Harris *et al.*, n. 11 above, 72; cf. the Rand Report, (Hensler et al.,) Table 6.15.

of Public Health and the Harvard Law School has, since 1984, been conducting extensive empirical studies of medical injuries and malpractice in the State of New York.[19] The State financed the study, and provided access to all relevant data under governmental control. The first part of the study aimed at obtaining reliable data on the incidence of injuries resulting from medical intervention (which the research called 'adverse events') and on the proportion due to the fault or negligence of the physician or other health provider. A second part examined the proportion of adverse events, both negligent and non-negligent, which led to claims for and payment of damages.[20] The massive scale of the study, and its meticulous attention to every methodological detail[21], are unlikely to be improved on for many years to come.

The crucial feature of the Harvard study is that medically qualified researchers were used to decide whether the medical treatment had caused an adverse event (that is, an unintended injury caused by medical management rather than by the disease process) and whether there had been negligence on the part of medical personnel in that causation. The judgments were made by members of the same profession as the potential tortfeasors. The determination of malpractice almost always rests on a medical judgement ('Did the treatment fall below the standard that normally should be expected from the practitioner usually caring for this kind of disease?').[22] Many difficult issues of causation and the appropriate standard of care had to be decided, but it is hard to believe that the medical researchers in the study would *over*-estimate the incidence of either adverse outcomes or negligence: their affinity with their professional brethren might lead to *under*-estimates, but we should be safe in accepting their findings as reliable and, if any bias were present, it would be towards the conservative side.

Doctors carefully studied the 1984 medical records of over 31,000 patients who had been discharged from fifty-one hospitals randomly selected in the State of New York. The study focused on patients in acute care hospitals, and assumed that this would pick up most cases

[19] *Patients, Doctors, and Lawyers: Medical Injury, Malpractice Litigation, and Patient Compensation in New York* (1990): The Report of the Harvard Medical Practice Study to the State of New York. This large report will later be published as a book, and further material from the study will be published as articles in learned journals.

[20] Other parts of the study surveyed the knowledge and perceptions of doctors about their potential tort liability (see below, 302), and measured the costs (medical expenses, lost wages, and lost household production) incurred by victims and their families, and the compensation they received from all sources.

[21] Extensive appendices to the report examine the statistical and survey methodologies, as well as legal and medical issues.

[22] See n. 19 above, pp. 5–16 to 5–17.

of medical mistakes causing serious injury which occurred outside hospitals, because the patient would be very likely to end up in hospital. The findings were that 3.7 per cent of patients suffered an adverse event (as defined above), of which 27.6 per cent were due to negligence. In other words, 1 per cent of the patients discharged from New York hospitals had been injured through some negligent medical management. (The incidence of adverse events is probably slightly underestimated because the survey could identify only those which were revealed by the medical records.) In each case, the assessment of negligence was made by at least two doctors, who followed a carefully designed and sophisticated procedure in which they separately reviewed the medical records. Each doctor ranked his views of causation and negligence on 6-point scales, so that the ultimate finding that medical managment had caused an injury, and that it had involved negligence, depended on the two separate findings averaging more than halfway up the scale. So a 'possibly . . . reasonably avoidable' error would not reach the threshold of negligence because two separate judgements by doctors had to *average* a higher score (3.5) than this, which was point 3 on the scale, *viz.* 'Negligence not quite likely: less that 50–50 but close call.' (The higher points were: '4. Negligence more likely than not: more than 50–50 but close call; 5. Strong evidence for negligence; 6. Virtually certain evidence for negligence'.) This method of ranking was designed to eliminate cases where the judgement could not be made with more than 50–50 confidence.

A further stage of the study was to establish the frequency of malpractice claims. The researchers used several separate data-sets and found that for every eight of the victims of negligence identified by the study, only one brought a claim for damages. In other words, eight times as many patients suffered a negligently caused injury as those bringing claims. A further finding was that only half the claims suceeded in obtaining damages, and that the delay after the injury before payment was made averaged six years. So the major result of the study, so far as deterrence is concerned, is the estimate that, for every sixteen patients who are injured by medical negligence in New York State, only one receives damages. This is a finding of great significance for advocates of the deterrent effect of tort liability. New York is a leading jurisdiction in the United States, a country where the highest number of malpractice claims in the world can be expected. This expectation arises from the easy and cheap access to legal services offered by the contingent-fee system,[23] and from the wide publicity

[23] But this system could exclude smaller claims if lawyers were unwilling to take on a case where the damages expected would generate too low a fee for the work involved.

given to these claims by the media; American victims of medical negligence are more likely than those elsewhere to know of the opportunity to claim damages and to overcome their natural reluctance to sue their doctor or the hsopital which treated them. If only one of these victims recovers damages for every sixteen cases of negligence identified by the medical profession, the proportion is most unlikely to be as high in the UK.

Such an empirical finding enables us to ask a new question—is the tort system worth preserving in this area of activity if it can identify only one in sixteen instances of negligence? The risk of being held liable, even if one is negligent, is so low (6 per cent) that New York doctors who learn these statistics need no longer be so afraid of tort liability. No one can now challenge the main finding that the true incidence of medical negligence is many times greater than the frequency of successful claims. The deterrent effect is so far below the optimal level that it raises the serious question whether this limited result justifies the cost of administering the tort system. The signal sent by tort law to the medical profession is that occasionally, in a symbolic way, they may be held liable for negligence, but that 94 per cent of the instances of negligence will not lead to liability. According to economic theory, New York doctors should, if they act rationally, discount the threat of liability by a massive proportion. The implicit message of the Harvard Study to patients and to society generally is that if they wish to maintain standards they must rely on many other mechanisms to hold doctors accountable. Standards should be maintained, and indeed improved (which is something tort law does not attempt to do), by a package of methods—by education (including post-qualification courses), by re-licensing at regular intervals, by peer review (regular medical audit by colleagues), by risk management by hospitals, and by better systems for enabling patients to complain and to initiate disciplinary action against doctors. Accountability to the public can be enforced simultaneously at different levels and by different methods.

The Harvard study also examined the reasons for no claims being made, even where there had been adverse outcomes of the medical intervention and strong evidence of negligence. The study showed that most of those who did not claim would have had claims of limited monetary value (which would therefore have been of only limited interest to the trial bar working for contingent fees). These were cases where the injury was minor (for example, complete recovery within six months) or the patient had only a limited life-expectation (aged over

The fact that only half of the claims succeed means that New York lawyers (invariably working for contingent fees) are paid nothing for half the medical malpractice cases they take on.

70). But this finding should not be used to say that the deterrent theory is operating in the more serious cases of negligence, because there is no necessary connection between the relative degree of fault and the relative seriousness of the outcome.[24]

Finally, the Harvard study included an attempt to use econometric analysis to measure the deterrent effect of malpractice liability. The analysis of the data failed to show any deterrent effect; but, on the other hand, it did not prove that there was no such effect. The data did not permit a comparison between a regime of tort liability and one of no liability, but they did permit a comparison of 'marginal incentives' in the experience of hospitals with different rates of both claims and injuries. The analysis, however, found no compelling evidence that hospitals with higher rates of tort claims subsequently had lower rates of medical injuries.[25]

The Knowledge and Perceptions of Doctors

A separate part of the Harvard study was a survey of doctors ('physicians' in American terms), both by postal questionnaires and interviews,[26] to discover their perceptions of the risk of being sued and of the impact of potential tort liability on the way they conducted their practice. Physicians themselves perceived the risk of being sued in a given year as three times greater than the actual risk of being sued (as shown by the main part of the study). This suggests that the symbolic effect of tort law may greatly exceed its actual impact. If there was a poor outcome of their treatment (for example, if a less-than-perfect baby was delivered) the physicians thought they stood a 45 per cent chance of being sued, whether or not they were negligent; if they believed they had acted negligently, they thought the chance of being sued increased to 60 per cent, not much higher than the 45 per cent. Apologists for deterrence may claim that this overestimate of the risk of being held liable will go some way to compensate for the low proportion of negligent actions which lead to payment of damages. But the whole of this effect will not persist when doctors learn the true risk, as demonstrated by the Harvard study. The false perception of the risk is also likely to affect medical practice adversely, by leading to doctors ordering more tests or reducing the scope of their practice.

The doctors saw the effect of the tort system as a psychological distraction rather than a factor which influenced the way they

[24] See also n. 17 above about the the UK position.
[25] This analysis is being pursued further by the Harvard group.
[26] A postal questionnaire of 739 physicians, and in-depth interviews of forty-seven.

practised. A claim against them caused them great distress, worry, anger, and frustration: 'a very insulting experience to go through.' The most severe reaction came from doctors whose cases had gone to a full trial, or had been reported in the media. In general, doctors thought that the severity of the sanction for malpractice depended on whether the media gave the case publicity or it went to a full hearing. Because they believed that malpractice claims arose from circumstances beyond their control, they felt unfairly punished.

Full interviews with forty-seven physicians obtained more detail about their attitudes toward malpractice liability. Most physicians accepted that they could make mistakes, but considered themselves to be competent. Since a finding of negligence was often treated by them as a finding of incompetence, they were unwilling to label mistakes as negligent, and did not accept that those outside the profession could identify negligence. A number of hypothetical cases were given to those who were interviewed so that the reasons for their judgements on causation, errors, and negligence could be examined in detail. The result was a considerable range of opinions on how the facts should be interpreted, showing the difficulties inherent in coming to decisions on these medico-legal issues.

The value of incentives can be diminished both if they are misconceived by those to whom they are directed, and also if the latter find it difficult to translate the signals into effective action. Virtually none of the doctors in the postal survey reported that they had modified their practices in the light of a particular malpractice suit. Any changes were due to the general malpractice climate and to the much more extensive range of tests becoming available. (The personal interviews provided more information about the increased use of tests: it is due as much to scientific and technological advances as it is to the practice of defensive medicine.) Most doctors did not believe that the tort system could play a role in preventing medical mishaps. One reason they gave was the great delay in incurring the legal sanction; another was the view that a malpractice claim usually concerned circumstances beyond the doctor's control. They believed that patients sued when they needed money or were unhappy with a bad or unexpected outcome of their treatment. It was a 'lottery' in which some failures to achieve an acceptable standard of care were punished, but not others. The tort system appears to stigmatize many actions which the doctors did not consider to have been negligent, but at the same time missed a good number of cases where there was negligence. The signal which doctors received from the tort system was, therefore, strong but unfocused: they saw a significant risk of being sued, whether or not they had been negligent. (This last finding may partly reflect the role of juries in the US, whose decisions on liability may be less predictable than those of judges sitting alone, as in England.) The doctors felt a 'malpractice' environment, but its impact on them was at a general and unspecific level.

Finally, the doctors were asked about the relative importance of various factors in helping to maintain standards of care in their practice. The influence of continuing medical education and of medical journals, and their relations with their peers, were rated as more important than the threat of malpractice liability; clinical care guidelines, standard operating procedures, and morbidity and mortality conferences were each rated as of similar importance to the malpractice threat, while external peer review was thought to be of lesser importance. They considered that the net of the tort system was cast too widely: the malpractice threat was an irritating nuisance rather than a useful method of quality control. They clearly preferred that the quality of their work should be assessed by another doctor from their own specialty.

This survey of an articulate professional group at the receiving end of tort liability does not suggest that it is having the effect desired by advocates of deterrence. The message actually received by New York doctors is vague, fails to educate them about specific risks to be avoided, and in some respects (for example, in equating negligence with professional incompetence) it is seriously misunderstood. The strong dislike which doctors may have for tort liability does not adequately explain their failure to draw the lessons which the deterrence theory expects them to draw from the imposition of liability. Even if tort liability were considered to have a useful symbolic role, as a demonstration in relatively few instances that society strongly disapproves of some categories of behaviour, this role is limited; first, because the court cannot itself see that publicity follows its rulings (the media comes to its own decisions on what is newsworthy); and secondly, because any serious case of negligence tends to be settled out of court, sometimes on terms requiring the victim to give no information to the media, even of the fact that there has been a settlement.

Compensation

Tort law was not designed to be a general system for compensating accident victims, and cannot be criticized for failing to be such a system. Since the nineteenth century, the law of negligence has openly discriminated between two categories of accident victims, those who could prove they had been injured by some one else's fault, and those who could not. The loss always falls on the victim in the first place, and the law decreed that it should stay there unless there was a justifiable reason for shifting it to another. Apart from the few instances of strict liability, the negligence of another was the only justification accepted by the law for compulsory loss-shifting.[27] This reasoning was seldom articulated in judgements, but it was always implicitly incorporated in them. This approach to loss-shifting deliberately left most accident victims to bear their own losses. If social justice demanded that they should receive help from others, this should not be channelled through individual tort liability, but rather through charitable funds or through governmental mechanisms designed to meet need directly, such as workman's compensation or social security.

In the twentieth century, many writers have maintained that a major goal of tort law is to compensate injured people.[28] The importance of this goal in the minds of legislators is shown by the fact that some groups of potential tortfeasors have been compelled by law to carry liability insurance; this compulsion was not introduced to protect motorists and employers from the risk of insolvency, but rather to ensure that money would be available whenever an accident victim could prove a valid claim in tort. But compensating injured people has never been the only goal of negligence law; it has been pursued only when the deterrence goal could be simultaneously pursued. When the two goals could be achieved together, the law imposed tortious liability: but if the facts showed only a need for compensation without a need to deter, no liability could be imposed. So the risk of fault-caused accidents was placed on those choosing to act, with the result that a decision to engage in an activity which was not itself unlawful could create increased risks to others, only part of which fell on the actor. A car driver knows that his choice to drive, and his choice of his annual mileage, will increase the risk of accidental injury to others, even in the absence of his negligence. But the law of torts focusses only on the *additional* risk created by any negligent driving at a specific location and at a specific time, not on the activity as such.[29]

Mechanisms designed simply to compensate injured and disabled people, such as first-party insurance or disability benefits under social insurance schemes, do not discriminate between them on the grounds of another's fault: the only grounds which they treat as socially acceptable are the relative needs of victims, the relative contributions which they have made to an insurance fund, or, in some cases, the

[27] Concepts of corrective justice may also have played a role: see above, 289.

[28] On 'loss-spreading', see J. G. Fleming, *An Introduction to the Law of Torts*, 2nd edn. (Oxford, 1985), 6–18.

[29] The special torts imposing strict liability are, of course, exceptions to this statement.

decision to give preference to whole categories of victims, such as with the industrial injuries and criminal compensation schemes. The surveys reported in this essay clearly establish how small a proportion of accident victims benefit from the tort system. They are a privileged minority whose need for compensation is not greater than that of other victims but who are fortunate in being able to take advantage of society's wish to use their need as a means to influence the future behaviour of people generally. But the award of damages is not the only way in which society can make a public example of careless injurers. Antisocial behaviour is stigmatized and deterred by a range of methods, such as criminal punishment, restriction of future activities (for example, a prohibition notice against a factory), deprivation of privileges (for example, suspension of a licence), or public censure or ridicule (for example, putting the offender in the stocks). Any reliance on tort to regulate behaviour has never been more than one method among many.

In deciding the future of personal injury tort law, the policy-maker must weigh both how few victims recover damages, and also the extent to which damages contribute to the aggregate compensation of victims generally. The Rand survey found that tort liability contributed only about 7 per cent of the total amount of compensation received by injured people from all sources in the US. The proportion was as high as 22 per cent in the case of road accident victims, but as low as 3 per cent for those injured away from work or the road. Another Rand finding was that through costs directly incurred, and through their reduced earnings, injured people and their households bear 38 per cent of the costs arising from all types of accidents in the US. The only (partly) corresponding figures for the UK were produced by the Pearson Commission which, on the basis of data for 1971–6, estimated that of the total amount of compensation from all sources received by injured people in the UK, about a quarter came from tort damages.[30] No simple comparison with the US is possible, however, since the Rand figures include first-party insurance for medical expenses, whereas most accident victims in the UK receive treatment under the National Health Service, the cost of which was excluded from the Pearson estimates. It should also be remembered that the value of the compensation provided by tort law is diminished by the delay in its receipt. In the Oxford survey, the average delay between the accident and payment of damages was 19 months; in the Harvard survey of medical malpractice, six years.

In the light of this data on the uneven coverage of victims, and the reliance of most on other forms of support such as sick pay or social

[30] Vol. I, para. 44.

security, the policy-maker should conduct a cost–benefit analysis of the tort system and ask whether it gives value for money. Are the proved benefits of the system, in providing some deterrence and some compensation, worth its cost? Could the same or greater benefits be obtained at lower cost through other mechanisms? Is the compensation provided by tort law administered in a cost-effective way? The high cost of administering the tort liability system is now clear: about half of the premiums paid for liability insurance actually reaches the pockets of victims, the other half being used to investigate claims and to pay the cost on both sides for legal, medical, and insurance services. This compares with the cost of administering social security benefits (6.25 per cent) or payments under a general no-fault scheme (7 per cent in New Zealand).

Conclusion

From the data presented in this paper, the reader is able to draw his own conclusions about the limited role of tort law. The writer believes that the data justify the conclusion that the tort liability system cannot contribute significantly to meeting either the goal of deterrence or that of compensating victims. The system suffers from an inherent weakness arising from its attempt to achieve both goals by a single mechanism; the attempt to meet either goal is seriously restricted by the need to accommodate the other goal. Both the US and UK have developed many other policy instruments which aim exclusively at one goal, and which can meet it more efficiently than can tort law. The basic question to be addressed by the policy-maker is whether personal injury tort law, a hybrid mechanism, is worth preserving in order to supplement these single-purpose mechanisms. Or does it make such a small contribution towards either deterrence[31] or compensation that it should be abolished for all injuries not caused intentionally? I believe that the impartial observer of the data given above, who has no vested interest in the present system, can give only an affirmative answer. The money now needed to support tort liability could be switched to support the single-purpose mechanisms, which could, with the injection of extra money, separately achieve the two goals even more efficiently.[32] It is encouraging that the scholar

[31] This paper does not challenge the concept of deterrence itself, but rather the effectiveness of the tort of negligence, as it works in practice, in deterring carelessness which causes personal injuries.

[32] Two recent books by American authors support this conclusion: R. Gaskins, *Environmental Accidents: Personal Injury and Public Responsibility* (1989); S. D. Sugarman, *Doing Away with Personal Injury Law: New Compensation Mechanisms for Victims, Consumers and Business* (Westport, Conn., 1989). See the review article by Harris, (1991), 11 *OJLS*.

honoured by the present volume argued along similar lines in his pioneering work on accidents.[33] But those who cherish traditional beliefs[34] will continue to ignore the accumulating evidence of how the tort system works in real life. They should reflect on the obstinacy of their spiritual predecessors who for many years continued to believe, despite the mounting evidence to the contrary, that the earth was flat.

[33] *Atiyah's Accidents, Compensation and the Law* 4th edn., ed. P. Cane (London, 1985).

[34] See the Pearson Commission Report, (n. 8 above), vol 1. para. 1716, which refers to one unidentified group within the Commission: 'Others among us hope, and believe, that there would always be a role for the tort system, whatever happened to no-fault provision. They would argue . . . that, despite the role of liability insurance, tort would continue to embody the socially valuable principle that, where a person negligently or intentionally caused injuries to another, amends should be made for the consequences of his fault; and that the continued existence of tort would, of itself, be some safeguard against a system of total dependence on the state.'

13

Negligence and Economic Loss

JOHN DWYER

In the April 1967 issue of the *Law Quarterly Review* Patrick Atiyah, then a Fellow of New College, published a characteristically thoughtful and lucid paper on 'Negligence and Economic Loss'.[1] In it he considered the effect of the then recent decision in *Hedley Byrne & Co. Ltd.* v. *Heller & Partners Ltd.*[2] ('*Hedley Byrne*') on what he described as 'the general rule that liability in the tort of negligence did not extend to purely economic loss'. Feldthusen in his monograph *Economic Negligence*[3] suggests that no such general rule then existed and that Atiyah's paper was influential in the development of the approach in England and the British Commonwealth which subsumed various categories of economic loss under a general rule.

Although Atiyah may not have been unique in his reference to such a general rule,[4] it is suggested that, following his paper, academic writers and judges fell into the habit of referring to a general rule against the recovery of pure economic loss in tort. What Atiyah did was simultaneously to confirm or establish that there had been such a general rule and to point out that *Hedley Byrne* constituted a significant departure from it. The plethora of litigation on these questions in the ensuing decades demonstrates the strong creative force of this conjunction of ideas.

In the decades since Atiyah's paper there have been many cases dealing with attempts to expand the law of negligence to cover pure economic loss. This paper attempts to outline the development of the common law in England and Australia with reference to the role that Atiyah's paper has played in that development. The cases are numerous, so that it is impossible to do much more than identify some significant features. The path towards and the retreat from *Anns* v. *Merton London Borough Council*[5] ('*Anns*') and *Junior Books* v. *Veitchi*[6] ('*Junior Books*') have been quite remarkable.

1 (1967) 83 LQR 248.
2 [1964] AC 465.
3 Toronto, 1984.
4 See e.g., Fleming *The Law of Torts* (Sydney, 1957), 182.
5 [1978] AC 728.
6 [1983] 1 AC 520.

It is difficult to compress the events of twenty-five years into a short compass. The law has been in a state of confusion and uncertainty, well described by Atiyah in 1988 when he remarked, concerning English tort law today, on the judges' 'floundering around with a total absence of theoretical help on an entirely ad hoc case by case basis'.[7] It is suggested, however, that this period of uncertainty may be coming to an end, and that clear principles are now emerging. Decisions such as *Murphy* v. *Brentwood DC*[8] represent a determined attempt by the House of Lords to restore certainty and clear principle to the common law.[9]

Some Background Considerations

Despite the persuasive moral force of the notion that persons who fail to act with reasonable care should be liable for any foreseeable harm caused by their conduct, the common law has always declined to adopt the position that it will protect plaintiffs from all of the consequences of negligent behaviour.

There has long been a reluctance at common law to permit recovery of pure economic losses in negligence actions. The sources of that reluctance have been various. In *Ultramares Corporation* v. *Touche*,[10] Cardozo J refused a claim for negligent misrepresentation against public accountants who negligently prepared a certified balance sheet for the Stern company which they knew the company would use to obtain credit. The plaintiffs lent money to the company, on the strength of the certified balance sheet, which was in substance lost when the company went bankrupt. The action failed because, as Cardozo J put it, to recognize a duty of care might '. . . expose accountants to a liability in an indeterminate amount for an indeterminate time to an indeterminate class'.[11] These words have been cited again and again. Indeed, courts have on occasion treated them as definitive of economic loss which cannot be recovered; such that if an economic loss could be shown to be sufficiently determinate as to amount, time, and class, recovery could be permitted.[12]

The use of the distinction between physical injury to person or

[7] Cassell Lecture, *Freedom of Contract and The New Right* (Stockholm, 1989), 30 (repr. in *Essays on Contract* (Oxford, 1990), 355).

[8] [1990] 3 WLR 414.

[9] See also *Governors of the Peabody Fund* v. *Sir Lindsay Parkinson & Co. Ltd.* [1985] AC 210 and *D & F Estates Ltd.* v. *Church Commissioners for England* [1989] AC 177.

[10] (1931) 255 NY 170, 174 NE 441.

[11] 255 NY 170, 179.

[12] See e.g., *Caltex Oil (Australia) Pty. Ltd.* v. *The Dredge 'Willemstad'* 136 CLR 529 at 593 per Mason J. *San Sebastian Pty. Ltd.* v. *The Minister* (1986) 162 CLR 341.

property and economic loss has been criticized by some, but it rests on the differing values attached to the protection of persons and their property from injury on the one hand and the protection of economic interests on the other. As Lord Oliver said in *Murphy* v. *Brentwood DC*:[13] 'The infliction of physical injury to the person or property of another universally requires to be justified. The causing of economic loss does not. If it is to be categorised as wrongful it is necessary to find some factor beyond the mere occurrence of the loss and the fact that its occurrence could be foreseen.' These differing values should not be seen as based on a primitive concern for material objects over non-material interests. As Atiyah pointed out, personal injury, unlike financial loss, can never be truly compensated for in money.[14]

There is a further reason for the distinction which follows from the existence of a free-market economy. A market economy is one in which financial 'harm' of some kind to some persons is to be expected, in that losses are likely to occur to individuals operating in the market. The less successful suffer financial harm, and foreseeable harm at that. Indeed, as Lord Reid noted in *Dorset Yacht Co.* v. *Home Office*[15] (*'Dorset Yacht Co.'*), it may be quite permissible to cause economic loss by deliberate action: 'Competition involves traders being entitled to damage their rivals interest by promoting their own . . . '

To allow recovery in tort whenever negligent behaviour causes foreseeable economic loss would create serious puzzles for a market economy. Misleading and deceptive conduct, whether fraudulent or negligent, calls for special treatment. Fair trading is not consistent with such conduct, so that the continued operation of the market may require recovery of loss in such cases. But apart from losses caused by reliance on fraudulent or negligent statements, a reluctance to allow recovery in negligence for losses that are purely economic is to be expected. So the question becomes whether there are any kinds of foreseeable economic loss which can be recovered in negligence, and on what basis.

In considering the effect of Atiyah's paper on the attempts by the courts to deal with economic loss in negligence cases it is necessary to say something about the pre-*Hedley Byrne* cases on economic loss, about *Hedley Byrne* itself, and about the cases after *Hedley Byrne* to which Atiyah referred. The discussion then turns to cases in various categories of economic loss where the influence of Atiyah's paper can be seen, culminating in the House of Lords' decisions in *Anns* and *Junior Books*. The retreat from *Anns* is covered less fully—there is much

[13] [1990] 3 WLR 414 at 446.
[14] (1967) 83 LQR 248 at 269.
[15] [1970] AC 1004 at 1027.

less explicit reference to Atiyah's paper in the cases, for one thing. But the decision in *Murphy* v. *Brentwood DC* makes detailed consideration of the post-*Anns* cases unnecessary.

The Pre-*Hedley Byrne* Cases on Economic Loss

Atiyah gave detailed consideration to the pre-*Hedley Byrne* cases on economic loss, including *Cattle* v. *Stockton Waterworkd Co.*[16] ('*Cattle*'), *Simpson* v. *Thompson*,[17] and *Morrison Steamship Co. Ltd.* v. *Greystoke Castle* ('*The Greystoke Castle*').[18] It is not necessary to cover that ground again.[19] It should be noted that the rule in *Cattle* was that a person who suffered economic or financial loss by reason of the negligence of another as a result of damage to or the destruction of property in which he had no proprietary or possessory interest, did not have a right of action.

In *Simpson* v. *Thompson*, most of the judgments in the House of Lords were based on issues relating to subrogation with which this paper is not concerned. Lord Penzance, however, was concerned to negative the proposition, put by counsel for the underwiters, that where a wrongdoer damaged a chattel, not only the owner but all those whose contracts with the owner were adversely affected could have a right of action against the wrongdoer. Although *Simpson* v. *Thompson* has not escaped criticism,[20] its authority has been consistently upheld in the courts.[21]

The Greystoke Castle, a case about general average contribution, was seen by some as marking a departure from the rule in *Cattle*, in that recovery of economic loss was allowed. The majority decision of the House of Lords was apparently based on the analysis that the cargo-owners and the shipowners were engaged in a common or joint adventure, so that acts involving general average expenditure were done on behalf of all.[22] The majority judgements all accepted the authority of *Simpson* v. *Thompson* but said that it did not apply to the case. The reasoning by which this result was arrived at is somewhat

[16] (1875) LR 10 QB 453.
[17] (1877) 3 AC 279.
[18] [1947] AC 265.
[19] Atiyah also referred to *La Société Anonyme de Remorquage à Helice* v. *Bennetts* [1911] 1 KB 243; *The Okehampton* [1913] P 54; *Elliott Steam Tug Co. Ltd.* v. *Shipping Controller* [1922] 1 KB 127; *Chargeurs Reunis Compagnie Française* v. *English & American Shipping Co.* (1921) 9 Ll. L.R. 464; *Best* v. *Samuel Fox & Co. Ltd.* [1952] AC 716; and cases concerning financial loss following personal injury.
[20] See e.g., P. S. James, 'The Fallacies of *Simpson* v. *Thompson*' (1971), 34 MLR 149.
[21] See e.g., *Candlewood Navigation Corporation Ltd.* v. *Mitsui OSK Lines Ltd.* [1986] AC 1, 17; *Leigh and Sillavan Ltd.* v. *Aliakmon Shipping Co. Ltd.* [1986] AC 785, 809; *Esso Petroleum Co. Ltd. v. Hall Russell & Co. Ltd.* [1989] AC 643, *per* Lord Goff at 665, Lord Jauncey at 676.
[22] [1947] AC 265, 280–1, 311.

obscure. As commentators, including Atiyah, have pointed out, there are significant difficulties in the application of the notion of joint venture and the result seems anomalous. Atiyah's suggestion that this case turns on doctrines peculiar to maritime law[23] was rejected in *Junior Books* by Lord Roskill.[24] However, in *Murphy* v. *Brentwood DC*[25] Lord Keith has now said that the case may be regarded as 'turning on specialities of maritime law concerned in the relationship of joint adventures at sea'. The case has not been accepted as authority against the rule in *Cattle* but rather as a particular instance of the recovery of pure economic loss.

Hedley Byrne & Co. Ltd. v. *Heller & Partners Ltd.*

As Atiyah pointed out, the judgments in *Hedley Byrne* paid little attention to the fact that the loss was purely economic. It will be recalled that the case concerned a claim in negligence against a bank for a credit-reference which would have succeeded but for the disclaimer of liability. The House of Lords overruled *Candler* v. *Crane Christmas & Co.*[26] and approved the dissenting judgment of Denning LJ in that case. In *Candler* v. *Crane Christmas & Co.* it has been argued that a duty of care only arose where there was a risk of physical damage to person or property. The majority agreed. Asquith LJ pointed out that *Donoghue* v. *Stevenson* had never been applied where the damage was not physical. Cohen LJ[27] quoted extensively and with approval from the judgement of Cardozo CJ in *Ultramares Corporation* v. *Touche*.[28] Denning LJ in his dissenting judgment had rejected the distinction between physical damage and financial loss, saying that once a duty of care exists, liability does not depend on the nature of the damage.[29] The House of Lords made virtually no attempt to reconcile its decision with the strong line of authority which applied the rule in *Cattle* v. *Stockton Waterworks Co.* This is not as surprising as it may now seem, having regard to the way the case was argued. Many of the cases which supported the rule were simply not cited. Counsel on both sides did refer to the *Greystoke Castle* and to American cases, including *Glanzer* v. *Shepherd*[30] and *Ultramares Corporation* v. *Touche*.[31]

[23] (1967) 83 LQR 248 at 254.
[24] [1983] 1 AC 520 at 540.
[25] [1990] 3 WLR 414 at 429.
[26] [1951] 2 KB 164.
[27] [1951] 2 KB 164, 202–7.
[28] (1931) 255 NY 170.
[29] [1951] 2 KB 164 at 179.
[30] (1922) 233 NY 236.
[31] (1931) 253 NY 369 also referred to were *International Products Co.* v. *Erie Railroad Co.* (1927) 244 NY 331; *Mulroy* v. *Wright* (1931) 240 NW 116; *Doyle* v. *Chatham & Phoenix National Bank* (1930) 253 NY 369; and *Edwards* v. *Lamb* (1899) NH 599.

In the paper referred to, Atiyah pointed out that little attention had been given to the impact of *Hedley Byrne* on the law relating to liability for pecuniary loss. He rejected the view that *Hedley Byrne* had abolished the distinction between physical injury and pecuniary loss. On the contrary, he appeared to favour the view that *Hedley Byrne* had not affected the general principle against recovery of pecuniary loss but merely illustrated an exceptional rule governing negligent misstatement about a financial matter. He went on to identify unsatisfactory and capricious features in the operation of the existing law and policy considerations which might bear on the development of the law. Atiyah demonstrated that economic-loss cases could no longer be satisfactorily dealt with by the simple application of the general rule against recovery, and indicated factors to be considered in deciding whether to apply the general rule in any particular case.

After *Hedley Byrne*

Following the decision in *Hedley Byrne* an attempt was made in *Weller & Co.* v. *Foot & Mouth Disease Research Institute*[32] (*'Weller's case'*) to argue that, since *Hedley Byrne*, physical injury or damage were not essential to found an action in negligence and that foreseeability of specific economic harm to specifically identified victims would suffice. It will be recalled that the plaintiff auctioneers sought to recover financial loss suffered from the closure of cattle-markets when foot-and-mouth disease virus escaped from the defendant's premises and infected cattle in the neighbourhood. Widgery J assumed that the loss was foreseeable and that the defendant's negligence caused the escape of the virus and thus the loss. Widgery J endeavoured to analyse the pre-*Hedley Byrne* cases in terms of a distinction between consequential loss and direct injury to person or property. He expressed the view that 'indirect' or 'consequential' or 'economic' damage had not been recovered because no duty of care had been owed to the plaintiff. On this analysis a duty of care would arise only where direct injury to person or property was foreseeable.[33] Thus Widgery J rejected the claim on the ground that the defendant Institute did not owe the plaintiff auctioneers a duty of care. Atiyah was critical of this conclusion,[34] suggesting that it was merely a semantic quibble to treat the question as dependent on the absence of a duty of care, rather than the distinction between physical damage and pecuniary loss. But it is

32 [1966] 1 QB 569.
33 [1966] 1 QB 569 at 587.
34 (1967) 83 LQR 248 at 259.

now well established that the key question is, in what circumstances will a defendant owe a duty of care to avoid financial loss to the plaintiff?

Widgery J's judgment in *Weller's case* was adopted by Roskill J in *Margarine Union GmbH* v. *Cambay Prince Steam Ship Co. Ltd.*,[35] a case of negligent damage to parcels of copra which the plaintiffs had contracted to purchase, where the plaintiffs did not own or have any possessory interest in the copra at the time of the negligent acts. The defendants successfully relied on the proposition that, before anyone can sue in tort for damage to goods he must prove that he had, at the time when the damage was suffered by the negligence complained of, either a proprietary or possessory interest. This decision has since been approved by the House of Lords in *Leigh & Sillavan Ltd.* v. *Alakmon Shipping Co. Ltd.*[36]

Economic Loss caused by Interference with the Supply of Water or Electricity to Businesses

Atiyah's paper had drawn attention to the Canadian decision in *Seaway Hotels Ltd.* v. *Cragg (Canada) Ltd.*,[37] a case of disruption to a business caused by the negligent cutting of an underground electricity feeder-line during construction works. The supply of electricity to the plaintiff's hotel was cut off. As a result, refrigerators and other equipment, air-conditioning, elevators, and some lights ceased to operate. Food spoiled and had to be thrown away. The dining-room and bars had to be closed, causing a loss of profits. There was some loss of rental of rooms. It was held that there had been actionable negligence towards the hotel on the basis that it was reasonably foreseeable that interference with the electric duct would cause damage to the persons who received the supply of electricity. As there was direct damage to its property, the plaintiff was entitled to recover all the damage resulting from the actionable wrong, even that part which arose solely by reason of interference with contractual relationships and would not be recoverable by itself under the rule in *Cattle*.

Following Atiyah's paper there was a series of disruption cases in which economic loss to businesses caused by interference with the supply of water or electricity was sought to be recovered: *Electrochrome Ltd.* v. *Welsh Plastics Ltd.*,[38] *British Celanese Ltd.* v. *A. H. Hunt (Capacitors) Ltd.*,[39] *SCM (United Kingdom) Ltd.* v. *W. J. Whittall & Son*

[35] [1969] 1 QB 219.
[36] [1986] AC 785.
[37] (1959) 21 DLR (2d) 264.
[38] [1968] 2 All ER 205.
[39] [1969] 1 WLR 959.

Ltd.,[40] *Spartan Steel & Alloys Ltd.* v. *Martin & Co. (Contractors) Ltd.*[41] The decisions in *Cattle*, *Simpson* v. *Thompson*, and *Weller's case* were applied by Geoffrey Lane J to reject a claim for economic loss in *Electrochrome Ltd.* v. *Welsh Plastics Ltd.*[42] The defendant's negligence caused the water supply on an industrial estate to be cut off. Because there was no water available to the plaintiff's factory, a day's production was lost. The loss was purely economic.

In the next reported English case after Atiyah's paper, *British Celanese Ltd.* v. *A. H. Hunt (Capacitors) Ltd.*,[43] the plaintiff was successful. The plaintiff's factory and the defendant's factory were on the same industrial estate. Metal-foil strips blown from the defendant's factory came into contact with bus bars at an electricity sub-station on the estate, causing a power-failure which brought the plaintiff's machines to a halt. As a result materials in some machines solidified and the machnies became clogged. The machines had to be cleaned before production could be started again. Materials and time were wasted and production lost. The plaintiff sued in *Rylands* v. *Fletcher*, in negligence, and in nuisance. Lawton J treated the case as one of physical injury to property with consequential loss of profits. He distinguished *Weller's case*[44] and *Electrochrome Ltd.* v. *Welsh Plastics Ltd.*[45] as cases where there was no foresight of injury to property and thus no duty of care. He referred to *Seaway Hotels Ltd.* v. *Cragg (Canada) Ltd.*[46] Although Lawton J did not refer to Atiyah's paper, it seems likely that it had influenced both the terms in which the issues were discussed and the outcome.

In *SCM (United Kingdom) Ltd.* v. *W. J. Whittall & Son Ltd.*[47] the defendant asserted as a general principle that foreseeable economic loss unaccompanied by injury to the person or damage to property did not give rise to a duty of care. Thus the general rule to which Atiyah had referred was apparently accepted (at least for the purposes of argument) by the profession. The defendant negligently cut a cable supplying electricity to a number of factories. The resultant power-failure caused current to be cut off for some hours. When the power was cut off SCM had molten metal in their machines which solidified. SCM's losses included the damage done to the machines and a day's production lost in consequence of that damage. The case was not, in fact, one of pure economic loss. The plaintiff had suffered physical damage to its machines and did not need to establish liability for pure

40 [1971] 1 QB 337.
41 [1973] 1 QB 27.
42 [1968] 2 All ER 205.
43 [1969] 1 WLR 959.
44 [1964] 1 QB 569.
45 [1968] 2 All ER 205.
46 (1959) 21 DLR (2d) 264.
47 [1971] 1 QB 337.

economic loss; and did not seek to do so.[48] Lord Denning MR was apparently keen to express his views on the general question. Winn LJ was also persuaded to make some observations going beyond what was needed to decide the appeal.[49]

Lord Denning was concerned to avoid a dichotomy between direct and indirect consequences relied on by counsel for the contractors, who based the argument on observations of Widgery J in *Weller's case*.[50] Atiyah, who was critical[51] of this part of Widgery J's judgment, had assumed that by 'direct' he meant physical, and by 'consequential' he meant pecuniary, although Atiyah pointed out that this was by no means clear. Atiyah also considered whether there was a valid distinction between direct and indirect pecuniary loss, pointing out that the distinction between direct and indirect consequences was generally thought to have been laid at rest by *The Wagon Mound*.[52] Lord Denning, in a passage which adopts Atiyah's argument (although his paper is not referred to), rejected the distinction between 'direct' and 'indirect'.[53]

Lord Denning characterized the issue about liability for economic loss as a question of remoteness rather than one of duty of care. He considered that it was plain that the defendant contractors owed a duty of care under *Donoghue* v. *Stevenson* to the factory-owners.[54] Lord Denning then turned to the question whether economic loss would be recoverable as well as the material damage, and took issue with Lord Devlin's remark in *Hedley Byrne* that he could find neither logic nor common sense in making a difference between them. In Lord Denning's view the basis of the rule in *Cattle* was that economic loss was regarded as too remote. Lord Denning was at pains to point out that economic loss was not *always* too remote, and that in some exceptional cases it was the immediate consequence of the negligence and thus recoverable. Examples given were *Hedley Byrne* and *The Greystoke Castle*. This approach left Lord Denning with the difficulty of providing a criterion for distinguishing between cases where economic loss was too remote and cases where it was recoverable. His solution (that the good sense of the judges would decide on a case-by-case basis)[55] was not entirely satisfactory.

[48] [1971] 1 QB 337 at 342.
[49] [1971] 1 QB 337 at 354.
[50] [1966] 1 QB 569 at 585.
[51] (1967) 83 LQR 248 at 262–3.
[52] [1961] AC 388.
[53] [1971] 1 QB 337 at 343.
[54] Ibid.
[55] [1971] 1 QB 337 at 346. Goodhart in a note on this case commented on Lord Denning's remarks about the good sense of judges: '. . . with the greatest respect, the fact that a judge has good sense does not explain the grounds on which he has based his decision.' (1971) 87 LQR 6, 10.

The question of liability for pure economic loss was again before the Court of Appeal in *Spartan Steel & Alloys Ltd.* v. *Martin & Co. (Contractors) Ltd.*[56] (*'Spartan Steel'*). Again the defendant contractor negligently caused an interruption in the supply of electricity to Spartan Steel's factory. When the power was shut off the plaintiff was operating an electrically powered furnace in which there was molten metal. Oxygen was used to keep the metal melted so that it could be poured from the furnace. The quality and thus the value of the metal was lowered (physical damage). Had that melt been completed as normal, the plaintiffs would have made a profit (economic loss due to the physical damage). Because they could not carry out more melts while the power was off, the plaintiffs lost further profits (pure economic loss). The plaintiffs claimed all three losses as damages. The defendants admitted negligence and liability for the physical damage, but denied liability for the economic loss. The plaintiffs relied on a doctrine of 'parasitic damages' by which damages not recoverable in themselves could be recovered if they could be attached to a claim for physical damage and were foreseeable. Atiyah had discussed 'parasitic' claims for financial loss[57] as an important exception to the general principle against recovery of economic loss. Although Atiyah was not the first to use this expression (which has been traced back to Street, *Foundations of Legal Liability*,[58] and which was discussed in terms by Harvey McGregor QC in his editions of *Mayne & McGregor on Damages*, beginning with the Twelfth Edition),[59] it does appear that Atiyah's article gave the term wider currency. The plaintiffs also argued for the wider proposition that pure economic loss was recoverable provided it was foreseeable.

Lord Denning MR, in characteristically forceful words, rejected the doctrine of 'parasitic damages':

> I do not like this doctrine of 'parasitic damages'. I do not like the very word 'parasitic'. A parasite is one who is a useless hanger-on sucking the substance out of others. 'Parasitic' is the adjective derived from it. It is a term of abuse. It is an opprobrious epithet. The phrase 'parasitic damages' conveys to my mind the idea of damages which ought not in justice to be awarded, but which somehow or other have been allowed to get through by hanging on to others. If such be the concept underlying the doctrine, then the sooner it is got rid of the better. It has never been used in any case up till now. It has only appeared hitherto in the text books. I hope it will disappear from them after this case.
>
> I do not believe there is any such doctrine.[60]

[56] [1973] 1 QB 27.
[57] (1967) 83 LQR 248 at 252.
[58] New York 1906.
[59] (1961) see paras. 110, 111.
[60] [1973] 1 QB 27 at 35.

McGregor suggests that getting rid of the terminology may not dispose of the doctrine.[61] It is beyond the scope of this paper to pursue the matter further.

On the question of a general principle dealing with recovery of economic loss, Lord Denning abandoned the stand which he had taken in *SCM* v. *Whittall*[62] that liability for economic loss was a matter, not of duty of care but of remoteness of damage. He now said that in some of the cases liability had been denied on the absence of a duty of care, whereas in others economic loss had not been recovered because it was too remote. He suggested that the better approach was not in terms of duty of care or remoteness but rather to consider the particular relationship in hand and see whether, as a matter of policy, economic loss should be recoverable.[63] He proceeded to identify policy considerations, including, in particular, that it was not sensible to saddle the contractor with enormous potential economic losses which could follow.[64] Lord Denning's discussion would appear to have been influenced by Atiyah's paper. Applying these policy considerations, Lord Denning rejected the pure economic loss element in the plaintiff's claim.

Edmund Davies LJ would have allowed all the losses claimed. In a dissenting judgment that was clearly greatly affected by Atiyah's paper, to which he referred several times, he rejected the general rule against recovery of economic loss. Edmund Davies LJ could see no basis for drawing a distinction between economic loss occasioned by the first spoilt melt and the four melts which were lost, and concluded that an action lies in negligence for damages in respect of purely economic loss, provided that it was a reasonably foreseeable and direct consequence of failure in a duty of care. It was not necessary for him to deal with the topic of 'parasitic damages'. The third member of the Court of Appeal, Lawton LJ, after an analysis of *Cattle* and the subsequent cases which Goodhart described as masterly,[65] adhered to what he saw as the clear rule against recovery of economic loss. He thus arrived at the same result as Lord Denning. He was not prepared to allow additional damages based on 'the so-called concept of parasitic damages'.[66]

An analysis of this case suggests that there was a real difficulty in drawing a distinction between the loss of profit on the melt affected by the cutting-off electricity and the loss of profit on the melts which could not be done while the power supply remained cut off,

[61] *McGregor on Damages* (15th edn.) para. 213.
[62] [1971] 1 QB 337.
[63] [1973] 1 QB 27 at 37.
[64] Atiyah had made a similar point (1967) 83 LQR 248 at 270–4.
[65] (1973) 89 LQR 10, 13.
[66] [1973] 1 QB 27 at 49.

particularly if recourse to a distinction between direct and indirect consequences was not permissible. The majority judgments did not provide any satisfactory basis for distinguishing between the losses, so that the difficulties which Edmund Davies LJ identified and developed undermined the persuasive force of the decision.

The end position reached in these cases of interference with the supply of water or electricity was that the part of the plaintiffs' losses which was characterized as economic loss was not allowed. The rule in *Cattle* was applied as a general rule against economic loss.

Other Developments in the Law of Negligence

While the question of recovery of pure economic loss was before the courts in these cases the law of negligence was changing in other respects. In *Dorset Yacht Co.*,[67] the plaintiff established the validity of a claim for damage to the plaintiff's yacht done by Borstal boys who escaped from the control of prison officers. The common law had long been circumspect in imposing liability for failing to control others. But it was entirely foreseeable that escaping Borstal boys would damage the property of persons in the neighbourhood.

The House of Lords held (Viscount Dilhorne dissenting) that the Borstal officers owed the plaintiff a duty to take reasonable care to prevent the boys from causing damage to the plaintiff's property if that was likely to result from a neglect of that duty; and that public policy did not require that the Home Office be immune from such claims. In a passage which foreshadowed a general expansion in liability for negligence, Lord Reid said:

> In later years there has been a steady trend towards regarding the law of negligence as depending on principle so that when a new point emerges one should not ask whether it is covered by authority but whether recognised principles apply to it. *Donoghue* v. *Stevenson* (1932) AC 562 may be regarded as a milestone, and the well known passage in Lord Atkins' speech should I think be regarded as a statement of principle. It is not to be treated as if it were a statutory definition. It will require qualification in new circumstances. But I think the time has come when we can and should say that it ought to apply unless there is some justification or valid explanation for its exclusion. For example, causing economic loss is a different matter; for one thing it is often caused by deliberate action. Competition involves traders being entitled to damage their rival's interest by promoting their own, and there is a long chapter of the law determining in what circumstances owners of land can and in what circumstances they may not may use their proprietary rights so as to injure their neighbours. But where negligence is involved the tendency has

[67] [1970] AC 1004.

been to apply principles analogous to those stated by Lord Atkin. cf. *Hedley Byrne & Co. Ltd.* v. *Heller & Partners* [1964] AC 465.[68]

Dorset Yacht Co. was not simply an extension of the law of negligence in itself. It represented a trend in the law which continued and accelerated thereafter.

Economic Loss caused by Negligent Manufacture of a Chattel: *Rivtow Marine Ltd.* v. *Washington Iron Works*

Atiyah had suggested that there was no reason to deny an action for financial loss to a consumer who buys a negligently manufactured chattel even where no physical damage was caused by it.[69] The question of the recovery of economic loss caused by the negligent manufacture of chattels was considered by the Supreme Court of Canada in *Rivtow Marine Ltd.* v. *Washington Iron Works*[70] ('*Rivtow Marine*'). Washington Iron Works designed and manufactured cranes for loading and unloading heavy logs on a barge operated by Rivtow Marine. Due to their negligence cracks appeared in the cranes such that they were in danger of collapsing. The barge was taken out of service and the cranes repaired. Rivtow Marine, who had purchased the cranes from a supplier, sued Washington Iron Works claiming negligent design, a failure to warn the plaintiff of the dangerous situation created by the error in design, which was or should have been known to Washington, and negligent statements. They sought to recover the cost of repairing the cranes and economic loss from loss of use of the cranes during repair.

The majority held that the manufacturer was not liable in negligence to Rivtow Marine Ltd. as the ultimate consumer, for the cost of repairing damage arising in the cranes themselves, nor for economic loss sustained from the repairs. But the economic loss caused by the necessity to carry out repairs during the busiest season, which could have been avoided by a warning of the defect, which would have permitted repair during the slack season, was recoverable. The manufacturer and the distributor had a duty to warn users of the necessity for repairs as soon as they became aware of the defects and the dangers. The duty to warn was founded on observations of Lord Thankerton in *Donoghue* v. *Stevenson*[71] concerning articles known by the manufacturer to be dangerous.

[68] [1970] AC 1004 at 1026–7.
[69] (1967) 83 LQR 248 at 276.
[70] (1973) 40 DLR (3d) 530.
[71] [1932] AC 562 at 602.

Laskin J dissented in part. He would have allowed the cost of repairs to the defective crane, as the repairs were to avoid the foreseeable threat of physical harm to the plaintiff. The case was not one where a manufactured product proved to fall short of promised expectations, but was one of a defect creating foreseeable risk of physical harm and economic loss to avoid such harm. The cost of repair could also be recovered on the basis of mitigation of damages.

Negligent Interference with Transportation: *Caltex Oil (Australia) Pty. Ltd.* v. *The Dredge 'Willemstad'*

The uncertainty concerning the general rule against recovery in negligence for pure economic loss, which had been generated by Atiyah's paper, had not been resolved when the question came before the High Court of Australia in *Caltex Oil (Australia) Pty. Ltd.* v. *The Dredge 'Willemstad'*.[72] The dredge had negligently fractured an oil pipeline in Botany Bay, which connected an oil refinery on the southern shore with the Caltex oil terminal on the northern shore. The oil refinery and the pipeline were owned by Australian Oil Refinery Pty. Ltd. ('AOR'). Caltex supplied crude oil to AOR for processing at the refinery and the refined product was delivered to Caltex either into a vessel at the AOR wharf or through the pipeline to the Caltex terminal. It was agreed that Caltex had suffered loss by having to provid alternative transport arrangements. Judgment was given at trial for the defendant on the ground that the damages suffered by Caltex were confined to economic loss and could not be recovered. Caltex appealed. The High Court held that Caltex was entitled to recover the loss as damages for negligence. All members of the court treated the case as turning on the question whether a person was entitled to recover economic loss sustained by damage negligently caused to the property of another. The influence of Atiyah's paper on the judgments is apparent.

There was general agreement among the judges that the issue of liability for economic loss could not be determined by simply applying the rule in *Cattle* against recovery. Nor were the approaches of the members of the Court of Apeal in *Spartan Steel* satisfactory. To varying degrees it was accepted, while acknowledging the reluctance of the common law to allow recovery in negligence of pure economic loss, that, in some exceptional cases, economic loss could be recovered. The

[72] (1975–6) 136 CLR 529. Smith in 1984 described the case as 'probably the most thorough canvassing in recent years of the issues raised by pure economic loss', J. C. Smith, *Liability in Negligence* (London, 1984), 52.

fact that the loss was foreseeable was not enough to make it recoverable. There was a clear desire to avoid liability in an indeterminate amount to an indeterminate class. Gibbs CJ and Mason J required a duty of care based on the particular relationship between the dredge and Caltex in which foreseeability of financial loss to the plaintiff as a specific individual was significant. Stephen J formulated his test in terms of proximity, a test which Mason J said was not satisfactory. Jacobs J adopted a novel approach in terms of immobilization of property based on a persuasive analysis of the authorities; but his approach has not been taken up in later cases.

Although *Caltex* accepted that the general rule against recovery of economic loss in negligence was not of universal application, and stands as an instance of the recovery of economic loss, it has not led to any widespread relaxation of the rule. Satisfactory principles by which to govern the question of the extent to which recovery of economic loss should be allowed have yet to be developed.

Liability in Negligence for Defective Buildings: *Dutton, Anns,* and beyond

There are now many cases in the law reports about liability in negligence for defective buildings. Because building is usually controlled by local-government authorities (who approve plans and specifications, carry out inspections during construction, and grant certificates of occupancy on completion) which have deep pockets when compared to builders, it has been sought in many cases to make the local authority liable when a building proves to be defective.

Such cases have involved the question whether defects in the construction of a building should be regarded as physical damage or as economic loss. That question was first raised in *Dutton* v. *Bognor Regis UDC*[73] ('*Dutton*'), which held that a local authority was liable to the owner of a house which developed structural defects due to inadequate foundations. The foundations had been inspected and approved by the building inspector but were unsound because they were built on the site of an old rubbish tip, as would have been detected but for the negligence of the inspector. The case is significant as the first in a line of cases making local authorities liable in negligence to building-owners for defects in buildings, which culminated in *Anns* v. *Merton*

[73] [1972] 1 QB 373. Space will not permit a full discussion of this case, which Atiyah has described as 'one of the most adventurous judgments given even by Lord Denning': in J. L. Jowell and J. P. McAuslan (eds.), *Lord Denning: The Judge and The Law* (London, 1984), 59.

London Borough Council.[74] But that trend has now been reversed. On the law as it now is, the Council would not be liable. In *Murphy* v. *Brentwood DC*[75] the House of Lords has now overruled *Dutton*.

In *Anns* v. *Merton London Borough Council* ('*Anns*'), the House of Lords held that a local authority could be liable for failing to carry out a proper inspection of the foundations of a block of flats to subsequent owners, for damage suffered when the foundations failed. The foundations had allegedly been constructed to a shallower depth than that approved by the local authority. The passage cited above from Lord Reid's speech in *Dorset Yacht Co.*[76] was applied, and the result in *Dutton* was said to be correct. Lord Wilberforce in the leading judgment appeared to base liability in negligence primarily on foreseeability of harm. In a passage which was to be cited many times he said:

> Though the trilogy of cases in this House—*Donoghue* v. *Stevenson* (supra), *Hedley Byrne & Co. Ltd.* v. *Heller & Partners Ltd.* (supra) and *Dorset Yacht Co. Ltd.* v. *Home Office* (supra), the position has now been reached that in order to establish that a duty of care arises in a particular situation, it is not necessary to bring the facts of that situation within those of previous situations in which a duty of care has been held to exist. Rather the question has to be approached in two stages. *First* one has to ask whether, as between the alleged wrongdoer and the person who has suffered damage there is a sufficient relationship of proximity or neighbourhood such that, in the reasonable contemplation of the former, carelessness on his part may be likely to cause damage to the latter—in which case a prima facie duty of care arises. *Secondly*, if the first question is answered affirmatively, it is necessary to consider whether there are any considerations which ought to negative, or to reduce or limit the scope of the duty or the class of person to whom it is owed or the damages to which a breach of it may give rise: see *Dorset Yacht* case (supra), per Lord Reid at p. 1027. Examples of this are *Hedley Byrne's* case (supra) where the class of potential plaintiffs was reduced to those shown to have relied upon the correctness of statements made, and *Weller & Co.* v. *Foot and Mouth Disease Research Institute* [1966] 1 QB 569; and (I cite these merely as illustrations, without discussion) cases about 'economic loss' where, a duty having been held to exist, the nature of the recoverable damages was limited: see *SCM (United Kingdom) Ltd.* v. *W. J. Whittall & Son Ltd.* (supra) and *Spartan Steel & Alloys Ltd.* v. *Martin & Co. (Contractors)* (supra).[77]

On this approach a prima facie duty of care would arise whenever it should reasonably have been contemplated that carelessness might

[74] [1978] AC 728.
[75] [1990] 3 WLR 414.
[76] [1970] AC 1004 at 1026–7. See p. 320 above.
[77] [1978] AC 728 at 751.

cause damage to another.[78] That prima facie duty of care could be negatived or limited in scope by policy considerations, but unless negatived would apply.

The damage to the house was said not to be economic loss but material, physical damage, such that expenditure necessary to restore the dwelling to a safe condition was recoverable on 'normal principle'.[79] Lord Wilberforce said[80] that on the question of damages he had derived much assistance from the dissenting judgment of Laskin J in *Rivtow Marine*,[81] which he described as being 'of strong persuasive force', and from the New Zealand case *Bowen* v. *Paramount Builders (Hamilton) Ltd. and McKay*,[82] but did not explain how this assistance had been derived.[83] The cause of action arose only when the state of the building was such that there was present an imminent danger to the health or safety of persons.[84]

Anns represented a fundamental shift in the law of negligence. The control exercised through the concept of duty of care had been significantly loosened. Now, whenever there was foreseeability of harm of any kind there would arise a prima facie duty of care with the onus effectively on the defencant to establish policy reasons why that prima facie duty should not result in liability. Atiyah's paper had not anticipated this development, and after *Anns* there was less reference in the cases to his analysis. *Anns* was immediately criticized for the excessive burden it placed on local authorities[85] and for the perfunctory nature of the discussion of the wider substantive issues involved.[86] *Anns* was, however, soon applied by the Court of Appeal in *Batty* v. *Metropolitan Property Realisations Ltd*,[87] where a developer and a builder were held liable in negligence to the purchaser of a house doomed to destruction by land-slip and thus unsaleable, for failure to carry out satisfactory investigations of the subsoil.

It soon became apparent that the approach adopted by Lord Wilberforce in *Anns* could be applied to greatly expand the scope of liability in negligence. The prima facie duty test had an inherent tendency to suggest that in justice the plaintiff should recover. This tendency was accentuated by the House of Lords continued

[78] There is a striking similarity between Lord Wilberforce's concept of prima facie duty of care and the ethical theory of prima facie duty developed by Sir David Ross in *The Right and The Good* (Oxford, 1930), 19 ff.

[79] [1978] AC 728 at 759.

[80] [1978] AC 728 at 760.

[81] (1973) 40 DLR (3d) 530.

[82] [1975] 2 NZLR 546 (space does not permit more extensive reference to this decision).

[83] [1978] AC 728 at 760.

[84] [1978] AC 728 at 760.

[85] Buxton (1978) 41 MLR 85.

[86] Wallace (1978) 94 LQR 60.

[87] [1978] QB 554.

disparagement of the floodgates argument, as, for example, in *McLoughlin* v. *O'Brian*.[88] The expansion led to some surprising results.[89]

Atiyah's Later Comments

In his 1979 Cambridge Lecture, 'Recent Judicial Developments in Private Law',[90] Atiyah took as his theme the gradual disintegration of the dividing-line between the traditional categories of tort and contract. His analysis was in terms of ideas developed in his then forthcoming book, *The Rise and Fall of Freedom of Contract*—the declining importance of consent and of protection of pure expectations in contract, and the increased protection accorded to reliance and to recompense for benefit. He also discussed cases showing the expansion of liability for omissions and then turned to recent cases concerning the recovery of damages for purely economic loss.

I turn finally to say something about the recent cases concerning the recovery of damages for purely economic loss. Here too there is a disintegration, or at least a blurring, or the dividing line between contract and tort. There has, after all, been nothing unusual about awarding damages for purely economic loss in contract. Indeed, this is the usual form of loss in contractual actions. But as is well known, in cases traditionally classified as tort, there has been felt to be more difficulty in obtaining damages for purely economic losses, though the difficulty has never extended to cases in which the pecuniary losses depend upon and follow some physical damage or injury.

The *Hedley Byrne* case provided the first major breakthrough on this point, for the decision in that case necessarily meant that there are at least some cases in which damages for purely pecuniary losses can be recovered in tort. But the problem of setting limits to the kind of case in which this is permissible was not, I think, very clearly perceived in the *Hedley Byrne* case. And since that decision the courts, both in England and the Commonwealth, have been gradually groping their way towards some principles to govern this difficult question.

Having noted the rapid growth in liability for negligent misstatements he turned to the problem of negligent acts which cause physical damage to one person and pecuniary loss to another. Although in England *Spartan Steel* was generally taken to deny liability for pecuniary loss in such cases, he noted the result in *Caltex*, suggesting that the spectre of unlimited liability to an unlimited number of

[88] [1983] 1 AC 410.
[89] [1983] QB 260. See e.g., *Acrecrest Ltd.* v. *W. S. Hattrell & Partners* [1983] QB 260 and *Dennis* v. *Charnwood Borough Council* [1983] QB 409.
[90] Toronto, 1981.

persons seems to loom very large. He repeated the argument against liability for economic loss based on loss distribution which he had put in his 1967 paper.[91]

He suggested that the most difficult questions of all were perhaps those arising from the negligence of a manufacturer or builder. Although approving of *Anns* and *Batty* from the point of view of improving consumer rights, he expressed difficulty with the argument that the loss in those cases was really physical and not pecuniary.

> Here again, the decision seems to cut right across traditional lines between contract and tort. For, it is plain enough, the plaintiff surely would have had no cause for complaint if he had bought the building with full knowledge of the defects, and paid a price which fairly reflected the value of the building as it stood. Thus, the plaintiff's right to sue the builder seems to depend on the terms of his contract with the person from whom he purchased it. Moreover, as pointed out by Lord Wilberforce in the *Anns* case there is the awkward possibility of subsequent buyers also suing the builder for the same negligence if they too buy in ignorance of the defects, the first buyer having pocketed the damages and failed to perform the repairs.

With regard to chattels, he said we were still at the experimental stage. *Rivtow Marine* was the leading decision, with the result that the law seemed to be on the brink of establishing different rules for buildings and for chattels. He concluded:

> But it is at least clear that the relationship between tort and contract will need to be defined anew in this field, as in so many of the others on which I have touched. Indeed, I am coming to hold the view that a total merger of contract, tort and restitution in a new law of obligations may not be far ahead. Certainly the case law of the last decade or so appears to be pointing in that direction.

The decision in *Junior Books* v. *Veitchi*[92] was to represent a striking endorsement of this view, even though the common law has since moved away from many implications of that decision.

Junior Books v. *Veitchi*

The question whether economic loss could be recovered in tort was before the House of Lords in *Junior Books Ltd.* v. *Veitchi Ltd.*[93] ('*Junior Books*'), where the continuing influence of Atiyah's 1967 paper may be seen from its citation in argument.[94] Specialist flooring-contractors had been engaged as nominated subcontractors by a builder to lay a floor in

[91] (1967) 83 LQR 248 at 272–3.
[92] [1983] 1 AC 520.
[93] [1983] 1 AC 520.
[94] [1983] 1 AC 520 at 530.

a factory. The building-owner sued the subcontractor in negligence alleging that the floor was defective. The building-owner claimed the estimated cost of re-laying the floor and associated financial loss such as the cost of moving stock and machinery, and loss of profits. It is noteworthy that the claim was for the negligently made floor itself and not for physical damage to property or to persons caused by the negligently made floor. There was no danger to the health or safety of any person nor to property. There was no statement or representation by the subcontractor nor reliance by the building-owner on any statement or representation. There was, however, obvious foreseeability of economic loss to the building-owner if the floor was defective.

The House of Lords (Lord Brandon dissenting) held that there was a duty in these circumstances to avoid foreseeable injury to the building-owner which extended to the economic losses consequent on the subcontractor's defective workmanship. The relationship between the parties was said to be sufficiently close to establish a duty of care which was not limited to a duty to avoid foreseeable harm to person or property and extended to a duty to avoid causing pure economic loss. The majority approach was greatly influenced by Lord Wilberforce's judgment in *Anns*, and in particular the passage set out above.[95] There was strong dissent from Lord Brandon, who saw the issue as being one as to the scope of the duty of care owed by the subcontractor. It was fundamental that the duty of care laid down in *Donoghue* v. *Stevenson* was based on the existence of a danger of physical injury to persons or their property. In the absence of any such allegation no cause of action was disclosed. He accepted that there could be claims in negligence in respect of pure pecuniary loss, such as a claim for negligent misstatement under *Hedley Byrne* or a claim for pecuniary loss reasonably incurred to prevent or mitigate inherent danger of damage to persson or property, such as that considered in the dissenting judgment of Laskin J in *Rivtow Marine*.

The decision has been described as 'the high point of recent judicial liberality in according liability for economic loss in England',[96] and was immediately subject to academic criticism.[97] It could well be said that the majority decision in *Junior Books* confirmed the trend which Atiyah had discerned in his 1979 paper. The decision could be described as one in which the limitations on recovery in contract presented by the

[95] See above, 324.
[96] I. N. Duncan Wallace, *Construction Contracts: Principles and Policies in Tort and Contract* (1986), para. 7.06.
[97] See e.g., J. G. Fleming, 'Comparative Law of Torts' (1984), 4 *OJLS* 235, 240–1. Atiyah expressed doubts about the wisdom of the decision in Jowell and McAulan, n. 73 above, 76.

doctrine of privity of contract were overcome by allowing recovery in negligence. The plaintiff could not have sued the subcontractor in contract because of the absence of privity. To permit recovery in tort achieved the same result in substance. The subcontractor was liable just as if for breach of contract.[98]

Reaction

Reaction soon set in. There has since 1985 been a strong move away from *Junior Books* and from *Anns*. It began in *Governors of the Peabody Donation Fund* v. *Sir Lindsay Parkinson & Co.*,[99] where Lord Keith sounded a note of caution about Lord Wilberforce's two tests in *Anns*. *Junior Books* has since been confined to the special proximate relationship between a building-owner and a nominated subcontractor and has been described as not laying down any principle of general application in the law of tort.[100] The relationship was sufficiently akin to contract to introduce the necessary element of reliance.[101] The dissenting speech of Lord Brandon has been approved as enunciating the principles applying in the general run of cases outside that relationship.[102]

The key decision in bringing about the change may be seen as that of the High Court of Australia in *Sutherland Shire Council* v. *Heyman*,[103] where all the judges of the court declined to follow *Anns*. It is not necessary to recite the facts of that case beyond noting that it was a claim by a subsequent purchaser of a house, which was damaged by reason of inadequate foundations, against the Shire Council for failing to ensure that adequate foundations were constructed. The claim was rejected by all the members of the court on the basis that, in the absence of reliance on it by the plaintiff, the Shire Council did not owe the plaintiff a duty of care. There was, however, no uniformity of approach to the question whether, in the case of defective construction of a building, the loss is to be characterized as physical damage or as economic loss.[104]

The reservations about Lord Wilberforce's two-stage test expressed

[98] See Fleming above where the decision is described as 'resorting to tort in order to correct perceived inadequacies of contract law'.

[99] [1985] AC 210.

[100] See *per* Lord Bridge *D & F Estates Ltd.* v. *Church Commissioners* [1989] AC 177 at 202.

[101] *Murphy* v. *Brentwood DC* [1990] 3 WLR 414 at 441.

[102] [1990] 3 WLR 414 at 441.

[103] (1985) 157 CLR 424.

[104] See 157 CLR 424 *per* Gibbs CJ at 446–7 *per* Brennan J at 493, *per* Deane J at 503–5. The reasoning of Deane J has since been described as incontrovertible by Lord Keith in *Murphy* v. *Brentwood DC* [1990] 3 WLR 414 at 428–9 where the passage is quoted in full.

by Lord Keith in the *Peabody Donation Fund* case[105] were echoed in other cases and by other members of the House of Lords. See *Ralph & Sillavan Ltd.* v. *Alakmon Shipping Co. Ltd.*,[106] *Curran* v. *Northern Ireland Co-Ownership Housing Association Ltd.*,[107] *Yuen Kun Yeu* v. *Attorney-General of Hong Kong*,[108] *Hill* v. *Chief Constable of West Yorkshire*,[109] and *Caparo Industries PLC* v. *Dickman*.[110]

Murphy v. *Brentwood DC*

The departure from *Anns* which seemed increasingly likely since 1985, has now been formally pronounced by the House of Lords in *Murphy* v. *Brentwood DC*.[111] The foundation raft of a dwelling-house failed. The owner carried out some repairs but could not afford the remedial work required and sold the house for less then half the value it would have had if free of defects. A claim under the principle in *Anns* against the local authority for negligence in approving the raft failed in the House of Lords. The House of Lords (accepting much of the analysis in *Sutherland Shire Council* v. *Heyman*) overruled *Dutton* and held that *Anns* was wrongly decided as regards the scope of any private law duty of care resting on local authorities in relation to their function in securing compliance with building regulations and should be departed from. On the same day as the decision in *Murphy* v. *Brentwood DC*, the House of Lords handed down their decision in *Department of the Environment* v. *Thomas Bates & Son Ltd.*,[112] another economic loss case concerning a defective building. *Murphy* v. *Brentwood DC* was applied and *Anns* again departed from.

The Law after *Murphy* v. *Brentwood DC*

The following propositions may be derived from *Murphy* v. *Brentwood DC*:

1. The rule in *Cattle* v. *Stockton Waterworks Co.*, that a third party cannot recover in tort for interference with his economic expectations or advantage resulting from injury to the person or property of another

105 [1985] AC 210.
106 [1986] AC 785 at 815 per Lord Brandon.
107 [1987] AC 718 per Lord Bridge.
108 [1988] AC 175.
109 [1989] AC 53.
110 [1990] 2 WLR 358.
111 [1990] 3 WLR 414.
112 [1990] 3 WLR 457.

with whom he has contractual relations, does not mean that a claim for damage that is purely economic is bound to fail. The critical question is not the nature of the damage but whether the duty of care extends in the circumstances to cover damage of the kind sustained, the nature of the damage being material to that question.

2. Pure economic loss unaccompanied by physical injury to person or property is not recoverable in tort in the absence of a special relationship of proximity.

3. A builder, in the absence of any contractual duty or of a special relationship of proximity, owes no duty of care in tort in respect of the quality of his work.

4. The builder of a defective building is in the same position as the manufacturer of a defective chattel.

5. On the principle of *Donoghue* v. *Stevenson*, a careless builder is liable where a latent defect results in physical injury to person or property; but is not liable in negligence for defects as such, nor for the cost of rectifying a defect which has become apparent before any injury or damage has been caused. The loss in such cases is purely economic and thus not recoverable in tort in the absence of a special relationship of proximity. To equate the damage sustained in repairing to make safe, with the damage which would have been suffered if a latent defect had never been discovered and had caused injury to person or property, is a fallacy.

6. A local authority in approving plans or inspecting buildings in course of construction to ensure compliance with building by-laws or regulations cannot be liable for a negligent failure to ensure compliance to an extent greater than the liability of the builder.

7. For a local authority to be liable at all in such cases, there would need to be a duty of care based on reliance as was explained in *Council of the Shire of Sutherland* v. *Heyman*; which requirement was not satisfied in the ordinary relationship of a local authority and the purchaser of a defective building.

Conclusion

As the cases considered in this paper show, the courts have contemplated, and in some cases allowed, departures from the general rule against recovery of pure economic loss referred to in Atiyah's paper. But in the end, the scope of the exceptions has been limited and the bright-line nature of the rule retained. The journey has been a fascinating one, as the judges have grappled with difficult issues.[113] The significance of Patrick Atiyah's ideas in the arguments and reasoning in the cases has been considerable. In the cases from *Spartan Steel & Alloys Ltd.* v. *Martin & Co. (Contractors) Ltd.* to *Junior Books* v. *Veitchi* there was repeated reference to Atiyah's ideas and to his 1967 paper. And the discussion since then has been conducted very much in terms of those ideas. At the same time, it must be said that the trend towards the breaking down of the distinction between tort and contract noted by Atiyah in 1979 seems, at least for the time being, to have been reversed.

What then does the future hold for economic loss? Has the expansion of tortious liability into this area which is predominantly the field of contract been permanently reversed or merely temporarily halted? It seems now to be the case that the rule against recovery of pure economic loss will in general be maintained. But the rule is not absolute, and it seems clear that in some negligence cases recovery will be permitted. Some progress has been made in establishing criteria for determining whether, in a given case, recovery will be allowed. Reliance is seen to play an increasingly important role. The confusion which for a time characterized the discussion was to a large measure caused by the departure from incremental development heralded in *Dorset Yacht Co. Ltd.* v. *Home Office* and established by *Anns*. The rejection of *Anns* by the High Court and by the House of Lords signals a return to a more cautious, traditional approach.[114]. Principles will still be required to guide that development. The attention now given by the courts to the concepts of expectation, reliance, and recompense for benefits received, which is in no small measure due to Atiyah's work, indicates a source for such principles. In his 1988 Cassel Lecture, Atiyah has suggested that non-consensual forms of liability can be legitimately developed so long as we do not tread on genuinely contractual ground.[115]. This suggestion could well serve as a guiding principle for future developments in the law regarding economic loss.

[113] See Markesinis 'Comparative Law—A subject in Search of an Audience' (1990) 53 *MLR* 1

[114] 157 CLR 424 at 481. *Caparo Industries PLC* v. *Dickman* [1990] 2 WLR 358 *per* Lord Bridge at 365, *per* Lord Oliver at 379.

[115] See n. 7 above, 32.

14

Libel and Constitutional Free Speech

JOHN FLEMING

Actions for defamation and invasion of privacy present a peculiar tension between a plaintiff's personality (dignitary) interests and the defendant's freedom of speech. These respective interests, especially the latter, are widely viewed as of constitutional significance, and often specifically protected by written constitutions. The purpose of this essay is to explore the effect this perception has on resolving the conflict between these interests: one the speaker's, the other that of the victim of speech. In particular, modern constitutional provisions guaranteeing freedom of speech and the press are apt to collide with traditional civil-law protection of individuals' reputation and honour, reflecting change from a value system of chivalry to one of democratic ideals. In several instances this clash has resulted in substantial modifications of the conventional private law.

Written Constitutions

The effect of constitutional guarantees of free speech on private law relations varies a good deal from one country to another. In some, like the US, such provisions can be directly invoked by defendants; in others, like France, a direct challenge to civil laws on constitutional grounds is greatly restricted and constitutional values are heeded interstitially. Again, some constitutional guarantees have been interpreted as addressed only to the legislator, inapplicable to private law relations, while others are given force *erga omnes*.

According to the liberal rationalist tradition of the eighteenth and nineteenth centuries, the function of constitutions was to protect the individual against state organs. Constitutional guarantees were expressed in terms of restrictions on state power, such as the US Bill of Rights command that 'Congress shall make no law . . . abridging the freedom of speech or of the press . . .' As a corollary of the contemporary concept of individual liberty, interpersonal relations remained immune to public imperatives. This limited view of the constitutional role is no longer universally accepted, with the result that constitutional guarantees are being increasingly applied to relations between individuals, such as those between a person defamed and the press. In German-speaking countries this construction is referred to as *Drittwirkung*, that is, third-party effect given to constitutional directives in their application to private law relations. This encroachment of public law into the sphere of private law, despite the traditional separation between the two in civilian systems, is supported by the recognition that in modern society the state shares power with other influential groups such as the press, trade unions, and large corporations, against which the individual stands in similar need of protection. Moreover, constitutional values should permeate the whole culture and influence the application and interpretation of law in general. Specifically addressed to the state, it binds the lawgiver as well as the courts to enforce the law in conformity with the constitutional directive.

A comparison between Canadian and American jurisprudence is illustrative of these different viewpoints. Shortly after enactment of the Canadian Charter of Rights and Freedoms in 1982, the Supreme Court of Canada was asked to invalidate a court injunction against unlawful secondary picketing. This it declined to do by construing the guarantee of freedom of expression as inhibiting only governmental action, not a court injunction based on common-law principles.[1] In addition to the fact that the Charter is in terms addressed to governmental action,[2] the Court was influenced by the liberal belief in preserving a private realm in which the individual did not have to submit to public virtues.[3] In so doing the Canadian court declined to follow the US model. For in the landmark, but admittedly controversial, case of *Shelley* v. *Kramer*[4] it had been held that an injunction enforcing a racial restrictive covenant

[1] *Retail, Wholesale and Department Store Union* v. *Dolphin Delivery* [1986] 2 SCR 573. Applied to defamation in *Pangilian* v. *Chaves* (1989) 54 Man. R. (2d) 163, 205 (burden of proof on justification).

[2] Section 32 expressly applies the Charter to governments.

[3] For an ensuing debate see R. Moon, *Process, Community, and the Canadian Charter of Rights* (1989) 39 *U. Tor. LJ* 410; P. Hogg, *The Dolphin Delivery Case* (1987) 51 *Sask. LR*.273. Generally: E. R. Alexander, *The Canadian Charter of Rights and Freedoms in the Supreme Court* (1989) 105 *LQR* 561. McIntyre J who delivered the principal opinion of the Court was a declared opponent of the Charter.

[4] (1948) 334 US 1.

between adjoining landowners was an unconstitutional exercise of state power. Government was implicated when the plaintiff invoked the coercive power of a state court contrary to the Equal Protection clause of the Fourteenth Amendment.

The Canadian court also held that the Charter did not apply to judicial application of rules of the common law (non-statute law)—again unlike the seminal decision of the US Supreme Court in *New York Times* v. *Sullivan*.[5] In that case it was held that the freedom-of-speech guarantee of the Bill of Rights applied to and modified the common law of Alabama by requiring proof of malice in an action by a public official against a newspaper. In contrast, Canadian constitutional law will have no direct bearing on the common law of defamation. While concerned with shielding private action from governmental interference, it creates an anomalous distinction between statutory and common-law rules. For it will be pure accident whether the challenged rule was or was not codified and therefore subject or immune to constitutional review.

In an important dictum, however, the Canadian court allowed that 'the judiciary ought to apply and develop the principles of the common law in a manner consistent with the fundamental values enshrined in the Constitution'.[6] Under this 'equity of the statute', courts, while not compelled, are *encouraged* to bring the common law into conformity. This approach provides a link to the highly developed German theory of direct and indirect (*unmittelbare, mittelbare*) *Drittwirkung*. Except where specifically authorized by the Constitution itself,[7] direct effect on private law relations is denied to it on principle, even when an incompatible rule of private law is being enforced by a court of law (that is, notwithstanding the contrary American view, courts are not regarded as organs of government for this purpose). On the other hand, constitutional values should permeate the whole society, and to this end enter private law through open-ended legal rules and concepts predicated on value judgments. An obvious breach-point is provided by the so-called 'general clauses', like *contra bonos mores*, appealing to contemporary public values, but also by many other rules susceptible to constitutionally inspired construction. This technique is particularly pertinent to non-contractual issues such as tort liability, representing public values much as does public law properly so-called; in contrast to contractual relations where private autonomy would justify a willingness to waive constitutional protection.[8] In extreme cases it justifies

[5] (1963) 376 US 254.

[6] [1968] 2 SCR 573, 603.

[7] As by GG Art. 9 III, sent. 2.

[8] This policy was first outlined in the 'Lüth case': BVerfGE 7, 198 (1958). See generally Maunz/Dürig/Herzog, *Grundgesetz (Kommentar)*, Art. 1 Abs III 127–133; Münch, *Grundgesetz-Kommentar*, 36–40.

even the recognition of new rights, such as a right to non-pecuniary damages for violation of privacy. In the upshot, the implementation of the constitutional right to freedom of expression and artistic freedom upon private relations has become a matter of course.[9]

Other countries, notably Italy,[10] treat the constitutional guarantee of free speech as directly applicable to interpersonal relations; both as a source for the protection of reputation and privacy, as well as a limitation in the interest of freedom of expression on claims for defamation and invasion of privacy.

Finally, the European Convention on Human Rights allows complaints against a Contracting Party for any violation within its responsibility, including injunctive orders of a court for defamation between private parties.[11] Britain has been censured repeatedly for violations of the Convention, though not hitherto for her defamation rulings. Most signatories, moreover, have incorporated this super-Constitution into their domestic law. For Austria this has led to spectacular modifications of her old-fashioned civil and penal code provisions, transfusing an authoritarian regime with democratic values.[12]

American and German Practice Compared

The United States and Germany have accumulated by far the richest experience of direct constitutional review in this sphere. While both countries subscribe to the same democratic values and therefore not surprisingly have reached rather similar resolutions of the tension between freedom of expression and the protection of personality, several distinctive features characterize their respective approaches.[13] These differences, as will be seen, are only marginally related to the fact that the one belongs to the common-law, the other to the civil-law family.

GENERAL DIFFERENCES

The first difference lies in the formulation of the constitutional guarantee of freedom of expression. The US Bill of Rights (First Amendment) prohibits 'abridging the freedom of speech or of the press' in unqualified terms. Neither it nor any other provision of the Constitution contains any express countervailing protection for individual dignity or personality. A fragile right to privacy has lately been discerned in the

[9] The German model is also followed in Austria and Switzerland.
[10] Followed in Argentina and Brazil.
[11] Art. 25. E.g. *Lingens* v. *Austria* (1986) 8 EHRR 407 (freedom of expression).
[12] In the aftermath of *Lingens* v. *Austria* (above).
[13] See also E. Barendt, *Freedom of Speech* (Oxford, 1985), ch. 6.

'penumbra derived from emanations of the Bill of Rights', but only as a vehicle for the controversial toleration of contraceptives and abortion, not as a counterfoil for freedom of speech. The seemingly unqualified formulation of that right has indeed supported the contention, vigorously advocated by two former justices of the Supreme Court (Black and Douglas JJ), that it is as absolute as it is expressed to be—without any qualification whatever and therefore overriding all other competing non-constitutional values such as the right to reputation and privacy. This has however remained a minority view.

By contrast, the German guarantee is specifically subject to restrictions (*Schranken*) found 'in the rules of general laws, legal regulations for the protection of youth and in the right to personal honour'. The last qualification is all the more significant because the right to personal honour is itself raised to constitutional status by another article of the Basic Law. What it postulates, therefore, is a balancing between competing constitutional values in which, at least on the face of it, each is entitled to equal weight. One might therefore be justified in expecting that German law would, at the margin, be more solicitous than American law in protecting personal reputation, honour, and privacy.

What is meant by 'general laws'? To allow ordinary rules of civil law without qualification to limit freedom of expression would stultify the constitutional guarantee. Rather, the judge must determine whether the particular rule of positive law is itself consonant with constitutional values. Before being given weight, it must be evaluated and construed in a sense sympathetic to freedom of expression (so-called *Wechselwirkung* or reciprocal effect). In short, the restriction is itself restricted. If the rule is designed to inhibit that freedom, it must be disregarded; if its purpose is to vindicate other significant values, like national security or the duty of loyalty and confidentiality of public servants, it deserves to be weighed in the balance in a spirit supportive of freedom of expression. Only very exceptionally would a law designed specifically to restrain freedom of expression qualify, as did the law prohibiting Nazi propaganda.[14]

A second difference between the German and American approaches is that German courts weigh the competing interests in an *ad hoc* manner, not abstractly but 'concretely', balancing for each case the gravity of the injury to the plaintiff's reputation or honour against the value or importance of the particular speech. By contrast, the American preference has been for categories, such as requiring proof of malice in all actions by public officials and public figures. Otherwise expressed, the balancing is reflected in general rules rather than required in relation to each individual case. This 'definitional' balancing, a pronounced

[14] The Lüth case', n. 8 above.

feature in general of American constitutional law, has been commended on two grounds.[15] First, it promotes predictability of decisions or at any rate facilitates the task of judging, particularly in an area where that task is shared with juries. This betrays a sensitivity to legal process, more pronounced perhaps in the common law than the civil law. Secondly, whether intended or not, this approach gives less emphasis to the particular harm the plaintiff happens to suffer and correspondingly greater support to free speech. This supposition is arguably borne out by comparison with certain German cases, such as *Mephisto* and *Böll* (below), in which the decision went for the plaintiff because of pronounced solicitude for the gravity of his injury.

UNITED STATES

Until 1964 defamation was not considered 'speech' at all within the prohibition of the Bill of Rights. Besides, until shortly before, that prohibition had been interpreted as applying only to Congress, not also to state laws, which are almost exclusively the *sedes legis* of defamation. It was the civil-rights struggle in the South that provided the occasion for the eventual intervention of the US Supreme Court in the celebrated case of *New York Times* v. *Sullivan*.[16] The New York Times had published an advertisement in support of the civil-rights movement, describing an incident of police abuse in Montgomery, Alabama, which contained trivial errors. The Police Chief, who had not been named personally, sued for libel and recovered an award of $500,000, which was upheld by the Supreme Court of Alabama. The occasion was politically charged, both in the sense that the article criticized an arm of government and that the Southern racist establishment was seen as employing state libel law in order to retaliate against the national press for publicizing racial suppression. The US Supreme Court unanimously allowed the appeal, implicitly affirming that the (federal) Bill of Rights reached to judicial orders enforcing the libel law of a state in 'private' litigation. The court held that a public official could not succeed in an action for libel without proving that the defendant was actuated by 'actual malice', that is, knowing that what he was saying was false or in reckless disregard of the truth.[17] Moreover, in addition to falsity, the plaintiff had to prove such malice with 'convincing clarity', a standard deliberately higher than the usual civil standard of proof on a balance of probability.[18] It thus overrode the

[15] M. Nimmer, 'The Right to Speak from *Times* to *Time*' (1968) 56 *Cal. LR* 935.
[16] (1964) 376 US 254.
[17] Mere failure to verify a report does not necessarily suffice. 'The defendant [must] in fact have entertained serious doubt as to the truth of his publication': *St. Amant* v. *Thompson*, (1968) 390 US 727, 731.
[18] Later decisions added that such findings were subject to searching appellate review.

prevailing common law in two respects, since the common law had required the defendant to prove truth and imposed strict liability without fault. True, there was no social value in a defamatory falsehood, but free speech would be unduly chilled if one honestly speaking about the conduct of a public official risked liability unless able to prove the truth. Public officials had the less reason to complain because they sought the public limelight and had superior access to the media for self-vindication compared with ordinary members of the public. Finally, commentary on the conduct of public officials peculiarly touches the public interest in a democratic society. Only knowingly uttering a defamatory falsehood could not be so justified.

The next step was to extend the malice rule to all 'public figures'.[19] These include both 'an individual [who] may achieve such pervasive fame or notoriety that he becomes a public figure in all contexts' and 'an individual [who] voluntarily injects himself or is drawn into a particular public controversy and thereby becomes a public figure for a limited range of issues'.[20] But later cases have made it clear that such a public character may not be lightly attributed, as, for example, to a merely locally well-known socialite or lawyer.

Next, the court extended the 'logic' of these categories to include the discussion of 'all matters of general public interest', including the conduct of a private individual, like a small smut-peddler involuntarily caught in a police raid.[21] This had the merit of shifting the focus to the matter discussed rather than the identity of the plaintiff, even if it opened the door more widely. But fissures in the Supreme Court were becoming apparent. On one extreme were the two justices, previously mentioned, who espoused the extreme view that no sanctions whatever were justifiable against defamatory falsehoods; on the other side was a group who thought that a constitutional standard was justified only for public officials or, at least, that a less stringent standard should apply to other matters of public concern. This moderate stance finally triumphed in the important case of *Gertz* v. *Welsh*,[22] which confined the *New York Times* standard of malice to public officials and public figures.

The court broke new ground, however, by extending the constitutional reach to private matters in other ways. For the first time it declared that states could not impose liability for defamation in general in the absence of 'fault', nor award damages for other than actual injury in the absence of 'malice'. The first reform corrected a source of widespread criticism of the traditional law, and most states

[19] *Curtis* v. *Butts, Associated Press* v. *Walker*, (1967) 388 US 130.
[20] *Gertz* v. *Welch*, (1974) 418 US 323, 351–2.
[21] *Rosenbloom* v. *Metromedia*, (1971) 403 US 29.
[22] (1974) 472 US 323.

have implemented the new constitutional rule by requiring proof of negligence, though some now postulate malice just as for actions by public figures. The second reform finally addressed the concern over the high level of damage-awards whose chilling effect on free speech had motivated the constitutional intervention from the start. The solution was to confine recovery to 'actual' damage (out-of-pocket losses as well as proven injury to reputation), eliminating 'presumed injury' which had allowed juries a free hand in awarding damages regardless of proof of injury. Banned also were punitive damages (again, in the absence of actual malice).

This multi-faceted decision was difficult to justify on principled grounds of constitutional theory. For how to reconcile the retreat from freedom of speech on matters of general public interest with constitutional concern in purely private defamation? As is not untypical of US Supreme Court jurisprudence, this pot-pourri represented compromises between different factions on the court in order to achieve a fragile majority sufficient for the occasion.

Gertz called for clarification in several respects. The most urgent was, were constitutional standards applicable at all to suits by private plaintiffs against other than media defendants? This issue came for decision in *Dun & Bradstreet* v. *Greenmoss Bros.*,[23] involving a false credit report. The court rejected any distinction between different types of defendant, but upheld the plaintiff's judgment on the ground that *Gertz*—at least in so far as it dealt with presumed injury and punitive damages—applies only to 'speech involving . . . matters of public concern'. The same qualification was applied in the next decision, which placed the burden of proving falsity on the plaintiff, contrary to the common-law rule,[24] and it will presumably be applied also to the requirement of 'fault'.[25] The withdrawal of constitutional involvement from the area of non-public concern lends some cohesion to the court's jurisprudence.

Finally, a dictum in *Gertz* by Powell J stridently proclaimed: 'Under the First Amendment there is no such thing as a false idea. However pernicious an opinion may seem, we depend for its correction not on the conscience of judges and juries but on the competition of other ideas.'[26] For some time this declaration was understood to create an absolute immunity for defamatory opinion and courts wrestled with how to distinguish opinion from factual allegations.[27] Recently,

[23] (1985) 472 US 749.
[24] *Philadelphia Newspapers* v. *Hepps*, (1986) 475 US 767.
[25] *Milkovich* v. *Lorain Journal Co.*, (1990) 110 S. Ct. 2695 at 2707 (Rehnquist CJ).
[26] (1974) 418 US 323, 339–40.
[27] See e.g. *Ollman* v. *Evans*, (1984) 750 F.2d 970 (D. C. Cir. *en banc*).

however, the Supreme Court resiled from this interpretation by holding that the dividing-line was not between fact and opinion, but between what can and what cannot be proven false. Ideas cannot, but an opinion may either be based on false facts or imply a knowledge of facts which are false.[28] This decision reverts to the traditional limits of the defence of 'fair comment', that is, comment or opinion based on true facts.

Perhaps the most drastic and controversial assertion of free speech was the decision to invalidate a (rare) state law requiring a newspaper to publish a reply by a person attacked in its columns.[29] In the court's view, this was an impermissible interference with the editorial function of what to publish, as much as telling what not to publish. Prior restraint has long been regarded as the most odious form of press censorship, totally impermissible even to interdict defamatory publications and condoned only for the protection of national security.[30] While a right of reply is generally unknown to the common law, it is widely available in civil-law countries and, like an order for retraction, regarded as a far less severe sanction than damages or fines.[31] Much more common is the *right* of retraction as a defence to liability, but this, being voluntary, raises no constitutional concern.

GERMANY[32]

As previously explained, the German Constitution requires essentially a balancing between two constitutionally protected interests: freedom of opinion and personal honour. It may arise in the context of criminal prosecutions, civil actions for damages (though these are much rarer outside Anglo-American communities), or demands for reply to offensive allegations. But notwithstanding the counterweight of the double protection of personal honour by the civil and constitutional law, doubts have been expressed whether, beyond false allegations of fact and misquotes, personal honour receives much protection at all today. Suggestive of the disparity of the two weights is at least a commonly voiced presumption in favour of free speech. These misgivings are exaggerated, as will appear especially in comparison with the US.

As frequently reiterated, the balancing process, dismissively called

[28] *Milkovich* v. *Lorain Journal*, n. 25 above.

[29] *Miami Herald* v. *Tornillo*, (1974) 418 US 241.

[30] See *New York Times* v. *U. S.*, (1971) 403 US 713 (*The Pentagon Papers* case).

[31] See Danziger, *The Right of Reply in the United States and Europe*, (1986) 19 *NYUJ Int L & Pol* 171, advocating an optional right of reply rather than one obligatory on the press. Neither in France nor Germany is the right frequently exercised.

[32] See esp. P. Tettinger, 'Der Schutz der Persönlichen Ehre im Freien Meinungskampf' (1983) 38 *JZ* 317.

the 'see-saw' (*Schaukel*) theory, has to focus concretely on the particular facts of each case. In order to avoid declining into arbitrary, *ex aequo et bono* adjudication, certain criteria have gradually emerged to help systematize the process. This development goes some way towards meeting the greater predictability of the US-style 'definitional' balancing, while retaining a measure of flexibility lacking in the American model. The following value-factors are influential:

1. Depth of intrusion into the sphere of the complainant's personality. This has an analogue in the American law of privacy,[33] but not of defamation. A distinction is drawn between a person's external honour, his reputation, and internal honour, his self-respect and sense of dignity. The latter, which is the specific object of protection under Article 1 of the Constitution, is excluded altogether from the balancing process. Examples are deliberate insults or vituperation, though one has to exhibit some fortitude in the light of today's level of public invective.[34]
2. Truth of factual allegations. The distinction between factual allegations and expressions of opinion is central. Only *Meinungsfreiheit* (freedom of thought) is protected. Because there is no social value in the propagation of untruths, repetition of false facts will be enjoined[35] without any need for balancing between the personality interests of the plaintiff and the defendant's freedom of thought. Misquotations were treated in the same way in the *Böll* case, where the Nobel Prize-winning author was falsely accused of having referred to the state as a 'manure heap'.[36] On the other hand, expressions of opinion are at the heart of public debate. And as in the US, the courts have been sensitive to the need for latitude in classifying allegations as opinion (*Meinung*). Thus, the description 'right-wing hate paper' was held to be opinion, dispensing with proof that the accusation was deserved in fact.[37] Even an expression susceptible of being proved either right or wrong, if in the context it is meant and understood as the speaker's opinion, is to be treated as such.[38] On the same lines, if comment (as is commonly the case) is inseparably intermingled with factual elements but is dominant, constitutional protection covers the whole.[39] Anti-

[33] See e.g. *Kappelas & Kofman*, (1969) 1 Cal. 3d 20.

[34] See e.g. the *Soraya* case, 1965 NJW, 685 (BGH 1964); the *Fernsehansagerin* case, (1963) BGHZ 39, 124 (sexual insults of TV female announcer).

[35] And gives a right of correction under the law of the various *Länder*.

[36] (1980) BVerfGE 54, 108. Accord: *Masson* v. *Malcolm*, (1991) 59 U.S.L.W. 4726.

[37] (1976) BVerfGE 42, 143 (*Deutschland-Magazin*).

[38] (1982) BVerfGE 61, 1 ('The CDU is the NPD of Europe', spoken in the course of a political campaign).

[39] BVerfGE 61, 1 at 9.

cipating the US Supreme Court, the burden of proof has also been cast on the plaintiff if the defendant can invoke the constitutional protection.

Special attention has been given to press publications in the heat of a current controversy. In determining the requisite degree of care in checking accuracy, for the purpose of civil liability allowance is due to the critical role of the press in remaining abreast of an ongoing debate. In this sense, organs of the 'responsible' press occupy a privileged position. Sensational news by the tabloid ('rainbow') press cannot be so justified.

Singularly problematical was the famous *Mephisto* case involving a novel by Klaus Mann, originally published in 1934 during his emigration, which portrayed a German actor/director who treacherously collaborated with the Nazi regime to aid his career. The central figure bore a close resemblance to a real person whose adopted son sought to suppress a German publication of the book in the 1960s, a few years after the father's death. The publisher invoked the freedom-of-art guarantee of the Constitution, which significantly is not restricted, as is freedom of expression, by the right of personal honour. The claimant, however, protested violation of the guarantee of the deceased's personal *dignity*, which enjoys absolute supremacy in the constitutional value-system.[40] The division of opinion on the court turned on whether the work was to be viewed as a fictionalized biography or as a work of art in which resemblance to a real person was a coincidental irrelevance, a portrayal of a type rather than a person. The court being equally divided, the injunction of the *Bundesgerichtshof* prevailed,[41] although its duration was linked to the rapidly fading public memory of the deceased. One of the dissenting opinions specifically compared the US Supreme Court's '*grosszügige Rechtsprechung*', but while the problem of the *roman á clef* has been repeatedly before American courts, it has not been considered on constitutional grounds.

3. Public interest. An important factor favouring immunity is that the impugned matter is one of serious public interest. It recognizes the important role of public controversy in a pluralistic society on social issues, not limited to politics, as similarly reflected in US Supreme Court jurisprudence. Any participant in public debates must accept negative criticism of his person and life-style.

[40] This right under Art. 1, unlike the right of personality under Art. 2, survives death. Under American common law, actions for defamation and invasion of privacy also abate on death; there is no independent equivalent to the 'right of dignity', the 'internal' aspect of honour previously referred to.

[41] (1971) BVerfGE 30, 173.

Reminiscent of the American special position of 'public figures', artists and other seekers of publicity in the popular press must also put up with its negative aspects. In particular, it is not required that the facts on which any comment is based be contemporaneously set out. Spontaneity as well as over-stimulation by the media deserve allowance for harshness and exaggerations in the clash of opinion.

That the public interest may well transcend personal aspects in a controversy was early illustrated in the *Schmid/Spiegel* case, where a judge successfully appealed against a fine imposed on him for an allegedly excessive retort to a press attack on himself.[42] Although his retaliation against the *Spiegel* magazine may have been unjustifiably vituperative as a self-defence against the distortion of his own political past, the fact that the issue affected judicial integrity and ethics demanded additional tolerance in the public interest.

4. Self-defence. Expressly acknowledged as a mitigating factor is that the offending speech was provoked. It need not even be in immediate response to a personal attack; the mere fact that in a matter of opinion the plaintiff had given occasion for adverse comment is sufficient.
5. Remedy. An important aspect, finally, is the remedy. The severer the sanction sought by the plaintiff, the more rigorous the demands on the constitutionality of the speech. Thus there is a clear distinction between ordering a retraction and an injunction: the former requires the speaker to withdraw his opinion, the latter, as also the right of reply, only looks to the future, leaving his opinion untouched. Non-pecuniary damages for violation of honour represent the strongest sanction, which can only be justified for grave fault or substantial prejudice to the plaintiff's personality.[43] This concern for the chilling effect of damages will strike strong resonance in American observers; indeed, it may explain the subtly differentiated attitude towards imposing liability on defendants: for in Germany, as in most other European countries, sanctions can be deployed against the defamer which are less than the large, sometimes crippling awards of damages, including punitive damages, available in the United States.[44] A

[42] (1961) BVerfGE 12, 114.

[43] (1981) BVerfGE 54, 129 at 135–6.

[44] In Germany damages for non-economic loss were not allowed by the Civ. c. (BGB); they were admitted in cases of defamation and invasion of privacy under the aegis of the constitution: the *Herrenreiter-Fall*, (1958) BGHZ 26, 349. For non-'material' damages generally see Stoll, 45 Juristentag, *Verhandlungen* I 1–164 (1964). In Austria non-economic

common complaint in many countries, however, is that the level of damages is inadequate to deter the sensational press.[45]

Severest is, of course, a criminal sanction, which requires correspondingly the strongest constitutional justification.

EUROPEAN CONVENTION ON HUMAN RIGHTS

Article 10 of the Convention provides that 'everyone has the right to freedom of expression', but also that the exercise of that freedom 'may be subject to such formalities, conditions, restrictions or penalties as are prescribed by law and are necessary in a democratic society . . . for the protection of the reputation and the rights of others . . .' The last-mentioned reference is to 'the demands of that pluralism, tolerance, and of that broadmindedness without which there is no democratic society'.[46]

The Court of Human Rights has been primarily concerned with free-speech problems other than ones impinging on individual reputation. Its basic approach in applying Article 10 has been close to the German, by insisting on individual evaluation of each case rather than categories.[47] Notably also, the formulation of Article 10 emphasizes that any countervailing 'restriction' must be '*necessary* in a democratic society', a phrase which has been credited to the inspiration of the famous 'clear and present danger test' under the US constitution. It demands not so much balancing as upholding 'a principle of freedom of expression that is subject to a number of exceptions which must be narrowly interpreted'.[48] On the other hand, like the German Constitution but unlike that of the US, the Convention explicitly calls for respect for the 'reputation and rights of others'.

In the principal libel case, *Lingens* v. *Austria*,[49] the Austrian court had imposed a fine and confiscation of the relevant newspaper edition for a derogatory comment on a prominent politician's response to criticism

damages were introduced by the Media Law of 1981 but limited to Sh.100,000 (US$8,000).

[45] E.g. Sweden and Netherlands. In Germany substantial damages are sometimes awarded, though small by American, even British, standards, e.g. DM40,000 in the *Böll* case. In France, large awards are not uncommon in order to punish a defendant who sought to make a profit out of scandal. An Italian statute of 1948 authorized the award of a 'major sum', in addition to compensatory damages, to persons libelled by the press. In England, where (as in the USA) juries determine damages, £1.5 million was awarded in one case in 1989. In Belgium civil, unlike criminal trials, are without jury, thus assuring more protection for the media.

[46] *Handyside* v. *UK*, (1976). Pub. European Court of Human Rights, Series A. No. 24 at 23.

[47] *Sunday Times* v. *UK*, (1979) 2 EHRR 245 at 281.

[48] Ibid.

[49] (1986) 8 EHRR 407.

of his tolerance of ex-Nazis in government. The European Court held this interference with the defendant's freedom of expression 'not necessary in a democratic society . . . for the protection of the reputation . . . of others', being disproportionate to the legitimate aim pursued. The impugned expressions were statements of opinion in a political context; a political figure was entitled to less protection than a private individual. 'Unlike the latter, the former inevitably and knowingly lays himself open to public scrutiny of his every word and deed by both journalists and the public at large, and he must consequently display a greater degree of tolerance.'[50] Furthermore, the Austrian code's requirement of proof of truth by the defendant[51] was irreconcilable with a proper distinction between statements of fact and opinion. Opinion was at the core of a democratic, pluralistic society.

This decision clearly aligns the European Court, and therefore commits all signatories of the Convention, to the liberal course charted by American and German constitutional doctrine. In some countries like France the impact of the Convention in the area here under discussion[52] will be negligible, because their domestic law already meets the Convention standards; but in others, notably Austria, it has already had a profound effect.

Other Countries

In many countries, as already observed, a litigant cannot directly invoke a constitutional guarantee in private litigation so as to contest, for example, the validity of a civil-law rule that stands against him. Thus in France, a statute may be challenged only prior to its promulgation before the *conseil constitutionel*; and in Canada, as already mentioned, the constitutional document has been interpreted as addressed only to the legislator and of no avail to contest a common-law rule. This does not, of course, preclude deference to the constitutional standard in the modulation and application of civil-law rules to the extent that the latter are flexible enough to permit such infusion. Such clearly has been the French experience, where the open-textured phraseology of the codes has enabled courts to shape the law in conformity to the historic free-speech guarantee of the Declaration of Human Rights, without the

[50] Contrast the recent *Barfod* case, 22 Feb. 1989 Ser. A no. 149, disputing the political character of a personal attack of bias against two lay judges.

[51] In civil claims the burden is on the plaintiff who, moreover, has to prove intent or negligence. But under the new Media Law, S. 6, the burden is on the defendant, though honest belief in the truth and appropriate care provide a defence.

[52] On other matters relating to freedom of expression, such as media control, complaints have been numerous.

need to strike down intractable civil-law rules with a constitutional gavel.[53] Likewise in Sweden, constitutional values over generations have worked themselves into the very fabric of the law, reinforced by the strong reliance on juries and the small awards of damages in defamation cases.

Conversely, direct constitutional review is most needed in order to overcome specific rules of the civil or criminal law stemming from a historical background no longer compatible with modern values. Intertia of the ordinary legislative process or respect for a revered code may have prevented reform by means of amending the archaic text, thus leaving no alternative to heavy-handed constitutional intervention to modernize the law. This was, as already mentioned, the situation in Austria, where judges welcomed the eventual intervention of the European Court on Human Rights, which freed them to transform their domestic law of defamation in the image of modern democratic values. Or, in the United States, constitutional intervention was mandated in order to uphold national values of free speech against a state 'establishment' wielding its own defamation rules in order to maintain its racist policies, coupled with need to curb runaway awards of damages, which are particularly 'chilling' to the media.

Finally, in countries without any written bill of rights, such as Britain, and some Commonwealth countries such as Australia and New Zealand, it would be idle to suppose that freedom of speech and of the press have not also long exerted a dominant influence in shaping and applying their common law and statutory law of defamation. Indeed, these values are counted among the prominent imperatives of their unwritten constitutions. Frequent statutory amendments and complete periodical reviews of defamation law attest to the importance attached to keeping the law abreast with changing social perceptions. The press is generally credited with considerable parliamentary 'clout' in advancing its own interest, as evidenced by its long-time success in opposing recognition of a discrete right of privacy. If, none the less, some aspects of the law of defamation appear less supportive of free speech than required by American constitutional doctrine, one may surmise that a major reason may be a difference in cultural values rather than the presence or absence of a formal constitutional text.

This supposition may be illustrated by a comparison of their treatment of 'fair comment'. Under English law, that defence is available only for comment on matters of public interest, honestly held and based on true (or privileged) facts. The burden of proving the truth of facts is on the defendant, which may jeopardize his sources of information. A strict view prevails in the classification of speech as

[53] See generally J. Morange, *Libertés publics* (Paris, 1985).

comment, little if any allowance being made for the interweaving of fact and comment in polemical contexts. Moreover, there is some authority that attacks on character are never a permissible subject of adverse comment for fear of deterring persons of honour from entering public life: a quaint survival of Victorian ethos at a polar extreme from the treatment of public officials in American and German jurisprudence. This aspect of the English law imports a more serious limitation on free speech, as it is linked to strict liability for factual inaccuracies and, in contrast to some other countries, politicians frequently re-fight lost battles in the courts.[54] Even without any constitutional prodding, let alone compulsion, this state of the common law was viewed in some Canadian and American jurisdictions as affording inadequate protection for public speech. Under some Canadian statutes it is a defence that the publisher on matters of public interest had reasonable grounds to believe them to be accurate, but this model was emphatically rejected in England by the Faulks Committee on Defamation in 1975, on the ground that the existing law represented a fair compromise between individual reputation and the free flow of information.[55] So also a number of American courts had modified the defence of fair comment long before the constitutional intervention. Thus, while in the United States the constitutional decision in *Gertz* merely validated and 'nationalized' the free-speech balance independently arrived at before in a number of states, it would be rash to surmise that a British court armed with constitutional power would have taken exception at the existing, much more restricted ambit of free speech,[56] given its repeated endorsements by a wide segment of public opinion.

Conclusion

The intrusion of constitutional guarantees for freedom of speech and of the press has served to adjust the civil law of defamation (and invasion of privacy)[57] to increased demands for free dissemination of information and public debate in today's democratic and pluralistic societies. Most prominent in charting this course have been the United States and the Federal Republic of Germany. Other countries have

[54] This is even more prevalent in Australia than Britain. See M. Newcity, *The Sociology of Defamation in Australia and the U.S.*, 26 Tex. Intern'l L.J. 1 (1991).

[55] Report on Defamation (1975), Cmd. 5909.

[56] In this respect. In others, English ground-rules can be more sensitive to the demands of the media, for example in not recognizing a specific tort of invasion of privacy or in not permitting next of kin to sue for defamation of the dead (contrast the *Mephisto* case, p. 343 above).

[57] Considerations of space preclude an examination of privacy in this context.

sought to live up to the spirit of their written or unwritten constitutions by accommodating their statutory and decisional law to the same demands, though their success has varied. The European Convention on Human Rights remains the ultimate policeman for member countries.

This tendency has straddled common law and civil law jurisdictions. More significant for the latter is the general shift from legislature to courts in implementing and developing that policy.[58] This role was made possible by the generally open-ended statutory or constitutional principles and by the legislative paralysis in solving the tension between rights of personality and the media. The courts had to fill this vacuum.

An inevitable consequence of the subordination of individual rights of personality to the larger value of free speech is the incremental power of the media. Europe, in contrast to the United States, has generally been more sceptical about the absolute claim that uninhibited free speech is the least costly way of disseminating worthwhile information. The irresponsibility of the sensational press in disregarding even such restrictions as the law still affords, supports that concern. But that is a story for another day.

[58] See F. Kübler, in G. Dworkin *et al.*, *Die Haftung der Massenmedien*, (Frankfurt 1972), at 136.

15

The Basis of Tortious Liability

PETER CANE

One of the most important, fruitful, and controversial lines of argument conceived by Patrick Atiyah goes as follows: it is an over-simplification to divide the law of obligations according to whether the obligation in question is imposed by law or voluntarily assumed. 'A more adequate and more unifying conceptual structure for the law of obligations can be built around the interrelationship between the concepts of reciprocal benefits, acts of reasonable reliance, and voluntary human conduct.'[1] In developing this argument Atiyah has concentrated on the law of contract, and he issued a very important disclaimer:

> I do not, of course, want to suggest that the whole law of obligations can be rewritten in terms of a few simple principles drawn from notions of benefit and reliance. Society and social and economic relationships are too complex in the modern industrial world for over-simplifications of this nature.[2]

In this essay I wish to test Atiyah's thesis by introducing complexity in the form of the law of tort.

Preliminary Points

Atiyah insists that the division of the law of obligations into contract law, tort law, and the law of restitution 'is designed largely for purposes of exposition and pedagogy'.[3] But it has to be admitted that the notion of a law of obligations consisting of what we now think of as the law of tort, the law of contract, and that part of the law of restitution concerned with restitution for wrongs (that is, for breach of legal obligations), is itself artificial. In the first place, there is no conceptual reason why such a notion should not incorporate the law of trusts, for example. Secondly, if we adopt the linguistically obvious

[1] P. S. Atiyah, *Essays on Contract* (Oxford, 1986), 42–3.
[2] Ibid. 42.
[3] Ibid. 52.

approach and define the law of obligations as being concerned with the creation and breach of *duties* as opposed to the creation of and interference with *rights*, we immediately see how 'mixed up' the law is in reality. For example, the law of contract is as much organized around the creation of contractual rights as with the breach of contractual duties; and the 'property torts' (trespass to land and chattels, conversion, and so on) are conceptually based on interference with rights rather than breach of duties. The fact that the work done by the property torts is not done by rules belonging to the law of property is itself a product of history rather than of any conceptual logic. Indeed, to the extent that rights and duties are correlative, there seems no compelling reason to classify any particular rule of law according to whether it is couched in terms of rights or duties. Obligations often protect and reinforce rights; if we seek to analyze obligations in isolation from the rights which they protect, the resulting analysis risks being incomplete. So, if we are to construct an integrated theory of contract and tort (at least), we must not take the word 'obligation' too seriously; in other words, an integrated theory of liability in contract and tort will not be an integrated theory of tortious and contractual *obligations* but an integrated theory of rights and obligations in contract and tort. Whenever, in what follows, the word 'obligation(s)' is encountered, the reader should bear this caveat in mind.

Furthermore, the word 'obligation' itself needs careful analysis. Two distinctions should be drawn. The first is between primary and secondary obligations.[4] In the law of contract, primary obligations are those obligations which are discharged by performance of the contract, while secondary obligations are those which arise upon non-performance of the contract (that is, most commonly, an obligation to pay damages). This distinction between performance and non-performance plays little part in the law of tort except in cases where there can be liability for failure to take positive action. Most primary obligations in tort are obligations not to act in the way the law defines as tortious.

Several characteristics of primary contractual obligations are worth noting. First, many such obligations are 'productive' in the sense that they are obligations to produce advantageous outcomes; but some (for example, contractual duties of care) are 'protective' in the sense that they are obligations to avoid disadvantageous outcomes. Secondly, most primary contractual obligations are owed to identified and specified individuals who have had dealings with the person subject to the obligation before the obligation arises. Thirdly, the content of primary contractual obligations is often defined quite specifically and in

[4] On this distinction in contract law see B. Dickson, (1989) 9 *OJLS* 439, 448–51.

some detail so that it is possible to know, in advance of performance, what will count as compliance with the contract, and when and how breaches of it might occur.

By contrast, the law of tort is predominantly protective, not productive. Secondly, many primary tortious obligations are 'unfocused', by which I mean that they can arise between strangers (that is, persons who may be unknown to or unidentified by each other, or who may have had no dealings with each other before the tort occurs); and also that it is difficult to specify in advance the conduct which they proscribe and the circumstances in which proscribed conduct may occur.

The second distinction to be drawn is between the basis or ground of an obligation and the content of that obligation. In other words, the reason(s) why a legal obligation is imposed in given circumstances may not explain its content, which may be justified by different reasons. To say that a person is under a primary obligation because she made a promise, or because she received a certain benefit, or because another relied upon her, or in order to protect some interest of the beneficiary of the obligation, does not tell us what she is under an obligation (not) to do. So, for example, duties not to damage property are imposed in order to protect the interests of the property owner, but we have to look elsewhere for an explanation of why the duty owed is strict or one of reasonable care, as the case may be. Again, secondary obligations in tort and contract are triggered and explained by breach of primary obligations; but the fact of breach does not explain the content of secondary obligations.

Furthermore, there is no necessary relationship between the ground of a primary obligation and the content of any secondary obligation to which non-performance of that primary obligation gives rise. A potent source of confusion in this area is the fact that the concepts of benefit and reliance can be, and are, used (both in contract and tort) to denote a measure of damages (that is, the content of a secondary obligation), as well as a basis for imposing primary obligations. Suppose that P relies to her detriment on a promise made by D: we might say that reliance is the *ground* of a primary (contractual) obligation resting on D, the *content* of which is defined by the terms of D's promise; and we might say that the ground of any secondary obligation resting on D is non-performance of that promise, but still leave open the question of whether the *content* of that secondary obligation should be measured by the content of the promise or by the amount of P's detriment.

Take another example: suppose that P is induced to lend money to C by a negligent misstatement made by D as to C's credit-worthiness, and P loses her money; and suppose, further, that if P had not lent the money to C, she could and would have invested it more lucratively elsewhere. If we assume, for the moment,[5] that the ground of D's (tortious) liability to P is P's reliance on D's statement, it does not follow that P will be limited to recovering from D the capital and interest not paid by C; in fact, there is much authority to support the proposition that P can recover the capital plus an amount equal to the return she would have made on the alternative investment—her expectation of gain from that alternative investment, if you like.[6] Here is a third example: suppose that P, as a result of negligent investment advice from D, makes an investment from which she expects to reap a profit of £X, but in fact she receives a profit of only £X − 2Y; suppose, further, that if P had not made this investment, she would have made another which would have yielded a profit of £X − Y. P sues D in contract (for breach of an implied warranty to take care) and in tort (for negligence). If we assume that the basis of the contractual liability would be *warranty*, and the basis of the tort liability *reliance*, one might expect the measure of damages in tort and contract to be different. But there is much authority for the proposition that, unless the court is prepared to hold that the adviser promised that P would reap a profit of £X, and that she did not simply promise to take care in advising on the value of the investment, P's recovery in contract will be the same as that in tort, namely £X − Y, not £X.[7]

With these distinctions in mind, let us now look more closely at Atiyah's three building-blocks of the law of obligations and their role in tort law.

Voluntary Conduct

Atiyah does not make it clear what he means by 'voluntary conduct', but the term appears to denote conduct the doing of which the law treats as a sufficient ground for subjecting the person doing it to a primary obligation to do or to refrain from doing some act. Making promises,[8] giving undertakings, executing a deed, signing a document containing promissory statements or undertakings, boarding a bus, borrowing money, taking goods from the shelf of a supermarket,[9] provide examples of such conduct. The word 'voluntary' is almost superfluous because it seems to denote little more than that the conduct was not done 'involuntarily', for example, in one's sleep.[10] The important thing is that the conduct be such that the law treats it as

[5] I will discuss this point further below.
[6] P. Cane *Tort Law and Economic Interests* (Oxford, 1991), 180.
[7] Ibid. 146.
[8] See P. S. Atiyah, *Promises, Morals and the Law* (Oxford, 1981), esp. ch. 6.
[9] For these last three examples see Atiyah, n. 1 above, 19.

a sufficient ground for imposing an obligation to act or refrain from action. An obvious distinction between 'voluntary conduct' as a ground of obligations, and 'benefit' and 'reliance' as grounds of obligations is that the former relates to conduct of the person under the obligation, whereas the latter two do not: 'reliance' refers, of course, to conduct of the beneficiary of the obligation; and 'benefit' refers to what the person under the obligation receives as a result of someone else's conduct.

Primary obligations generated by voluntary conduct in this sense are a common feature of the law of contract (and the law of trusts) but occur only rarely, I believe, in the law of tort. The only primary tortious obligations which are said to be based on voluntary conduct are the duty to take care in making 'statements' for the accuracy of which the speaker has 'voluntarily undertaken responsibility'; and obligations to take affirmative action which rest on 'voluntary undertakings' to act or on regular courses of conduct.[11] But I will argue below (in the section on reliance) that voluntary undertaking is not normally the juristic basis of obligations to take care in making 'statements'. An express undertaking to act may be a ground for imposing liability for inaction; but if an undertaking to act is 'implied' then it is usually, in effect, a fictitious undertaking imposed for reasons which are typically unexpressed. In the vast majority of cases, the justification for primary tortious obligations is the desire to protect interests which the law considers worthy and needful of protection from certain types of conduct (or inaction). The law of tort gives people very little scope for defining for themselves which interests will receive its protection or how and to what extent they will be protected. By contrast, the law of contract, through the medium of the concept of 'voluntary conduct', gives people considerable (although very far from unlimited) power to define their obligations or, conversely, to specify the interests which they are prepared to further or protect, and the ways in which they will do this.

At one point Atiyah suggests that the concept of 'voluntary conduct' is relevant to explaining the liability of the driver of a motor vehicle to a road user injured by his negligent driving because the driver is 'voluntarily on the road, voluntarily driving his car'.[12] At one level this is true: the act of driving subjects the driver to certain legal obligations; indeed, the deliberate doing of almost any act can attract legal

[10] Ibid. 20. But, in Atiyah's view, duress does not negative voluntariness: (1982) 98 *LQR* 197; (1983) 99 *LQR* 353 (an answer to Tiplady (1983) 99 *LQR* 188).

[11] As, for example, in *L. Shaddock & Associates Pty Ltd* v. *Parramatta City Council* (1981) 36 ALR 381.

[12] Atiyah, n. 1 above, 41.

obligations.[13] But this misrepresents where the emphasis falls in our justifications of the liability of car drivers to other road users:[14] it falls not on the fact that someone has chosen to drive a car, but on the fact that driving is a dangerous activity, the negligent conduct of which is likely to interfere with the rights and interests of others. To point out that the driver deliberately took his car on to the road adds little force to the justification. By contrast (to take one of Atiyah's examples), the fact that a person has deliberately taken (or is taking) a bus-ride is the very basis of her obligation to pay the fare.

One of Atiyah's main arguments is that 'voluntary conduct' is the source of some, but by no means all, primary contractual obligations. My argument here is that 'voluntary conduct' rarely provides a sufficient justification for the imposition of primary tortious obligations. Such obligations are usually imposed as a way of protecting specified rights and interests against certain types of conduct (as defined by legal rules).

Reciprocal Benefits

Given that our aim is to develop a conceptual structure for an integrated understanding of contract and tort law, the word 'reciprocal' is unduly limiting. It conveys an idea of mutuality or intended exchange of benefits. This idea gives a reasonable account of situations where the benefit in question was obtained with the consent of the plaintiff and on the understanding, either explicit or implicit, that it should be paid for. But it seems inappropriate in cases where D secures a benefit from P without P's consent as a result, for exmaple, of tortious exploitation of P's property. It seems even less apposite in cases where, by committing a tort,[15] breach of contract,[16] or other legal wrong against P, D reaps a benefit from a third party. If D refuses to perform her contract with P because she would rather perform for C, then any chance of reciprocity between P and D is destroyed. If D reaps a profit by defaming P or by betraying P's confidence, any notion that requiring D to disgorge her profits satisfies the demands of reciprocity seems grotesque; even more so if a trustee makes a profit

[13] '. . . nearly all tort liabilities arise in the course of the performance of voluntary actions', *Ibid*.

[14] Furthermore, as Atiyah points out, the basis of the driver's obligation is essentially the same whether the liability is technically tortious or contractual.

[15] Not all torts give rise to restitutionary rights: see Cane, n. 6 above, 317–9, 321–6.

[16] The basic rule is that breach of contract does not give rise to restitutionary rights; but it has been argued that some breaches of contract should, and I will assume for the purposes of the discussion that this is right: Birks [1987] *LMCLQ* 241.

for herself by misappropriating trust property, or if a fiduciary makes a profit for herself by exploiting the fiduciary relationship. Legal obligations often arise where the defendant has acquired a benefit at the expense of the plaintiff; but the notion of reciprocity only seems appropriate in cases where the benefit was obtained with the plaintiff's consent, and where the basic obligation is, therefore, to pay for it (that is, essentially, in actions for the price or for a *quantum meruit*). Where the benefit has been obtained without P's consent and where the basic obligation is to restore[17] or disgorge the benefit, the notion of reciprocity seems out of place.

Therefore, a distinction should be drawn between what might be called 'consensual benefits' (that is, benefits acquired with P's consent) and 'non-consensual benefits' (that is, benefits acquired without P's consent). Non-consensual benefits are not-infrequently recoverable in tort actions, and so an integrated theory of tort and contract should speak of 'benefits' rather than of 'reciprocal benefits'.

This distinction between consensual and non-consensual benefits relates closely to the distinction between primary and secondary obligations. The receipt of consensual benefits may provide a sufficient ground for imposing a primary (contractual) obligation to pay for the benefit, although the amount to be paid may not be equivalent to the value of the benefit. On the other hand, the receipt of non-consensual benefits does not provide a sufficient ground[18] for imposing primary obligations (either in tort[19] or in contract), but the value of benefits received as a result of breaching a primary obligation may provide the measure (or content) of a secondary obligation to pay damages.

Reasonable Reliance

It is particularly important to avoid confusion by distinguishing clearly between reliance as a measure of damages—the so-called 'reliance interest'—and reliance as a justification for imposing obligations. Even if the basis of D's primary obligation is promissory, P may claim, and be awarded, damages representing loss suffered (or gains foregone) in reliance on the promise. Conversely, the fact that D's secondary obligation is to pay damages for 'reliance losses' does not mean that

[17] Whether *in specie* or not.

[18] In tort, whether a person was acting for his own benefit may be relevant to deciding whether he acted tortiously or not. For example, other things being equal, conduct is more likely to be held to be negligent if it was done for the defendant's benefit than if it was done for the benefit of 'the public': see e.g. *Daborn* v. *Bath Tramways Motor Co. Ltd.* [1946] 2 All ER 333.

[19] Most (secondary) tortious obligations to disgorge non-consensual benefits arise on breach of a primary obligation not to interfere with property rights.

her primary obligation is based on the fact that P has detrimentally relied on her. Our present concern is with reliance as a ground of obligations.

It is useful to distinguish between three types of reliance. P may rely on D by conferring a benefit on her (for example, a loan made on the basis of a promise to repay); I shall call this 'benefit-reliance'. Or P may suffer some loss by relying on D (for example, making a bad investment as a result of a misstatement of fact); this, of course, is called 'detrimental reliance'.[20] Finally, if D says he will do X, P may rely on this in the sense that he believes that D will do X, and expects D to do X, but neither suffers any loss as a result nor confers any benefit on D on the strength of his belief; cases of waiver of debts provide classic examples of this form of reliance. There is authority for the view that a promise to accept part-payment of a debt may be binding even if the debtor suffers no detriment in reliance on the promise, and confers no benefit on the creditor in return for the promise.[21] But if the debtor has simply passively enjoyed the benefits of the promise, it seems strange to say that the promise is binding *because of her reliance on it*; if it is binding, it is so because, given the circumstances in which it was made, it would be unfair to allow the creditor to renege. It is also clear in English law that reliance in this third sense cannot create legal liabilities either in contract or in tort.

Benefit-reliance provides another way of looking at cases of consensual benefit, and so we need consider it no further. Our concern here is with detrimental reliance. The role of detrimental reliance in contract law is a matter of much dispute, which we need not consider in detail. The important and contentious question is whether action by P, as a result of which she suffers detriment, can give rise to a primary obligation to perform a promise or undertaking, if the action in question was not done in response to a request by the promisor and was not intended as the price for the promise, but was merely done in reliance on the promise. Atiyah is the chief modern proponent of the view that unrequested detrimental reliance on a promise or undertaking can found liability for failure to perform that promise or undertaking.

What is the role of detrimental reliance in tort law? It is often assumed that detrimental reliance is a ground of certain primary tort obligations. But there are at least two arguments which must be considered before this assumption can be accepted. The first concerns liability for negligent misstatement, and it says that the basis of the

[20] These two categories will, of course, overlap, where P relies on D by conferring a benefit on D.

[21] See G. H. Treitel, *Law of Contract*, 7th edn. (London, 1987), 104.

liability is a voluntary undertaking of responsibility by the speaker, not reasonable reliance by the hearer.[22] In other words, a person will be liable in tort for negligent misstatement only if, in addition to making a false statement, the speaker also accepted legal responsibility for any want of due care in making the statement. The main reason for preferring undertaking of responsibility to reasonable reliance as the basis of such liability resides in the observation that it might be quite reasonable for a person to rely on the truth of a statement without checking it for herself, in circumstances where it would not be reasonable for the person relying to think that the speaker was accepting legal liability for the truth of the statement because, for example, she had expressly disclaimed responsibility for its truth.

This argument cannot, however, be accepted. Take, first, cases in which there is no express disclaimer of responsibility: whenever (as will almost always be the case)[23] the alleged undertaking of legal responsibility is implied rather than express, the relevant legal question is whether, in all the circumstances of the case, it is fair and reasonable to allow the plaintiff to sue the defendant. Since this is essentially an evaluative question for the court, nothing would seem to be gained by insisting that any liability imposed is referable to a fictitious undertaking by the speaker, as opposed to the reasonableness of the hearer's reliance on the speaker; however it is framed, the real question is, should the defendant be held liable?

The argument seems, at first sight, much stronger where there is an express disclaimer of responsibility. How, it might be asked, could a legal obligation arise when the speaker has expressly disclaimed responsibility for the accuracy of the statement? A short answer is that legal obligations are ultimately imposed by law, not by actions of the parties: the law can ignore a disclaimer if it chooses to do so. A longer and more satisfactory answer goes as follows: in tort, as in contract, it may be socially undesirable, in certain circumstances, for a person to be allowed to say that she will do X but also to exclude legal liability for failure to do X; or to be allowed to say that Y is the case but also to exclude legal liability for the truth of Y. And if this is undesirable, then it would be equally undesirable to allow a person to say that she will do X while at the same time accepting no (legal) obligation to do X; or to assert Y while at the same time refusing to stand by the truth of Y. This argument forms the basis of Section 13 of the Unfair Contract Terms Act 1977 which, *inter alia*, renders ineffective provisions which seek to exclude any obligation to do X rather than to exclude liability

[22] Feldthusen, *Economic Negligence* (Toronto, 1984), ch. 2.

[23] An express undertaking of responsibility could justifiably be treated as a ground of liability.

for not doing X. And that section was interpreted in accordance with the logic of my longer answer in the tort case of *Smith* v. *Bush*.[24] It may be reasonable for a person to rely on a statement made by another, and to expect to be able to sue her if it turns out to be false, even if the other attempts to exclude any duty to take care or any liability for failure to take care.

The second argument is that reliance by the plaintiff is not a ground of liability in tort, but is only a link in the (factual) causal chain between negligence and loss in certain cases. If the plaintiff can trace a causal chain from the defendant's negligence to her loss without reliance by her on anything said or done by the defendant, she can recover (provided all the other elements of liability are present). In relation to the vast majority of tort actions concerning personal injury and property damage,[25] this statement seems so obviously correct as hardly to need expression. The problem arises in relation to purely economic loss: there is support in the cases for the proposition that liability in tort for such loss only arises in circumstances which can be subsumed under the principle of liability first enunciated in *Hedley Byrne* v. *Heller*.[26] This was a case in which, on the assumed facts, the loss was suffered and only suffered because the plaintiff relied on the defendant's (undertaking of responsibility for the accuracy of its) statement. As a result, it is often asserted that reliance by the plaintiff is relevant to the issue of liability, and not just to causation. In this light, cases such as *Ross* v. *Caunters*[27] and *Ministry of Housing and Local Government* v. *Sharp*,[28] in which liability was imposed for purely economic loss in the absence of reliance by P on D, appear anomalous. They have seemed particularly troublesome in a number of recent cases in which courts have been asked to impose liability for failure by D to warn P of a risk of loss and of the desirability of taking precautions against such loss. In such cases, it is said, there can be no liability in tort in the absence of an undertaking to warn and (as a matter of causation) detrimental reliance on that undertaking.

However, courts in these failure-to-warn cases have been prepared to accept the principle that reliance may not always be a precondition of liability for purely economic loss, and rightly so. There is no logical inconsistency[29] between, on the one hand, refusing to impose liability

[24] [1990] 1 AC 831.

[25] Including actions in which the allegedly negligent act consists of a statement: *Clay* v. *Crump* [1964] 1 QB 533.

[26] [1964] AC 465.

[27] [1980] Ch. 297.

[28] [1970] 2 QB 223.

[29] Although there may be inconsistency in terms of policy, since omissions which cause physical loss are often actionable even in the absence of undertakings to act.

for economic loss resulting from failure to speak or take other action in the absence of an undertaking to speak or act (which undertaking would not, as a matter of fact, cause damage unless relied upon); but on the other hand, being prepared to impose liability for negligent words or conduct which cause loss to P without reliance on D by her. Such a difference of approach can be justified logically in terms of the distinction between doing and not-doing. Furthermore, recent negligence cases contain statements which support the conclusion that (assuming D was negligent) the test of liability for purely economic loss is the same whether or not, on the facts of the case, reliance is a necessary link in the causal chain. Liability is now seen to rest, even in cases where liability would once have been seen as based on (reliance on) an (implied) undertaking of responsibility, on a cumulative combination of deference to precedent, foreseeability of damage, 'proximity of relationship between the plaintiff and the defendant', and considerations of fairness, justice, and policy. If the plaintiff suffered loss as a result of reliance on the defendant, this may help to establish the degree of proximity required to justify imposition of liability for economic loss, but this is not the only way of establishing such proximity.[30] Conversely, the mere fact that the plaintiff relied on the defendant will not lead to the imposition of liability on the latter, as *Caparo Industries plc* v. *Dickman*[31] clearly shows. One way of making the latter point is to say that it must have been reasonable in the circumstances for the plaintiff to rely on the defendant without seeking some other protection for her interests.

Considerations of policy and fairness may be subsumed under the head of proximity of relationship between the plaintiff and the defendant (for example, in *Caparo* v. *Dickman* such considerations were relevant to deciding whether there was a sufficient degree of proximity between an auditor and prospective shareholders); or they may be treated as having independent force (the immunity of barristers falls under this head, as do 'floodgates' arguments, and arguments that defendants should be protected from too heavy a burden of liability for economic loss). In other words, it is now openly admitted that the basic question in any tort action is one of policy: should the plaintiff be given a remedy? In some cases, this question would never fall to be answered if P had not relied on D, because otherwise P would have suffered no loss. But in no case does the fact (or absence) of reliance answer the question of whether the defendant should be held liable.

[30] See esp. *Murphy* v. *Brentwood D.C.* [1990] 3 WLR 414, 445–6 *per* Lord Oliver of Aylmerton.

[31] [1990] 2 WLR 358.

Reliance is neither a necessary nor a sufficient condition of liability for purely economic loss.

This analysis also seems right for the oldest of the modern forms of tort liability for misstatements, namely deceit. Here, loss is a precondition of liability, and so reliance is necessary to complete the causal chain. But the *basis* of liability is the obvious moral case for protecting people from and discouraging fraud.

If I am right in saying that the presence or absence of reliance can only determine the issue of causation in tort cases, does this have any ramifications for the earlier brief discussion of the role of reliance in contract, where I assumed that reliance *per se* could be a ground of liability, and that it was not just a causal precondition of actionable loss being suffered? In the typical contract case, reliance by P on D's contractual undertakings is part of the causal chain. Indeed, so typically is this the case that it goes without mention.[32] So what distinguishes contractual liability based on detrimental reliance on an undertaking from contractual liability for failure to perform a paid-for undertaking is not the presence of reliance in the one case and its absence in the other. The distinguishing difference is whether the undertaking was paid for; that is, whether consideration was given for it. In English law, the paradigm of an enforceable undertaking is the paid-for undertaking. But both the law of tort and the law of contract recognize that sometimes it may be unjust not to award a remedy for failure to perform a relied-upon undertaking even though it has not been paid for. In a market economy, payment has great legal significance. But distortions in the operation of the market justify the law sometimes in awarding remedies for breach of undertakings even in the absence of payment. This would suggest that any integrated theory of the law of contract and tort would need to pay careful attention to the role of payment as a ground of obligation: when will a person be legally liable for failure to do X even though she was not paid for her undertaking to do X? And when will a person be legally liable for failing to do X properly even though she has not been paid for her undertaking to do X (properly)?

In terms of legal categories, contractual liability is usually liability for failure to perform paid-for undertakings; but exceptionally, liability for failure to perform gratuitous undertakings is treated as contractual. Conversely, while tort is usually identified with obligations imposed regardless of payment, tort liability may arise out of nonfeasance or misfeasance of obligations paid for by P (as in *Smith* v. *Bush*)[33] or in

[32] For a theoretical discussion of the pervasiveness of reliance in contract law see S. Stoljar [1988] *CLJ* 193, 207–12.

[33] [1990] 1 AC 831.

cases of concurrent liability in contract and tort. Furthermore, the fact of payment may help to justify, and at the same time constrain, the imposition of tortious liability: in concurrent actions the general rule is that no wider obligation can be imposed on D in tort than can be justified by the rules of contract law. Again, in *Smith* v. *Bush* the fact that the house-purchaser had, in effect, paid for D's survey, strengthened the case for holding D liable to P for negligence in conducting the survey. So the distinction between paid-for and gratuitous undertakings does not coincide with the distinction between tortious and contractual obligations. But the role of payment is of great importance to any integrated theory of tort and contract law.

The concept of payment may be seen as marking a distinction between those areas of life where market values tend to predominate, and those areas of life where, to adapt Lord Atkin's famous phrase, values of neighbourliness play a part. Central to much of the modern law of tort is the question of whether the plaintiff ought to have protected herself from loss (or captured D's gain) by making a contractual (that is, a market) arrangement; and, conversely, whether the law of tort ought to come to P's aid and impose a gratuitous obligation on D in P's favour. But this analysis of obligations in terms of payment has its limitations, too. Can it realistically be said that when D undertakes to do X in return for some consideration, she is also being paid to assume the battery of secondary obligations which the law of contract imposes? And in what sense is a promisor being paid not just for her express undertakings but also for any implied undertakings the law may impose?

Stock-taking

The somewhat surprising position we have reached is that neither receipt of benefits nor reasonable reliance is an important ground of tortious liability. This is not to say that these concepts do not help us to understand certain aspects of tort law: damages can be awarded in tort for benefits secured by the defendant, and sometimes even if the plaintiff suffered no loss as a result of the tort; and specific reliance plays a part in the analysis of tort law exactly because tort does sometimes impose liability for statements. But neither benefit nor reliance appear to be important grounds of tort liability. Again, while the concept of payment must play a part in any account of tort and contract law, it does not by itself provide a key to the understanding of contract and tort.

I have also argued that the concept of 'voluntary conduct' which is used to justify certain primary contractual obligations, plays relatively little part in the law of tort. It is clear, then, that we will need to utilize some more concepts if we are to develop an integrated theory of tort and contract liability. I want to suggest that we need concepts of two broad types: these are concepts which enable us to discriminate more between different *types* of conduct; and concepts which enable us to distinguish between different types of *protected interest*.

Types of Conduct

'MISREPRESENTATION, WARRANTY AND ESTOPPEL'[34]

This set of distinctions is central to an understanding of contract law. Warranties are a type of 'voluntary conduct' as defined and discussed earlier. Misrepresentations, on the other hand, are not voluntary conduct in this sense but are, rather, an example of the sort of conduct which can constitute breach of a primary obligation to make accurate statements, and which can trigger secondary obligations. The distinction between misrepresentations and warranties is obviously important to an understanding of the relationship between tortious and contractual liability for statements which induce contracts.

Estoppels can arise out of promises, other statements, or conduct. The concept of estoppel in contract law bears a number of different meanings; but in essence, estoppel allows the creation of contractual rights in circumstances where some condition normally required for the creation of such rights is not satisfied. In other words, estoppel prevents a defendant from arguing that she is under no contractual obligation, when her argument to this effect is seen as lacking merit.[35] In a sense, the concept of estoppel is used to plug what are seen as gaps in the concept of 'voluntary conduct'. Estoppel has no real equivalent in tort law, although cases of tortious liability for the malicious exercise of legal rights bear some similarities: the law sometimes recognizes that doing that which is permitted by law may properly attract liability if it is done for an improper purpose.

Warranty is the hallmark of contractual liability; and it is only contract law which gives a remedy for purely innocent misrepresentation: tort requires fraud or negligence. In other words, strict liability for statements which induce contracts does not lie in tort. The only example of strict tortious liability for statements is defamation.

[34] Atiyah, n. 1 above, ch. 10.

[35] The objective test of contract formation is a sort of estoppel: J. Raz (1982) 95 *Harv. LR* 916, 935–6.

ACT-LIABILITY, OUTCOME-LIABILITY, AND FAULT

The set of distinctions I am about to discuss is relevant to the definition of 'breach of obligation' and hence to the content of primary obligations. Sometimes the law imposes liability for a particular act or omission regardless of its consequences; this is usually referred to as 'actionability *per se*'.[36] Such liability is imposed where the act in question is seen as interfering with a legal *right*. Breaches of contract (that is, interferences with contractual rights) are, in theory at least, actionable *per se*; although in practice, a remedy for breach of contract will be awarded only if it has already inflicted, or will likely inflict, some injury on the plaintiff or deprive him of some intended contractual benefit. Actionability *per se* in the common law of tort is restricted to the tort of trespass and to the award of an injunction. Normally, damage (consequential upon the tortious act) is the gist of an action in tort.

Outcome-liability is much more important; here the act or omission the doing of which attracts liability is defined to include a reference to its actionable consequences. Thus, liability for intentional action is liability for doing an act intending that it should have certain consequences, or with reckless indifference to the occurrence of such consequences; liability for negligent action is liability for doing an act which one should have foreseen (or 'contemplated') would have certain consequences; and liability 'strict as to consequences' (to coin a phrase) is liability for doing an act which has certain consequences, even if those consequences were unforeseeable. These distinctions based on outcome are most often subsumed under the heading of 'remoteness of damage' which is an aspect of the content of secondary obligations. In tort, intended and foreseeable consequences are never too remote; in contract, intended and contemplated consequences are never too remote. Unforeseeable consequences may give rise to liability in both contract and tort by virtue of the distinction between 'kind' and 'extent or manner of occurrence' of damage; and in some torts (such as deceit) the test of remoteness expressly allows recovery for unforeseeable consequences.

Next we must distinguish between liability for deliberate acts, liability for non-deliberate acts which the reasonable person could have avoided by the exercise of reasonable care ('careless acts'), and liability for non-deliberate acts which could not have been so avoided (liability

[36] It should be noted, however, that this term is used in two different senses in the law of tort. Apart from the sense referred to in the text, in the law of defamation the term is used to mean 'actionable without proof of special damage'. In the sense used in the text, defamatory statements are *not* actionable *per se* because the definition of 'defamatory statement' includes a reference to its (likely) consequences.

'strict as to conduct'). Contractual liability is either liability for carelessness or liability strict as to conduct. Liability for deliberate conduct seems of little importance in the law of contract because of the rule that exemplary damages are not available in contract actions. Birks argues that restitutionary remedies (other than actions for the price or a *quantum meruit* which are, of course, allowed) ought to be available for certain calculated breaches of contract,[37] but the general rule is against restitutionary as well as punitive awards in contract. Much tort liability is liability for deliberate acts, some is for carelessness; liability strict as to conduct is relatively rare in the law of tort.

The traditional basis of the distinctions between different types of outcome-liability and different degrees of fault is moral: the moral case for liability for deliberate and intentional conduct is easy to understand. The case for strict liability is more problematic; as is the case for liability for careless and negligent acts, given that the tests of carelessness and negligence do not require that the defendant could personally have done otherwise or foreseen the consequences of his actions. These forms of liability are often justified by arguments of distributive, as opposed to corrective, justice; but Honoré has recently made a convincing case for such liability in terms of commonly held moral views about personal responsibility.[38] The economic case for drawing these distinctions is weaker because the economic aim of maximizing welfare requires, for its fulfilment, that all activities bear the costs they generate regardless of the moral quality of any particular activity. On this view, the answer to the lawyer's question of which activities ought to be encouraged and which discouraged depends not on the moral quality of an activity but on whether its economic benefits outweigh its economic costs (including the losses it inflicts) plus the costs of imposing liability (process costs).

MISFEASANCE AND NONFEASANCE

This distinction (which, like the last set of distinctions, relates to the content of primary obligations) is fundamental to an understanding of the interrelationship of tort and contract. Even given the difficulty of clearly distinguishing, for legal purposes, between misfeasance and nonfeasance, it is true, as a generalization, that nonfeasance is more likely to be actionable in contract than in tort because the courts are relatively unwilling to impose duties to act on persons who have not undertaken to act. This is one area in which the distinction between self-imposed and externally imposed obligations is important. Indeed,

37 [1987] *LMCLQ* 421.
38 (1988) 104 *LQR* 530.

in one recent tort case the Court of Appeal took the view that a contractual obligation to take positive action would arise only if it was expressly stated or could be implied on the basis of a test of necessity (to give the transaction business efficacy), or applying the officious-bystander test.[39]

So far as the law of tort is concerned, duties of positive action are recognized for three main reasons: first, in order to require persons who are in exclusive control of premises or processes to take steps to ensure that those premises or processes are not physically unsafe; secondly, in order to encourage professionals positively to exercise their skills; and thirdly, to satisfy the expectations of persons who have relied on non-contractual undertakings to take positive action or on regular courses of conduct.

Types of Protected Interests

MEASURES OF COMPENSATION

The distinctions I will now discuss relate to the content of secondary obligations. As I said earlier, there is no necessary connection between the basis of any primary obligation and the content of the secondary obligation(s) to which breach of that primary obligation gives rise, or between the basis and content of secondary obligation(s). In some cases (although relatively rarely in contract or tort) the secondary obligation may be to perform the primary obligation; if so, a remedy of injunction or specific performance (or, if coercion is unnecessary, a declaration) will be appropriate. In such cases, the basis of the secondary obligation will, presumably, be the same as the basis of the primary obligation.

But where the secondary obligation is to pay money we cannot assume that the basis of either the primary or the secondary obligation will dictate the content of the secondary obligation. A secondary obligation to pay money can take one (or a combination) of three possible forms. The first is to compensate for losses suffered; such losses may be divided into reliance losses and consequential losses, but this distinction is of no juristic importance because it only rests on a factual difference between cases in which reliance forms a link in the causal chain and cases in which it does not. Losses can also be divided into physical (damage to person or tangible property) and economic; and economic losses can be divided into losses consequential upon

[39] *Bank of Nova Scotia* v. *Hellenic Mutual War Risks Association (Bermuda) Ltd.* [1990] 2 WLR 547.

physical damage, and purely economic loss. Consequential economic loss tends, for legal purposes, to be treated in the same way as physical loss. The distinction between physical and economic loss is relevant (both in contract and tort) to the question of remoteness of damage; but in tort, it is also very relevant to the basis of primary obligations: duties of care to avoid economic loss are much less common than duties of care to avoid physical damage. In contract, the distinction between physical and economic loss seems to have little relevance either to the basis or content of primary obligations.

The traditional basis for imposing a secondary obligation to compensate for losses suffered is clear and straightforward: corrective justice demands that if P is made worse off by the wrongful conduct of D, D should reinstate P to her former position. Losses[40] are never irrecoverable. Some economic analysts of law, for whom deterrence of wrongful conduct rather than corrective justice is the primary goal, draw a distinction between private loss and social loss. Because economic analysts see the prime goal of the law as the maximization of *social* 'wealth', then if a loss to an individual is not a loss to society overall, but only represents wealth which has been transferred from one person to another (that is, if one person's loss is another's gain), then the law should ignore that (purely private) loss. But different economic analysts disagree about which losses are purely private; and English courts, at least, have shown no signs of explicitly recognizing the distinction between private and social losses, although some decisions may be consistent with it.

The second form of the secondary obligation to pay money is restitutionary. A restitutionary obligation may be one either to restore or pay for some benefit received from the plaintiff, or to account for or disgorge some benefit received, at the plaintiff's expense, from some third party. Such obligations are recognized in both tort and contract, but it is by no means the case that both restitutionary obligations attach to every tort or breach of contract. This indicates that the case for imposing restitutionary obligations is not as strong as that for imposing an obligation to compensate for loss suffered. The explanation for this, in traditional terms, is probably that to require D to disgorge benefits which do not represent a loss to P is seen as being, in some sense, penal, and so inconsistent with the basically compensatory aim of the common law. In other words, corrective justice, which provides the most fundamental basis of secondary monetary obligations in contract and tort, only supports restitutionary obligations when the benefit in

[40] That is, legally recognized losses; not all losses are compensatable: for example, mere grief. Compensatable losses correlate with interests considered by the law as worthy of protection.

question also represents a loss to P. But if one is prepared to fashion secondary monetary obligations to achieve other goals, such as deterrence of wrongful conduct (however defined), then restitutionary obligations seem more justifiable. The purpose for which the law of tort is most prepared to impose such obligations is the protection of property rights. In the English legal system, which lacks a written constitution and in which a reasonably well-developed public law is a very recent phenomenon, private-property rights have been seen as the most sacrosanct interests recognized by law, and so as most worthy of the extra protection which restitutionary obligations can give.

The third form of the secondary obligation to pay money is to make good unfulfilled expectations of future financial gain. A distinction needs to be drawn between the gain which was expected on the investment actually made and the hypothetical gain which could have been made on the next best alternative investment. The latter may be recoverable in tort from a negligent investment adviser, for example; but the former is never recoverable in tort. The former may be recoverable in contract, but only if the promisor warranted that the gain would be realized; otherwise only the latter will be recoverable even in contract.

THE RANGE OF LIABILITY

I argued above that reliance by the plaintiff is not, in fact, a basis of liability in tort. The bases of liability in modern tort law are evaluations of the moral quality and social and economic value of different types of conduct, and evaluations of the moral, social, and economic strength of different types of invaded interest. But these concepts of invaded interest and sanctioned conduct do not, by themselves, specify the *limits* of liability. Neither tort law nor contract law is content to treat factual causation as defining the limits of liability. Various devices, such as remoteness of damage and 'proximate cause', are used to draw narrower limits. Another device is 'proximity' of relationship between the plaintiff and the defendant. Privity is the basic contractual notion of proximity; a 'privy party' is one to whom promises, undertakings, or warranties have been made or given, and who has paid for such promises, undertakings, or warranties.

But there are two extremely important qualifications to the operation of the doctrine of privity. The first is that the law sometimes allows contractual provisions expressed to exclude or limit liability (most commonly tort liability) to have effect as between parties one of whom is not privy to the contract containing the provision: if a contract between P and C purports to protect D from liability, this provision may well be held to be effective if P tries to sue D. Furthermore, in certain circumstances, a protective clause in a contract between D and C may prevent P suing D (usually in tort) for conduct amounting to a breach of that contract. The juristic basis of this qualification has been expressed differently at different times; but in the end, the basic issue is whether the (proximity of the) relationship between the parties is such that it would be unfair to allow P to sue D in the face of the exclusion clause. That the strict rules of privity have been relaxed in this context is not surprising: it has been recognized for over thirty years that an occupier can modify his liability for the state of his premises to lawful visitors by means of non-contractual notices, provided that reasonable steps were taken to bring the notice to the visitor's attention; this test of notice also plays an important part in judging the effectiveness of contractual modifications of liability; and the Unfair Contract Terms Act 1977 assimilates contractual and non-contractual exclusions.

The second important qualification to the doctrine of privity is that where D has a contract with C, P may be able to sue D in tort in respect of conduct which constitutes a breach of that contract, provided there is a sufficient degree of 'proximity' between the parties. This principle, which underlies the decision in *Donoghue* v. *Stevenson*,[41] forms the basis of much (although by no means all) of the modern law of negligence. It is important to note that the principle in *Donoghue* v. *Stevenson* is not just concerned with so-called 'contracts for the benefit of third parties'. Any contract between a manufacturer of goods and a supplier is very unlikely to be intended (in any meaningful sense) to benefit the consumer. Furthermore, liability under the principle does not depend on the plaintiff having given value for the goods (or services),[42] whereas proposals for the recognition of 'third-party beneficiary contracts' tend to require that the third party gives value, so as to prevent third-party beneficiaries being put in a better position than promisees.

The meaning of proximity in the law of tort varies according to the plaintiff's interest; in other words, the concept of 'proximity' helps to define the notion of 'legally protected interest' and, hence, the incidence of primary tortious obligations. Victims of tortiously inflicted bodily injury[43] (but not mental injury) are always proximate; proximity for the purposes of actions arising out of the death of another is defined by statute.[44] Persons whose property is tortiously interfered with, whether by being damaged, appropriated, or exploited, are always proximate; but persons who complain of loss resulting from

[41] [1932] AC 562.

[42] Although *Smith* v. *Bush* [1990] 1 AC 813 shows that the giving of value may strengthen P's case in tort.

[43] And deprivation of liberty.

[44] Fatal Accidents Act, 1976.

interference with another's property are almost never proximate so far as the common law of tort is concerned.[45] The same is true of persons who complain about the quality of acquired property.[46]

So far as contractual rights are concerned, proximity and privity coincide in cases where concurrent actions in tort and contract lie; but in other cases of interference with contractual rights, proximity usually requires that the tortious conduct was 'aimed at' the plaintiff. This is also true of contractual expectancies,[47] except where the tortious conduct consists of a misstatement which induces the making of a contract. In the latter case, proximity and privity coincide if D is P's contracting party. In other instances, proximity for the purposes of the tort of deceit involves an 'aiming at' the plaintiff. But proximity for the purposes of the tort of negligence rests on an amalgam of two ideas: the degree of knowledge which the defendant had, or ought to have had, of the identity of the plaintiff and of the nature of the transaction into which she was about to enter; and, particularly in cases where the alleged negligence was committed in the course of exercising statutory functions, the ends which the function being performed was designed to achieve. A similar concept of knowledge serves to define proximity in relation to tort actions in respect of interference with non-contractual expectancies.[48]

The case law is not, as yet, very illuminating on the question of knowledge. All that can be said with any degree of certainty is that the defendant need not be aware of the plaintiff as a named individual; it may be enough that she is a member of a known and identifiable class. On the other hand, the transaction in question needs to be defined fairly narrowly: the defendant must have known (or have had means of knowledge) of the transaction in quite specific and narrow terms. The main aims of the demanding test of knowledge are to prevent tort liability being too heavy; and to encourage people to look to means of protecting their interests other than tort law.

TYPE OF INTEREST

It should be clear from this that some classification of protected interests is of great importance to the understanding and exposition of tort law: the incidence of primary tort obligations and the content of

45 *Morrison Steamship Co. Ltd.* v. *Greystoke Castle (Cargo Owners)* [1947] AC 265 may be an exception, but it may be based on principles of maritime law.

46 *D. & F. Estates Ltd.* v. *Church Commissioners* [1989] AC 177; *Murphy* v. *Brentwood D.C.* [1990] 3 WLR 414. *Junior Books Ltd* v. *Veitchi Co. Ltd* [1983] 1 AC 520 and *Smith* v. *Bush* [1990] 1 AC 813 may, but need not, be viewed as exceptions.

47 By which I mean the chance or expectation of making an advantageous contract in the future.

48 By which I mean the chance or expectation of realizing a future gain otherwise than by making a contract: for example, the chance of receiving a legacy under a will.

secondary tort obligations are both a reflection of the interests which the law considers worthy of protection. But analysis of protected interests tends to be neglected in discussions of tort law, which typically focus on the definition of tortious conduct. This emphasis on sanctioned conduct may partly be a result of the fact that the conduct which triggers tort liability, the beneficiaries of tort obligations, and the circumstances in which they arise, tend to be less specifically defined in advance than contractual obligations;[49] and also of the fact that the content of primary tort obligations is simply a corollary of the definition of tortious conduct. But no account of tort law can be complete without careful analysis of the interests protected by it; and no integrated account of the law of obligations will emerge without proper analysis of the rights and interests which the obligations protect.

At least seven different types of interest can be identified: the interest in personal (that is, physical and mental) health and safety; dignitary interests (reputation and liberty); interests in (tangible and intangible) property; interests under existing contracts; contractual expectancies; non-contractual expectancies; and an interest in the preservation of monetary wealth. The very fact that tort law is a system by which a variety of interests can be legally protected means, at the very least, that neither tort law, nor the law of property or contract, can be properly understood in isolation.

The Purpose of an Integrated Theory

Any integrated theory of tort and contract law must be based on enough concepts to enable us to understand both components. I have argued that the concepts of voluntary conduct, benefit, and detriment are, by themselves, insufficient to this task. But there can be no doubt of the value of developing a catalogue of such concepts, if only because the law of contract and tort interact in a number of different contexts. The most obvious are liability for defective products, premises, and services; liability for misstatements which induce contracts; tort liability for interference with contractual relations and contractual expectancies; and the impact of contractual provisions on tort liability. The value of a catalogue of the concepts underlying tort and contract liability is, however, not just that it helps us analyse the interaction of the two

[49] Conversely, the fact that the typical primary contractual duty is quite specific in content may partly explain why, for example, little more than ten out of 800 or so pages in the seventh edition of Treitel's *Law of Contract* are devoted to explicit discussion of what amounts to breach of contract.

bodies of law, but also that it helps us understand the basic differences of focus and emphasis, the result of which is that the two bodies of law interact rather than merge.

I do not believe that it matters much, in most cases, into which juristic box any particular obligation or liability is put. No matter how we classify the law, the messiness of reality will always prevent the classifications remaining watertight. The important thing is to realize that the categories of the law are not, and could not be made, self-contained; and to seek to understand their interactions and similarities with other categories, as well as their differences. One of the greatest contributions Patrick Atiyah has made to legal scholarship is to teach us this lesson; and in particular, to show us that the apparently inexorable and self-contained logic of 'classical contract law' was spurious. A degree of disrespect for received categories of legal thought can be both illuminating and liberating; and it is for this insight, perhaps, that we owe Atiyah most.

Patrick Selim Atiyah

A Bibliography of his Publications, 1954–1990

BOOKS AND PAMPHLETS

1957 *The Sale of Goods* (London, Pitman, 1957), xxv, 206 pp.

1961 *An Introduction to the Law of Contract* (Oxford, Clarendon Press, 1961), xii, 246 pp.; Clarendon Law Series (corrected repr. 1966).

1963 *The Sale of Goods*, 2nd edn. (London, Pitman, 1963), xxvii, 252 pp. (repr. 1964 and 1965).

1966 *The Sale of Goods*, 3rd edn. (London, Pitman, 1966), xxviii, 284 pp.

1967 *Vicarious Liability in the Law of Torts* (London, Butterworths, 1967), lxi, 452 pp.

1970 *Accidents, Compensation and the Law* (London, Weidenfeld & Nicolson, 1970), xxviii, 633 pp.; Law in Context (repr. 1973).

1971 *Consideration in Contracts: A Fundamental Restatement. An Inaugural Lecture delivered at the Australian National University, Canberra, on 29 July 1970* (Canberra, Australian National University Press, 1971), 61 pp. (repr. (with revisions) in *Essays on Contract*, 1986 and 1990).

An Introduction to the Law of Contract, 2nd edn. (Oxford, Clarendon Press, 1971), x, 290 pp.; Clarendon Law Series (repr. 1975 and 1977).

The Sale of Goods, 4th edn. (London, Pitman, 1971), xxxii, 356 pp.

1972 *Review of Insurance in Relation to Road Safety* (Australia, Expert Group on Road Safety, 1972), iv, 242 pp.

1975 *Accidents, Compensation and the Law*, 2nd edn. (London, Weidenfeld & Nicolson, 1975), xxii, 646 pp.; Law in Context (repr. 1978).

The Sale of Goods, 5th edn. (London, Pitman, 1975), xxxii, 358 pp.

1978 *From Principle to Pragmatism: Changes in the Function of the Judicial Process and the Law* (Oxford, Clarendon Press, 1978), 33 pp. An inaugural lecture delivered before the University of Oxford on 17 Feb. 1978 (repr. (1980), 65 *Iowa Law Review* 1249–72).

1979 *The Rise and Fall of Freedom of Contract* (Oxford, Clarendon Press, 1979), xi, 791 pp. (repr. in paperback with corrections, 1985).

1980 *Accidents, Compensation and the Law*, 3rd edn. (London, Weidenfeld & Nicolson, 1980), xxiv, 695 pp.; Law in Context.

The Sale of Goods, 6th edn. (London, Pitman, 1980), xxxvii, 423 pp.

1981 *An Introduction to the Law of Contract* 3rd edn. (Oxford, Clarendon Press, 1981), x, 335 pp.; Clarendon Law Series.

Promises, Morals and Law (Oxford, Clarendon Press, 1981), 218 pp. (repr. in paperback, 1982).

1983 *Law and Modern Society* (Oxford, University Press, 1983), viii, 158 pp.; OPUS.

1985 *The Sale of Goods*, 7th edn. (London, Pitman 1985), xxxvi, 448 pp.

1986 *Essays on Contract* (Oxford, Clarendon Press, 1986), vi, 363 pp. (corrected repr. in paperback, 1988).

1987 *Form and Substance in Anglo-American Law: A Comparative Study of Legal Reasoning, Legal Theory, and Legal Institutions* (with Robert S. Summers) (Oxford, Clarendon Press, 1987), xx, 437 pp.

Pragmatism and Theory in English Law (London, Stevens, 1987), xii, 193 pp.; Hamlyn Lectures, 39th series.

1989 *Freedom of Contract and the New Right: 1988 års Casselföreläsning* (Stockholm, Juristförlaget, 1989), 35 pp.; Juridiska Fakulteten Stockholm, Skriftserien, 20 (repr. in *Essays on Contract*, 1990).

An Introduction to the Law of Contract, 4th edn. (Oxford, Clarendon Press, 1989), xxiii, 495 pp. Clarendon Law Series.

1990 *Essays on Contract* (Oxford, Clarendon Press, 1990), vi, 396 pp. (repr. of 1986 edn. with new chapter).

The Sale of Goods, 8th edn. (London, Pitman, 1990), xxxiv, 571 pp.

ARTICLES, ESSAYS, NOTES

1954 'The relation between the provocation and the resentment' (1954) 17 *Modern Law Review* 459–61.

1955 'The aged, impotent and poor' (1955) 18 *Modern Law Review* 76–8.

'Charitable Trusts (Validation) Act 1954' (1955) 18 *Modern Law Review* 152–5.

'Maintenance and common interest' (1955) 18 *Modern Law Review* 292–5.

'A re-examination of the *jus tertii* in conversion' (1955) 18 *Modern Law Review* 97–109.

1956 'The right to reject goods for breach of condition' (1956) 19 *Modern Law Review* 315–18.

'*Sid Ahmed Mohamed* v. *Sudan Mercantile Co.*' (1956) *Sudan Law Journal and Reports* 55–9.

'*Sudan Government* v. *Bakheit Adam Mohammed* and the Recovery of Lost and Stolen Property Ordinance 1924' (1956) *Sudan Law Journal and Reports* 46–54.

1957 '*Abdel Gadir el Baloula* v. *El Saggay Agricultural Scheme*' (1957) *SLJR* 17. (1957), *Sudan Law Journal and Reports* 95–7.

'*Couturier* v. *Hastie* and the sale of non-existent goods' (1957) 73 *Law Quarterly Review* 340–9.

'*Hassan Khalil Suleiman* v. *El A'Gib Ali*' (1957) SLJR 10; '*Christos Simos* v. *Mohamed Ali Ahmed*' (1957) *SLJR* 11. (1957), *Sudan Law Journal and Reports* 94–5.

'*A New Sales of Goods Bill*' (1957) *Sudan Law Journal and Reports* 107–41.

'*Rouchdi Boutros* v. *Christos Simos*' (1957) *SLJR* 8. (1957), *Sudan Law Journal and Reports* 93–4.

'*Sudan Government* v. *Hirachand Jeraj Shah*' (1957) *SLJR* 77. (1957) *Sudan Law Journal and Reports* 97–8.

1958 'Equitable relief in contracts of hire purchase' (1958) 5 *Business Law Review* 71–3.

'The Infants' Relief Act 1874—a reply' (1958) 74 *Law Quarterly Review* 97–104.

'Injustices and anomalies in the law of hire purchase' (1958) 5 *Business Law Review* 24–38.

'Legal education in the Sudan' (1958) 4 *Journal of the Society of Public Teachers of Law* (NS), 137–42.

'Public benefit in charities' (1958) 21 *Modern Law Review* 138–54.

'Re Gillingham Bus Disaster Fund' (1958) 74 *Law Quarterly Review* 489–90.

'Some problems of family law in the Sudan Republic' (1958) 39 *Sudan Notes and Records* 88–100.

1959 'The liability of infants in fraud and restitution' (1959) 22 *Modern Law Review* 273–91.

'Rescission of a contract of sale of goods' (1959) 22 *Modern Law Review* 76–80.

1960 'Commercial law in Ghana' [1960] *Journal of Business Law* 430–7.

1961 'Mistake in the construction of contracts' (with F. A. R. Bennion) (1961) 24 *Modern Law Review* 421–43.

1965 'Causation, contributory negligence and *volenti non fit injuria*' (1965) 43 *Canadian Bar Review* 609–37.

'Loss of buyer's right to reject in contracts of sale' (1965) 81 *Law Quarterly Review* 487–9.

'Thoughts on company law philosophy' (1965) 8 *The Lawyer* 15–21.

'The transfer of title by non-owners' [1965] *Journal of Business Law* 130–41.

'Trespassers on railway lines—a further note' (1965) 81 *Law Quarterly Review* 186–92.

1966 'Law Reform Committee: twelfth report' (1966) 29 *Modern Law Review* 541–5.

'Company law and partnership' [1966] *Annual Survey of Commonwealth Law* 443–64.

1967 'Misrepresentation Act 1967' (with G. H. Treitel) (1969) 30 *Modern Law Review* 369–88.

'Negligence and economic loss' (1967) 83 *Law Quarterly Review* 248–76.

'Company law and partnership' [1967] *Annual Survey of Commonwealth Law* 461–88.

1968 'Conceptualism triumphant in the Court of Appeal' (1968) 31 *Modern Law Review* 332–7 [Case note: *United Dominions Trust (Commercial) Ltd.* v. *Eagle Aircraft Services Ltd.*]

'Judicial techniques and the English law of contract' (1968) 2 Ottawa Law Review 337–62 repr., with revisions, in *Essays on Contract*, 1986 and 1990.

'Misrepresentation', 'Personal, Incapacity', 'Corporations and Unincorporated Associations', 'Assignments', 'Death and Bankruptcy', in *Chitty on Contracts*; 23rd edn. (Sweet & Maxwell, 1968). vol. 1, *General Principles*, chaps. 6, 8, 9, 18, and 19; 'Loans and Interest', 'Suretyship', in *Chitty on Contracts*; 23rd edn. (Sweet & Maxwell, 1968), vol. 2, *Specific Contracts, chaps. 9 and 13.*

'Company law and partnership' [1968] *Annual Survey of Commonwealth Law* 529–54.

1969 '*Baker* v. *Willoughby*: an addendum' (1969) 85 *Law Quarterly Review* 475–6.

'British Columbia Royal Commission on Automobile Insurance' (1969) 32 *Modern Law Review* 547–51.

'Collateral benefits again' (1969) 32 *Modern Law Review* 397–407.

'Compensation for personal injuries' (1969) 119 *New Law Journal* 653–4 and 863–4.

1971 'Compensation for the injured' (1971) 34 *Modern Law Review* 432–6.

'Loss of earnings or earning capacity?' (1971) 45 *Australian Law Journal* 228–33.

'Misrepresentation, warranty and estoppel' (1971) 9 *Alberta Law Review* 347–85 (repr., with revisions, in *Essays on Contract*, 1986 and 1990.

1972 'Accident prevention and variable premium rates for work-connected accidents'—I. (1975) 4 *Industrial Law Journal* 1–11.; II (1975) 4 *Industrial Law Journal* 89–105.

'Bills of lading and privity of contract' (1972) 46 *Australian Law Journal* 212–6.

'Res ipsa loquitur in England and Australia' (1972) 35 *Modern Law Review* 337–46.

'Restraint of trade—contract—restrainable by injunction at suit of third party' (1972) 46 *Australian Law Journal* 235–6 [Case note: *Buckley* v. *Tutty*].

'*Watt* v. *Rama*. Negligence, unborn infants and the duty of care' [1972] *University of Western Australia Law Review* 159–61.

1975 'Consideration and estoppel: the thawing of the ice' (1975) 38 *Modern Law Review* 65–9.

1976 'Conceptual construction' (1976) 39 *Modern Law Review* 335–6 [Case note: *Esso Petroleum Ltd.* v. *Commissioners of Customs and Excise*].

'When is an enforceable agreement not a contract? Answer: when it is an equity' (1976) 92 *Law Quarterly Review* 174–80.

1977 'Mistake', 'Misrepresentation', 'Duress and Undue Influence', 'Personal Incapacity', 'Corporations and Unincorporated Associations', 'Joint Obligations', 'Death and Bankruptcy', in *Chitty on Contracts*, 24th edn. (Sweet & Maxwell, 1977), vol. 1 *General Principles*, chaps. 5, 6. 7, 8, 9, 17, and 20; 'Suretyship', in *Chitty on Contracts*, 24th edn. (Sweet & Maxwell, 1977), vol. 2 *Specific Contracts*, chap. 12.

1978 'Contracts, promises and the law of obligations' (1978) 94 *Law Quarterly Review* 193–223 (repr., with revision, in *Essays on Contract*, 1986 and 1990).

1979 'Compensation orders and civil liability' [1979] *Criminal Law Review* 504–9.

'Consumer protection—time to take stock' [1979] *Liverpool Law Review* 20–44.

'Promises and the law of contract' (1979) 88 *Mind* 410–8.

'What now?' in D. K. Allen and others (eds.), *Accident compensation after Pearson* (London, Sweet & Maxwell, 1979), 227–55.

1980 'Judges and policy' (1980) 15 *Israel Law Review* 346–71.

'Liability for railway nuisance in the English common law: a historical footnote' (1980) 23 *Journal of Law and Economics 191–6.*

'No-fault compensation: a question that will not go away' [1980], Insurance Law Journal 625–40; (1980) 54 *Tulane Law Review* 271–93.

1981 'Further random reflections on the Ontario proposals and some comments on Professor Ziegel's paper' in J. S. Ziegel (ed.), *Workshop on Commercial and Consumer Law* (Toronto, Butterworths, 1981), 18–27.

'Recent judicial developments in private law', in *The Cambridge Lectures: Selected Papers based upon Lectures delivered at the Cambridge Conference of the Canadian Institute for Advanced Legal Studies, 1979* (Toronto, Butterworths, 1981), 9–29.

'Reflections on some differences in the common-law tradition between the Commonwealth and the United States', in J. S. Ziegel (ed.) *Workshop on Commercial and Consumer Law* (Toronto, Butterworths, 1981), 113–20.

1982 'Economic duress and the "overborne will"' (1982) 98 *Law Quarterly Review* 197–202.

'A legal perspective on recent contributions to the valuation of life', in M. W. Jones-Lee (ed.) *The value of life and safety: proceedings of a conference held by the Geneva Association* (1982) 185–201.

'The theoretical basis of contract law—an English perspective' (1982), 1 *International Review of Law and Economics* 183–205 [review article of A. T.

Kronman and R. A. Posner, *The Economics of Contract Law*, 1979] (repr., with revisions, in *Essays on Contract*, 1986 and 1990).

1983 'Comments on Professor Waddams' paper' (1983) 8 *Canadian Business Law Journal* 10–18.

'Duress and the overborne will again' (1983) 99 *Law Quarterly Review* 363–56.

'Lawyers and rules: some Anglo-American comparisons' (1983) 37 *Southwestern Law Journal* 545–62.

'The legacy of Holmes through English eyes' in *Holmes and the Common Law: A Century Later* (Cambridge, Mass., 1983), Holmes Lectures, 1981. Harvard Law School occasional pamphlets 10, pp. 27–73 (repr. (1983), 63 *Boston University Law Review* 341–82; extract repr. in *Essays on Contract* 1986 and 1990).

'Mistake' 'Misrepresentation', 'Duress and Undue Influence', 'Personal Incapacity', 'Joint Obligations', in *Chitty on Contracts*; 25th edn. (Sweet & Maxwell, 1983), vol. 1, *General Principles*, chaps. 5, 6, 7, 8, and 17; 'Suretyship', in *Chitty on Contracts*; 25th edn. (Sweet & Maxwell, 1983), vol. 2, *Specific Contracts*, chap. 12.

1984 'Contract and tort', in, J. L. Jowell and J. P. W. B. McAuslan (eds.) *Lord Denning: the Judge and the Law* (London, Sweet & Maxwell, 1984), 29–77.

1985 'Common law and statute law' (1985) 48 *Modern Law Review* 1–28.

'Contract and fair exchange' (1985) 35 *University of Toronto Law Journal* 1–24 (repr., with revisions, in *Essays on Contract*, 1986 and 1990).

'Economic loss in the United States' (1985) 5 *Oxford Journal of Legal Studies* 485–90.

1986 'Form and substance in legal reasoning: the case of contract' in Neil MacCormick and Peter Birks (eds.), *The Legal Mind: Essays for Tony Honoré* (Oxford, Clarendon Press, 1986), pp. 19–44 (repr. in *Essays on Contract*, 1986 and 1990).

'The Hannah Blumenthal and classical contract law' (1986) 102 *Law Quarterly Review* 363–9.

'Medical malpractice and the contract/tort boundary' (1986) 49 *Law and Contemporary Problems* 287–303 (Spring 1986).

'The "neutrality" of contract law' (1985–6) 35 *Kings Counsel* 7–11.

1987 'American tort law in crisis' (1987) 7 *Oxford Journal of Legal Studies* 279–301.

'Tort law and the alternatives: some Anglo-American comparisons' [1987] *Duke Law Journal* 1002–44.

1988 'Judgments in England', in *La sentenza in Europa: metodo, tecnica e stile: Atti del convegno internazionale per l'inaugurazione della nuova sede della Facolta, Ferrara 10–12 Ottobre 1985* (Padova, CEDAM, 1988), 140–58.

1989 'The binding nature of contractual obligations' in D. Harris and D.

Tallon (eds.), *Contract Law Today: Anglo-French Comparisons* (Oxford, Clarendon Press, 1989), 21–38.

BOOK REVIEWS

1955 J. Crossley Vaines, *Personal Property*, 1954 (1955) 18 *Modern Law Review* 523.

1962 R. M. Goode, *Hire Purchase Law and Practice*, 1962 (1962) 7 *Journal of the Society of Public Teachers of Law* (NS) 95–7.

1966 S. Stoljar, *The Law of Quasi-Contract*, 1964 (1966) 29 *Modern Law Review* 347–9.

1969 A. M. Linden (ed.), *Studies in Canadian Tort Law*, 1968 (1969) 10 *Journal of the Society of Public Teachers of Law* (NS) 232–4.

1970 G. Calabresi, *The Cost of Accidents*, 1970 (1970) 44 *Australian Law Journal* 297–8.

1976 J. O'Connell, *Ending Insult to Injury*, 1975 (1976) 45 *University of Cincinnatti Law Review* 340–6.

K. C. T. Sutton, *Consideration Reconsidered*, 1974 (1976) 92 *Law Quarterly Review* 625–7.

1977 G. Gilmore, *The Death of Contract* 1974 (1977) 71 *American Political Science Review* 636–7.

1981 Charles Fried, *Contract as Promise: A Theory of Contractual Obligation*, 1981 (1981) 95 *Harvard Law Review* 509–28 (repr., with revision, in *Essays on Contract*, 1986 and 1990).

Barry Reiter and John Swan, (eds.), *Studies in Contract Law*, 1980 (1981) 5 *Canadian Business Law Journal* 245–52.

1983 *The Principles of Social Order: Selected Essays of Lon L. Fuller*, 1981 [1983], *Duke Law Journal* 669–93 (repr. in *Essays on Contract*, 1986 and 1990).

Keith S. Rosenn, *Law and Inflation*, 1982 (1983) 132 *University of Pennsylvania Law Review* 187–94.

1985 John Bell, *Policy Arguments in Judicial Decisions*, 1983 (1985) 33 *American Journal of Comparative Law* 342–7.

LETTERS

1955 Correspondence (1955) 18 *Modern Law Review* 595.

1987 Correspondence (1987) 50 *Modern Law Review* 267–8.

EDITORIAL POSITIONS

Member of Council and Editorial Committee of *Sudan Law Journal and Reports*, 1956, 1957; General Editor 1957.

General editor *Oxford Journal of Legal Studies*, 1981–6.

Index

miss me